ELINOR WYLIE

Elinor Wylie,

A Life Apart

A BIOGRAPHY BY

Stanley Olson

The Dial Press

James Wade

NEW YORK

Published by The Dial Press/James Wade
1 Dag Hammarskjold Plaza New York, New York 10017

Grateful acknowledgment is made to Alfred A. Knopf, Inc. for permission to quote from the copyrighted works of Elinor Wylie.

Excerpts and photographs from *Elinor Wylie: The Portrait of an Unknown Lady* by Nancy Hoyt; copyright 1935 by The Bobbs-Merrill Company. Renewed copyright 1962 by Nancy Hoyt. Reprinted by permission of The Bobbs-Merrill Co., Inc.
"Sonnett in Answer to a Question" by Edna St. Vincent Millay: From *Collected Poems,* Harper & Row. Copyright 1939, 1962 by Edna St. Vincent Millay and Norma Millay Ellis.

For excerpts from the letters and papers of Elinor Wylie grateful acknowledgment is made to Mrs. Edwina Curtis Schiffer and the following archives and collections:
The University of Texas, Humanities Research Center; Princeton University Library; The University of Chicago, Joseph Regenstein Library; Henry W. and Albert Berg Collection, The New York Public Library, Astor, Lenox, and Tilden Foundations; University of Virginia Library; Collection of American Literature, Beinecke Rare Book and Manuscript Library, Yale University; The Charles Patterson Van Pelt Library, University of Pennsylvania; Martha Foote Crow Collection, George Arents Research Library for Special Collections at Syracuse University; Special Collections, Morris Library, University of Delaware; Charles Roberts Autograph Collection, Haverford College Library, Haverford, Pennsylvania; Eunice Tietjens Papers, The Newberry Library, Chicago; The Sophia Smith Collection, Women's History Archive, Smith College.

Quotations from the letters and papers of Horace Wylie in the Henry W. and Albert Berg Collection, The New York Public Library, Astor, Lenox, and Tilden Foundations, used by permission of Michael Marsh.

Quotations from *From Another World* by Louis Untermeyer used by permission of Harcourt Brace Jovanovich, Inc.

Quotations from the unpublished diaries of Edith Olivier used by permission of Rosemary Olivier.

Quotations from the letters and papers of William Rose Benét used by permission of James Benét.

Quotations from the letters of Rosemary and Stephen Vincent Benét copyright 1978 by Thomas C. Benét, Rachael Benét Lewis, and Stephanie Benét Mahin reprinted by permission of Brandt & Brandt Literary Agency, Inc.

Manufactured in the United States of America
First printing

Design by Winston G. Potter

Library of Congress Cataloging in Publication Data

Olson, Stanley.
Elinor Wylie : a life apart.

Bibliography: p. 366
Includes index.
1. Wylie, Elinor Hoyt, 1885-ND1928—Biography.
2. Authors, American—20th century—Biography.
PS3545.Y45Z8   811'.5'2   [B]   79-15425
ISBN 0-8037-2316-4

To My Parents

Acknowledgments

This biography of Elinor Wylie has been made possible by the generosity and cooperation of many people and libraries, especially Elinor's own family, who have steadily offered assistance while not always subscribing to my opinions about her. They are: Mr. and Mrs. Sydney Schiffer, Mrs. Constance Hoyt Easton, and Mr. and Mrs. Henry M. Hoyt.

Others to whom I would like to acknowledge my appreciation and gratitude are: Sir Harold Acton, Mr. and Mrs. Leonard Amster, Miss Liz Archibald, Mr. Julian Bach, Miss Patricia K. Ballon, Mrs. Eugenia Bankhead, Sir Cecil Beaton, Mrs. Sybille Bedford, Professor Quentin Bell, Miss Laura Benét, Mr. James Benét, Mr. Thomas Benét, Mr. Scott Bennett, Mr. Austin C. Benton, Miss Grechen Bloch, Professor and Mrs. Fredson Bowers, Mrs. Donna Brown, Miss Mildred Brown, Miss Claudia Bruce, Mrs. James Branch Cabell, Miss Gill Coleridge, Miss Joan St. C. Crane, Mr. James Cummins, Miss Ellen Datlow, Miss Jane Davies, Mrs. Rosemary Dawson (née Benét), Miss Babette Deutsch, Miss Elaine Dickinson, Miss Susan Edmiston, Miss Ros Edwards, Mr. C. W. Folgate, Miss Patricia Gallagher, Mr. Donald Gallup (Curator, Collection of American Literature, Beinecke Rare Book and Manuscript Library, Yale University), Mrs. Angelica Garnett, Mr. David Garnett, Mr. and Mrs. M. R. Gethin, Canon C. Leslie Glenn, Mrs. John D. Gordan, Mr. Giles Gordon, Mrs. Clair Gorman, Mr. S. Hamilton, Sir Rupert Hart-Davis, Mrs. T. P. Hazard, Dr. Evelyn Helmick, Mr. and Mrs. R. Hibbert, Miss Joan Hofmann, Mr. Michael Holroyd, Dr. Bonnie Sue Homsley, Lady Hutton (née Young), Dr. Judith Isroff, Mrs. Arthur James, Mr. P. M. Jago, Mr. Alfred Knopf, Mr. Ernest Kroll, Dr. Mary Lago, Miss Nancy Lazar, Mrs. Henry Goddard Leach, Mr. R. W. B. Lewis, Miss Susan Loppert, Mr. George Loveland, Mr. Russell Lynes, Mr. Michael Marsh, Mrs. Robert Mathew (née Young), Mr. James T. Mayock, Mrs. Patricia McCandless, Dr. A. Parks McCombs, Mrs. Helen de Selding Melcher, Mrs. Nancy Milford, Miss Hope Mirrlees, Miss Sarah Morris, Miss Hélène Mullins, Mr. Robert Nathan, Mr. L. W. Newell, Mr. Nigel Nicolson, Miss Rosemary Olivier, Dr. A. R. Olson, Mrs. Louisa O'Neill, Señora Janetta de Parladé, Mrs. H. Partridge, the late Professor Norman

Holmes Pearson, Mrs. John Peltz, Miss Katherine Anne Porter, the
Hon. Mrs. Philipps (Rosamond Lehmann), Dr. Nancy Potter, Miss
Salisha Richmond, Mrs. P. K. O. Riordan, Professor J. Albert Rob-
bins, Mr. James Romer, Miss Lin Root, Sir John Rothenstein, Mr.
John Rudman, Miss Robin Rue, the Hon. Sir Steven Runcimann,
Dr. A. T. Schwab, Mr. Desmond Shawe-Taylor, Miss Hilda Sher-
man, Mr. Richard Shone, Mr. John Saumarez Smith, Mr. Conrad S.
Spohnholz (Director, The MacDowell Colony Inc.), Dr. and Mrs.
Alan Stolow, Dr. Lola Szladits, Mr. Robert H. Taylor, the Hon.
Stephen Tennant, Mr. G. H. J. Thomalin, Miss Anne Tyrell, the late
Louis Untermeyer and Mrs. Untermeyer, Miss Gillian Vincent, Miss
Emma Walker, Mrs. J. Crawford Ware (née Woodhouse), Dame
Rebecca West, Mrs. Edmund Wilson, and Mrs. Jeanne Ballot Win-
ham.

I would also like to thank The Alderman Library, University of
Virginia; The George Arents Research Library, Syracuse University;
The Astor, Lennox and Tilden Foundations, The Berg Collection,
The New York Public Library; The Beinecke Rare Book and Manu-
script Library, Yale University; Bryn Mawr College Library; The
Baldwin School; Condé Nast Publications, Inc.; Dartmouth College
Library; Doubleday and Co., Inc.; Harcourt Brace Jovanovich; The
Gotham Book Mart; Haverford College Library (Charles Roberts
Autograph Letters Collection); Heywood Hill Bookshop; The
Houghton Library, Harvard University; Humanities Research Cen-
ter, The University of Texas; Judges' Library, United States Court
of Appeals for the District of Columbia Circuit; Alfred A. Knopf and
Co., Inc.; The Library of Congress; Lockwood Memorial Library
(Poetry Collection), State University of New York at Buffalo; The
National Book League (London); The Newberry Library; Oster-
hout Free Library; The Overbury Collection, The Wollman Library,
Barnard College, Columbia University; The Poetry Society of
America; Princeton University Library (The Robert H. Taylor Col-
lection); The Joseph Regenstein Library, University of Chicago; The
University Library, The University of Delaware; The University
Library, The University of Illinois at Urbana-Champaign; Smith Col-
lege Library; The Charles Patterson Van Pelt Library, University of
Pennsylvania; Vassar College Library; Westminster City Public Li-
brary; The Wyoming [County, Pennsylvania] Historical and Geo-
logical Society.

Finally, I am also deeply indebted to Mrs. Frances Partridge for
her steady assistance and tireless corrections and to Mr. James Wade
for his well-tested patience.

Key to abbreviations in the text:

(B)—refers to The Berg Collection. See *Notes.*

(Y)—refers to The Beinecke Rare Book and Manuscript Library, Yale University. See *Notes.*

( )—when Elinor Wylie herself has dated a letter, parentheses are used.

[ ]—when the author has dated a letter, brackets are used.

(n.d.)—indicates that a letter is undated.

Book One

1885-1910

*. . . I expect to end my days begging my bread
through seven cities which will dispute,
possibly to the point of actual bloodshed, the
honour of having been my birthplace. The
unromantic aspect of New Jersey will I hope
cause no one to believe the Somerville Myth,
for such it will be designated; the other six
cities will probably be Philadelphia,
Washington, New York, London, Paris and
Persepolis. . . . Or perhaps the seventh will be
Petit Andelys, where the proximity of Chateau
Gaillard coloured all my youthful dreams with
romance.*

—Elinor to Horace Wylie
July 20, 1923 (B)

CHAPTER ONE: 1885

§*i*   *"It don't look human."*

The country lanes were obscured by snow. The newlyweds shivered in the back of a sleigh that moved haltingly from Boundbrook to Somerville, New Jersey. Bells chattered all the way. It was the late afternoon of February 1, 1883.

Anne (Nancy) McMichael was barely twenty-two. She was not ravishingly beautiful, but she was certainly attractive. Her face was drawn along more masculine lines than feminine. Youth turned this feature into plainness; old age would make her look distinguished. What she lacked in height she made up in extreme assurance. She knew the full power of dressing conservatively. Henry Martyn Hoyt, Jr., was twenty-seven. Educated at Yale (Class of 1878) and the University of Pennsylvania, he had trained as a lawyer and was recently employed as a cashier at the United States National Bank in New York. Tall, strikingly handsome, a tireless walker and talker, he seemed a model of exuberance, yet his emotions were obscure. Unlike Nancy, he kept his feelings largely to himself; he was essentially mysterious while not appearing to be. They had been married the day before in Philadelphia.

From Somerville they moved on to New Haven and Cambridge. All Nancy remembered about her honeymoon was the cold and the snow, and the embarrassment of being summoned to her husband's room by a servant. The Hoyts took rooms at 37 Fifth Avenue (at 10th Street) in New York. The austerity of rough new handtowels, a copper-bottomed bath, tiny rooms, and a rigidly tight budget was only slightly mitigated by a Turkey carpet, meals taken at the Brevoort House, and a huge black maid, with no teeth, who never stopped whistling. While Henry sat at his post in the bank, Nancy would trudge down to Washington Square and watch the heavily furred socialites, installed in fabulous sleighs, glide by. Being a Philadelphian seemed to mean much less in New York than it did at home. Nancy felt inconsequential. But not for long, for by May 1885, reasons of economy had forced the Hoyts out of New York. They went to Somerville again, this time to settle. In Somerville Nancy was less inconspicuous; she needed less money, and she was pregnant.

They signed a two-year lease on a new frame house in Cliff Street, which cost some $20 a month. The house, which had a verandah, was situated in about an acre of garden with a quince tree, grape arbor, apple trees, and strawberries—all of which were superintended by a hired man. The house was austere, even by Nancy's newly adopted standards: no plumbing or heating, save for highly undependable iron stoves. The walls, Nancy remembered decades later when she wrote her memoir "Your Father and I, or The Crow's Children; The Simple Annals of Our Early Years" (Y), were "washed in pale-colored calcimine—less costly than paper." Everything about the place seemed designed to save money. They bought some new furniture, hired a black maid who appeared at dawn, took in a cat who guarded the garden, and started housekeeping for the first time. They ate strawberries for breakfast, then Henry rushed off to catch the 7:48 train to New York while Nancy fought with the hired man, who "was determined to plant onions. I, as firmly, wanted two more rows of peas. Haughtily ending on that final order, in due time two grand rows of onions came up." They moved in a White Mountain ice-cream freezer and the McMichael family mahogany cradle.

The summer was very hot. Nancy went to bed to await the arrival of the baby, expected no later than mid-August. The Cliff Street house baked in the sun and pigeons sought refuge in the shade of attic windows, as did doves, whose constant cooing sounded appallingly like labor groans. The monthly nurse raced up and down the stairs mistaking the birds' noise for what she hoped was Nancy's, but the days rolled by and there was still no sign of the baby.

Mrs. McMichael traveled up from Philadelphia to witness the event. As Nancy had been born on her grandmother's birthday, Mrs. McMichael concluded that she would celebrate her own birthday—August 21—this year with the birth of a granddaughter. The women were certain the child would be a girl, if only it would be born.

The monthly nurse sat knitting throughout the month of

August. Mrs. McMichael sat at a cousin's house nearby, waiting while Nancy rested. Mrs. McMichael's excitement over the impending event turned into annoyance with the inconsiderate delay. Her birthday came and went; the child would not now be named after her, as Nancy had been after her grandmother. Henry went to Philadelphia and the doves continued, disconcertingly, to coo. September began as hot as August. Finally, on September 7, after considerable difficulty, a daughter was born to Nancy and Henry. Nancy described her daughter as "small and pink and pretty, [a] wax doll of a baby."

After Mrs. McMichael's choice for the baby's name, Lucie, had been discarded, the parents could not decide on any other. By the time they registered the birth, on October 11, the baby was still nameless. Nancy was determined that her daughter should have a McMichael name; Henry was determined on an appropriate Hoyt one. Finally they compromised: Elinor Morton—Elinor after Henry's mother and Morton after Nancy's father.

When Elinor was scarcely a month old she was taken to be shown off to her grandparents. The tour got off to a dismal start when they missed the Philadelphia train and had to wait on the platform at Boundbrook for two hours. When they reached the Hoyts, Mrs. Hoyt had something to say about every aspect of Elinor's care. The bath temperature was too hot. No matter how much lettuce Nancy ate, that would not prevent her giving Elinor colic. In the end she gave Nancy a "stout volume" on baby care; by the time they moved on to the McMichaels', the nurse had given up and resigned.

They returned to Somerville at the beginning of winter, which was to become unusually severe. The stoves had to be coaxed to give what heat they could. The windows were rimmed with ice. Snow drifted under the door and sifted through the keyhole. The bedrooms were so cold that water froze in the jugs. In the morning Elinor was bathed in front of the smoke-free wood-burning stove in the kitchen while Henry shoveled snow before catching the train. In the afternoons Mama (Nancy) would take Elinor off to visit various neighbors. Her favorite stop remained Cousin Carrie's, where she had frequently visited as a bride. Mama adored the house, which was full of gleaming brass and well-polished Colonial furniture. The old black cook bustled about the place rocking with laughter over everything Mama said; and she adored Elinor, whom she said was "fat as a mole." Other members of the family were less charitable about the baby. One young cousin ushered up to the cradle in dour solemnity blurted out: "It don't look human."

By the spring Mama was getting bored with housekeeping, tired of Somerville. The monotonous flow of the same faces made her long for some change. The only immediate change was that Papa (Henry) began to commute to Philadelphia, where he was establishing a law practice.

§ *ii* *Down to the Puritan marrow of my bones . . .*
There is something in my very blood that owns
Bare hills, cold silver on a sky of slate,
A thread of water, churned to milky spate
Streaming through slanted pastures fenced with
stones.

—Elinor Wylie, "Wild Peaches"

Philadelphia had for the last six decades been the home of the McMichaels, and more recently also of the Hoyts. Since the McMichaels had risen swiftly, in the span of three generations, in Philadelphia society, they could cavalierly place themselves on an equal footing with the Hoyts' eleven generations in America. The air around Chestnut and Walnut streets was heady with arrogance, and the McMichaels were easily intoxicated. Despite their own distorted appreciation of themselves, they were a distinguished family—but no less so than the Hoyts.

"I could kick Simon Hoyt in the slats, the bastard, for leaving Somerset in 1628," Elinor once moaned to William Rose Benét [October 15?, 1928] (Y). Three hundred years after Simon's departure, Elinor managed to solve the mystery of his parentage. Simon was the first American Hoyt; the

earliest known mention of the name itself stretched back to
1418, to a baker in Curry Rivel, Somerset—one John Hoyt.
There are, however, some nineteen variations of the name.
After Simon Hoyt alighted from the deck of either HMS
Abigail or HMS *George* at Salem, he began an itinerant career
that subsequently distinguished him as being among the first
settlers in Charlestown, Dorchester, and Scituate, Massachusetts, and Windsor and Fairfield, Connecticut. Finally his travels came to an end in Stamford, where he died. He halted long
enough in one of these places to marry Deborah Stowers, and
then another "Goodwife," with whom he produced ten children and collected cows, horses, swine, and "tabacca," as well
as taking possession of and selling reaches of land.*

Four generations stayed securely in Connecticut, until
toward the end of the eighteenth century when one adventurous member moved his farming equipment from the concentration of Hoyts south to Kingston, Luzerne County, in Pennsylvania, where Elinor's direct ancestors remained with only
minor shifts to the east or west.

The early Hoyts farmed. Their lives revolved around the
farmer's calendar; they participated briefly in local militias that
were mustered for various skirmishes in the Revolution. Their
real interest rested in the church, where they sat uncomforta-
bly erect as deacons and in other capacities. The only notable
variations in their lives were geographic, and their unbridled
procreation and longevity bear witness to brute stamina. Not
for eight generations did the Hoyts leave the land: Henry
Martyn Hoyt (1830–90), Elinor's grandfather, became a lawyer.

The long line of Hoyts that preceded Elinor failed to live
up to the meaning of the word "hoyt" or "hoit" (c. 1594),
which was simply "to indulge in riotous and noisy mirth" or
"to act the hoyden" ("hoity-toity" is a derivation). Steeped in

---

*To celebrate this otherwise undistinguished man, the Hoyts collected *en
masse* at Stamford, Connecticut, in 1866. Some 500 descendants of Simon
(Elinor's father—then ten years old—among them) sat piously in Stamford
Church listening to endless genealogical papers and lengthy conjectures
about Hoyt antecedents. The proceedings were published later in the same
year, edited by D. W. Hoyt, as *Record of the Hoyt Family Meeting.* He also
compiled *A Genealogical History of the Hoyt, Haight, and Hight Families* (1871).

Puritan sobriety, they could hardly indulge in frivolity, although a real warmth and humanity emerged in Elinor's
grandfather, who remarked in a booming voice to the Hoyt
gathering in Stamford (1866): "none of our name has
achieved eminent distinction among the great ones of the
world; and none has given us unpleasant notoriety among the
base ones of the world."

Henry Martyn Hoyt was admitted to the bar in 1853,
after a false start three years earlier when he taught mathematics briefly. Armed with legal documents, he helped to organize the 52nd Regiment, Pennsylvania Volunteers. He rose
through the ranks, was taken prisoner of war twice, led the
night assault on Fort Sumter over which he raised the victori-
ous U.S. flag (he kept it as a souvenir of the occasion), and was
elevated to the rank of Brevet Brigadier General: "the title is
a harmless brevet as brigadier-general," he pointed out in
1866, "—a little out of the region of mere 'militia generals,'
—perhaps nothing to have 'sot [sic] much pride onto.' " The
momentum of his Civil War career carried him to such posts
as temporary judge of Luzerne County (1867), Collector of
Internal Revenue two years later, chairman of the Republican
State Committee, and ultimately to governor of the state from
1878 to 1882—posts which he held while also fulfilling his
duties as husband to Mary E. Loveland (whom he married in
1855) and the father of five children. Henry Martyn Hoyt, Jr.,
Elinor's father, was the eldest.*

---

*The other children were Maud Buckingham Hoyt (1859–1931), George
Loveland Hoyt (1861–62), John Sidney Hoyt (who died the same year he
was born, 1866), and Helen Strong Hoyt (1871–1944). Neither of Elinor's
aunts married. Helen Strong Hoyt taught English at Bryn Mawr College
and retired to California before her death. She caused a scandal among the
respectable Main Line residents by dressing as a man and driving her own
coach and pair through the district.

George Loveland, a second cousin to Elinor, wrote to the author (July
9, 1975) that Maud, "the older of the Hoyt aunts, helped bring up my father
after his mother died. She apparently lived in the Wilkes-Barre area for
some time, but moved to Paris before World War I and remained there
during the whole of that war and for several years after the war helping
nurse wounded French soldiers.

". . . A Wilkes-Barre friend of mine, whose grandmother was a great
friend of Maud Hoyt, remembers Maud Hoyt well. She reports that she was

The lineage of Nancy McMichael was long and, though
undistinguished, sufficient to guarantee her a place in the
Daughters of the American Revolution and establish her as a
Colonial Dame. Through marriage, her ancestors were connected with some of the oldest American families. The first
generation on American soil became far more memorable
than for that fact alone. Subsequent generations reclined un-
memorably for a couple of centuries, lacking any distinction
other than the fact of their birth.

The one exception was Nancy McMichael's first recorded
ancestor, Issac Easty (alternately Este, Esty, etc.), who was
born in England and settled in Topsfield, Massachusetts,
around 1650. In 1655 he married Mary Towne, one of eight
children born to William Towne of Yarmouth. In the spring
of 1692, Goodwife Easty, aged fifty-eight, found herself arrested and interrogated on the accusation that she had tormented several young girls of Salem through her arts as a
witch. Also figuring among the accused during the Salem
witch hysteria were Mary Easty's two sisters, Rebecca Nourse
(or Nurse) and Sarah Cloyse.

About a month after her arrest Goodwife Easty was
released from prison and then hastily taken back into custody.
"I was confined," she wrote in her petition to the governor
after her second trial,

a whole month upon the same account that I am condemned now,
then cleared; and your Honors know two days later I was cried out
upon and now I am condemned to die. The Lord above knows my
innocence and in the great day it will be known to men and angeles
[sic]. I petition your Honors, not for my own life, for I know I must
die and my appointed time is set; but the Lord he knows it is that, if it
be possible, no more innocent blood may be shed, which undoubt-
ably cannot be avoided in the way and course you go in. . . .

---

a most amusing person, rather avant-garde. At 15, she went to dinner with
her mother and Maud Hoyt in London. She remembers Aunt Maud had
cocktails and smoked. She dressed rather unusually but not in men's clothing.

". . . It might be of interest, and probably of little surprise, to you that
her Hoyt aunts greatly disapproved of Elinor's marital behavior or misbe-
havior—or so I gathered from my parents—but were secretly proud of her
renown in literary circles."

Goodwife Easty and her sister Goodwife Nourse were hanged on September 22, 1692.*

Nancy McMichael's maternal ancestors married into the Kimball and Pengilly families, two of America's most distinguished by means of their longevity. By the sixth generation after Issac Easty, the McMichaels came into the line.†

Nancy McMichael's father could scarcely boast seventeenth-century antecedents on American shores; the best the genealogist could do for these McMichaels was to identify Irish ancestors, who came to America in the late eighteenth century. They managed to replace social history with energy, which raised them to importance and respectability, all in the space of one man's lifetime—that of Morton McMichael (1807–1879), Elinor's great-grandfather. He was born in Bordontown, New Jersey, and was educated at local schools until his family moved to Philadelphia, where he studied law.‡ At the age of twenty he was admitted to the bar. But his real

*The full text of Mary Easty's petition can be found in Charles W. Upham's *Salem Witchcraft* (1867), vol. 2, pp. 327–8. Goodwife Easty and her sisters were not readily condemned by the "Circle Girls" who instigated the great Salem witch hunt. But when the girls fell about in fits (two of them were epileptic), the local doctor judiciously diagnosed that they were bewitched. The girls then refused to name the source of their ailment—until they received Tituba's (the Salem vicar's maid) proscription for a remedy: four ounces of rye meal, mixed with children's water, rolled in the shape of a biscuit, baked in ashes and then fed to a dog. If the dog became ill, the girls would name their bewitcher. The girls went on to name dozens. See also William Nelson Gemmill, *The Salem Witch Trials* (1924), Chapter XIV.

†The complicated line of Anne McMichael's ancestors is as follows: Issac Easty married Mary Towne. Their son, Issac (1656–1714), married Abigail Kimball; their son Moses married Eunice Pengilly in 1736 and moved, ultimately, to New Jersey. Their daughter, Rebecca Easty, married Martin Thomas; their son, Moses Thomas, married first Anne Dover and then Mary Nice. Moses Thomas's daughter by his first marriage, Ellen Thomas, married Morton McMichael in 1856. Ellen and Morton McMichael were the parents of Anne McMichael Hoyt and thus Elinor's maternal grandparents. The first five generations of this line are chronicled, in some detail, in *Colonial and Revolutionary Lineages of America* (New York, 1950), a volume which is more august than accurate. See pp. 437–9.

‡He generously, and erroneously, credited the University of Pennsylvania with his legal education; fifty years later, in 1877, the University of Pennsylvania credited *him* with an honorary degree.

career spanned three fields and over five decades. He moved from editorship of the *Saturday Evening Post* to ownership of the *North American* by way of the *Saturday Courier, Neal's Saturday Gazette,* and *Godey's Lady's Book.* He rose from police magistrate in the early 1830s to mayor of Philadelphia from 1866 to 1869, stopping briefly on the way as sheriff. President Grant asked him to become minister to the Court of St. James and he was mentioned as a possible vice-presidential candidate —posts he chose to escape by touring Europe instead. An ardent Republican, he brought the full weight of his conservative principles to bear on every aspect of Philadelphia life. His ambition was curbed only in the privacy of his library. There he amassed a substantial collection of books, spent hours writing unmemorable poetry, and reading.

Nancy's grandfather had been content with overtly manipulating the thoughts and policies of Philadelphia through his own newspapers and elected office; his son, Nancy's father, was no less immune to the lure of power but his influence was considerably smaller. Morton McMichael, Jr. (1836–1904), confined the expression of this urge to the significant forces of profit-and-loss ledgers in the First National Bank of Philadelphia, which he helped to found.* He supervised the use of vast sums of money for others, and managed to amass for himself a fortune through skillful investment. He took over his father's *North American.* He took over his father's library, steadily enlarging it. And he took over his father's willfulness. When Nancy's elder brother, another Morton McMichael, made what was considered an unsuitable marriage, he was summarily banished to Europe.

The dual forces of power and energy in the McMichael line were neither lost nor dissipated by the time Nancy was born in 1860. She managed to modify each strain until they were suitably refined. Her love of control and power focused narrowly on a few rather than many, but the force remained substantial. She drew on endless reserves of subtle ruthlessness, which she directed at her family. She sent a chill spirit of independence through her children while craftily maintain-

*In 1955 Morton McMichael's bank merged with the First Pennsylvania Bank—a firm that has, today, no knowledge of Morton McMichael.

ing strict control over their bank accounts. Like her father, she successfully exploited the power of debit and credit. Unlike her father and grandfather, her scope of influence, ordained by the limits of her sex, was considerably smaller, but no less frightening.

The shadow of famous and powerful fathers loomed heavily over the lives of Morton McMichael, Jr., and Henry Martyn Hoyt, Jr.; more so perhaps on the McMichael side. Money cushioned a good portion of that weight, and Nancy's father rose to Clover Club prominence. He shared the paternal devotion to poetry (his father boasted of having been complimented by Edgar Allan Poe for his own poetry). He inherited his father's relentless energy, even if it often meant competition with him. And he carried on his father's exaggerated admiration for conventionality and staunch Republican ideals. The Hoyts were also avid Republicans; and probably through Nancy's efforts both families, which her marriage united, nurtured a disproportionate affection for the details of their genealogies. When she was invited to submit her lineage to *The Compendium of American Genealogy,* Nancy even managed to make up a few extra generations, and to overlook one ancestor who might have brought Jewish blood into the line.

§iii   *Illness*

Papa (Henry), like Somerville itself, was caught between the conflicting interests of New York City to the east, and Philadelphia, somewhat further, to the southwest. His career as assistant cashier at the United States National Bank was coming to an end, in part due to the financial panic that had forced the move out of New York before Elinor was born. Mama (Nancy) longed for them to move to Philadelphia. For the moment, however, her activities centered exclusively on Cliff Street.

The kitchen garden was planted. Neighbors called, bringing welcome fresh-baked cakes and unwelcome cream-

colored tuberoses: "I simply had to burn them after dusk fell,"
Mama confessed decades later in her autobiography, "so op-
pressively sweet their smell; heavenly on the night air but
deadly indoors." She neglected her passion for lawn tennis for
the lawn. There was watering in the evenings—not only of the
grass but the house as well in an attempt to keep cool. She
waited for the butter woman to call, and the milkman, who
also brought them chickens. Cool drinking water was hauled
from the deep recesses of a nearby well. Somehow, Philadelphia seemed a long way off.

Her parents thought the same. Elinor was sufficient attraction for the McMichaels to undergo the tedious journey
from Philadelphia some Sundays. The New York train
dropped them at Boundbrook. They then had to make their
way to Cliff Street in a horsedrawn carriage, arriving hot,
tired, and dusty, and full of complaints about the considerable
inconvenience. The McMichaels, who came more often than
the Hoyts, begged their daughter to return to Philadelphia.

In April 1887, with one month remaining on the lease of
the Cliff Street house, the Hoyts moved, not quite all the way
to Philadelphia but to one of the fashionable stations west:
Rosemont, suitably rural, yet definitely Philadelphian. Mama
remembered the house, at 1227 Lancaster Road, as "brick
. . . very cozy and pretty." Certainly more substantial and
luxurious than Cliff Street, it was a somber affair, solid, rising
just over two stories in the newest red brick. The bricklayer's
art had superseded any that an architect might have had. The
front door was shielded by a wood verandah, and the kitchen,
also in wood, had been annexed to the back. Once inside there
was little of interest or comfort. The rooms were coolly formal, lacking both elegance and imagination.

Lancaster Road did offer a suitable location—close to the
turnpike and train, in "an unattractive part of Rosemont"—
and some modern luxuries: "when 'a bath in a china dish'
began to be advertised, we could not resist it," Mama admitted, "so one was put in. . . . Then gas was brought along the
turnpike, and we must add that."

Mama was adding to the family. Scarcely had the windows of the new house been cleaned and the carpets beaten
than Mama gave birth to Henry Martyn Hoyt, III, on May 8,

1887.* "He was red and bald and a perfect duck for sweetness and good temper," she wrote, ". . . He was so jolly, fat and rosy." As soon as Henry could walk, he would wobble after Elinor and a chain of ducks would waddle after him. He had been told to feed the neighbor's ducks—a task he managed only by failing to feed the crackers entirely to himself. He adored Elinor, and the servants adored him.

The first winter at Rosemont was the year of the great blizzard. "It out-blizzarded all the others before or since," wrote Mama. One Sunday she took Elinor and infant Henry off to Philadelphia to visit their McMichael grandparents, while Papa prudently stayed at home. By the late afternoon the snow had halted most of the activity along the Main Line, and the next morning all trains ground to a standstill. "When we looked out in the morning it was piled and drifted in long smooth waves like sand dunes. Over the steps and fences and paths. It still fell steadily all day long." Snow packed every sill and doorway of the house, but they managed to stay warm. They were completely trapped for two days. "For us, it was all an adventure, but lives were lost in this great storm."

As they were treated to an excess of snow in the winter, so one summer they enjoyed too much heat: "A much worse thing for us came on a quiet summer evening when your father and I were sitting reading indoors. We heard the cry 'Fire,' and started up." The wooden kitchen at the back of the house had caught fire. Mama leaped up the stairs to Elinor, who was sleeping in her crib; Papa dashed for his infant son, asleep in his carriage downstairs. The neighbors formed a bucket brigade and the valuables from the house were piled on the front lawn. People milled about watching. Men ran back and forth in a flurry of totally unproductive activity, but only the kitchen was burned. "Henry never woke up at all, but Elinor sat up sedately," and drank some milk offered by a young girl. The fire had started through the cook's carelessness. It provided Mama and Papa with an excellent opportunity to rebuild—and to add a nursery.

*Three and a half decades later Mama's memory became haphazard. In 1921, on the publication of Henry's *Dry Points; Studies in White and Black*, she dated his birth as either "10 or 20th May."

The kitchen was rebuilt with an enormous pantry, and above it the new nursery: "the real triumph," Mama remembered. "It had windows to face the morning sun, and a large bay window to get all the sunshine from midday on. In this window was a seat running round at the height for children to use . . . honorably established by Henry and Elinor as their own domain. Here they had undisturbed possession." The place was heated by an open fire and furnished with a rocking horse, miniature parallel bars with a safety mattress, and a various assortment of high and low chairs plus a stout table. A set of back stairs led conveniently down to the kitchen, and both Elinor and Henry would hurl "their silver cups down these stairs, on the pretext of wanting more milk." It was a snug place.

In the spring of 1889 Mama retired to her bed again. On May 22, she and Papa had another daughter, Constance. The news reached Elinor and Henry when they were concentrating on a game of "boat," which involved sitting in a cramped position and paddling furiously. The nurse interrupted them to display their new sister. They registered only mild astonishment before returning to their game. Constance was "a plump, brown, baby, with big grey eyes. She was regarded by the other two as a pampered and superfluous addition to *their* nursery," claimed Mama. It was a status she would never quite manage to shed for the rest of her life.

As the newest member of the family, a great deal of the attention formerly lavished on Henry and Elinor now turned to Constance. Elinor and Henry retaliated by ignoring her. Constance fought their alliance with kicks and bites, which both thought neither fair nor orthodox: *they* refused to indulge.

Elinor did, however, indulge in hours of tilting back and forth on the rocking horse. Dressed summer or winter in a heavily starched white frock, her chestnut hair crowned with a gilt paper crown, she would recite some verse she had heard in an endearing lisp.* Other activities were less exciting.

*One poem Elinor chanted high atop her painted horse, Mama remembered, began: "Open the gates and draw the curtain;/ Here comes something fine—that's certain./ Louder the band begins to play,/ Open the gates and clear the way."

There were the daily hair-brushings during which Elinor was obliged to stand still for what seemed to her an eternity—a half hour—while Mama recited stories. "Elinor had beautiful hair," Mama pointed out, "like your father's—fine and soft and thick, and compared to mine, fair. I was very proud of it." Elinor's favorite story was about two fairies: Brownie, who represented thrift and prudence, and Silver Wing, who was the opposite. Characteristically, Elinor preferred "Sirly Wing," as she pronounced it.

Even at an early age Mama struggled to persuade her children of their superiority. The mere facts of their birth were not enough to establish what she considered their proper position. Instead, she trapped her son and daughters in a suffocating sense of respectability and preeminence. Consequently they grew up in an atmosphere of isolation. The children's activities were subject to the same scrutiny as the servants'. Individuality was fostered by their unusually formal dress and by the endless assertions of excellence that excluded everyone else. Mama felt obliged to nudge the course of nature since she felt she might not live long enough to see her children grow up. It was a tactic that would prove disastrously successful.

In the spring of 1892 Mama used the excuse of a maid's departure to close up the Lancaster Road house, and take the three children, along with their nurse Mary Ann McDonald, to visit their grandparents. While at her father-in-law's home in Wilkes-Barre she absent-mindedly drank some tapwater. She soon developed a fever and a throbbing headache. A doctor was called in, quickly diagnosed Mama's illness as influenza, and sat on Elinor's favorite toy—a fragile bird in a cage that squeaked each time one touched the bottom of the cage. Mama's illness seemed to get worse. She telegraphed Papa that she was coming home, stopping at her parents' in Philadelphia on the way. Mrs. McMichael took charge of everything when Mama and the children arrived. She begged her daughter not to rush back to Rosemont with the two new maids, but rather to send the children on ahead with Mary Ann. Mama would not listen; she insisted on getting back to Lancaster Road. There she began to feel steadily worse and went to bed.

The children were not impeded by their mother's illness.

Elinor and Henry raced around the garden, poking their
fingers into rabbit hutches. When Constance ate a crayon,
thinking it some sort of special chocolate, Mary Ann rushed
to Mama saying that Constance had been poisoned and then
ran out to fetch a doctor. He prescribed an alum in jam for
Constance, then turned to examine Mama. She said it was
nothing more than grippe, but the doctor diagnosed typhoid.

Nurses moved in and the children moved out. Mama lay
in bed for three weeks, occasionally receiving a few select
callers. Papa read to her each evening. She soon began to feel
better. She ate a few strawberries and the children came to see
her. Then, all of a sudden, "I had a heart attack," she wrote
in her autobiography. "Well there I was, *in extremis*—two
doctors, three nurses, on eight-hour shifts, life hanging by a
thread. The thread held. I began to get better. It was slow
work getting well. . . . The convalescence would fill a book;
it was so long. The truth is, it changed my view of life. . . .
Every value was changed." The convalescence was indeed "so
long"—it would last nearly six decades.

The immediate effect of her double illness was that she
was "thin as a sapling," hairless, and very haggard. A friend
came to visit and suggested, heartlessly, that Mama read *Ethics
of the Dust*. The children carried innumerable white stones to
her bedroom, for decoration. They looked on, hardly tall
enough to see over the bed, somewhat suspicious of the gravity of her illness, which she tried to impress upon them. The
routine of their life was utterly changed. Their silence was
vital to Mama's recovery; in fact, every element of their life
was linked to the potential loss of their mother's. The enter-
tainments became more subdued. Their nurse read to them in
front of the nursery fire. As Mary Ann rocked back and forth
in her chair, Constance squirmed and fidgeted, while Henry
and Elinor sat in stonelike silence. She would recite Irish
ballads and folk songs, mysterious and frightening stories of
Ireland, full of grass and damp. She would tell them of her
childhood and of her family's farm.

Mary Ann became the most important figure in the children's life. She was "a treasure," costing precisely $4 a week.
"She had a long face and a mouth that looked as if a draw-

string had puckered it"; an imposing figure, no longer young, she had "the kindest heart." As a child Mama had met Mary Ann, and admitted frankly, "I was rather afraid of her." But when she came to work in Lancaster Road, the fear turned to real affection. Mary Ann was born in County Antrim, and despite decades in America seemed to ignore the ocean that separated the two countries. She could scent out a fellow countryman in the most unlikely places and would talk for hours about Ireland as if they were cousins. Her highest compliment was to credit people with some Irish quality: Papa was dubbed an "Irish nobleman." Her accent never diminished; if anything, it grew stronger. She ruled the nursery like some aging Isolde, defending her tea and sugar against Constance's raids. She sat with a lavishly illustrated Bible on her lap, reading and narrating tales, so transfixing the children that Henry persisted for years in pronouncing biblical names with an Irish accent.

Mama's illness cast a shadow over every aspect of the life in Lancaster Road. Her role as mistress assumed a ghostlike quality; she cast a somber spell on everything. She was completely withdrawn from family life, becoming a distant, and somewhat forbidding, figure. Papa did not seem to make up for Mama's absence. Indeed, he had very little impact on his children. Mama's illness only made her more important. She discovered that inactivity could have very powerful effects. The most unfortunate residue of her new position was the fact that her emotional involvement was as withdrawn as her physical presence. She had a fear of exhausting herself—a fear that was so great she ended up doing very little. Her children, at first frightened of bringing on another attack, soon became frightened of her. The threat of death convinced Mama that any investment in life was an empty gesture—and an extravagant waste of energy. Instead of using herself, she managed to use the people around her.

Another effect of Mama's illness was that Papa could not be allowed to waste precious hours traveling up and down the Main Line. So for the winter of 1892–3 the Hoyts closed Lancaster Road and moved to the cramped comfort of a narrow house in Locust Street, in the heart of Philadelphia. "It was nice to be in town with friends get-at-able again," Mama explained, "but I did not attempt to go out much." Her husband went out daily to the Investment Company of Philadelphia, where he had risen steadily from treasurer to president in 1890, with the help of a law degree and family influence. Philadelphia was now, mercifully, parent-free. The McMichaels had left for Devon on the Main Line earlier that year. General Hoyt had returned to Wilkes-Barre to take up his law practice after the death of his wife in 1890. There still remained the constant family visits, but Mama felt she was finally home, after some eight years.

The "Burtonage," as Elinor called the house, had a large library added to it which got the afternoon sun. It was here that Mama, wrapped in shawls, spent most of her time. The children were strictly superintended by Mary Ann. Every morning she would lead Elinor and Henry across Rittenhouse Square to school. Constance insisted on going as well. One day Mary Ann turned up at school to find Constance being led away by one of the boys, who calmly explained that he liked her and wanted to take her home. By comparison, Elinor and Henry behaved extremely well. They took themselves very seriously, especially at school.

Papa and Mama had a stern view of education. When Elinor began to draw, they engaged a pretty young girl to instruct her and Henry in clay modeling and various other skills. Both children loved it: "Made superior mud pies, representing birds, beasts, and fishes—if you overlooked a certain sameness in the results," Mama noted. The real skill their art tutor taught them was to sing children's songs—in German. Papa read a prose version of the *Odyssey* to them, which Constance hated. Grandfather McMichael, whom Elinor nicknamed "Dada," adored reading to Elinor. Everyone seemed to read to the children. Every night they would have a story before going to bed. The nursery was littered with books. All this reading only managed to keep Elinor from learning to read herself. Somehow that instruction had been overlooked, and Elinor did not read until she was five: "rather later than usual," Mama claimed, "—more especially in so clever a child."

By spring 1893, the Hoyts had moved back to Lancaster Road. Keeping up a fast recuperative pace, Mama detoured on her way home to spend two weeks in the new Bryn Mawr Hospital: "just to rest," as she explained, in a pink "memorial room." It all suited her perfectly. Doctors and nurses were gratifyingly concerned, but this medical activity spread to Lancaster Road, where both Elinor and Henry, as if in competition with the professional invalid, came down with the measles. Mary Ann threatened them with unmentionable consequences if they dared to put their feet on the floor. Mama cut short her stay at Bryn Mawr to come home to her own bed during the measles epidemic. Syrups, draughts, and powders lay ready in the nursery, while restoratives and cordials went to Mama's room. The children recovered rapidly. Mama, predictably, refused to shake off her complaint; then Constance, exerting her independence, came down with the measles in her turn.

The winter months in Philadelphia had failed to cure Mama; instead, they resulted in further exhaustion. The doctors merely sighed that a complete change was now required. Papa and Mama sailed for Liverpool, while their "lambs" stayed at home under the supervision of an Irishwoman (from County Antrim and, even more to Mary Ann's liking, a member of the gentry) employed for the purpose. Two months later Mama and Papa were back, laden with souvenirs of London, Paris, and Switzerland, to return to their old routine: Papa to work and Mama to bed.

CHAPTER TWO: 1892

§ *i*   *"I am going to be a great artist!"*

From the age of four Elinor was taken every summer to Mt. Desert Island, a short distance off the coast of Maine. It was largely unspoiled. Inns and houses did not detract from the rustic beauty. The stretches of sandy beaches were relieved by stone promontories and carved into bays and inlets. Footpaths laced grassy hills that rose into higher slopes, which in turn descended into calm ponds. The vegetation was thick with ferns and abundant with balsam, fir, and maple trees. The variations of the sky made every moment of the day astonishingly beautiful. The air was fragrant with pine and juniper. And for Mama there was no hint of illness. "The air is so tonic you do not tire, the sun so warm you do not chill," she pointed out. "The American summer is at its best there. . . . Those summers in Maine were an insurance against illness, lasting through the winters, I believe."

The first summer the Hoyts headed north, in 1889, they sailed overnight from Boston. The passage was smooth and easy, ending at Bar Harbor. There they stayed in a small cottage called the Birch Tree Inn presided over by Captain Rodick and his red setter. The dog kept watch over Mama and the children, who slept in her bedroom on the second floor. The menu was limited but hearty, and included blueberry pies and doughnuts that were "the best ever," Mama confessed. Constance, hardly two months old, slept away the summer in a large washbasket, and Elinor and Henry ran freely in and out of the place. Sometimes Elinor, straining to sit still, and Henry, squirming with excitement, would bob about in a small boat skillfully rowed by Papa. Or they would spend the mornings on the beach building sandcastles. While the children slept in the afternoon, Papa strode vigorously through the woods. At the end of the summer they boarded the boat back to Boston. Everyone but Papa was seasick. One experienced passenger equipped herself with a paper collar cov-

ering the shoulders and chest that rustled ominously throughout the voyage. The following summers they took the train to
Mt. Desert Ferry.

Education resumed with tutors returning to the house in
Rosemont. Then, in 1892, Elinor was enrolled in Miss Baldwin's School for Girls at nearby Bryn Mawr, but withdrawn
again when Mama decided to go to Philadelphia to recuper-
ate. With Henry, and later Constance, Elinor was tutored by
Miss Virginia Graeff; the courses, due to the ages of the students, were restricted. In fact, the tuition was simply another
name for removing the children from the "Burtonage" for
Mama's peace and quiet. The arrival of the Hoyt children at
Miss Graeff's was unvaried. Mary Ann delivered them, "unbuttoned long leather leggings, hung up wraps, smoothed
roughened hair, provided kerchiefs," then "with a regal wave
of her hand," Elinor would dismiss her, saying, "Now, you
may go, Mary Ann . . . don't eat up the time." Such behavior
astonished Miss Graeff. The moment Mary Ann left, Constance burst into tears. Elinor calmly explained: "Oh, don't
mind her, Miss Virginia, she always has to have her cry out."
Neither Elinor nor Henry paid the slightest attention to Constance, even when the wails rose to a crescendo. As abruptly
as it had begun, the crying stopped, and the lessons got under
way. Along with a few other children, they took a form of
kindergarten course. Painting and drawing figured largely in
the routine. Elinor loved to draw, Miss Graeff remembered
years later, "and probably exhibited designs, boldly drawn
with great splashes of color. I remember one of Uncle Sam,
stalking over a mountain, which gave her great delight.

" 'I am going to be a great artist!' she announced delight-
edly, as she showed it to me."

§ *ii   When I was seven years old I had a primer:*
The immaculate bosom of the mother-tongue
Flowed milkily in mercy to the young,
Dispensing balsam to the infant dreamer . . .

Profuse and fabulous appeared the page
On which your youngest lessons were emblazoned:
Enchantments that unlock a crystal cage;
An alphabet with astral fire seasoned;
These are the characters of that largesse
Which give the lavish greater to the less . . .

—Elinor Wylie, "Dedication"

The following year Elinor enrolled in Miss Baldwin's School again, where she stayed for four years. Even Bryn Mawr, one of the focal points of Cassatt's grand design for the Main Line, had distinct Hoyt connections. Scarcely eleven years before, in 1881, Mama had joined other suffering Philadelphians in the summer exodus to the old Bryn Mawr Hotel, an enormous yet austere mansarded building, with vast wooden verandahs and spacious lawns spread before it. Here she and her family had spent the summer, and her courtship by Henry Hoyt had begun. Henry, himself sweating under the final cramming for his law degree, took the train down from the Governor's Mansion in Harrisburg, where he was also acting as his father's secretary, to be with her for weekends. And it was at the old Bryn Mawr Hotel that he proposed to her.*

At Miss Baldwin's, painting and drawing were considered secondary to the intellectual skills. Miss Florence Baldwin began her school in 1890 when she was twenty-nine. It was founded on the revolutionary principle of preparing girls for a university education; the courses were specially designed for the entrance examinations to Bryn Mawr College. In fact, graduation from Miss Baldwin's waived the necessity of examinations altogether for Smith and Wellesley colleges. Flo-

---

*"I managed to occupy the time," Henry confessed to Nancy after one such visit [June 20, 1881], "until my train started last night with reading, and reserved in the luxury of my sorrow, the pain of parting for the distance from Philadelphia to Bryn Mawr. There I tried vainly to catch the light from your window, although I was partially comforted with a glimpse that I imagined came from the shutters of your father's room. Afterwards, notwithstanding a strong undercurrent feeling of bereavement, I dwelt persistently and happily on the inexpressible sweetness of the evening with you, and stayed my heart by the thought of seeing you again." (B)

rence Baldwin was an energetic woman, constantly changing the curriculum and instituting new policies for the school she headed until 1906 when she retired. "I realize," she said, when she stepped down, ". . . that for the last two or three years I have made no new aggressive plans for the school, that I am merely carrying on what I have already done. . . . I take this to indicate that I have finished what I have to do for the school. . . ." From the start she gave her school academic standing, and, more to Mama's liking, social acceptability. Mama was not convinced that college education was suitable for girls; in fact, she loathed the idea of girls going to a university. She was unimpressed that Miss Baldwin prepared students for higher education. She was interested only in the soundness of reading and general education. She held the belief, like her sister-in-law Helen Strong Hoyt, that "schools & colleges are the last places to send girls . . . for the primary reason that they leave out training in goodness in the old religious sense."

Miss Baldwin's School was located in a modest wood building that had housed the builders and the architects of the Main Line in the seventies and eighties, "within three minutes' walk of the station." There it remained during Elinor's years as a student until 1897, when the school moved across the street to Frank Furness's radical hodge-podge of brick, iron, and shingle that replaced the old Bryn Mawr Hotel, destroyed by fire.

The courses were divided among three departments: Primary, Intermediate, and Advanced, with tuition payable half-yearly in advance ranging from $50 to $150 a year; music and painting lessons were extra. At Miss Baldwin's, Elinor embarked upon a stern school régime. From 9:00 to 1:40 each day, with thirty minutes' recitation demanded in each course, Elinor studied Arithmetic, Inventional Geometry, Geography ("North and South America. United States. Map Drawing and Moulding"), Observation Lessons on Plants and Animals, French, Drawing (which involved clay modeling and writing as well), and Gymnastics, held under the watchful eye of Miss Anna Goodwin Baldwin, Florence Baldwin's sister. But the chief concentration of the course was on English: "A prominent place," the prospectus emphasized, "is given to instruction in English; the aim throughout the course is to cultivate an appreciation of what is good in literature, and to teach the pupils to use clear and forcible English."

The reading was wide and varied. Shelley was considered "good in literature." "I first read 'The Cloud' and 'The Sky-lark,'" Elinor recalled some thirty-four years later, "in my Third Reader, and I think I was seven years old. This was the same winter when my innocent young mother read 'Christabel' aloud to me. My admiration for it was so nearly pure horror that 'The Skylark' was a great consolation after dark. 'If we were things not born to shed a tear'; even a child can understand those words." Five years earlier she admitted that the "pure horror" of "Christabel" scared her into "seven fits."

A year after the shock of "Christabel" and the soothing influence of "The Skylark," Elinor wrote her first poem:

> The sun had sunken in the West
> The lights of the day had fled
> The moon upon the quiet sky
> Her peaceful beams had shed.
>
> Slowly the silver crescent rose
> O'er meadow, hill & dale,
> It lit the ocean's broad expanse
> And shone upon a sail.

The summer that poem was written the Hoyts deserted the Birch Tree Inn for Asticou, perched in the recess of Northeast Harbor, south of Bar Harbor: "the woods were divine. . . . At Asticou you were right at the woods and yet within a stone's throw of the water too." For ten subsequent summers they returned to Asticou, slightly more primitive than Bar Harbor, and a great deal smaller. Summer was passed in the standard occupations—walking, reading, sailing, rowing, and bathing. Strolling through the woods was hard work with the constant impediment of "ferns as high as your waist, sweet fern, bunchberries, with first white blossoms and then red berries. . . . No snakes. . . . Chipmunks, full of curiosity, run along watching you with their bright eyes; squirrels (red ones) scold at you from the trees and even pelt you with pine cones." Rainy days and evenings forced one inside, to read. The hotel's library was a haphazard collection of books discarded by previous guests. "Nearly every year a book-shelf was added," Mama remembered. For Elinor the summer was the most important time of the year, and the most enjoyable.

The young girl lived in a safe and ordered world. Mama never relaxed her absolute control; Elinor was rarely free enough to question anything. Less than question, she never even doubted Mama's authority. As a result, her behavior was characterized more by reacting than inventing. She managed to carry her actions to extraordinary lengths, but she was cautious to keep an eye open for approval, a word of praise.

Mama selected Elinor's friends, and Elinor resisted her by tempting these friends into indecorous behavior. Her energy and enthusiasm could subvert even the most careful instructions. Since her friends were "approved," they could play without the calming influence of governesses or nurses. One such friend was the daughter of T. Whister Brown, a friend of Papa's, who lived in Villanova. Agnes Brown and Elinor would meet approximately once a week, either with Elinor arriving in Villanova under the protection of a coachman or Agnes bouncing over to Rosemont in a dogcart, a contraption Elinor ridiculed mercilessly. It was much greater fun to go to the Browns'; the large barn behind the house was loaded with things that were strictly forbidden. "I was very carefully brought up by my parents," Agnes later confessed, and "would not dream of breaking any rule." Elinor actively opposed Agnes's caution, teasing her, laughing at her, and goading her by saying: "Oh, you're just an old Quaker!" Elinor never stopped until she got Agnes to do what she wanted.

The barn was a marvelous place: hay spilling over the loft, ladders, ropes, and a few mice. Elinor raced up the ladder and tossed herself down onto the hay; Agnes resisted. She was called more names, there was a great deal more sarcastic laughter: "Elinor kept forcing me to act against my parents' wishes . . . [she] was quite athletic; she did anything she wanted to." Elinor's astonishing combination of fearlessness and energy was enough to tempt Agnes more than the taunts. In the end both girls rushed around the barn, jumped off ladders, swung on ropes, and hid in the hay. Then they played with Agnes's enormous collection of pets—rabbits, cats, and

mice—all greatly loved by Elinor. There was no end of the
games to be enjoyed at the Browns'.

Agnes's visits to Lancaster Road were the exact opposite.
Each visit began with Agnes being ushered up to Mama's
room, and Elinor warning: "My mother's always ill." Mama,
recumbent, was an intimidating person for a child—"judging
all the time, not helping for one minute to bring out things in
her children. Yet she did want you to be Elinor's friend."
They would exchange a few uncertain words, and were then
dismissed to their games. Despite the prodding and teasing
that laced their friendship, Agnes adored Elinor and admired
her. She always looked forward to seeing her. Yet there was
one thing alarming about Elinor: "she could lie like a trooper.
She lied willingly and yet, one wasn't too surprised. Nothing
was too strange in connection with Elinor."

§iii   *"Anemia and Apoplexy"*

For Elinor, life at Miss Baldwin's School was a period of no
hesitation, a period of assurance. The only surprising thing she
ever did was to enter the schoolroom through the window.
She was boisterous and she was energetic. For her biographer
there is very little material, and even that is hardly out of the
ordinary. The scraps that remain yield scant evidence of what
was to follow. There was a certain precocity, but with literate
parents and grandparents bearing down on her, it assumed
only a mild and charming sophistication—particularly in the
case of one short story she wrote when she was nine.

"A Narrow Escape," written in 1895, deals with a quartet
of young mice: "Sleek-sides made his sister Silverskin cry by
pulling her tail and that naughty boy, Squeaky hurt poor little
Pinkears very much by trying to use her as a ball." The young
mice sit listening to their grandfather—"meditatively licking
his whiskers"—relate a tale of danger from his own youth.
The story manages to convey a hint of Elinor's extraordinary
awareness of color and light, and also to suggest the vanity that
was later to make her notorious. "A moon-beam fell in

through a broken slat in the window and fell like a strip of silver carpet on the floor. In it lay a bit of looking glass and I stood admiring myself in it." (B)

The year "The Narrow Escape" was written, the Primary Department of Miss Baldwin's School moved around the corner to a new building in Morris Avenue. The building housed a large study room, gymnasium, studio, and various classrooms. "Great care," the prospectus read, "has been taken to secure a good light and ventilation in all the rooms, and there are open fires throughout the building." But Elinor's life reflected the shifts at Lancaster Road more than the subdued events of the classroom. Mama's health and Papa's career were alternating influences in the household, taking them both away from their children. After four years as president of the Investment Company of Philadelphia, Papa returned to private law practice again in 1894. Mama's health was cautiously guarded, mostly by herself, and by the three children. In spite of her remoteness, her importance in their life increased. They mistook Mama's apparent nobility in withstanding illness for loving devotion, and Mama encouraged the misapprehension. Papa was even more shut off from her; his interests began to wander from his family, and Mama felt that she was too ill to draw him back. Like all McMichaels, she was part steel, part fire—frightening, yet clever in the extreme. Luckily for her, her own father—Dada—took her illness as seriously as she did.

When he himself went off to Europe in the spring of 1897, Dada sent his daughter money to buy her a change of scene. On the spur of the moment, Mama recalled, "I planned to take the three children to see Washington." Both she and Papa had adored Washington, ever since a brief visit there in the autumn of 1896. The five of them traveled without a nurse, staying at the Willard. The first night in town they dined with an old classmate of Papa's who had been an usher at their wedding: John Addison Porter, then Secretary to the President.* "After dinner," as Mama related the episode,

*John Addison Porter's brief life (1856–1900) was a chronicle of ambition and failure. He graduated from Yale in 1878 and was for ten years editor and proprietor of the Hartford, Connecticut, *Post.* He was a member of the

"[Porter] & your father went out & I went up-stairs with the children. . . . It was late when Harry [Papa] came in, and he was quite excited by a suggestion John had made to him—He said there would be an Assistant Attorney General position vacant soon, and that if your father could get the backing of his two Senators from Pennsylvania, he might get the appointment. 'Would you be willing to have me take it?' " Papa asked Mama. She answered quickly, " 'sure.' "

The appointment came through by the summer. The children were taken to see President McKinley, who handed each of them a red carnation and spoke a few cordial words. Mama and Papa were extremely pleased. Elinor was not; it meant leaving Rosemont and Miss Baldwin's School. "I miss you dreadfully," Elinor wrote (May 30, 1897) to her science teacher, Tirzah Nichols (herself fresh from teachers' college when she went to Miss Baldwin's), before news of the impending move reached her.

. . . On Saturday I was playing you were there [Lancaster Road], and the children didn't understand. Henry asked me to play buffalo hunt, and he didn't know why I wouldn't, until I told him. I guess he likes you, for he said, when we were talking about a little house up in a tree, where we could have lemonade and gingerbread and little gold things, that are very like little flies, that I could have you whenever I wanted.

Do you mind me writing to you? Because it seemed such an awfully long time to next Fall?

After spending the summer with Mama in Bar Harbor, the children were packed off to the McMichaels' house, now back in Philadelphia, at 205 S. Twenty-second Street, while the new house in Washington was made ready. Elinor was

Connecticut General Assembly and was several times a candidate for governor at the Republican conventions. As Presidential Secretary he was hastily removed. In Arthur Wallace Dunn's *From Harrison to Hardy*, 2 vols. (1922) Porter's appointment is discussed: "It was not a happy selection. Mr. Porter knew very little about Washington and less about public men. He was of very little help to the President and for the most part he buried himself with the social side of the White House life and other matters of little importance" (vol. 1, pp. 208–9). Eventually Porter became "a kind of social secretary in the White House," as W. C. Spielman explains in *William McKinley: Stalwart Republican* (1954), p. 103.

sorry to leave Miss Baldwin's. School was her private preserve. There she could distinguish herself, and there she was
happy. "I am coming back," she wrote to Miss Nichols (November 14, 1897) from Philadelphia,

on Friday to say good-bye to you and everybody else. And I'll come
up to the book closet and say a private goodbye to you. You don't
know how sorry I am to go away from you, how dreadfuuly [sic]
awfully, and you don't know how much I love you. I hope you will
be a little tiny bit sorry. But then, whatever you *say*, you must *know*
that there are a very great many of me, and only one of you.

Two weeks after Elinor wrote this letter to her science
teacher, she moved to Washington. The Hoyts took a house
at 1516 K Street, near to John Porter's, where Papa had stayed
throughout the summer. The Department of Justice, located
at McPherson Square, was less than a block away. Mama's only
memory of the house was that it "had quite a good back
garden . . . climbing roses & honeysuckle & even quite large
trees, so it was very open & pleasant." Mama also remembered
that she brought two maids with her from Lancaster Road.
Elinor seemed only to remember Miss Baldwin's School:
"This certainly can't be called a letter," she confided to Miss
Nichols (November 27, 1897), "because it dont say or tell
anything. Only its something written on a peace [sic] of paper.
If you answer this *please* tell me who sits next you in Science.
. . . I'm not going to write what I think because in the first place
I don't think anything, and in the second I *won't* be sentimen-
tle [sic]."

Life at K Street was scarcely distinguishable from that at
Lancaster Road. At the age of twelve Elinor was enrolled in
Mrs. Flint's school—"a small and very select tutoring school"
located near Connecticut Avenue. At first she did not like it
much. "When I heard about the Cantata," she wrote to Miss
Nichols two days after Christmas, "I wished more than ever
I was still at Bryn Mawr. But except for school I like Washing-
ton *very* much."

But Elinor's opinion of school changed rapidly as she
came under the influence of her English teacher—Miss Carolyn Arms—and her father's library. Miss Arms was more critical of Elinor than Miss Nichols. She wrote to Elinor, "You are

unstable as water," an assessment Elinor took seriously and
attached to her mirror. She increased her own small library—
which already included a vellum-covered Shelley in the Variorum edition (two volumes) and a "claret colored Keats"
(both given to her by Dada)—by stealing *The Oxford Book of English Verse* from Papa. "Thanks to it," she remembered in
1921, "I used in those days to sup with Landor and Donne."

Elinor has left only one scene illustrating the effect of
these two influences, and even that is heavily shaded with
romanticism. "It was September in Washington," she recalled
in a piece written three decades later,

and the air was warm and sweet as if all the grapes and peaches of
Maryland and Virginia had flavored it to my taste. I stood before the
smallest bookcase in the library, and from its shelves I drew Trelawny's "Recollections." The window was wide open; there was
plenty of light and soft autumnal wind in the room. I did not move
except to turn the pages. Even the black leather chair was too far
away from the scene within the covers of the book. I stood quite still
and turned the pages, and the curtains blew in at the window and
a few golden leaves blew in between them.

Elinor remained at Mrs. Flint's for three years at least (no
records of the school now exist). Photographs of her at the
time show, inaccurately, her meticulous appearance, and more
accurately, her beauty. Dressed invariably in white (as she
herself dressed her fictional heroine Jennifer Lorn decades
later), with her chestnut hair braided or ribboned, she stood
in alarming confidence with a poise that was reinforced by her
height. Elinor's beauty, which rose in adolescence, was an
active thing. It rested on posture, movement, and demeanor.
She did not possess the robust prettiness that was to make
Constance so famous in Washington, but she had a certain
austerity, refinement, and perhaps frailty that was no less impressive. Her features were remarkable only in combination.
She was, as those who knew her then confirm, very striking.
One observer wrote: "she was the most beautiful person I had
ever seen." Away from the camera, Elinor was far from meticulous about her appearance. She had a casual disregard for her
beauty, her clothes, and her hair. She was taller than most of
the other girls in her school, and there was a hint of awkward-

ness in her posture. Her dresses never managed to stay tidy throughout the day. She was even less particular about her room at K Street. Upstairs, next to Connie's room, it was strewn with wrinkled handkerchiefs, stockings, and gloves. Her desk, which Mama and Papa had given her for her first Christmas in Washington, was a riot of scraps of paper, nibs, and ink. Order was the enemy.

By April 1899 space presented another problem in the K Street house. After nearly a decade, Mama felt that her heart had improved enough to undergo the strain of having another child. On April 4 a second son, Morton McMichael Hoyt, was born. The event was endured with the same nobility, laced with suggestions of martyrdom, as Mama's other births. Now the children were old enough to appreciate the disrupting effect of her withdrawal into pregnancy. Three years later, on October 1, 1902, the final addition was made to the family—Anne McMichael Hoyt.

At the beginning of September 1902, Elinor and Connie (aged seventeen and thirteen respectively) had been sent off to the Devon Inn, Devon, in Pennsylvania to stay with the McMichaels while waiting for the arrival of their sister. "I am *most awfully* glad," Elinor wrote to Mama (October 2, 1902),

that the little stranger has come at last, and particularly pleased that it is a girl. You can imagine how delighted we were when the telegraph arrived this morning. Now, darling, can you tell us pretty soon when we are to come home and see you again? Of course I know that as yet it is much easier that we should be away. . . . And then I also want to see the dear little new sister, though that is of secondary importance, I must confess, dear, because she is not quite such an intimate friend of mine as you are . . . you *must* name it Nancy, just Nancy. . . . At least always call it Nancy. It is queer that none of us have managed to get named after the best person in the family and this little lady really should be. Please do. (B)*

As the population of the Hoyt household increased, the K Street house grew more and more cramped. After the birth of Nancy the family moved to 1701 Rhode Island Avenue, where they remained. Mama's control was as absolute as ever. Emotional blackmail became her favorite weapon in battling

*Anne was always known as Nancy.

with her children, who were, not surprisingly, developing
very strong personalities. Elinor possessed Mama's ambition
and Papa's keen intelligence. Henry had his father's love of
reason and fairness, and recoiled in shyness against his
mother's dominance. Constance proved most clearly the Hoyt
beauty and Mama's perverse self-indulgence. She was Mama's
declared favorite. All three children were perhaps too aware
of their mother, and certainly too ignorant of their father.
Elinor rarely mentioned her father as she grew older. He
seemed not to exist in the scheme of things that Mama so
readily manipulated. (After his death, Mama would almost
obliterate his memory.)

Mama was strong, yet not strong enough to overcome the
impulses of doubt that sometimes betrayed her. She once left
a suicide note for her children to find. After she heard what
they had to say, she decided not to try it again. "I have given
birth to a generation of vipers!" she once snapped.

Mama's whole life was her children. As Elinor, Henry,
and Constance grew older and began to drift away from her,
she let Papa back into her bedroom. Then children became
her career. For a period of almost four decades her supremacy
at Rhode Island Avenue would remain inviolate. The traffic in
the nursery was extraordinary. Mama's interpretation of her
matriarchal role meant that her children grew up to be less
than satisfactory parents, and she was provided with a steady
flow of grandchildren to superintend once her own children
left. In actuality Mama commanded the nursery steadily from
1885 until her death in 1951.

In 1901 Elinor's English teacher Carolyn Arms and her
colleague, Mrs. Jessie Moon Holton, left Miss Flint's school to
start up their own. Mama would not let Elinor follow Miss
Arms until Mrs. Flint had an opportunity to reorganize her
school without the benefit of her two most promising teachers.
Then Mama relented, and in September 1901 Elinor was enrolled in the new Holton-Arms School, a small school of about
twenty girls aged between fourteen and eighteen years old,
located in Hillyer Place.*

*In 1906 the school moved to new quarters built to Mrs. Holton's specifica-
tions at 2125 S Street, where it remained until 1963. That year it moved

Elinor's affection for Miss Arms and for her school is best read in the only surviving document of her years at Holton-Arms School: her report for the final term, ending May 1904. She earned the highest marks possible in History, Political Economy, Astronomy, Shakespeare, English, and French. She did only slightly less well in Deportment—a B+; and in Science, which she took for one month, a B. By all accounts Elinor was an excellent student. Family legend has it that she memorized *Hamlet* in two weeks and was capable of remembering almost every poem she read. Certainly she displayed unusual powers of concentration. The only description of Elinor as a schoolgirl at Holton-Arms comes in a letter Papa wrote to Mama, then in Philadelphia with Morton and Nancy, in 1902 or 1903: "The girls [Elinor and Constance] started in at school today, in high spirits, and returned tonight with the usual assortment of new books & new tasks. Elinor has just completed a letter in French to Alice Miller, a task set by the Professor, and she & Maude [Hoyt] are delighted with the cleverness & cuteness of the production." (B)

When Theodore Roosevelt became President after the assassination of McKinley in 1901, he retained McKinley's cabinet intact. Eighteen months later, on March 31, 1903, he promoted Papa to the office of Solicitor-General. When Taft became President, he elevated his Yale classmate to the new office of Counsellor of the State Department (in 1908). As Solicitor-General Harry Hoyt was an adviser to the Supreme Court, specializing in antitrust and security matters. When he was elevated to Counsellor, he was concerned with international legal problems—tariff schedules and reciprocity negotiations with Canada. He fought big business and monopolies. He was, as one observer noted after his death, extremely well suited for public office, having "a cool, quiet detachment from the heat and passion of every-day questions and debates." He was astonishingly conscientious and dedicated to his work, publishing an

to Bathesda, Maryland. Enrollment today is approximately 500 girls. Elinor's two sisters also attended Holton-Arms.

enormous number of papers on the intricate interpretation
of the law, Unfortunately, the qualities that distinguished
him in his career were extremely ill-suited to family life.
The "cool . . . detachment" carried over into his relationships with his family, leaving the children almost exclusively to Mama. While Papa's standing in government increased every year, his authority at Rhode Island Avenue
decreased. Mama, however, was satisfied with the improvement in their social position, which in Washington was
linked to governmental power.

Elinor was the first child to fall victim to Mama's constricting sense of social position; she was now, at the age of
seventeen, a debutante. Mama sent her off to Philadelphia
to further her education under the watchful eye of Dada.
In the early spring of 1903 Elinor followed a grueling routine—through the Academy of Fine Arts to look at the Sar-
gents, plus interminable teas, luncheons, and dinners. It
was a disastrous plan. Elinor begged to come home, to be
released from this sort of tuition. But her traveling and social education continued.

In May, Elinor and Connie sailed for Europe, chaperoned
by Dada, who at the age of seventy controlled his young
granddaughters feebly, yet successfully. They made a stately
and leisurely progress through Germany, Holland, Belgium,
France, and England. In Paris the girls spent their afternoons
sitting to Marie Berger, a portraitist who depicted them in
such languid poses that she avoided anything close to a likeness. When the enormous pastel, commissioned by Dada, was
hung in Rhode Island Avenue, both Elinor and Constance
hotly denied that they might have been the subjects. They
renamed it "Anemia and Apoplexy"—Constance being the
former, Elinor the latter. The picture became a figure of fun,
and in the twenties Elinor renamed it "The Sweetbread Sisters."*

In London they stayed at the Hyde Park Hotel, in rooms
overlooking Rotten Row. Their mornings were given over to
sightseeing, and their evenings were spent at the theater. "Tonight we are going to see 'Dante,' " Elinor proudly an-

*The portrait is now at the University of Virginia.

Elinor
Wylie

nounced to Mama [July 18, 1903], "which I am sure will be very interesting and certainly very unusual. We have a box from Sir Henry [Irving]—and Conny and I are secretly hoping that he will give us some flowers like the other time." (B) Sardou's *Dante* turned out to be "dull"; the real pleasure for Elinor was sitting in the Royal Box and being served ices by a footman between the acts.

Dada's friendship with Sir Henry Irving stretched back for two decades to when, in 1883, Sir Henry went on his first American tour. In December of that year the Clover Club gave him a reception at the Bellevue Hotel in Philadelphia. Morton McMichael was one of fifty-three guests. Sir Henry was greatly moved by the occasion, and said in return: "I hope I shall have the pleasure of welcoming some of the members of this club whenever they cross the water . . . I will endeavor to make some return for this unexpected welcome."* Dada's annual visits to London gave Sir Henry ample opportunity not to forget him. Morton McMichael became a regular guest at the Beefsteak Club, and his final visit to London with his granddaughters proved his most successful. Sir Henry's secretary, Bram Stoker,† was particularly impressed by the beauty of both Elinor and Constance as they were led into dinner by their grandfather.

"We went to a supper," Elinor wrote to her mother about two weeks before sailing home [July, 1903] (B), "Sir Henry gave after the last performance of Dante the other night. It was a lot of fun—one saw lots of theatrical and literary people. They looked tremendously usual and respectable—just like *plain* ladies and gentlemen. Some of

*His chance came three months later after a performance of *Much Ado About Nothing* at the Chestnut Street Opera House on March 19, 1884. Among those present as the guests of Sir Henry Irving was Elinor's paternal grandfather, Governor Hoyt.

†Bram Stoker (1847–1912), educated at Trinity College, Dublin where he received an Honors Degree in Pure Mathematics. He joined the Irish Civil Service where he stayed until 1878, when he came to London to join Sir Henry Irving as manager of the Lyceum Theatre. He is best known as the author of *Dracula* (1897) and was the author of some fifteen other books, among them a two-volume memoir of Sir Henry Irving (1906) and a pamphlet on *The Duties of a Clerk of Petty Sessions in Ireland* (1879).

them were quite young and awfully nice, too, and every
one of them was quietly dressed and well bred." The vision of Elinor and Constance Hoyt so impressed Bram
Stoker that he dedicated his novel *The Jewel of the Seven
Stars* (1903), to them, and failed to spell Elinor's name
properly. Like the Berger portrait, Elinor never mentioned
her appearance in this book.

While her mornings and evenings bustled with activity,
her afternoons were steadily empty. Dada needed his rest,
which included Elinor and Constance as well. "The only thing
that really irritates me," she moaned to Mama from Paris
(June 2, 1903), "is the half-witted convention which makes it
impossible for me or two young girls to take walks by themselves—for I love to walk and some of these wide tree bor-
dered avenues look very delightful and alluring—much like
Washington only new and unexplored. It makes me furious.
I have not walked at all—that is, not what I call walking—since
I landed." And just as Elinor and Constance were getting
accustomed to this leisurely pace toward the end of their tour,
Dada decided to take them up to Scotland, stopping at York
on the way. Elinor was delighted by this unexpected burst of
energy in her grandfather, reporting to Mama: "I am awfully
glad we are going—and, except for such paltry considerations
as more dirty clothes and less washing, it is quite a perfect
plan."

Elinor displayed little aptitude as a traveler. She lost
her keys and all her money the night before she left America. She *"despised* that slow boat," the S.S. *Kroonland.* She
did not enjoy looking at pictures. Yet she did admit to her
mother, "We really have had the most perfect time imaginable, and enjoyed every minute of it thoroughly. I only
wish you had been with us. I was delighted to find *everything* much nicer than I expected it would be—except perhaps the Rhine which has been modernized lately." Mama
and Papa planned to meet up with their daughters in London, but at the last moment Mama preferred to stay with
Morton and Nancy at Asticou. Henry sat for his entrance
examinations to Yale that summer, and after passing, went
on a long motor trip in "the Olds."

Papa met Elinor and Constance and Dada the first week

in August when they docked in New York, then took his daughters up to Asticou where they spent the rest of the summer. In September Elinor returned for her final year at Holton-Arms and began to move through the exhausting rituals of being a debutante.

CHAPTER THREE: 1905

§ *i*   *God knows the ways of innocence are steep*
And difficult to climb . . .
                —Elinor Wylie,
        "With a Bare Bodkin"

Washington—like much of Boston—was built on reclaimed swampland. Its society was founded on the progeny of vulgar Colonials who became sophisticated after four generations, and who lived, it seemed, for gossip. With its broad avenues and narrow minds, expansive parks and constricted etiquette, Washington was for Mama a very comfortable home. Until the arrival of Theodore Roosevelt in the Executive Mansion, Blue-Booked Washingtonians rarely gave the President a glance: " 'the brilliant diplomatic society' was supposed to make up for the social short-comings of the Administration," Edith Wharton noted in her *Age of Innocence*. Yet, despite the continual mandatory shuffle of calling cards, Washington remained a calm and restful place. In 1926 Elinor remembered it as possessing "delightful quietness"; the ambiance was lethargic and distinctly Southern.

Freed from the protection of school, Elinor found herself plunged into the elaborate matrimonial stakes. The routine of "coming out" was a complicated ordeal. First came tea for the elderly members of the family, followed by "the first dinner party before the debutante dance, which will end the suspense," Nancy Hoyt pointed out, "as to whether she is going to be a success." The pre-dance dinner guests were selected for their eligibility, and Elinor's parents had a great deal of trouble finding enough young men. The procedure culminated in a cotillion attended by "all the young men you were supposed to know." "I can remember Elinor," Nancy wrote, "pink and white as a sea-shell, in coral tulle," emerging from the ordeal " 'luminous and radiant' " and, as her beauty ordained, an unquestioned success. Cotillions and balls headed a hectic social season of luncheons, teas, dressmakers' *39* appointments, and dinners. It was not a routine at all suited to Elinor. She held back, tentatively. She enrolled in the Corcoran for art lessons, but quickly withdrew. When Mama asked her if the model wore any clothing, Elinor replied slightly too candidly, "Yes, some blue side-combs in her hair." She entered into a college course in philosophy, but never managed to attend with any regularity. She continued to read, and persisted in writing poetry. The poems she wrote between the summer of 1902 and the summer of 1904, eleven of which were collected as "Juvenilia" in *Incidental Numbers* (1912), demonstrate nothing more than youthful romanticism with some precocious touches of irony and sarcasm. They are little more than interesting specimens that foreshadowed more important work. She herself was embarrassed by these poems and told very few people about them.

As the eldest of three daughters, the pressure to get married was fierce. Spinsterhood was an embarrassing state and the family had two unmarried aunts who brought no credit to the Hoyts. Elinor was virtually shoved at men. Unlike Connie, she was very shy in company of potential husbands. She rebelled against Mama's ambition for her, took up with unsuitable men, and seemed to care very little about marriage.

Elinor's adolescent romantic adventures have only been hinted at, not by her, but by her sister eleven years after Elinor's death. "Before she came out Elinor had no beaux, but several admirers. Among them were a red-headed witty boy slightly in disgrace with his own family, and a lame, intellectual youth who went to church every Sunday in order to come home with Elinor afterward and talk about books. . . . At eighteen she was slightly austere. . . ."

Elinor's shyness, coupled with her burgeoning vanity, drew her to the underdog. It became a family joke, and as she grew older it turned into a habit. In the 1920s William Rose Benét wrote to her that it was one feature in her character he not only warmed to, but could always rely on. Yet while she was a debutante it was not an attractive tendency. The arrogance fostered at Rhode Island Avenue did not overwhelm her timidity sufficiently. She had to *appear* assured and confident; her casual neglect of proper social connections was per-

plexing even to the Hoyts. Elinor was caught in a difficult trap.
She was forced to act out of character. Her teachers begged
her to continue her education; Mama forced her into society.
Neither option intrigued her sufficiently.

Success at the cotillion had to be topped with marriage,
and Elinor seemed to be moving toward that end. "About this
time," Nancy Hoyt wrote under Mama's instructions,

there occurred an interlude in a conservatory, almost as idyllic as the
one in *Jennifer* [*Lorn*]. The tall, fair young man was just as much a
person of race as many of Elinor's future sub-heroes. . . . He was just
such a person as one would have expected her to marry. The fragile
romance was conducted on technically classic lines from the rowboat
above the cool emerald eel-grass at North-East Harbor, to the actual
conservatory with pink and white striped curtains in Washington,
D.C. Something happened; mildly embittered because this so suitable union did not occur immediately, Elinor rushed off and without
the knowledge of my parents, became engaged to a nice-looking and
well-born young suitor with a bad temper, who had been courting
her unsuccessfully for a year or more.

This was all Mama wanted to reveal about Philip Hichborn.

§ *ii*   *"Mrs Hichborn*—ha!"

Mama had a good reason to keep Philip Hichborn out of
Nancy Hoyt's biography of her sister—Elinor had married a
madman. Almost nothing is known about him. Elinor forgot
him very easily, and she rarely mentioned him.

If Nancy Hoyt's veiled hints about Philip Simmons Hichborn are correct, he caught the Hoyts completely by surprise
and Elinor on the rebound. He was the eldest child and only
son of a Boston family that traced its paternal line back to Paul
Revere. Born in 1882, Philip Hichborn was three years older
than Elinor. His father was Rear-Admiral Philip Hichborn and
his mother was Jennie M. Franklin. When his father was appointed Chief Constructor of the Navy in 1893, the family
moved to Washington. Unlike his father, Philip Hichborn, Jr.,
ignored a naval career and entered Harvard in 1901, moving

on after graduation in 1905 to study law at George Washington University until he qualified in 1908. His career at Harvard was far from memorable, save that his classmates found him disconcertingly charming, that he was a member of the Hasty Pudding Club, and that he was editor of the *Harvard Lampoon*. His law practice, which began as an assistant in the highly distinguished office of the Attorney-General, quickly lost its reputation when he went on his own. He was competent, but little more.

In the best Hoyt tradition he was as much given to outdoor activity as indoor: he was an accomplished sportsman and socialite. He was addicted to riding and hunting, played an adequate game of tennis and bridge, and danced extremely well. Tall, elegant, impeccably mannered with flashing eyes, dark hair, he cut an altogether dashing figure at cotillions and clubs. Mama and Connie were quite overpowered by his appearance. Fourteen years after his death Mama remembered him as "a Rudolph Valentino." Henry meekly accepted him into the family, without liking him; Papa darkly refused to see much merit in the man. And Papa was correct; for there was, alarmingly, an unattractive side to his character. There was no question that Hichborn loved Elinor, but the expression of this affection gave way to violent fits of jealousy and hatred. These unmanageable outbursts of temper destroyed any relationship they might have shared. What made it worse were his attempts to control his tantrums. Marrying Elinor had a calming effect, temporarily.

Elinor and Philip Hichborn were married on December 12, 1906, quietly at Rhode Island Avenue. The ceremony was presided over by Bishop Satterlee and Henry was best man. President Roosevelt came. And, apart from the collection of relatives, Henry brought a friend from Yale, William Rose Benét. The couple went to Boston, stopping in New York on the way for their honeymoon.

It was a rapturous beginning: "didn't they give us a wild farewell," Elinor wrote to her mother from New York [Dec. 13, 1906] (B). "Still it was fun I think but you should have seen the way the confetti stuck to us—no disguising our status I guess." They stayed at the Holland House at Fifth Avenue and 13th Street, where they had a "fine big room and bath

. . . I love N.Y. They have *grand* things to eat here and my
sore throat is *all* gone. . . . Phil is an angel and says he hasn't
felt so well for weeks. I am *fine*. Wasn't it a pretty wedding?
. . . Write me a letter—to *Mrs Hichborn*—ha!"

They went shopping for a pink silk petticoat. They had
luncheon and tea at the Waldorf, and they went to the theater.
On their last night in New York they had "a grand farewell
dinner at Sherry's . . . all by ourselves . . . I never had such
a lovely time in my life and really Phil is absolutely *perfect*,"
Elinor told her mother [Dec. 17] (B).

It was a status he did not retain. Elinor was soon pregnant.
The alternation of Phil's moods became more and more pronounced, as if somehow linked to Elinor's advancing pregnancy. He was plunged into deep depressions, relieved sometimes only by petulance. He became enraged over the smallest
things. He shouted at Elinor; called her names. He stormed
about their house in N Street, and then as quickly as these
perverse moods gripped him they would disappear and Phil
became kind and gentle. To all outsiders they presented a
facade of complete harmony, appearing to conduct their life
with affection for one another. There was no hint of madness
lurking behind the facade.

"Phil can ride every morning," Elinor wrote in one of
her few letters during the first year of her marriage [June 6,
1907] (B). "—which is the time I want him off my hands—
and in the afternoon we go to the club together and he plays
tennis. I suppose every man out there has asked me why I
don't." Phil's other way of entertaining his wife during her
sixth month of pregnancy, while he was enjoying freedom
from his law studies, was to make her sit in a "very small and
very smelly" motor launch in the hot sun. Elinor did not
complain, and according to her sister, "did her very best to
like these outdoor amusements."

Marriage was not a progression for Elinor; she was neither absorbed into her husband's life nor any longer part of
Rhode Island Avenue. She was isolated and her early pregnancy only increased her unhappiness. She had no time to get to
know her husband, or adjust to married life, before becoming
a mother. Phil aggravated the difficulty even more by becoming very jealous of the baby who was not yet born. Elinor tried

to hold on to her mother, but Mama would not allow it.

The Hoyts left Washington for the summer, first for The Homestead, Hot Springs, Virginia, and then for Europe in July. Mama thought it the right thing to do, to leave Elinor and Phil alone together for the first time. They promised to be home in time for Elinor's twenty-second birthday and the birth of her baby, due shortly thereafter. This promise did not make Elinor feel any happier: " 'I thought I would die,' " Mama reports Elinor saying in her account of Elinor's marriage, "The Naked Truth." (B) " 'I was so frightened, I stood on the steps and watched you all drive off, and I thought, "I won't ever see any of *them* again." ' " Elinor confessed that she was not frightened about having the baby, but by being left alone with Phil.

Her mother could not understand; "to be sure you were cheerful," she told Elinor when she heard this out-burst, "and looked pretty, and went about, but it was always a mite [?] daunting—Then you both are so young, and the baby's coming so quickly, not much time to get used to each other. . . ." Phil's outbursts came as a complete revelation to Mama. Elinor explained that he "has been so strange, and so irritable for ages, just bad tempered, I thought. He does of course rave at me about nothing, and I suppose he could say I am excitable too, you see I do get perfectly wild, I am so scared . . . I think he simply hates me . . . and being married at all, at least that is what he always says." Then there were frantic outbursts that had nothing to do with Elinor: "he says he cannot ride on street-cars, or take a taxi, or go to the country club, because all the men employed by all three, in-sult him, or despise him, because they believe he is un-manly." All this forced Elinor to the undeniable conclusion: "I think he is crazy." She was proved correct one year later.

Like Shelley, Philip Hichborn III was born less than ten months after his parents' marriage, on September 22, 1907. "My first news is," Henry wrote groggily from bed where he was recuperating from chicken pox to Bill Benét at Yale (September 24, 1907) (Y), "—Elinor's child was born last night and they're both getting along finely. You must now treat Nancy with the respect due an aunt under five years old." It was an easy birth, with no complications. In attendance were,

of course, a battery of supervising nurses and a cluster of eager
female members of the family. "Beeyup," as the baby was
called, was placed in the McMichael mahogany cradle that
Elinor herself slept in as a child. The nurse bullied Elinor a
great deal, frightened Mama, and blocked any changes in the
established routine of the household she ordered.

The arrival of the child brought Elinor little happiness; he
only seemed to complicate her life with her husband. Late in
October she had a conversation with her mother, fully revealing for the first time what she had hidden so well. Before she
confessed, Elinor extracted a painful promise from Mama:
"Swear you wont tell anybody . . . no, no, no *swear.*" The true
nature of her marriage came out; she begged Mama for help,
knowing there was very little Mama could do without telling
Papa.

Elinor: "If it wasn't for baby I could tell [Papa] but now how can
I?"

Mama: "Promise or no promise, I would have to tell your father, but
he isn't well, he is dreadfully depressed."

Elinor: "No, it wouldn't do me any good and he would be angry,
he hates him [Phil] anyway."

Hitherto any worries Mama had about the success of Elinor's
marriage were explained by Elinor's extreme youth. The re-
spective families had no idea all was not well. This startling
news was not easy for Mama to contain. Even overlooking the
fact of her promise, she could not tell her husband. "Well as
it happened," she recalled, "he was absent, sent away for his
health, a nervous breakdown, and at the moment in New
Mexico." The only solution was to wait—"Perhaps it would
disentangle itself." "Being optimistic by nature," Mama
thought of herself, "fairly young still, and fondly loving babies
herself, this grandmother could not quite despair of some
solution—A new and painful idea, tends to cloak itself like this
—there is such a thing as being too *bad* to be true, as well as
too good."

While Mama hoped, Elinor and Phil concealed all out-
ward signs of discord. Six weeks after the birth of her baby,
Elinor stood at Rhode Island Avenue to receive the guests for
Connie's "coming out" tea. Mama remembered her looking

astonishingly beautiful, and almost the same age as her younger sister. The house was full of flowers—orchids from the White House and roses from the German Embassy. The event was as much a triumph for Elinor as it was meant to be for Connie. Elinor announced that she was back in Society, after her confinement.

And so the elaborate charade began. Phil toyed with his new law practice by day, and wrote some charming but inconsequential short stories in the evening. "Phil had a short story accepted by the Metropolitan," Henry wrote to Bill Benét (n.d.), "and its [sic] going to appear in the June number. I don't think its much of a story, but its well written, and easily good enough for contemporary magazine stuff. He sent them another which I think *is* really good and not a bit 'Philish.' " (Y) By "Philish" he meant slight racing and hunting tales, full of outdoor stuff with some occasional delightful touches. The stories were distinctly unmemorable, no matter how hard the United Hunts Club of America tried to make them otherwise when they sponsored a collection in 1912 entitled *Hoofbeats*. Unlike Phil himself, Elinor rarely mentioned these stories. Elinor did no writing. For both of them it was "a life filled with gaiety—," Mama assessed, "constant dinners and dances and meetings with young people their own age—No drinking to amount to anything—Wine with dinner, occasionally champagne with supper."

But by autumn 1908, the veil of secrecy was lifted for all to see. Phil suffered a serious concussion after falling from his horse and the dangerous signs of mental imbalance could be hidden no longer. Weeks later, "with his own consent and that of his parents a famous doctor at Johns-Hopkins was consulted." The doctor announced that Phil was suffering from "dementia-praecox." Henry passed on the news to Bill Benét: "Phil has nervous prostration, or some Egoist's disease like it, and will have to go away and get better. Hell!" The result was, as Horace Wylie later wrote (April 16, 1910), that Phil "neglected her [Elinor] so, poor child"; he was "(nearly crazy) & in the Winter they had left the baby & gone to that hole Pinehurst which she hated."

While Elinor thought her place was beside her husband in "that hole" during his convalescence, Mama sacrificed her

own holiday to look after Elinor's child. Henry became very
worried about his mother. "I am really very much troubled
about her condition," he wrote to Bill Benét. "You see she's
got such indomitable nerve, and takes on herself such a lot of
our burdens, that she's used up, and even now I fear it would
be impossible to make her go, because she thinks she ought
to stay here and take care of Elinor's baby." The baby, by
contrast, was the healthiest member of the family, "growing
big, and healthy and handsome and good tempered."

The knowledge that Elinor's suspicions about her husband's mental state were correct did not relieve her strain. In
many ways it only increased it. The need for duplicity was
greater now; she had to appear more loving and understanding than before. She had to stand by him. She was tied more
closely to him, at least for appearance' sake. As a result, Elinor
herself was beginning to suffer from this painful tension. Her
blood pressure became alarmingly high. She became extremely nervous—"essential hypertension" was her doctor's
verdict. She started to have painful headaches, often migraines, which were not helped by her perverse refusal to
wear spectacles. The headaches grew more and more severe
as she grew older, but they date directly from the complications of her marriage to Hichborn. She always had bromides
in her purse and learned to ignore the pain, which she was
never entirely free from. She accepted it as part of life, just as
she accepted that "barely decent cheerfulness" was required
throughout the worst stages of her life with Phil.

§ *iii*   *"Reason is not the goddess of emergencies."*
                                          —Elinor Wylie,
                              The Venetian Glass Nephew

Washington was not a town for anonymity; everyone knew, or
seemed to know, everyone else. Society was guided by its own
Baedeker: The Blue Book. The season revolved not around
governmental fixtures, but the weather. Summers were passed
far to the north. Toward the end of September, after the heat
and dust had cleared away, Washingtonians breezed home.

In every respect Washington was a small town; provincial to the point of petty, and petty to the point of microscopic. Neighbors provided what passed for entertainment and diplomats provided a transfusion of titles to stale guestlists. It was a discouraging world, a suffocating world, and unlike Mama, Elinor felt it deeply.

Washington might have been bad enough, but coupled with the difficulties of marriage to Philip Hichborn, it became intolerable. Elinor's existence was circumscribed by home, husband, and baby. There were few, if any, recesses from the tiresome régime. As Mrs. Philip Hichborn she was expected to play bridge, drink tea, and converse for innumerable hours; she loved tea, hated her companions, and never quite mastered bridge. Again she found herself ill-suited to her new role. Thus she was poised to jump at the merest hint of escape, no matter how reckless or foolhardy. As it happened, Horace Wylie's timing proved ideal.

"I thought at once," Horace Wylie later wrote of Elinor (April 16, 1910) (B), "she was the most beautiful person I had ever seen I really almost gasped. Just what as a boy I had dreamed that my love should look. After I had seen her a couple of times more I discreetly followed her. . . ." To Horace, Elinor soon became infallible; to Elinor, Horace was attentive. It all began as a magnificent dance. The pace quickened as time went on, fed by fear of discovery. Philip continued to waver between petulance and depression, alternately disliking and tolerating his wife. Elinor sought Horace's wife Katharine out as a confidante; the horrors of marriage to Phil were placed, unwelcomely, before her. Every movement Elinor made was watched by Phil—she was answerable to him for everything. Any advance she made toward her son only enraged him more. The N Street household pushed her where her emotions alone were not strong enough to draw her: toward Horace Wylie. The progression involved directly and indirectly nearly a dozen people.

Horace Wylie led an enterprising life. He pursued his career on the baize at the Metropolitan Club and the rolling shaved grass at the Chevy Chase Club, and his achievements were the result of admirable professionalism at bridge and golf. He was an ardent gamesman, accomplished in surmounting the challenges of chess, the stock market, the turf, and good conversation. His life rotated easily and majestically around affairs of little consequence. His intelligence was exercised in reading, and in dressing carefully.

Horace succeeded, at various times, in stretching his genealogy to include the duc de Richelieu, Jean de Brienne (leader of the Fifth Crusade, king of Cyprus, and later Emperor of the East) and Rollo of Normandy. More recent in his version of his family tree was Napoleon (undoubtedly a connection engineered through an undeclared bastard). His affection for Michelet and Mirabeau no doubt had something to do with this extraordinary feat of heraldry. Somewhat closer to home, he was the product of a background that for two previous generations had enjoyed high public office, social standing, and considerable achievement. His great-grandfather left Ireland in 1776 to farm in Pennsylvania. His grandfather, Andrew Wylie (1789–1851), moved further west to dedicate himself to education and God, becoming the first president of Indiana College in 1828 (in 1838 it became Indiana University), and moving from Presbyterian to Episcopal pastor in the space of three decades. Horace's father, Andrew Wylie, Jr., was no less energetic. He began his law practice in Pittsburgh and even after the great fire of 1845 had destroyed all his papers, his enthusiasm remained undampened. That year he married, moved to his in-laws' home in Alexandria, Virginia, and started his career again. In 1863 President Lincoln appointed him Justice of the District Circuit Court of Appeals and he moved to an imposing brick mansion on what was later known as Thomas Circle, in the center of Washington.

Horace's mother, Mary Caroline Bryan, provided him with the French lineage he loved to expand. Yet the Bryans were more closely associated with the history of Virginia: her uncle was governor of Virginia, U.S. senator, Secretary of War, and minister to England; another uncle was a Justice of the Supreme Court; her father retired from the state senate to the less demanding office of postmaster. Mary Bryan Wylie was an extraordinarily beautiful woman, with dark eyes and hair. She was noted for saying precisely what she thought, and for her aversion to eating meat, except for chicken breasts.

Horace Wylie was born September 16, 1868, when

his mother was forty-two and his father fifty-four. He was the only child of seven to survive. He was very spoiled, and though the Wylie intelligence passed to him, he regarded it somewhat too casually. When he sat for his Yale entrance examinations in 1885 he forgot his pencil. But, as he admitted at the time, "Knew [Latin] passage by heart 1st through exams. 1st through French essay 20 minutes allowed four hours." Rapid in translation, he managed to fail handwriting. After Yale he went on to Harvard Law School; in 1892, after he was graduated, he went on a world tour. His only memory of the journey was that he contracted cholera.

Back in Washington fully recovered, he prepared to practice law. He had cards engraved, a sign made, and an office furnished—which was about as close as he ever came to being a lawyer. He caught typhoid and went to bed. Just as he was beginning to recover, his doctor pronounced him well enough to walk a mile. Wylie took him at his word, suffered a severe relapse, and impaired his eyesight irreparably.

Horace Wylie suffered from an intemperate weakness for beautiful women all of his life. Despite the distance enforced by etiquette and his faulty vision, women were a sharp stimulus to his imagination. He would stare, and he would chase. It was a compliment, but often an embarrassing and annoying one. Luckily, Horace had a taste for selecting women who would love him, and a talent for making women love him. In 1895, at the age of twenty-eight, he married Katharine Hopkins: "she had the face of a Madonna," he recorded in his diary (B). It was a match that surprised no one. Both bride and groom were prominent in the same social set and had known each other for some time. And it was, in fact, a very happy marriage. They lived in the Thomas Circle house with Horace's father, and their four surviving children (Katharine had borne six children). But marriage and family life were not enough for Horace; he needed a fresh transfusion of feminine beauty, and Elinor provided it.

Though Katharine never lost her beauty or her charm, she was no longer unobtainable, no longer mysterious. Elinor was both. She was an uncharted territory that Horace explored with convincing and exhausting ardor. "Just to show her that I lived to see Her," Horace began in his private memoir about Elinor (B),

in different ways: One day I made up a story that a Furnace Man had applied to me for a job & had given the Hichborns as a reference. I went to "the Admiral's" house (where Elinor was living) and saw her on that pretext. It was a hot day about 2.30 P.M. I had to talk loud to Elinor because Mrs the Admiral was listening. There were a few whispered words I think. A day or two later I told Elinor that it was all made up about the Furnace Man. So you see I must have been making love to her.

And another time, before he left Washington for the summer of 1908, he cruised around town in his automobile ("First year Franklin") searching for her. He was almost on the point of abandoning the search when she appeared, "looking lovely," in a $2.50 dress. She then rode around the block with him and Horace volunteered that "she was the most beautiful thing in life or art." Elinor turned to him and replied, "If I thought you meant that I should be very sorry for you." It was this same sort of romantic urgency that won the love of his third wife, Mrs. Eleanor Marsh. At the age of fifty-two he wooed a woman half his age reciting, at considerable length, the charms of her hair and wrists.

Elinor was extremely vulnerable to Horace's attentions. Her life with Phil was completely without romance; he paid considerable attention to her presence, but not to her person. He found Elinor an extremely shadowy creature, becoming each day more evasive and private. Phil's temper grew increasingly erratic and Elinor began to see her husband only as someone to avoid.

Horace breezed into her life, scattering the gloom. After many years of watching her, practically spying on her, he was finally introduced to her at a cotillion the beginning of 1908. "She was sitting," Horace remembered (April 16, 1910) (B), "against the east wall [at Rauscher's] not many seats from the door . . . I told her at once how I had admired her as a girl. . . . We got on well that year but I found her hard to talk to & thought her mind rather empty & not clever. My Lord! what an Ass I was!"

Throughout the season of 1908 Elinor noticed Horace

increasingly. He managed to get himself invited to the dinners and balls she went to; he engineered, sometimes by the most devious means, to run into her in the street. She was pursued with the utmost reluctance—and fascination. "I first found out that she was clever this way," Horace wrote.

I met her on F. St. and she dived into a shoe store (Burts) . . . but told me she had just bought tickets at the Columbia for that night. I looked at the tickets, went & bought one for myself right in front of hers. She & Phil came in after I did that night & P attracted my attention (ha ha) by touching me on the shoulder I think. In the entre act I made some reference to *Arms & the Man* & Elinor to my amazement had read it. She said she had read all of Shaw. She said one did not "have to be such a high brow" to have done that. I joked her on the lowness of her forehead & for the first time knew she had a mind. Was it not strange that I could see her so often and not know that she was clever, witty or well read?

Horace now became even more ardent.

By 1909 their intimacy had forged ahead. In a tactic to blunt Phil's suspicion, Elinor penciled notes so illegible, so cryptic, and apparently so inconsequential on scraps of paper that only Horace's amatory diligence could decipher them. Horace received her messages in the safety of the Metropolitan Club and kept everything, with annotations, in the vault of the American Security and Trust Company. Only when he was too ill to get to the vault did he destroy any of her letters, and even then he noted the fact at a later date. Horace's attentiveness was extraordinary; it lingered flatteringly on the most minute details: "I kissed Elinor first," he records with scientific precision, "on the 15th May, 1909 between 12 & 1 P.M. in my motor up the road from the ford in Rock Creek Park."

One month later Horace left Washington with his family, in his "2nd year Franklin (no chauffeur)," for the North Shore, Massachusetts. Elinor hastened north to Asticou with Phil and her son and a collection of Hoyts. Before he left Horace gave Elinor a pearl stick pin which she had remade as a ring, "paying for the exchange with some old jewelry." And Elinor wrote "Song—For You" for Horace to celebrate his gift (later she revised and published it as "Song" in *Incidental Numbers*):

My love, before he went away,
Gave me a ring to keep—
I smile at it when I am gay.
I kiss it when I weep;
I wear my shining ring all day
And if the night is long, I lay
My lips to it and sleep.
(A sweet and blessed sleep)

Because my ring is smooth and bright
Because I love it so
I keep my hands as clean and white
As newly fallen snow
As pale rose-petals plucked at night—
The angels' hands, in God's own sight
Are scarce so white, I know.
(Scarce so milk-white, I know)

My lover, when he went away,
Left me a memory—
It is so sweet it seems to me
Through golden hours and through grey
Yes, when I laugh, and when I pray,
It still shines steadfastly.
(Brightly and steadfastly)

It is so beautiful and white
I strive with every act
To keep my soul as clear a light
As cleanly set apart.
I think the holy angels might
Look down on me from Heaven's height
And envy my pure heart.
My pure and happy heart.

The May kiss and summer separation changed mere gestures into real affection. Play acting gave way before Horace's romantic scrutiny of Elinor's activities. And Elinor, for her part, was not without an ability to amplify the simplest event, layering it with some amorous meaning. She was beginning to enjoy this idea that she might be in love. On Sunday, October 17, Elinor and Horace were members of a large luncheon party. After the men retired to the smoking room, Elinor, in Horace's words, "tried to hold the match until it was all burned i.e. shifting the end held when necessary to see if someone loved her." Her first attempt failed, and on the second, "she changed the end of the match while it was almost red hot to ensure its being all consumed. It burned her so badly! Even burnt a piece out of her nail. She kicked her chair . . . with her little heels it hurt so but she held on."

This telling incident was not an auspicious start to a week of separation "to gradually get used to what must be this winter." [October 20] (B) On Monday Elinor sent Horace a perfumed note begging him not to worry about her burnt finger: "you don't know what a relief it is to be burnt *that* way." Tuesday she managed to bruise a finger, which left her so shaky she had to have a restorative hot chocolate. Horace spotted her going into Hughes' and nonchalantly went in himself to buy some peppermints. He sat down next to Elinor and prescribed Jane Carlyle's letters for her nerves; they arranged to meet the next morning when he would give her the book. Wednesday morning Elinor raced over to their favorite spot on 15th Street to tell Horace that she had to accompany Mama to the dentist and could not stay. She said she would meet him at the end of the Connecticut Avenue car line at 10:55 that morning. She did not appear, but scrawled two quick notes to Horace addressed to his club, one saying: "I am so unhappy I have not looked in the glass but I think my hair is white . . . ." Finally they met that afternoon, and Elinor told Horace that Phil "was cross to her" about her injured fingers. Horace noted: "she liked to tell me . . . to see me mad with him about it."

From burnt and bruised fingers in the early part of their "separation" week, Elinor had moved on to major ailments by the weekend with a sinus attack. "Dear," she wrote to Horace on Friday [October 22, 1909] (B),

I *am* a coward but Xmas (or sinus) comes but once a year and is necessary to make allowances. Indeed I am ashamed of myself but I *cannot* bear it—really . . . never *never* have I been so near the end of the rope—I *can't stand* it. I must see you for a short time—a short time is best I think—tomorrow—Saturday. . . . If I see you for five minutes and you tell me I am brave—or good—I don't need *both*—I can live. . . .

Their "five minutes" together expanded into two and a half
hours, which was fitting culmination to the week of separation.
"Saw her every day," Horace chronicled. "Except one & then
I saw *her* & did not speak through fortitude."

The following week they tried again, and were much
more successful. Elinor only demanded constant declarations
of love to bolster her willpower: "please think of me *very*
hard," she directed Horace [November 2] (B), "and love me
a great deal—I need it . . . I want to be quite sure you are
loving me *with all your might.*" Then she added, in ink, that
he would be able to catch a glimpse of her the next morning
when her carpets were aired.

Now that they had tested their strength, they prepared to
experiment more boldly. By the end of November they were
planning to have lunch together. The first attempt was a miserable failure; Elinor could only stay until twelve thirty—"she
cried and wanted to stay with me anyway but it was wiser to
go after a nibble at the quail (she doesn't like fried oysters)
We had lovely roses. We hid the champagne under leaves but
someone found it and the roses," Horace remembered. Two
days later, December 1, they were more successful. They
motored out to the place of their first kiss, Rock Creek Park,
which they both affectionately referred to as "Arcadia," where
Horace again prepared the scene. He decorated the bushes
with violets and Elinor said: "it looks like a hat shop in Eden."
Then she lay down on the ground, took a bromoseltzer for her
headache, and "got well (or so she said) right away." They
both made themselves comfortable, adjusting their furs and
rugs, and Elinor recited the first part of a long poem she had
written: "Peace on Earth Good Will to Men or the Devil Take
the Hindmost." Horace read two poems by William Morris.
Then they ate lunch: "We did eat Pâte and quail and drink
Mumm '98 Selected Bruit [sic] and we pretended that we
must go as usual at 1.15 or 1.30 we really went at 3.30.
. . . She had on her best dress and the waist I liked. She took
her hair down for a little while. It had been recently washed
and was very light and very beautiful . . . all day she was
perfect." (B) This is the only evidence Horace reveals of their
intimacy after nearly two years. His notations on Elinor's letters are surprisingly, and constantly, accurate down to the

smallest detail. He is a very reliable recorder of a relationship in which the trappings of romance almost seemed of greater importance than any substantive activity.*

Elinor retained the status of *"perfect"* throughout the welter of canceled appointments, postponed meetings, and detonated plans. The calendar for December, after their lunch, proved consistently thwarting to them. The season vaulted from dinners to cotillions, luncheons to teas—appearances had to be maintained unimpeachably upright. It was a difficult time for furtive encounters. And it was, annoyingly, a time for family cohesion. "I have been thinking it over," Elinor wrote to Horace (December 8) (B), ". . . and I am afraid we must put off our picnic. . . . Honestly I couldn't be happy for fear the turkey hadn't come or one of the people telephoned to say they were dead. I don't know if you quite realize how awful it would be of me in either of these circumstances not to be home." She could not leave home on Christmas Eve either, as she was certain her absence would be missed by someone in the household. She gave up the idea of having a private Christmas tree with Horace in Arcadia. Instead, she satisfied herself with a Christmas Eve waltz with Horace and sending him her favorite gift—photographs of herself.

The New Year began, like the final week of 1909, with prolonged separation. They did have their tree in Arcadia, but it was closely followed by Horace rushing off to New York: "I am missing you frightfully already for a whole week!" she confessed to him (no date) (B), "—I suppose it would have been d—d cold in Arcadia this morning but not for me as I should have worn your fur coat!" Then toward the end of January they came perilously close to being discovered. "We were sitting in 'Arcadia,'" Horace wrote later that same day, Friday (January 28, 1910) (B), "when Pierre Lorillard rode by on horseback. He jumped the fence further on but rode round the same way again. He did not seem to see anyone & I am sure did not in the least recognise us. Elinor kept whispering 'I'm going to die.'" When they returned to town Horace learned that they had not

*Elinor admitted that they had not "sinned"—clearly referring to sex—as late as December 1910.

been discovered, and Elinor went to bed with a bad headache.

Toward the end of the winter Elinor and Horace had reached a plateau in their relationship; a pattern in the Arcadian idyll emerged. Private meetings and public encounters performed a gentle counterpoint. There appeared to be no tension. They managed to interweave their lives with the distracting obligations of family. The arrangement of their existence became easier, less hectic, and less emotionally charged. Somehow the attraction between them equalized, becoming less frenetic. Horace was content with the harmony of the current duet; so was Elinor, temporarily. She still managed to overplay many incidents and he remained cloyingly attentive. Once charmed and flattered by Horace's reckless behavior, Elinor was occasionally annoyed, and she could not disguise her fear. Her own behavior became exaggerated. Horace caught a cold after a picnic in "Arcadia" and stayed in bed for five days. Elinor thought at once that he had died. She was speechless with joy when he finally telephoned her. Then she wrote two letters to him in rapid succession, one of which Horace labeled "The Scolding Letter" before he deposited it in the bank vault [February 25, 1910]: "I was sure you were dead or going to be—and it would have been my fault. . . . I love you—you can't know how much—are you really all right—can you *ever* forgive me? Do you realize what an unhappy life is in store for you—of being fussed over by me forever? . . . you mustn't *Think* of coming out in a machine for a week at *least*—I shall think of you every second. . . ." (B)

Then the static nature of their relationship became more pronounced, and complicated: possessiveness was slowly taking over all other feelings. Elinor's furious outbursts when she met Horace were smoothed away by letters of apology she wrote when they were apart. Excuses filled her letters. Every action was put down to love—"It was all love," she said in an attempt to brush aside one of her many tantrums. Restraint did not come easily to her and she often exercised it when it was too late. She found caution only slightly easier, and even her idea of caution flirted with danger.

In order to see Horace more often, Elinor set out to become friends with his wife. It was an enterprising tactic, making use of propriety as a cover for her attachment to

Horace. Phil too was immediately drawn into her schemes. Elinor was not jealous of Katharine; she liked her. She knew that Horace did love his wife, yet for the past four months she was beginning to forget. The Lorillard episode shocked her quickly into remembering. She told Horace to send his wife some flowers. She reminded him that he must stay at home more often, run fewer risks. And by Valentine's Day, Elinor herself was helping Horace. She "asked me for money," he wrote (February 14) (B), "to buy valentines for Margin & Katharine [Horace's daughters, aged five and seven] she sent them lots and used some of her own money although she had enough of mine. . . . Katy sent her an Oxford Book of French Verse with well known ones marked and 'I don't like de Musset do You?' written."

The Hichborns and the Wylies quickly became friends. From March to June (when the Wylies went abroad), they met on an average six times a month. Their enforced society worked admirably. They dined together; Horace chauffeured them around Washington; they met at the Chevy Chase Club. Elinor and Katharine composed poems together, and played various word games. Katharine listened patiently while Elinor droned on and on about Phil, the horrors of her marriage, and herself. It was a brand of intimacy Katharine preferred not to indulge in. She confided in her diary when Elinor finally left that Elinor's confessions were extremely unwelcome, in fact embarrassing, for her. To Elinor herself, however, she courteously offered the only possible advice—that she must leave Phil. The constant appearance of the Hichborns at Thomas Circle was far more pleasant for Horace. One evening, he recorded, "After sitting at Thomas Circle from 9.15 to 12.45 . . . Elinor when Katy said something about my being old [forty-two] said 'He might look old to *you*' E. *was sweet.*"

At this crucial stage of painful inactivity, Mama came forward with a most unwelcome proposal. She planned to sail to England with Elinor at the end of April. She suspected nothing of Elinor's affair with Horace, but she did know that she had to take Elinor away from Phil, at least for a short time. The idea might even have originated from Papa, since he was anxious to support his daughter and help her make a success of her marriage, but unlike Mama did not rule out the possibil-

ity of divorce. Elinor's confession to Mama could not possibly
have been kept secret from him for nearly two and a half years;
Elinor was incapable of hiding her feelings for so long even
if her mother could.

Horace was extremely upset by the idea. "My love is to sail to England on the 30th," he penciled forlornly at the Metropolitan Club (April, 16, 1910) (B). ". . . She told me this morning   I will put down some of the beginnings now because I think it may hurt too much to do so after she is gone." He went on to write eleven pages. The threat of separation led to a burst of profound remorse—the pattern of their lives for the last eighteen months was revealed. He took up the pages, folded them, and sealed them away in the bank.

Then, as suddenly as Mama had managed to place herself and the ocean in the center of things, events called the sailing off. On April 27 Philip's father, Admiral Hichborn, suffered a cerebral hemorrhage. He survived three days, and on May 1, he had another stroke, which killed him. Aged seventy-one, Admiral Hichborn had been in retirement for the last nine years.*

The days waiting for her father-in-law to die left Elinor exhausted and depressed. There could be no escape from Phil, no matter how brief, now. The demands of mourning sent her not to her husband, or her mother or father, but to Horace, the person least in a position to help her. "I look to you always for tenderness & wisdom & strength—will you help me to be good?" she asked in one of the four notes she sent to him the day after the Admiral's death (B). "Will you help me to do all I can for this poor boy [Phil]? I want to be kind to him—poor poor child I am so sorry for him—won't you try to be sorry too? My dear I am asking a great deal of you but you must help me." "Listen my dear," she wrote in another note,

*He began his naval career as a shipwright's apprentice, moving on to carpenter of the clipper ship *Dashing Wave*, on which he sailed from Boston to the Golden Gate in 150 days. Hichborn was given a commission in the Navy in 1869 for his work in shipbuilding, and rose quickly through the ranks. He invented the Franklin lifebuoy (named after his wife) and the Hichborn balanced turret (used on battleships to prevent the vessel from rolling sideways when the guns were aimed to one side). He became Chief Constructor of the Navy in 1893 and held the post until 1901.

don't be unhappy—it is only that I can't see you so often—because this thing that I have to do I must do with all my time all my strength and as much of my heart and soul as is mine to use—but do you suppose that I do not need you even more than before . . . nothing can ever be to me what you are and even though at this time I am trying to do all I can for someone who needs something I can give them—don't you know that I know you *always need me always*—don't you my dear?

Oh God I don't know what to do but you will tell me and whatever happens you'll always love me won't you?

These appeals to Horace were not enough to provoke the displays of affection she demanded, insisted upon having. He held back, needing to see Elinor in order to release his affection. But she remained withdrawn. She was being Mrs. Philip Hichborn for perhaps the first time since Horace had fallen in love with her. Instead of reassuring Elinor, sending her letters, or trying to see her, Horace went to bed with a severe headache.

"I am *so* worried about you," Elinor blurted out (B),

—how is your headache—have you got the grippe again? Why haven't you passed my house—are you angry? Please don't be it is more than I can bear—that—do you think it is easy for *me* not to see you? Do you think *I* am happy? Must I tell you what I know to be true—that I will *always* love you—don't you know that my heart is *breaking* yes really. . . .

Again there was no reply. Katharine came to her instead. Mrs. Wylie paid a formal call on Elinor the day after the Admiral's death, and then lunched with her the following day. Still there was not a word from Horace. Elinor wrote to him again (as always care of the Metropolitan Club), this time in her wildest scrawl: "If you don't get well I shall come and make you. I cannot think of anything in this world but your headache. How can you have one for five days—are you giving it to yourself on purpose. . . . Have *I* made you ill—don't you know I love you?" But it was not a headache that kept them apart; Horace had gone to Baltimore to the races.

The deep mourning of May was a recess from both active deceit and Elinor's intolerable status as Mrs. Hichborn. Phil had meaning for her because he needed her. He had, for the

first time in years, real appeal: the appeal of isolation and
sorrow. It supplied a new meaning to a relationship that was
no longer a marriage. The Admiral's death did nothing more
than delay Elinor's displays of strained tolerance with her
husband and her emotional outbursts to Horace. She rose
wonderfully to obligation. She missed Horace enormously,
but knew that their meetings would be out of place. She was
even able to marshal her emotions sufficiently to simulate
kindness, warmth, and generosity. She was unselfish in her
reaction—unselfish at least until she was tested when Horace
and his family were to sail to England. Then, in the sorrow of
being parted from Horace, all of Elinor's noble feelings about
Phil were brushed aside. She became frantic, even more hysterical than she had been about his headache. Horace calmly
accepted the parting, as he had accepted so many other things,
and looked forward to his holiday. This did not soften Elinor's
reaction in the least.

On Sunday, June 6, Elinor sat down and wrote a long
letter for Horace to keep during the crossing. She hid it
among her own cases that were being packed to be sent on
ahead to Maine. Phil came into her room and began—as Horace later noted on the envelope—"nosing around a trunk
tray." He found the letter and Elinor begged him not to read
it. He read it anyway, but mercifully "thought it a make-
believe thing." He did not suspect the real nature of the letter
(in part due to Elinor's deliberately illegible handwriting), but
Elinor tore it up "before his eyes as if in nervousness," just to
prove how meaningless it was. The next morning Elinor and
Horace went to "Arcadia" and stayed there, saying goodbye,
for three-quarters of an hour. Later that day (June 7) Elinor
wrote him a note in pencil: "I am afraid you are very sad but
dont be my dear dear I love you   I will always love you my
own beloved I kiss your dear hands and your dear eyes
Good bye my dear God bless you." (B)

The summer of 1910 seemed free of danger for them both.
Horace was in England, staying at The Old Hospital, Rye,
with Katharine and the children. Elinor was in Maine, buf-
feted between her mother and her mother-in-law, and trying

to keep both her son, nearly three years old, and her husband under some control; her son proved slightly more cooperative. Mama guarded Papa, who was dangerously overtired. And Henry, after returning from his visit to the Benéts' in California, superintended young Morton, just nine years old, who constantly threatened to fall into the ocean at Asticou. It was a summer of unrelieved domesticity for everyone. For the first time since Elinor had known Horace, she was free of the distraction from her family life. She did not like it. She had grown accustomed to living with danger and the predicament excited her. Now her only excitement was the prospect of moving into a new house at 14th Street and the obligations imposed upon her by her husband and son. She longed to see Horace again, and for the escape he would provide.

The Wylies returned to America at the end of September. Katharine went to Naragansett Pier, Rhode Island, and Horace rushed to Washington from New York. He telephoned Elinor at once and arranged to meet her at eleven o'clock. "She disappointed me a little," Horace remembered after their reunion, in a memoir he entitled "The Return from Abroad"; "didn't seem to love me as much as I had expected. . . . (Also she said not to Kiss her yet please as we went into the woods.) All that afternoon & next morning I was very unhappy." (B) They met again by accident on 16th Street the following day. "She blushed crimson," asked Horace not to go to Naragansett Pier, and said: " 'I have missed you terribly.' "

About a week later Horace did decide to join his wife in Rhode Island, and Elinor got a letter off to him just in time for them to meet before he left. "Listen my dear," she wrote [October 5, 1910],

if by any merciful chance you *do* understand and *haven't* gone—then tomorrow 10.30 15th [St.] and O how I hope I shall see you then my dear I do miss you. I never felt worse in my life—see how selfish I am but you don't mind since you know I love you. If you get this come a little early so when I get there I won't have to wait long if your [sic] not there—that's mixed up but you see what I mean my dear—O *please!!* hope you haven't gone. (B)

Before putting this letter in the vault, Horace added candidly:
"All Elinor's trouble in this note was only that she wanted to
see me."

Their second meeting was scarcely more successful than
the first. When she heard Horace say he was leaving to join
his wife, Elinor was frantic. She overlooked the simple fact
that she herself was planning to go to Pomfret to visit Mama,
and that she had already deserted Horace for four days to visit
friends. She became extremely irritable and petulant. After
they parted, she was embarrassed over her outbursts. "O
well," she sighed later that day, having learned that her journey to Pomfret was canceled,

now I am being punished for having however unwittingly made you
suffer so frightfully those four days. My dear when I heard you say
you were going tonight I could have cried & cried and begged you
to stay one day longer. . . . I am quite alone without you for how
long—? That is the worst part—I don't know—and O I didn't want
you to leave me! (B)

Elinor realized now that her life could not continue as it
had prior to the summer. She was not willing to play her real
emotions for Horace against nonexistent ones for Phil. Yet
she felt quite incapable of action, so she turned to Horace for
some sort of solution. He listened patiently to all she had to
say, her complaints and her anger. Then he answered calmly
that they would, in time, adjust to an existence founded on
lies. He was perfectly content with the arrangement as it
stood. He tried to understand Elinor's frustration, but he was
not unhappy and he was not dissatisfied. Unlike Horace, Elinor was not willing to lie any longer. When they met, her
affection for him was displaced by doubts and questions. The
fantasy they had both enjoyed was being rapidly transformed
into harsh reality, and their once pleasant encounters were
poisoned by Elinor's anxiety. They could not go back, and it
seemed that they could not go ahead.

Elinor eased the strain by making imprudent confessions
to anyone who would listen. Katharine Wylie was one of many
who were sworn to secrecy before Elinor unfolded the horrors
of being Mrs. Philip Hichborn. She presented an impressive
case. Katharine again responded with the verdict Elinor had

set out to get: she must of course leave Phil. Such advice, Katharine herself admitted, was offered with the greatest reluctance and in complete ignorance that her own husband figured in Elinor's life. Mama consistently maintained that appearances must be preserved (her life exemplified this perfectly). Elinor had married Phil and she must stay his wife. Mama did not subscribe to Papa's much more generous conclusion—that Elinor must get a divorce. Papa listened with no less sympathy than Mama, and his response was much more understanding. He fully appreciated his daughter's suffering, knowing only too well the hardship of duplicity.

Papa did not have to stray far from his own predicament to understand his daughter's. For many years he himself had had a mistress.* His long and frequent absences from home Mama attributed to nervous strain, and the children were kept completely ignorant of the fact during his lifetime. Even if Papa had wanted a divorce, it would have ruined his career.

But Elinor was a different matter. Papa disliked Phil intensely. He also knew that the Hichborns were no strangers to divorce. Phil's sister, Martha, had married James G. Blaine —a divorced man—in face of considerable opposition from her parents. Her marriage to Blaine lasted two years and it was Admiral Hichborn who successfully steered his daughter through the complexities of divorce. Martha later remarried without too much scandal attaching to her. So Papa started to gather material to help Elinor obtain a divorce. He was her only ally at Rhode Island Avenue.

Yet Elinor's emotions were strangely incompatible with her behavior. In her long discussions with Papa about dissolving the marriage to Phil, she never told him about Horace. When Papa reached the conclusion she wanted to hear, she merely interpreted it as approval for her love of Horace. Similarly, she used Horace to convince herself that she could no longer stay married to Phil. The whole situation was com-

*It has been impossible to identify the woman. She was, it was rumored, a secretary in the Department of Justice. The garden of her house backed onto the garden at 1701 Rhode Island Avenue, so it was just a short walk across. She only came to the Hoyts' house once, when Papa lay dying. Mama refused to let her in.

plicated by vital omissions in her recital of the facts when
asking people for advice. The strength of her love for Horace
was only amplified by her urge to escape Hichborn. She overlooked the fact that her happiness would mean great suffering
to others: Phil would be completely ruined by her desertion,
and she conveniently forgot the penalties that would have to
be paid by her son.

Divorce had lost much of its stigma in the past few
decades, but it still spelled disaster to such prominent families
as the Hoyts and Hichborns—especially in Washington. It
would be impossible to calculate the full effect. Society had a
far greater respect for submission to one's obligations than for
the pursuit of personal happiness, and happiness bought at
other people's expense could never be forgiven in any circumstances.

Elinor believed that Horace alone held the key to her
happiness. In her confused thinking she calculated only that
leaving Phil meant she would go to Horace. Her mind raced
ahead, completely disregarding the obstacle of Horace's marriage to Katharine. Horace, in turn, was infected by Elinor.
He had caught her peculiar form of analysis. Yet he knew that
Katharine would not give him a divorce, and did not even ask
her for one. He said nothing to anyone. His affection for
Elinor forced him to include desertion of his family, regardless
of his natural opposition to the idea. So Elinor managed to
push him into a solution of *her* problem, obliging him to
sacrifice his perfectly comfortable life in Washington and making him turn his back on his children. Worse still, she did not
fully recognize what she was doing.

In October 1910, Horace decided that they must run
away together. Elinor had planted the idea in his head, but
she was so astonished when he actually proposed it that she
could not even bring herself to mention the subject in a
letter. It was not an attempt at secrecy; she was too frightened. She could not appreciate that she was pushing Horace beyond his desire. She was also fascinated. On October
19 Horace received a letter written in ink so as to under-
score the gravity of its content. He disregarded Elinor's instructions at the top of the page—"Please tear this up"—
and wrote on the envelope: "This so far is the saddest [let-

ter] It is also the most loving." "My dear," Elinor's letter began,

for God's sake think this thing over because if it should be true it is asking so frightful and unprecedented a sacrifice of you—I cannot bear to think of it—I cannot think of it without crying. My dear love we had better not try to have any happiness against such odds as that —you couldn't *couldn't* love me under such circumstances—ah truly I know best about it my dear—I know you would grow to hate me. I wish so that I were dead   couldn't you possibly let me off my promise—surely this is different—and it would simplify things so. As the matter rests—of course there is no proof—it seems impossible that everything is not fatally blasted for us—and yet to conceive of living without you is torture. I love you more than I ever did—no I would rather live without you than ask that [of] you—o my dear please think about it—I will never break my promise to you but I would rather lose you than have you endure such a thing as that for me. Ah my dear I love you so much. (B)

Elinor was shocked by what she had done. At first when she heard Horace's idea she could not believe her ears. But now that Horace had the idea, he would not let go of it, ever. He was being brave, noble, even audacious—all of which suited his romantic idea of love. The proposal was directly out of a plot for a Gothic novel. At forty-two he was prepared to sacrifice everything for Elinor. His matter-of-fact calmness was surprising; Elinor's wild oscillations were not. Her vanity responded to the magnitude of Horace's daring, and she wavered between fear and a sense of flattery. But the fear only increased the attractiveness of the scheme. It was a form of attention she had never received before. The entire relationship had been engineered for some momentous display, not on her part, but Horace's. She had led him to it, but told herself—and indeed believed—that this was not so. Running away would mean freedom, the freedom to accept Horace at a very high price. Her essential selfishness could not hide the recurring and unsettling consideration that she might be more in love with the prospect of escape from Hichborn than she was with Horace. But the two situations were now inextricably linked and Elinor could no longer separate them.

They decided to leave Washington at the first auspicious moment. They held their breath, waiting and hoping—very

soon they would elope. Then, suddenly, Papa fell gravely ill.
He broke off his negotiations with the Canadian government
over reciprocity laws, rushed back to Rhode Island Avenue,
and was immediately confined to bed on Monday, November
14. Dr. Baker was called in from Wilkes-Barre for consultation. Elinor rushed between her new house in 14th Street and
Rhode Island Avenue. Henry was summoned. Mama sent
cables to Connie every day, giving steady reports on Papa's
condition.* Accustomed as Elinor had been to the ill health
Mama enjoyed, she was alarmed by her father's sudden illness
—and by the obvious affect it had on her plans to leave. She
begged Horace on Friday (November 18),

dont worry about me or even, my dear,—since you are after all
human—about yourself—nothing is changed—and if it cant be—
next Tuesday—which it cant—it will none the less be—whenever
the time is ripe. What a selfish thing for us to think—but we must
think it. . . . Everything may come out all right but no matter what
happens I am yours forever and ever. Don't forget to love me I am
awfully lonely. (B)

On Saturday Papa's condition began to deteriorate rapidly. Mama, Elinor, and Henry stayed with him continuously. By midnight they realized that there was little hope. His
pulse was much weaker. Finally, at 8:20 on Sunday morning,
he died. The cause was peritonitis, aggravated by a perforated
ulcer. Next month he would have been fifty-four, only twelve
years older than Horace.

Rhode Island Avenue was in deepest mourning. For the
second time in six months the Hichborns had death to contend
with. Elinor was stunned. It had happened so quickly, so unexpectedly. All hope of elopement (and divorce) vanished. The
sorrow of her father's death put everything else aside. On
Monday there was a private funeral service in Washington.
The following day his body was interred at Forty Fort Cemetery after funeral services at the Episcopal Church in Wilkes-
Barre. Before leaving for Pennsylvania that Tuesday (November 22) Elinor wrote to Horace, "If we must bow to the
inevitable let us do so politely. Nevertheless if it is any com-

*On March 30, 1910, Connie had married the Baron Ferdinand von Stumm
and two months later sailed to Germany with him.

fort to you—I might as well tell you that I have no interest in life whatsoever—except that I hope I shall see you on Monday at eleven—on 15th [St.] My dear don't be unhappy." (B)

Papa's death did not impede her plans; it accelerated them. She made the fatal discovery that he had a mistress. Mama could no longer keep it a secret. And that discovery alone, she admitted years later, gave her the strength to carry through her elopement. "Elinor described the scene of this discovery with great feeling," Rebecca West wrote in 1953, "and always expected me to take it for granted that when you found out that your father had been in love with someone not your mother, why, *of course,* you left your own husband; you just had to, you were so upset. Quite beyond argument. It was something she could no more help than her blood pressure."

The elopement became more urgent. While Elinor's behavior grew more and more chaotic, Horace appeared calmer than ever. He closed his various bank accounts. He moved slowly and methodically, preparing the paper work required for departure. Both became cautious, concealing the frenzy each endured. The first two weeks in December were filled with canceled meetings and changed plans. After one of their rare successful meetings, Elinor's optimism was quickly renewed. She wrote to Horace on turquoise paper in a flourish: "The color of *hope* This paper my dear. I am Thinking you are frightfully *relieved*—is it possible—really you must be honest with me you know. . . . Did you mind my teasing you this morning? You wouldn't if you knew that I admired overcoatlessness as an idiosyncracy [sic] of *yours.* " (B)

They kept their plans very dark; no one was let into the secret. And no one was more ignorant than Phil, who suspected absolutely nothing. He was settling into the new house, determined to make it a home for Elinor and his son. "There has been nothing for a long time," he wrote to Mama (December 13, 1910) (B),

that pleased me so or given me such pride and satisfaction as the new house I feel exactly as Bee [Beeyup] does when he says "That all [?] you know about our beautiful parlor!" It seems more beautiful every day to me. . . .

Some day, perhaps not right away, and yet perhaps not so far away either I shall find myself and then the little things that have upset Elinor and me will seem very trivial indeed and will cease to be.

I have always had a strong feeling that I should succeed some day, but every day I realize more and more that first I must succeed with myself and I believe just a little that I am winning.

But the plans were already set. Elinor and Horace decided to leave Washington separately, meet later, and sail from Canada to Liverpool. They chose Friday, December 16, as the day, giving them the safety of the weekend to slip out of the country. The actual details of their departure are unknown. But according to family legend, they in fact drove out of Washington together, abandoned his car, and boarded a train for Canada. Mama was astounded that Horace left his car behind. The third Mrs. Wylie, in her memoir of Horace, claims that they bought steamship tickets for the SS *Château Frontenac,* which was sailing from Montreal to Liverpool. Elinor and Horace boarded the ship at St. John's, New Brunswick. Among Horace's papers was a baggage ticket from the "Frontenac" stating his room number, 1653. But it is more likely that the "Frontenac" referred to is the hotel of that name in Quebec. There is no record of a SS *Château Frontenac.* In any event passenger liners rarely sailed so far north in the winter.

The one thing Horace insisted was that they must, at all costs, avoid any family confrontations. In Elinor's nervous state she might say or do anything; she might even turn back. Horace was delighted by the plan, constantly issuing advice to Elinor. Somewhat impulsively she sent off one last letter to him:

O my dear—do you mind my writing you a long perfectly unnecessary letter?—without my glasses! But really I must I am so nervous I think I shall fling the inkstand through the window if I don't have the relief of expressing myself to you. O dear I am so nervous. How can you like to be. I suppose it is the nux.* Damn it! I am awfully unhappy—and it will be so long before I see you. Nothing double about that—no twenty drop threat—only it seems

*Nux Vomica: the seed contained in the pulpy fruit of the East Indian tree that yields strychnine. A popular pick-me-up.

forever till Wednesday.* Don't worry—I think a calm and conventional old age is what you have to look forward to. I hardly think we'll go. Fraid not. O Lord what fools we are. Nice dear good fools —but O of the first water. My gracious *what* an ordeal! I really minded horribly—did you. But you were spared some of it. If only I had listened to you—but ah it is still the child and the express train isn't it? How *can* I stand it? Wouldn't you really ever forgive me? "If we meet I shall pass nor turn my face"—your sentiments I suppose. O my God its the wages of sin—don't you see it—mental and spiritual sin though we've committed no actual one. Can't you make me see it your way—please my dear show me how silly I am. I am very unhappy. And so nervous Why *do* you allow *yourself* to be so nervous by the way—it is very distracting. . . . Really and seriously my heart's in my mouth all the time—that's the only way to describe it.

Ah my dear—listen—I'll try not to be so wild—don't worry about me—I love you so my dearest love—I want to see you—to cry I suppose—it's rotten to write you letters like this—but by Wednesday I'll be more sensible—very gay and amusing perhaps. My darling I only care for you out of everything in the world—do you think you can ever make me get out of this hideous nightmare and be happy? Because otherwise I shall kill myself and that's rather a pity isn't it? O my dear dear love please make me believe you—and save me. (B)

Elinor left a note for her husband; Horace left one for Katharine. In Atlantic City where Mama was resting after the death of Papa, she received a letter from Elinor postmarked Grand Central Station in New York. She opened the letter, read the words: "don't let this kill you . . . I have run away," and instantly fainted. Later she wired to Henry, who rushed to New York, where he met Phil. The *Mauretania* had docked at the 14th Street Pier in New York that morning—Friday, December 16—and was to sail at six the next evening in a record-breaking attempt to cross to Liverpool. Everyone thought they would be on the ship. Henry and Phil met at the pier to examine the passenger list, and all the people boarding.

*Perhaps five days after they left Washington separately, Wednesday December 21. The few hints Elinor gives in this letter are completely inconsistent with family legend, newspaper accounts, and subsequent research. The days following December 16 are a complete mystery. This is one of the few letters Horace left without helpful notations.

They called at Horace's club, various hotels, everywhere,
Mama later wrote. They found no trace of them.

The newspapers went wild. Pictures of Elinor and Phil
and their son, who changed gender and age with each new
report, appeared on front pages up and down the East Coast.
Reporters demonstrated a bizarre sense of geography and
chronology. They had Horace and Elinor placed in various
cities at the same time. They besieged the Hoyts, Hichborns,
and Wylies for statements, but managed only to get quotes
from Phil's law partner, from Henry, and a very reluctant
cable from Mama. Katharine Wylie stayed at home and said
nothing. Her brother, Captain Hopkins, flatly refused to issue
one syllable to the press. Pestered to distraction, Mama finally
wired a "dignified" statement to the *New York Herald Tribune:*
"though ill and unable to join her daughter," the December
24 story ran, "she was fully aware that her daughter in her
unconsidered action in leaving her home would turn to her,
where she could count on love, sympathy and understanding.
She did so and Mrs. Hoyt can only deplore unfriendly and
unfounded attacks on her from certain journals." The "certain
journals" were the *New York American* and the Washington
Post—both of which ran front-page reports December 22 of
the "coincidental" disappearance of Elinor Hichborn and
Horace Wylie.

The day of the first newspaper reports Mama wrote to
Katharine Wylie on her black-bordered stationery, "You must
try and like me . . . I hope Horace will realize what he has
done." Nearly a week after she had injudiciously telegraphed
the New York newspaper, she regretted it, confessing to Katharine (December 30), "Of course my statement to the papers was silly. . . ." If Mama's comments to the press were
"silly," Phil's were nothing more than an attempt to buy time,
time to find Elinor. He calmly asserted that his wife was "suffering from a nervous collapse" and was in a Philadelphia
sanitorium.

Mama told Katharine she was doing everything she could
to trace the pair. Even President Taft volunteered his help,
writing to Mama (December 26, 1910) (B): "If I can do
anything, I will, for my sympathy with you is deep and beyond
expression. But, my dear Mrs Hoyt, I have no knowledge

where W— is—If I did, I might use the diplomatic or consular corps to try to bring him to a sense of the awful course he is pursuing. I'll talk with Secretary Knox about the matter. . . ." Constance was alerted in Stuttgart. Private detectives were hired. Everything was being done not only to trace the couple but to bring them back. Horace and Elinor had left America in a fog of conflicting reports. They were finally together, yet far from safe.

Book Two

1911-1920

. . . I am quite naturally & deservedly exiled.
—Elinor to Mama
May 10 [1912] (B)

*It is as if he [Horace] had piled up a big
wall around Burley & Durmast & the Forest
& the two of us—(with plain Hell outside as
I'm absolutely aware) & kept running around
night & day, as I tell him, filling up holes,
mending cracks, & polting away at dragons
with his gun—never stopping but doing it all
so guiltily that I forget it is a fortified peace I
live in. But I don't really forget, you know,
darling, that it's Hell outside.*
—Elinor to Mama
May 28 [1912] (B)

CHAPTER FOUR: 1911

§*i*   *But I shall not repent me of*
       My sin—the promise stands;
       I never shall deny my love,
       My soul is in His hands.
       —Elinor Wylie, "From Whom No Secrets are Hid"
       (April 1911)

The year 1911 began with astonishing confusion. Whispers of
Elinor and Horace's movements were shrouded in rumor and
originated from the activities of the Hoyts. Everyone thought
that Mama or Henry would rush to Elinor. Washington eagerly awaited any word of the fugitive couple, welcoming the
most incredible stories and anticipating their imminent return.
Katharine Wylie enlisted her friends' support and begged
them not to cut Horace when he returned. Her private detectives cabled her that Horace and Elinor had been seen at
Shepheards Hotel in Cairo the second week in January.
American newspapers had them placed anywhere from England to Monte Carlo. The couple's rare communications to
America were issued with no return address.

On January 20 Horace sent Katharine a letter from London. He begged her not to keep the children from him, and
offered to give her $10,000 a year. Katharine immediately
contacted English and French friends to be on the lookout for
her husband. Letters were sent to him care of the U.S. Express
offices and various American banks in both countries. The
ignorance of their location and travels at once provided the
couple with an excellent cover and also laid the foundation for
the myth that surrounded Elinor for the rest of her life. Like
the exact details of her departure from Washington, the early
weeks in Europe, alone with Horace, are a mystery. Neither
Elinor nor any of the injured parties ever revealed exactly
what happened.

Constance, who left Washington in June, was in Stuttgart,
pregnant, very bored, and short of entertainment, being at-

tached to the German Embassy, where her husband was secretary. Mama instantly informed her of Elinor's elopement. "This awful thing is almost beyond my understanding—" Connie wrote back (January 4) (B) after Mama's return from the Brighton Hotel in Atlantic City to Washington. "I can imagine Elinor, desperate as she was, doing *anything* but that. . . . I have such a pathetic letter, mostly about you and me, written a few days before that act of madness." "I don't ask any more questions about Elinor," Connie added to her mother on January 16 (B), "because I am waiting to see you. It is all one unanswerable question to me anyhow—it doesn't go with her character as we all knew her surely. Doesn't it seem strange and terrible to think of our perfectly unconscious goodbye last June. . . ."

When Connie first announced that she was pregnant, Mama volunteered to come to Stuttgart. Papa's death and Elinor's flight did not change her plans; she seemed even more eager to sail to Germany. Since Connie predicted the baby's arrival some time in the second week in February, Mama sailed on February 4 for Cherbourg, "running it close." With her were Henry, Morton, Nancy, a nurse—and Beeyup: "Poor little Beeyup, poor little cheerful boy," Connie wrote (January 4) (B), ". . . Poor Phil—I cannot help feeling very very sorry for him. I know what cruel agony he must feel." Ten days later she asked Mama, "Won't Phil miss Beeup [sic] terribly? I should think he would find it hard to let him go."

While Katharine tried to get Horace back by telling him his friends would not turn against him, Mama's plan was to use Elinor's obligation to her son as a threat of emotional blackmail. Though she claimed there was "no real or authentic news" of the couple, she must have known something to drag the child across the Atlantic. And she was right. When she was out one day from Cherbourg, she received a radiogram announcing tersely, "Will meet you in Paris." There was no signature, but Mama knew the source.

The Hoyts docked at Cherbourg. Constance sent her butler ahead, who was, at best, only partially useful; he did not speak French, and he was unfamiliar with Cherbourg and Paris. In Paris, where Mama and her "caravan," as Connie called her traveling companions, stayed only a few days,

Mama at last came face to face with Horace and Elinor.
    Her impressions of Horace were far from enthusiastic.
"The man an utter stranger to the family as yet—smooth,
quiet, with a guarded face, a look seemingly open." What
transpired between the three those few cold days in February
1911 can only be guessed at from Mama's sketchy notations
in her memoir. "Promises of protection for the future, the
certainty of a speedy divorce from wife and husband, an immediate marriage, life abroad—No real grounds to stand on."
Mama did not understand Elinor; after meeting Horace, she
found it difficult to try; their optimistic, not to say idiotic, ideas
were more than she could grasp. The entire arrangement was
sordid. Their plans seemed pathetically unrealistic, and the
belief that all would turn out satisfactorily once they married
was simply wrong. Divorces were unlikely, and establishing
anything like an acceptable life abroad was out of the question.
Horace and Elinor could never escape the scandal they foolishly
believed they had left behind in Washington. They would have
to be careful, always. No one could possibly overlook Elinor's
desertion of her son. Even if Mama thought she might make
Elinor realize what she had done, there was no time. As mysteriously as Elinor and Horace appeared, so they disappeared.
    Mama and her "caravan" went on to Stuttgart, stopping
at the Hotel Marguardt, "one of the least annoying features
of this beauteous spot," as Connie sarcastically informed
Mama (January 14) (B). ". . . All strangers live there, quite
often for months." Elinor was undaunted by the sight of her
son. Mama took him to stay with his aunt Connie. "Tumm,"
as Connie affectionately referred to her husband, was called
constantly to Darmstadt to fill the diplomatic ranks attending
the visit of Czar Nicholas II or to a seemingly endless number
of court functions. Stuttgart, Connie wrote to Mama, was
populated exclusively by dull people. There was no relief from
the tedium, first of teas, calls, and parties, and then of her
enforced confinement. She spoke chiefly of the sables Papa
and Mama had given her as an early Christmas present and of
Blank's (the cook at Rhode Island Avenue) brandy snaps. Still,
she apparently believed that her marriage was a success.
    Carl Heinrich Friedrich von Stumm was born February
25, 1911. Less than two weeks before the birth of her nephew,

Elinor left Paris for London. The interview with Mama had upset Horace. Gradually the incompatibility between his emotions and behavior became evident. On February 12 he wrote to Katharine from London: "I am fonder of you than ever in my life. . . ." It was an extraordinary statement in face of his actions. He thought, in a curious and generous way, that such declarations comforted Katharine. But more than courtesy, the comment proved that he was suffering from reservations. As Elinor's dependence on him grew, he turned back to his wife. Yet he could no more return to Katharine than he could desert Elinor. He was torn between desire and obligation, and quickly managed to confuse the object of each appeal. He began to believe that his obligation now lay in Elinor's direction, and his desire pulled him back to Katharine. Trapped by his own uncertainty—which had been to a large degree brought on by Mama's disapproval—his remarkable talent for disregarding the facts was faltering.

Horace's solution was as easy to him as it was impossible to Katharine: he would have both Elinor and Katharine. "Would you and the children care to live in England?" he innocently asked Katharine, ". . . we could try it for the summer. . . . You must let me support you." Katharine was furious. She refused to allow him to assume a generous posture: he *must* support her and his children. She pointed directly to his legal obligation and told him that he must return to Washington.

It took two months for Horace to realize fully what he had done, and even then he persistently refused to grasp the full gravity of his actions. He simply could not understand Katharine's objection to coming to England. She would not have to see Elinor, he pointed out. He could be with her and his children during the week and with Elinor at the weekends. This compromise was surely better than banishing him from his children forever? It was precisely this sort of naïveté that made Elinor love him and that ruined his life. He appeared so certain, so confident, and yet beneath the surface was a strong vein of absurdity. Elinor found it both charming and infuriating.

For the moment there was nothing else for Elinor and Horace to do but travel. They were in constant fear of being

seen and exposed. Every move they made had to be carefully
thought out. The strain was slowly dispelling any euphoria.
Horace shaved off his mustache in a clumsy attempt at disguise. They headed back to Paris, and then followed Mama
into Italy, stopping at Monaco on the way.

Horace continued to write to Katharine, and her responses to his brief notes filtered through to him. He replied
to her refusal of his summer suggestion [March 20, 1911]
from Paris: "I will not leave Elinor. . . . But there is nothing
else I wouldn't do for you." Five days later he wrote again
from Monaco that his will was made, leaving everything to
Katharine; and, he went on, Elinor would not be in England
so there was no obstacle to Katharine's sailing. Almost as an
afterthought he reminded his wife later that same day [March
25]: "I will not desert her [Elinor] . . . I will do anything but
desert her." On and on the correspondence went—Katharine
refusing to see Horace until he left Elinor, and Horace flatly
refusing ever to do so. But they continued to write even after
they recognized this essential impasse.

Horace's vacillation kept emotions at a high pitch. Just as
he was trapped by his own confusion, so Elinor was caught
between her dependence on Horace and Mama's steady reminders of her duty to her son. Instead of solving anything,
her elopement with Horace had created untold complications;
she could not be sure of him until he made up his mind about
Katharine. Family obligations threatened his love for Elinor.
Horace was powerless to affirm his love for Elinor through
marriage. That was clear. Yet it was precisely that that was
required. Mama insisted upon it; convention demanded it; and
Elinor wanted it. Paradoxically, both Elinor and Horace had
a great respect for convention; yet they found themselves
outside it.

They met Mama again in Rome: "a reappearance,"
Mama noted in her abbreviated style, "more evasions less
security, endless worry and anxiety, they left us as unexpectedly as they had appeared—". By the early spring Horace
gave way completely to remorse. He had to return to Katharine. Mama read this as "a new, utterly new, development";
his optimism had completely vanished.

Horace sailed to New York from Cherbourg at the beginning of April 1911, alone. Elinor went with her family to Stuttgart to wait. Mama, disconcertingly, took Katharine's side in the whole matter. She said Horace's place was, of course, at his wife's side, no matter how uncomfortable it might be. Even with her daughter's future at stake, Mama came down firmly on the side of convention. Elinor received some insight into the way Katharine herself must have felt five months earlier. To complicate matters further, the President's influence could not keep the story from the Washington papers.

Horace's idea of returning to Katharine had stemmed from the same sort of good manners that prompted his declarations of love in February. He believed she must be allowed to argue her own case, that Elinor had an unfair advantage over her by being at his side. Katharine had suffered, and he owed her at least the courtesy of making an appearance at Thomas Circle. He refused to predict the outcome of his interview with his wife; nor could he tell Elinor when he planned to return.

Elinor found little sympathy in the Hoyts' suite at the Hotel Marguardt. She was very unhappy. She spent her afternoons with Connie, Tumm, and their baby, Carlo. Often she would escape to be alone, walk, and sketch. One Sunday [April 14] she sketched the Stuttgart Tower and sent it to Horace, adding: "I drew it to show I was brave & was taking an interest in life but forgive me if I cannot help seeing you & you only in everything. O my dear *you* are my life I cannot help it." (B) Onlookers found it difficult to take Elinor's side during Horace's absence. Her brother-in-law Tumm said that Horace rushed back to Katharine "to save his skin" after ruining Elinor. Mama, in turn, refused to be generous. She resolved to sail home on May 6, with or without any news of Horace's decision. She hoped to force Elinor's hand, and again she was defeated because she was not firm.

"I have just heard from Mama," Elinor wrote to Horace two weeks after her Stuttgart Tower letter,

who is all turned around again poor woman—that she will wait if I want her to, probably anyway—& not sail till June 3rd. Of course it is too late to let you know & I feel guilty beyond the power of words . . . she has, as I suppose you heard—been on Katy's side lately & that is one reason I felt so deserted & lost & cabled you "what shall I do?" Of course at that time with the family against me—& sailing on May 6th & urging me to come—with them & you sailing just about the same time *with your family*—what chance had I for the one last time of seeing you that I hoped for as a damned soul hopes for —what, I wonder? I simply didn't know what to do—I was really & absolutely not only in despair but utter confusion—& so I cabled you —& rather to my fright for I feared I *must* be lessening your chances of success—you cabled that you were coming   I know you will never believe me—never forgive me—& yet I promise you that in the whole matter I have been, though perhaps stupid with fright & unhappiness—perfectly honest & conscientious, and it is only because of the *entire change* not only in the family's plans but in their *whole attitude* that I am put in the position of a liar, a cheat, a coward & a meddler . . . you see poor Mama . . . thinks I am pitiful & love you so & am so unhappy—& so quite unexpectedly offers to wait & see if theres any hope for me. And so you needn't have come *nearly* so soon, after all. . . . (B)

Horace's plan of attack on Thomas Circle was certainly vague. The first stage of his offensive was a half-hearted attempt at total reconciliation, which involved whisking Katharine and the children off to Europe for their summer holiday. He knew it would be ineffectual and probably lead to total separation. Katharine agreed to Europe on the single predictable condition that there would be no contact with Elinor. Horace hastily agreed, then cabled Elinor that he was coming to Europe—cautiously advancing his plan to see her alone in Paris. He explained calmly to Katharine that he was sweeping away her enemy. Katharine knew, as Elinor herself was learning, that what Horace said and what he did were not in harmony. His protestations only amplified her doubts; but for the moment she was willing to travel with him through Ostend, Geneva, and Zurich. She had no other choice.

Elinor heard nothing of these plans until she received Horace's cable, itself a reply to a frantic one sent by her. She expected him back in Europe about the last week in April. She thought he was returning to his wife. Katharine was less certain. Horace had slipped in and out of America swiftly. By the third week in April he was back in New York, staying at the Astor Hotel before sailing to Liverpool "on the Cunarder

[*Carmania*] as Henry White," as he wrote to Katharine. On April 21 he sent two letters to Katharine, one giving the details of his sailing, the other containing a pressed rose. He was eager to see Elinor again.

When Horace docked at Liverpool he was greeted with a flood of letters and cables, all from Elinor, and all filled with doubt, fear, and a perverse sense of confidence. She was frightened of the answer he was bringing to her. She wanted to meet him at the dock, but her sister and brother-in-law flatly refused to allow it: "I dare not 'sneak off' it would scare them all so," she confided to Horace [April 25] (B). "They think it wouldn't be safe travelling so far alone & might even miss you & so I have had to give in. . . ." The compromise she reached was to take the train from Stuttgart to Paris the following Friday and meet Horace at the Hôtel Crillon, where she reserved a "small room & bath" with a salon for herself, fully expecting to move into larger accommodation when Horace arrived. "Of course I do not know if you intend to play the part of Joseph you funny child but I know what I intend, & it is quite determined upon & not to be altered by even your intention of leaving me again in four days—that intention which I warn you I will do my best to prevent you carrying out. Do not worry about that however—nothing tragic is to be feared from me at first, anyway. . . ." For the moment she was simply content with the prospect of seeing Horace again. She knew he would be tired. She knew that any scene must be avoided. She was willing to avoid the news that he brought back to her—"why should I think of these horrors?—They are all, (at least for the present & that is what concerns me)— dispersed & driven away by the tremendous & overwhelming joy I feel when ever I think I am going to see you again."

Her "overwhelming joy" lasted until Thursday. "Yesterday," she scrawled to Horace on Friday [April 28] (B), "at 6 P.M.—my trunks about to be taken to the station overnight & my ticket bought—intending to leave at the bright hour of 6:58 A.M. Today—I get a telegram from the d—— Crillon as follows 'Sorry cannot accommodate you on the 28th accident happened' Do you or do you not think it sounds fishy? I do rather. Well I was *wild*. . . ." She sent off four cables. Two went to Horace—one asking him to telegraph her in Stuttgart

on landing, and another asking him to make plans for both of
them to meet in Paris—both sent, she confessed, "in conster-
nation & witsendedness (as usual)." Then she telegraphed
Cunard to find out when the *Carmania* was supposed to land,
and discovered that she had until Sunday to make some alter-
native arrangements. In the same emotional state she sent off
the last cable, this one to the Crillon, asking when she might
have rooms. Her "witsendedness" was aggravated by the fact
that the von Stumms were setting off for the Crillon on Tuesday, followed by Mama and the family, who were also staying
in Paris before they sailed, having changed their plans for the
third time. "Family may sail 6th [May] after all—o gibber
gibber!" This all meant that Elinor had less time to convince
Horace to stay with her.

And then, "almost simultaneously with the arrival of the
Crillon telegram" at the Hotel Marguardt came the delivery
of three copies of the Washington *Post* (dated April 15) at
Connie's house, which ran the story, in a garbled fashion, of
Elinor and Horace's elopement. "Aren't the papers lovely to
me?" Elinor wrote to Horace [April 28].

Aren't you ashamed to be connected with SO INFAMOUS A WOMAN?
But no, my darling boy that wouldn't be like you, to hate me for
what I can't help & mind as much as you, quite—some people to the
contrary not withstanding. But O my poor lamb—I *am* the sorriest
for you, always. Don't think I'm insane flippant or (please darling
you know me better than that) "cheap" to talk so gaily—I am really
rather upset. . . .

She calmed down sufficiently to warn him that there might be
a third cable awaiting him in Liverpool to tell him she had
managed to get rooms at the Crillon after all, "in which case
you will go straight there, but I fear the hope is small."

Horace's brief appearance in Washington breathed new
life into the dying scandal. Merely by trying to settle relations
with Katharine, he revived the interest. Every time the story
was told in the newspapers, a new and stronger hint of moral
outrage crept in. Elinor had betrayed her class; Horace was
just as guilty; and all Washington and New York was excited
by the two criminals. Elinor tried to take the newspaper stories
lightly. She had expected them, but she was caught off guard

by their severity. She knew they would be inaccurate, and realized her reputation was ruined, but the idea that she should be turned into "news" sent a shudder through her. She believed her motives were creditable; the newspapers saw them as notorious. Yet the uncertainty of Horace's decision crowded out all thoughts of shame, for the moment.

The next part of 1911 was as confused as the first, complicated by further, more intricate, participation of the Hoyts, Hichborns, and Wylies. Horace arrived in Paris exhausted, without having reached any conclusion whatsoever. He was prepared to wait and told Elinor she must do the same. His plans, as vague as they were, required that Elinor must again stay out of the way. With Horace appearing to favor Katharine, Elinor was pulled, with Mama's help, back to Phil. Throughout her stay in Europe, Mama was in communication with her son-in-law. He begged her to plead his case, and according to Mama, "reproached himself bitterly, sorrowfully, could not understand, begged her [Elinor] to return." All was forgiven, with thousands of miles separating them. Elinor could no longer disregard his appeals, especially in face of Horace's actions. Finally, by the beginning of May, she had decided to sail back to America with Mama, closely followed by Horace, who would returned to collect Katharine and his children for their holiday. Elinor and Horace parted from each other with the promise that they would be married; he gave her an engagement ring to prove it. Then he lied to Mama, assuring her that he was in fact returning to his wife. "Anything I can ever do you may command," he wrote to her (May 23, 1911) (B). "In the event of your staying in Washington next year I will stay away. I can answer for myself and I will use my best efforts to have Mrs. Wylie stay away also. I feel sure I can make her do so." The only thing Horace achieved by his extreme indecision was to silence opposition. He also gave himself more time.

After docking in New York, Elinor headed straight for Rhode Island Avenue where Henry tried to protect her against prying newspapers. He was not successful. "Mrs. Hichborn to Reach Home To-day" ran the headline in the *New York Herald Tribune* for May 24. That same day she wrote to Horace, who was staying at the Astor Hotel in New York

before sailing on the *Vaterland* back to Europe, that she
planned to stay in Washington "a couple of weeks longer
. . . I have lots of books & I love the house." She too was
planning a summer holiday, but had not decided where.

Though Phil had promised to take her back, as soon as
she got to Washington, he abruptly changed his mind: "she
might not see the child," Mama recorded, "her husband intended to divorce her, naming the older man [Horace] as co
respondent." Beeyup was taken to Thorn Cliff, Black Rock,
in New Hampshire, with his father and grandmother. "The
position," Mama calmly stated, "was delicate, if not desperate." Even Hoyt relations avoided them.

Elinor managed to derive strength from adversity. "Listen my poor boy," she wrote to Horace (May 24) (B),

—little as I can do for you now (O my darling) at least I can tell you
what is true & what you will be gladdest to hear—that I am all right,
that, after the first horror of the idea, I don't mind being here, that
I am not only trying to be brave & strong for you but succeeding
. . . whatever troubles & worries & hardships you have to bear, you
need not, honestly & truely [sic], worry about my "going down" or
getting sick or despairing because I have promised myself, for you,
not to. . . . You know always, by your own heart, what is in mine.
You are everything to me just as I am everything to you & it is only
for each other, & in hope of our heart's desire, that we can do this
thing.

By "this thing" Elinor meant waiting, waiting until Horace
had acted out his charade. She came alive only when writing
to him. Her existence was monotonously simple: "I'm perfectly well & eat & sleep splendidly & can *read poetry*   I pray
all the time & love too & it helps a lot. I know you have been
praying for me otherwise I couldn't be so brave. You have all
my prayers & all my love dearest dearest dearest. I am so glad
we're engaged. . . . Goodbye till London mail my own darling."

Like most of May and early June, the summer was spent
in complete solitude. Mama avoided Mt. Desert Island for the
seclusion of the Jackson Falls Hotel, Jackson, New Hampshire, in the White Mountains. Her children were with her.
Elinor complained to Horace that she was "pilloried" there.

The boredom was intense; he started to imagine that Horace might desert her, that he might be reconciled with Katharine. Her routine of walking and reading was supplemented, as in other times of great stress, by writing—writing poetry for Horace. She dispatched a "sonnet to plead again for me, in my hour of need—& your hour of trial":

—In the Wood

I know that you will come to me, my dear;
I have not cried, I have not even prayed
I am not lonely, I am not afraid
I know there is not anything to fear
Because you kissed me when you left me here
And told me to be patient. I have stayed
Quite still, & in all faithfulness obeyed
Without a question & without a tear.

But I am tired now, & it is late
The morning & the golden afternoon
Are gone, & deep in the night the Forest stands.
A little wind is blowing & I wait,
My heart so sure that you are coming soon
My hands outstretched to clasp your warmer hands.

Both Elinor and Horace knew how they planned to end their separation, though their families remained completely ignorant. The problem still remained how to achieve that end. Horace clouded all his activities in mystery and unpredictability; Elinor herself was beginning to doubt his resolve. Return sailing accommodation from London was hard to get that summer, but he managed to reserve an early passage for himself and his eldest son Andrew, who had to be back in America for the beginning of school, leaving Katharine and the other three children to follow. Because their ship docked in New York several days before Andrew was to enroll in school, Katharine demanded that Horace should not see Elinor before Katharine herself returned to New York. Horace agreed —then put Andrew in a hotel alone before speeding up to Jackson. His appearance at the Hoyts' "quiet mountain place, miles from the rail-road," stunned Mama. She thought no one had the address.

Again events moved quickly. No sooner had Horace

pledged that he had returned once and for all to Elinor, than he was back in New York to meet his wife off the *Kaiser Wilhelm,* which had sailed from Southampton on September 20. He met Katharine on the pier and assured her that he had made good his promise. Then he took her and the children to their suite at the St. Regis Hotel, which he had filled with white roses. That night he scrawled a note to Elinor announcing that he would see her the following day, September 27. When Katharine woke the next morning, she found no Horace, but three notes. "if I were to stay with you now," one said, "it would be the act of a dastard and a murderer. You and the children *would be cut off from every friend and from your home* and *I would* not allow *this* even *if this were all.* I mean every word I have written. But that is not all, I have placed Elinor where she has lost *everything . . .* & if I desert her now it would be madness or death." The third note began with the heading "The Last Word," and added cryptically, "I meant what those flowers meant." Katharine's baggage tickets were enclosed. It was December 16, 1910, all over again. She had had no warning that Horace had been play-acting for the last three months. She thought that he had returned to her.

Instead, Horace returned to Elinor. He went up to New Hampshire, and there he encountered Mama's grave disfavor again. She presented formidable opposition. "Every argument, command, entreaty was used," as she recalled, "in vain." For a brief moment, however, she believed she had won the day. Elinor consulted the train schedule she had penciled on the back of one of Horace's envelopes and asked Henry to take them to the train, where she would say goodbye to Horace. But she told her brother the moment she stepped into his car that she was leaving. As soon as they got to the station, Elinor calmly crossed the platform onto the train. Instead of waving goodbye to Horace, she turned and waved to Henry. No amount of argument could keep her from Horace. Again they ran off to Canada to sail for England where, Mama noted, "in quiet rural surroundings the next act of this so tragic drama was played out."

This time they left in their wake not bewilderment, but anger. It was clear that Horace had lied, steadily and consistently, to everyone. Katharine again pleaded for him to re-

turn, complaining that her health, ruined by the first elopement, was now completely gone. She asked for Mama's help:
"With your help, you appealing to Elinor & the children & I
appealing to him—I think we might succeed. I am no more
reconciled than the day they went. It gets worse and worse for
me." It also got worse and worse for the Hoyts. Anonymous
letters arrived at Rhode Island Avenue; people turned away
when they saw Mama in the street. The newspapers concocted
the story that there had been an elaborate plot between Elinor
and Phil to carry out this second and more painful elopement.
Nothing had improved for anyone save Elinor and Horace.

§ ii   "into a rut"

The Atlantic crossing, their second in ten months, was a
foretaste of the next four years. For the first time they had an
inside cabin, Elinor was not the "stewardess's darling," and
the weather was appalling. Elinor read Arnold Bennett's *Buried Alive* to Horace. He responded with "more improving but
equally nice literature. . . . He seems to know more than ever.
To breathe the same air is educational. There is no help for
it, I adore him," Elinor confessed to Mama [October 1911]
(B). A month later she amplified this sentiment: "He is even
more wonderful than he used to be, & I don't know *how* much
I shall love him eventually—certainly I do more & more every
day. The amount I learn from him of history, literature, general information & (as I think) high philosophy (in this case
more friend than foe) is without end."

Elinor knew her mother's attitude and had no wish to
read it in her letters. She gave her mother no return address,
saying they were traveling around too much to tell Mama
where to write. She confessed that she was too frightened to
write to Connie. Elinor's first letter to Washington was an
aggregate of remorse. She realized the shame she had brought
on Rhode Island Avenue for the second time. She took all the
blame: "If it has been too dreadful for words, it was I that did
it to you, & deliberately, so that remorse for that would only

sound insincere, since I chose to do it." She let Mama know that she herself was paying the penalty as well.

They moved around aimlessly, completely uncertain about where they would go, forced to be on guard the whole time. After landing in Liverpool, they spent a night in Chester, then moved on to Leamington Spa—much safer, they thought, than pressing on to London. Elinor had a suit made out of the same material as Horace's dressing gown. They went sightseeing. For the first time they were concerned about money. Elinor felt her reduced circumstances, especially with a much grander hotel (The Regent) in sight of their own (Manor House Hotel). She tried, unconvincingly, to put on a brave face: "$4,000 a year we have. But it will be more, later on, & at present it is plenty. Even in travelling, to be wineless, cableless, even bath-*room*-less, is certainly just as much fun. . . ."

"It is the earnest desire of both our hearts," she added in the same letter, "to get into a rut & stay there. I suppose we don't deserve it one bit. . . . I feel as if the peace, which undoubtedly exists like a delightful atmosphere over all this English country, was so undeserved by us, & yet we benefit by it. Graceless creatures."

For the moment they had no idea where to find their "rut." They carried their money around in "our hip pocket, having no bankers." Their search was interrupted by Horace's concern over Elinor's health; her headaches returned with renewed pain and were becoming, as she confessed the next month from Oxford [November? 1911] (B), "a nuisance to me in lots of ways." A soothing campaign—"We read all we can, & we are the most tremendous walkers. We have worked up to about ten miles a day, truly"—did nothing to relieve them. Horace took Elinor off to consult Sir William Osler* in Oxford, who diagnosed that her headaches were directly linked to her blood pressure; if the pressure could be reduced, the pain would vanish. By the end of the month Elinor joyfully

*Sir William Osler (1849–1919), was Regius Professor of Medicine at Oxford and author of some ten medical books on subjects as varied as cerebral palsies in children and stomach cancer. He was famous as a diagnostician.

announced to Mama: (Thanksgiving, 1911) (B): "It is quite amusing to see how *everything* fits into Osler Theory. He was quite funny the way he asked if I'd led 'a fairly reasonable' life & had few troubles, because you see it is worry & excitement & unhappiness & such things that *make* extra pressure. You see how perfectly it all explains itself."

Unwittingly, Elinor gave herself away; she could not divulge her illness without revealing that she was not as content as she made out. Her health was the real index to her state of mind, not her letters. She never actually lied to Mama, though she skillfully omitted to tell the complete truth. Yet her letters were her only confessions.

Because of her dependence on doctors, the West Country was ruled out. London was impossible. Brighton or Bournemouth were more likely stops on their search for a home. They wanted to be in a small town, close to a larger one. As it turned out, Burley, in Hampshire, fitted these requirements perfectly. Bournemouth was some nineteen miles away and the New Forest provided them with ample protection as well as isolation. They found Durmast Cottage in the beginning of November, but there was one drawback: they would have to wait two months before taking possession as the owners wanted to stay on through Christmas before going out to India. They took the house anyway, and began the first tentative steps to establish themselves.

"Mrs H. Waring is my name at the bank, of course," Elinor told her mother (November 10) (B). The choice of their assumed name was Henry's suggestion. Before they boarded the train in New Hampshire in 1911, he had said to them: "You have got to keep your own initials, and you assure me that you must change your name. Well, try Waring! I got the idea from, 'What's become of Waring, since he gave us all the slip?'* . . . Make it Waring!" They opened an account at the First National Provincial Bank of England in Bournemouth. That was their address for all letters, and they could safely ask Mama to write to them, finally, after six weeks.

They searched for another place to pass the two months. Burley was so small it had no hotel. Bournemouth was *"stuffed*

---

*The quotation is from Browning's poem "Waring."

with consumptives" and therefore impossible. They decided

to cross the Channel to France, even though Elinor was in no mood to travel. She had had enough of it and longed to settle down. Her letters to Mama became a "sort of wicked Baedeker" as they progressed through cathedral country, stopping at Amiens, Rouen, and Lyons. She loathed it all. She detested the French, and her feelings were manifested in something "like a fever blister" on her nose (not unlike Mama, who developed one inside her nose). "I might as well tell you as a joke on me that *I* must have had it . . .", she wrote to Mama (December 15) (B), "a fine cure for vanity! . . . If it doesn't entirely go away I'll have it fixed in England—you wouldn't like to trust a French doctor at your *face!*" But worse awaited her in Lyons.

There they received their first communication from America. It had been sent on from Bournemouth. The letter was from Mama, addressed not to Elinor but Horace, and it substantiated their worst fears, which had been aroused by Mama's continued silence. According to Mama, Katharine was broadcasting some serious accusations: that Elinor had "compelled" Horace to desert his wife and that she had been left without sufficient income to raise her children.* She

*Horace answered these charges in his reply to Mama from Lyons [November, 1911] (B): "I regret extremely that you have had additional suffering placed upon you. As to the statements made to you by Mrs Wylie I will say that you know that I returned to Elinor Because I loved her and also felt that my first and greatest duty was to her. You know I was not compelled to. As to the money matter if it will not too much annoy you I should like to give you the facts. I left in Mrs Wylie's name in the American Security & Trust between nine & ten thousand dollars. I directed Riggs National Bank to transfer to her three hundred shares of common stock of the American Tabacco Co. I deeded to her the Thomas Circle property and ten tenement houses. I also transferred to her six thousand dollars of bonds. The Tabacco pays $40 a share a year (has been earning $80). The houses give about $1200 a year, the bonds $300   Total = $13500. From this she must pay $2250 interest on borrowed money secured by the Tabacco—and taxes about $1000 so it works out thus. . . . Net Income $10250   Besides the above she has in her own right about $1500 a year from her father's estate. She and the family lived last year at the rate of $8400 a year. She also has the Thomas Circle House to live in. Also she has $10,000 cash to start on. . . . If I have made myself clear you will I think agree that a sufficient allowance has been made her."

topped these intimations with, as Elinor put it (November 23) (B), "threats of—revenge practically." Elinor explained that if any of Katharine's letters should reach them, which was most unlikely as she had neither their pseudonym nor their address, "they will be burned unread, & if they continued, we would change our address & name if necessary."

Mama's vulnerability concerned both Elinor and Horace far more than Katharine's threats and accusations. "But for you," Elinor wrote (November 23), "left by us unprotected against the brunt of her anger, it is too awful. We both feel this strongly. . . . Indeed I do not minimize my wrong-doing, but I think it rather pitiful, & a commentary on her hardness and violence, that she should have reduced you to almost apologising for daring to love such a monster as I."

Elinor was fully aware that she appeared unconscionably selfish to Mama, and knew that her letters to Washington were designed to crowd out the enormous guilt that assailed her. It was in desperation over Mama's silence that she poured out her feelings in the Thanksgiving (1911) letter (B):

I would so love to be good but I can never be *that,* I know, & I perfectly understand that the sort of small self-sacrifice, good-temper & consideration which we delight in showing to each other, is only a luxury, & no more *good* than eating ice-cream (but far nicer for us!)

You see I do not deceive myself, & I realize that the barely decent cheerfulness I managed under Phil was far harder & of more worth than all the angelic amiability I simply can't help towards (my dear) Horace.

She sympathized with Mama, and hoped that Mama might, if she were aware that Elinor appreciated the gravity of her action and status, somehow come round. She longed for a kind word from her. The isolation was having more serious effects even than depression—Elinor's strength seemed to be running out.

It still remained for them to return to England and make the final preparations for moving into Durmast Cottage. They had to stop at Paris on their way back in order not to retrace "our steps to the most horrid extent," referring to the constant fear of being discovered by private detectives, newspaper reporters, or any visiting Washingtonians. Every move they made was calculated to avoid a potential confrontation. They stayed on the Left Bank because the Right Bank was popular with Americans. They got back to England, reported to Sir William Osler in Oxford for a brief consultation, then went on to London. There they bought belated Christmas presents: "picture books for the children—even one perhaps which *could be kept at your house,"* Elinor suggested to Mama (December 15), "—& given by Nancy to Philip [Beeyup], not to take home—& these will do for New Years presents." They planned to stay in London for only two days, but ended up staying on at the Savoy until the end of the year. Elinor's health was getting more troublesome. She wrote to Mama (December 29) (B) that she was "unwell & therefore had to stop my nice medicine [for the high blood pressure] . . . So, I have had several days of rather bad headache." Horace's idea of rest and convalescence was to continue Elinor's instruction. "Horace is going to teach me . . . [indec.] half an hour at the Kensington Museum [the Victoria and Albert]—all the different annoying furniture periods so I'll know them forever, he says. Just because it bores me to hear about them . . . & not know one from which."

The stay in London was very quiet—"theatres & restaurants being as much out of our scheme of life—& pocket—now as if we were in the Sahara." It was a fitting end to a year of intense activity—according to Elinor's calculation, Horace had traveled 27,000 miles in 1911. They had run away for the second time and brought scandal back to their families.

On Christmas Day they indulged themselves: Horace gave Elinor a dress and she gave him an encyclopedia—"an extravagance we had promised ourselves from the beginning." They celebrated the New Year quietly in Bournemouth, and took possession of Durmast Cottage on January 7, 1912.

§ *iii*   *Hibernation in the Home Counties*

Elinor's only correspondent was Mama. She was still too frightened to communicate with Connie, who was now in Rome. She searched the Rome notes of the *Herald,* "just to hear of her. Naturally I don't dare write to her. . . ." Connie's husband made certain she did not. He wrote a scathing letter, addressed not to Elinor but to Horace, expressing the anger he shared with Henry who was, Tumm explained, too cautious to vent his feelings himself. "From what I hear from America you seem to think," wrote Tumm (October, 1911) (B),

that you have not yet brought sufficient dishonor upon your wife and children as well as upon my sister-in-law and her family. I am sorry that my sister-in-law seems pliant to your wishes and does not appear to realize that you—having left her once to save your skin—are liable to repeat the performance at any time . . . should I ever chance to run across you over here I will under any circumstances apply my cane or whatever is handy to your face in a manner you will not easily forget—the right treatment for a cad in mine and all gentlemen's opinion.

If Elinor thought her family might forgive her, such a letter convinced her she had a very long time to wait. And if such letters from her family could filter through "the Warings'" manifold defenses, the idea of what might be lurking unopened at "different guessed-at addresses" was hardly thinkable. Her caution became even more extreme; she concealed her address even from Mama. The knowledge of their exact whereabouts was safe with no one. In a fit of anger, Mama might give the secret away. Elinor did not even address the envelopes to America herself since her handwriting was too well known to prying eyes. Horace addressed the letters and posted them from either Bournemouth or Southampton, to avoid the Burley postmark. Such circumspection meant that all outward communication was erratic. Inbound letters were scarcely less so. Mama's infrequent letters were routed from the Bournemouth bank, through the Royal Bath Hotel, then on to Burley (a mistake on the bank's part because Elinor gave her last address, before moving into Durmast, as the hotel). It provided ample camouflage. Despite the time required for letters to reach her, Elinor still gave way before the gravest forebodings: "I am hoping that you are not writing," she wrote to her mother (January 19, 1912) (B), "because you think it wiser not to, & not because you are angry with me."

When Washington letters did arrive, they caused little

pleasure. Mama's contained the mortifying information that
Tumm's opinion was widespread. There were endless assaults
and persecutions, first from Hoyt and McMichael relations
who beleaguered Mama with unwelcome judgments on Elinor: "think of [them] openly siding with the charming young
martyr, Phil," Elinor responded, "—& O well, if only, as
Horace says, Phil would marry _one of them!_" Then there were
the deserted spouses, Katharine and Phil, who offered a
stream of comments.

Hichborn got in the first and most damaging shot—on
January 8, 1912, he made good his threat of the previous May
and filed for absolute divorce, naming Horace Wylie as co-
respondent. The following day the news was in the Washington papers and the international _Herald,_ which Elinor read. "I
am afraid it is very hard for you. Why couldn't he do it else
where?" she asked Mama [January 10] (B). ". . . it is disgusting." The morning of January 19 the _New York Herald_ arrived
at Durmast Cottage

with a full account. Really it is too terrible to think of how bad it
must be for you. Of course I am helpless—& really too utterly
scot-free to feel selfrespecting on that score. If only I could do
something for you but you must be tired of hearing me say _that._

What _is_ this idea about the abhorrent name [Hichborn]? Does
he suppose I _want_ to use it? . . . Had I known all this was happening,
I wouldn't have praised everything so & been so cheerful in my
letters, particularly about Horace whom you must despise—still you
would rather know that to me he is an angel, anyway. What it was
to have him beside me this morning when I saw that gorilla-like face
in the paper no words can say. (B)

Phil thought that Elinor's disgrace had ruined the Hichborn name, and he was determined to deprive her of it. Along
with the name went her son. Phil demanded that he too must
be completely cut off from her. "I am glad," Elinor commented wistfully to Mama, "you see Philip [Beeyup]—I
couldn't have, I know, & I suppose I _never_ shall, but can't quite
believe it. Kiss him for me—seriously I mean please do."
Beeyup was placed in the joint care of Phil's sister Martha
Pearsall and "Mrs. the Admiral"; between these two stalwart
ladies Mama managed to sneak occasional visits to her grand-

son. The Hichborns detested any remnants of Elinor's influence, no matter how slight, on the child. But while Elinor resigned herself to the fact that she was denied her son, Mama refused to give up.

All Washington was agog with gossip. Phil, prone to his own mental problems anyway, decided to quit the capital and start a new life in California—with his son. The news surprised Elinor; she had hoped that any love she might still possess for her son could be filtered through Rhode Island Avenue. Now that course was closed to her:

It will be too terrible if Phil takes Philip west—I can't *believe* such a thing will happen—& wait till I know it's true. Anyway, as you say, he'd *never* stick it out, in the world. Philip is too sweet & adorable to say he loves me—poor lamb—but I suppose to him I am a mythical person . . . do you suppose he loves me by *instinct?* I would give anything for a picture of him, though I suppose I should shed bitter tears over it. I wonder if I will *ever* see him again. If *only* he is not dragged away from you & Nancy, it would be enough. (B)

Katharine, knowing the surest means of contact with her husband was through Mama, made certain that Mama realized what she felt. Whatever Katharine had to say to Horace, Mama passed on to Elinor. And Elinor answered Mama for Horace in return:

Mrs W. is mistaken. Her letters get no further than London. We ran up the other day & found two thin ones, which we promptly tore up *unread.* That was all. Receiving no answer, I think she will stop, if not, there will simply be a spring tearing-up UN-READ the next time we go to London . . . however she may boast to you, she will never really know what became of them. I am sorry to sound cruel, but it is the only way, & you know we determined upon it long ago.

Overlooking what she herself had done, Elinor believed that Katharine alone held the key to her happiness. Everything rested on the belief, naïve as it was, that if Katharine would give Horace his freedom, the past could be completely overcome. Katharine had refused to give Horace a divorce, yet Elinor was still optimistic: "If only K. would ever divorce poor Horace I *might* hope for other children. . . ."

Burley, Hampshire, lies on the southwest side of the New
Forest, which was, for Elinor, "next to North East [Harbor,
Maine] the most beautiful place in the world." And the New
Forest was strangely reminiscent of Maine. Perched between
Southampton Water and the Avon, it stretches for some
93,000 acres of wilderness. Dating from 1079 (when William
the Conqueror established it as a hunting ground), it is severe
and wild terrain—a mixture of heath, marsh and forest, full of
oaks, yews, beeches, and holly. Semi-wild ponies meander
across land that boasts some of the rarest breeds of plants in
England, among them wild orchids. The place is infested with
rabbits—not rats, as Nancy Hoyt claimed in 1935.

The village of Burley, as Elinor remembered it some
eleven years later, was "the most fairy-book place in the world
. . . there were sherry-glass elms with rooks in them, and a
beechwood which was pink and purple in April, and bright
holly bushes which were covered with scarlet berries in November." Village life centered on a primitive inn, all red and
white, called the Queen's Head. Up the road was the church
and churchyard, which overlooked an enormous grazing field.
Durmast Cottage,* secluded but less than a mile from the
heart of town, was so close to the golf course "you could toss
a biscuit from its front door" to it. The footpath to the church
was arched in ancient trees. The house itself was protected by
laurels that surrounded the front garden, and a hedge of holly.
Elinor began to see holly through every window and eventually she nicknamed Horace "Holly." The house faced south
and the northern exposure looked onto a well-stocked kitchen
garden. The Bowens had scattered the lawn with bulbs, "&
later with our little apple orchard & big solitary pear-tree—*not*
in the hedge—& plenty of roses it should be delightful," said
Elinor shortly after moving in [January 10] (B). Even though
they moved in the dead of winter, Elinor found it difficult to
control her enthusiasm:

Anything lovelier than the wood behind the house with the ground
white, & white powdering on every tree, it is impossible to imagine,

*Captain John Cuthbert Grenside Bowen bought Durmast Cottage, then
technically called Durmast Lodge, in 1908. Elinor and Horace rented the
property from him. In 1937 the name was changed to Durmast Cottage;
today it has reverted back to Durmast Lodge.

with the turquoise sky & no leafless trees except for the lovely beech, all the rest being the brightest green, huge gorse bushes covered with brilliant yellow flowers, & shining holly trees—as tall as good-sized maples. . . . No dark pines or evergreens to lower the key—simply blue & white & yellow & vivid green. The holly tree, perhaps because it is alive & growing, is as light as jade. . . . (B)

She was no less pleased with the inside of the house. "I think I keep house very well & economically—(the truth is, I always did, only the odds were against me)—& our cook is a wonder," she reported to Mama. Apart from "the cooklet," who was a "comparatively mature person of twenty-two" named Savrina Waterman, there was a "pink & white & very meek" maid of nineteen called Catherine, and a gardener and his wife to look after "the Warings." "We also have a pretty little cat-kitten . . . fluffy like an angora, but of plain tiger markings," whose major occupation was following the maid around by day and chasing his shadow by night. A tame robin completed the ménage: "he comes right in the front door, calmly walking. He is so nice that one cant be superstitious & discourage him. He taps with his beak on the dining room window for bread . . . & he doesn't mind our standing right there, watching him eat it off the sill."

Still, Horace remained Elinor's prime source of pleasure. She expounded his virtues *ad nauseam* to Mama, longing to win her round. Mama could not withstand the force of Elinor's ceaseless praise, and very quickly relented, volunteering that she liked Horace. "Dear Horace"; Elinor sighed,

thank you for saying you are fond of him, darling. Even if his decision was wrong he is happy in believing it to be right to stand between me & the world that, because of him, is my enemy. He is changed—I know he has found strength & I cannot think it a wicked strength when it is my comfort & protection. I dont think his happiness is all selfish—I think he now really has the quiet *courage of his convictions,* & also it makes him happy to know that he can, & does, do everything for me . . . & he seems good to me because he IS good —to ME! . . .

Elinor protested too much. The excessive language was as alarming a signal as her headaches. The isolation was impossible to deny, the solitude boring. There is a false note running throughout her letters to Rhode Island Avenue. She tried to

convince Mama—and herself—that she was happy. She
thought that through sheer effort she might persuade herself
Horace was enough to replace the absence of so many other
people. But Elinor was essentially social; she had known no
life other than a very busy one. Now she was plunged into a
completely uneventful existence. The result left her off balance. What she told Mama and herself was a meek confession
of martyrdom: "we are simple harmless & quiet people who
merely have a natural genius—& love—for pleasing each
other! That's all. . . . But—! look at the other side! What is one
to think? I know what most people think . . . that we can't be
good." Gradually Elinor was withdrawing into an elaborate
form of guilt; no letter was without some disclosure that she
knew the severe consequences of her actions. She undercut
every declaration of pleasure and contentment with a poisonous indictment of either her selfishness or villainy. Every moment of happiness, no matter how brief, had to be paid for.
She had trapped herself in a moral vise.

As the year progressed she developed physical symptoms that contradicted her declarations; her health deteri-
orated while her happiness, she protested, was steadily increasing. The headaches returned and her lethargy
increased. She attributed everything to the weather. That
first winter in England was "the coldest weather England
has had for forty-five years—that's some cold—& have
lived to triumphantly tell the tale." Horace predicted there
would be a coal strike and laid in ample supplies. He
warned the other locals, and very few people in Burley
were short of coal. "We have had endless fun out of our
efforts to keep warm—very successful efforts, too,—& have
emerged into nice spring like weather—I with no cold at
all. . . . Our rooms are so tiny that we can keep them very
warm, though with coal fires. . . . My hoofs got chilblains
from being too much toasted in front of fires. . . ."

From "unromantic childblains" she moved back to tor-
menting headaches. What a mercy, she wrote to Mama on
March 7 (B), that Horace, unlike Phil, did not force her to
exercise:

I often walk around the links with him which I love but I need never
be pestered to play any game again . . . because of my arterial

hypertension or stick in the mud. This is fine—I can walk all I want, so long as I dont run up hill, but I need never ride, or play tennis, or stand on my head. . . . But O if I'd known about that excuse before —authoratively, I mean! Now I dont need it in the least, with this angel of a Horace.

Elinor's headaches were becoming an important feature of her life. The signs of essential hypertension had first appeared shortly after her marriage to Phil, and her blood pressure soared to dangerous heights when she was in her mid-twenties. Phil had laughed at her each time she complained of headaches, so that she was forced to ignore their regular appearance. Now, with so little else to occupy her, she gave way before them. One day they were *"miraculously* better," requiring but one bromoseltzer for the entire day; the next they raged with unremitting force. She was immobilized by them, had to increase the medicine, and so made the symptoms worse when they returned. Yet she claimed that Horace alone worked better than any bromoseltzer. "My headaches as I told you," she wrote to Mama, "are better than they have been for five or six years. I think myself it is more peace, happiness, & a reasonable life than Osler, though doubtless he helped. Anyway it IS Horace."

But the continued threats and slights from Washington overwhelmed the effect of any kind of antidote. She could not shake off the need to fight. Though Katharine's letters ceased —"there were no more Katy letters," Elinor wrote her mother after a trip to London (March 7) (B), "though it has been three or four weeks since those torn-up ones got there. So, we felt very much pleased & encouraged"—another quite unexpected enemy crossed her path. Her brother Henry seemed to take over where Katharine left off in the Washington battles. He had become engaged to Alice Parker, a tall elegant creature he had met in art school. Her family expected the wedding to take place in London, and Mama started making plans to come to Europe, both to attend the wedding and to travel on to Italy to see Connie. Then the plans were abruptly changed—because of Elinor. The wedding would take place in America after all. Elinor could not overlook the implications of the move: "If the Parkers decided on America because they were afraid of my being in England would give

them trouble [sic] they really are *brutishly* stupid," she railed
(March 18) (B). "Fancy *my* trying to butt in! However, they
may have had other reasons only I suspect them of fearing *I*
would turn up. Fools!" It was just another in the long string
of attacks on her. She appealed to Mama not to give up her
intention of sailing to Europe. Could she not still come after
the wedding? Elinor was desperate for some sign that she was
not completely cast off from her family. The gesture would
have to come from Mama. "Of course you would adore it
here, but I suppose you wouldn't want to come to me. Still,"
she added forlornly in the same letter, "as I've said, we could
manage it somehow. And you *would* love this place. The country is the *only* place to live, as I now see." It was certainly the
only place where Elinor could live.

Mama did not come. She fell ill again. And she sent as her
ambassadors, of all people, Henry and Alice, who were married in April. Surprisingly, Elinor rose to the occasion with
considerable delight: "It will be wonderful," she told Mama
(May 28) (B), "to see 'one of us' though I wish it were *you.*"
Henry and Alice began their honeymoon in Spain; after wandering through the Prado in Madrid, they headed north for
England. The visit, so longed for and anticipated, was not a
success. Four years later, when Katharine finally relented and
sued Horace for a divorce, Henry was asked to make a thor-
ough deposition, and his ammunition was drawn from this
visit. He gave the evidence Katharine needed.

Henry was caught in the middle of the scandal Elinor
provoked. As the eldest son he was expected to act for Mama,
no matter how unpleasant the task might be. It fell to him to
shore up the debris of the family Mama held so dear. As she
got older, she placed more and more importance on family
unity, which only seemed to disintegrate increasingly around
her. Henry's distasteful task was further aggravated by
Mama's strange equivocalness regarding her eldest son. She
could be astonishingly unfeeling and vicious toward him. She
adored Connie, then Elinor, and made it obvious that she had
little regard for Henry. Yet she never hesitated to make demands on him. Mercifully Henry, of all her children, was the
most sensitive to other people and his character reacted
against Mama's coolness. He was the most generous of the

children. Yet, by being forced to act for Mama, he ended up acting against his own nature, becoming another casualty of Elinor's selfishness and Mama's sternness. The female members of his family even tried to turn him against his new wife.

Henry and Alice arrived at Durmast Cottage on Wednesday, July 10. "I was awfully glad of course—but it meant a rush which has been unremitting ever since," Elinor reported to Mama two days later (July 12) (B). Both Elinor and Horace were delighted by the first intrusion of family into their life for nine months. The painful reminder of Tumm's declaration that Henry detested Horace created a strained atmosphere. But Elinor, the ardent housekeeper, was quite pleased to give herself up to the "wild scurry" demanded by guests; as in her letters to Mama, she was anxious to plead her case by example. Henry and Alice saw proof of her happiness. She was afraid her brother did find her "oldfogyish & dull"—a result of a quiet rural existence, she professed. For their part, Henry and Alice were "in raptures over the place, as a paintable one. Well, it *is* heavenly." Elinor darted around, "quite fussy & middle aged tidying up rooms behind them & secretly hating their never-ceasing cigarette smoke." Elinor was not so secretive, however, about detesting Alice's extreme slimness. "Really you know she is rather a scarecrow as to figure, but she is quite certain that she is the highest ideal of beauty, & condoled with me as to my *thickness* . . . I suppose I weigh 15 pounds more than I did last summer . . . what do *I* care?" Alice's final verdict on her notorious sister-in-law was that she was "thrilling." Elinor was not flattered: "In reality it is my chiefest cause for self-congratulation that I am no such thing, but very normal & quiet & in a sort of heavenly irradiated 'rut.' "

The visit passed smoothly enough, if without much warmth. Elinor still awaited the final move from Mama. If she could only visit, Elinor would know all was forgiven though not forgotten. The house emptied, and Elinor moved into the garden: "At present picking my sweet peas keeps me rather busy. . . ."

While Elinor was extolling the virtues of gardening, Philip Hichborn was moving in complete darkness—a darkness cast

by his own imbalance and intensified by the steady flow of
rumors that reached him about Elinor. As Elinor had predicted, he did not stay in California. By the third week in
March 1912, he had returned to Washington. The attempt at
independence had defeated him. He moved back to his
mother's house. His divorce proceedings did little more than
revive the accusation and scandal he longed to escape. He had
thought that divorce would bring him peace; it was doing
precisely the reverse. Having chosen to give Elinor up, the
newspapers would not allow him to do so. Report after report
appeared affecting not Elinor and Horace but Phil.

The divorce proceedings moved slowly. Phil's freedom,
though certain, had to wait. As in December 1910, the newspaper reports were wildly inaccurate as to times and places.
When Mama fell ill in March 1912, the newspapers stated that
she had gone to Rome to see Connie. In fact, Connie had come
to Washington and Mama was recuperating from some foot
ailment. Elinor was stated to be pregnant, languishing in a
romantic spot just motor-launch distance from Monte Carlo.
The child was, of course, Horace's. Such stories could not be
taken lightly, least of all by Phil. Or by Society: the Social
Register judiciously removed Phil, Horace, and Elinor from
its rolls on January 1, 1912. Washingtonians and New Yorkers
read every Hichborn-Wylie report as entertaining fiction; Phil
saw them as added proof for his continued depression. He
could not shake off his mood. Everything seemed to feed his
sadness. Even before Phil had gone to California, Katharine
had met Phil in the street and was so astonished by his deteri-
orated appearance, she asked him what was wrong. The answer was as surprising as the question: "The rent," Phil said
tersely.*

*According to Dr. Nancy Potter's astute Ph.D. thesis on Elinor (*Elinor
Wylie: A Biographical and Critical Study,* Boston University, 1954), p. 27,
Katharine Wylie staunchly refused to grant a divorce "until Elinor Hichborn would bear a child out of wedlock." Such a condition would almost
certainly guarantee that Horace would never return to her. The Monte
Carlo reports that Elinor was pregnant meant, or at least suggested, that
Horace and Elinor's marriage would take place. If, as Dr. Potter suggests,
these false newspaper reports prompted Hichborn's final depression, it leads
one to believe that he still held out for Elinor's return. The theory seems
very plausible if one were able to discount Phil's madness.

Phil returned to Washington from California late on Tuesday, March 26. The following day he headed straight for his office, where he worked for several hours. After lunch he called at his sister's house to collect Beeyup, then aged five, for a ride, ending up at his mother's house (1707 N Street NW). He left Beeyup there and went to call on his sister again, telling his mother he intended to stay on there for dinner as well. Around five o'clock he arrived at 18th Street and found neither the butler nor his sister but two maids who had been left in charge. He told the parlor maid that he would wait for his sister in the library. He climbed the stairs to the small library and locked the door. Instead of picking up a book, he withdrew a sheet of paper and swiftly scrawled a note in pencil. Calmly and deliberately he then pulled out a revolver, raised it to his temple, and fired. The bullet passed through his head, embedding itself in a mirror on the wall. The shot, heard in the servant's hall, was ignored; the maids thought it was a car backfiring.

When the library door was forced open by the police shortly after Martha Pearsall (his sister) returned home at six thirty, Hichborn's body was found sprawled out on the floor, the pistol some inches from his hand. After a life of relative insignificance, it was a final irony that the police, lawyers, and doctors who paraded through the library to certify death should overlook his note. It was brief. All that was revealed of its content stated: "I am not to blame for this. I think I have lost my mind. . . ." He was twenty-nine years old.*

Newspapers up and down the East Coast could not afford to overlook the unfortunate climax they had inadvertently encouraged. The *New York American* splashed a large picture of Elinor on its front page, not even bothering to reproduce one of Phil on subsequent pages. The *New York Herald* more generously ran pictures of them both. No matter how the various stories were written, the guilt rested firmly upon Elinor.

*There is an astonishing similarity between this scene and the death of Ralph Marvell in Edith Wharton's novel *The Custom of the Country* (1913), Chapter XXXVI. Hichborn's death was reported in the international *Herald* and Edith Wharton could have read about it.

But Elinor, normally given to so much emotional excess,
kept her feelings to herself. She said little, and wrote less.
Mama took to her bed again.

"I knew this would happen some time," Elinor wrote to
Mama from Cambridge (n.d.), "& that I would be blamed—
it is too dreadful for you to have a child who is CALLED a
murderess, but, dearest, you know, DONT YOU, that I'm not
really? I am perfectly well, & NOT going to have a baby in the
least, on my word of honor. . . . I only write this to ask you
to love me & to tell you how I love you. Am I not, PLEASE,
just as much as ever your Elinor?" (B)

Though she kept silent about Phil, Beeyup was in her
thoughts now more than ever. He was shunted from grandmother to grandmother, aunt to aunt, and played with an
uncle who was only six years older than he was. The Hoyts and
the Hichborns engaged in a perverse tug-of-war over him.
Mama was prepared to go to court to get custody. Elinor
advised her from Burley (April 4) (B): "It isn't fair to you to
keep going over the various aspects of this painful thing. Except this—remember that if anything happens to poor Mrs
Hichborn, Philip is INFINITELY more yours, legally, equitably
& morally than Martha's."*

Elinor waited over a decade before giving her final justification for Phil's suicide. "Of course," she said to Carl Van
Doren in 1925, "if Philip had killed himself over me, he could
not have waited over two years to do it."

The best expression of what she felt was not evident in
words but in her symptoms. The headaches returned, more
strongly. As soon as the Hichborn news reached Durmast
Cottage, Elinor was "dragged (that's rather ungrateful to the
poor darling!)" by Horace to Cambridge and London to consult specialists for her "awful" headaches. The verdict was "to

---

*About eight weeks later (May 28) (B) Elinor added, "Naturally it is a great
blow about Philip. I don't want you to think . . . that I was urging you *to*
take it into *court*. Of course you mustn't & cant dear. Only I suppose I was
trying to assure you that your claim was stronger than *Martha's*. Maybe I'm
wrong. God knows—but I *cant* believe anyone would give him to *her* rather
than *you*. Poor dearest Mama, it *cant* be possible—think of her. Of course
all of that is frightfully *cruel* of Mrs. H. I think, so far as my opinion is worth
anything."

try some electric business as a last resort. . . . Of course I am convinced," she confided to Mama (May 10) (B),

that staying still makes them as well as they'll ever be, & naturally the last thing that happened increased them somewhat. Well, now I am passed on to a Bournemouth electrocutor & have to go 3 TIMES a week   a horrible bore. . . . The truth is, I always have a splendid week or ten days in the month, & the rest is rotten, but only physically so, as I am perfectly & blissfully happy with Horace, & will be as long as I am with him.

They could not have selected a better place for "staying still" than Burley. In the extreme isolation there unwanted publicity simply could not reach them. Elinor enjoyed almost no village life. There were occasional visits to neighbors, all very courteous and unrevealing. No one had the slightest idea who she was or what she had done. Elinor spent her time dismissing the past and filling the present with minor Durmast Cottage excitements. Her hours were passed in the complicated geometry of flower arrangement, attempting a few putts on the links with Horace, watching him grease the new car every morning before his bath, or teaching the "cooklet" how to fry mash. Boxes of books arrived at regular intervals from London lending libraries. She read steadily through Meredith, Trollope, old issues of *The Cornhill* and *Punch.* She always had a newspaper in front of her, and read every report she could find of the sinking of the *Titanic.*

This endless list of activities filled her letters to Mama. Mama for her part could not overlook that Elinor was getting very tedious, and very uninteresting. She urged her to start writing again. Indeed, Elinor herself confessed: "I have lots of time for reading & writing." Only the latter was not making much headway. "I *will* write for you," she promised Mama, "even if it has to reflect housekeeping & country, & not be poetry. You see I am so busy & so happy." Every suggestion Mama made regarding literary activity was countered by some excuse. The idea of a collection of old poems, polished up, met with silence. To the chance of some novel, Elinor protested (April 18) (B): "If only my headaches would go away, I would really write you a novel* since you want it. Maybe when I'm

---

*There was in fact a "novel" which Elinor sent not to Mama but to Connie, in the late summer of 1912. She informed Mama (August 26) (B): "I sent

older they will, & it is something, isn't it, to practice cooking
against an emergency."

Mama returned to her plan to print a slender volume of
Elinor's early verse—she even offered to pay for it. For the
first week in June, while repairs on the house were under way,
Elinor and Horace went off to France. Before leaving for Caen
by car, she asked Mama: "Do you realize the poems would
cost about $200? And how could we get them into any kind
of circulation? The London agent of your man refused them.
However, if you wish it, it can be done privately—but to what
end?" Mama did wish it. She dispatched "a mass of money
which I suppose is for the poems" through Henry, who was
still in London at the end of July. "We must go up to London
to see about them," Elinor explained (July 31) (B), "& will
probably wait a while until it is emptier of Americans." The
excuses continued. How should authorship be handled: "If we
were not discovered but continued to live in Burley," asked
Elinor, "would poems have to be concealed from possible Mrs
Dents [her only close acquaintance in Burley] all my life, or
not? Tell me, darling, what you truly think, & I will take your
decision as final." Mama suggested "anon." By the middle of
August they had still failed to get to London, but Elinor assured Mama (August 13) (B): "In September we shall go up
to London for a few days to see about the poems & for Horace
to give me furs for my birthday." Negotiations dragged on.
The project required the stamina of Mama herself, who finally
arrived in October 1912. It was approximately a year since she
had last seen Elinor.

Mama brought Nancy with her. Elinor had cautioned her
not to bring a maid, fearing that even trusty "Maid Marion"
might say something indiscreet to the "cooklet" or Catherine.
Elinor treated Nancy, now eleven, more like a daughter than
a sister. She carted her off to Sunday School, took her to

Constance the Crane books & my 'novel' but I believe they were lost as I've
heard nothing. Probably considered a seditious document, coming from
England." All trace of this MS has been lost, but Mama did remember
something about it, as did Nancy Hoyt in the 1930s when the first biography
of Elinor was written. Nancy recalled the first chapter as "amazing," dealing
with a young girl in Paris. She says that Connie passed various chapters on
to a friend in Rome who promptly lost them. Elinor never mentioned the
MS again. Nancy Hoyt dates the "novel" 1914. See Hoyt, pp. 49–50.

massive teas, and they both went for walks across the New Forest. Meanwhile Mama set to work getting the poems into print.

Incidental Numbers was the title Elinor selected for her collection of twenty-five poems dating from 1902 to 1911. An elegant little volume, bound in blue-gray boards, it was modeled on William Clowes & Sons' edition of Blake's *Songs of Innocence;* the same firm printed Elinor's book. About sixty copies were ready toward the end of the year. The book was a gift from Mama.*

The lease on Durmast Cottage was drawing to a close, and the Bowens were due back from India. At this point Horace fell ill. He had suffered regularly from a winter cough that usually turned into "grippe," so they decided to spend the winter in some warm, or at least mild, climate. They went to Bournemouth en route for France, but his cough got worse. On December 14 they went up to London, where he managed to complicate the cough by contracting food poisoning. They stayed in London for five days, then headed down to Folkestone. There Elinor finally persuaded Horace to see a doctor. He had lost fourteen pounds in ten days. Elinor was frightened, but Horace assumed that he looked "more romantic!"

*When Nancy Hoyt's biography of Elinor came out, mentioning that Mama paid for the printing, Horace disputed the point. He wrote in the margin of his copy of the biography that he paid for the edition. He must have forgotten the furs. He also noted that though negotiations were carried out from Burley, they collected the copies in London on their way to France at the end of 1912. Elinor gave him a copy of *Incidental Numbers* for Christmas 1912 inscribed: "Some little sound of unremembered tears." Horace gave it to his third wife, and it is now in the Berg Collection. Horace did supervise the printing of the book. All copies, save about a dozen, were sent to Mama in Washington. Elinor asked her to keep a few "to distribute in my old age."

Carl Van Doren made a great point about the coincidence that Philip Hichborn's *Hoofbeats* appeared the same year as *Incidental Numbers,* suggesting that there was something more than mere coincidence involved. There was. Elinor was too bored to write, so she did the next best thing. It might be added that Hichborn's book was sponsored by the United Hunts Club of America—an organization that was most unlikely to inform Elinor of their tribute to its late member. Phil's book was published in 1912. The earliest anyone in America could have seen *Incidental Numbers* was the beginning of 1913.

They reached Paris on December 23 and stayed on there for a "gay & cheerful" Christmas. Elinor took time off from her Florence Nightingale routine to buy two wildly extravagant dresses: one in "thick brocaded crepe de chine, pale silvery blue with silver embroidery," and the other "dark sapphire blue & gold." The evening of December 27 they boarded the train for Pau—the place celebrated by Dornford Yates for its excellent golf links. The usual precautions in their itinerary remained: "if we see anyone we know we will leave at once for Spain—it is on the way—but if not will linger a while for the sake of golf which is very good & just what Holly needs. . . ." she told Mama on December 27 (B).

CHAPTER FIVE: 1913

People seem surprised that I am not
bored, but I never dream of being. I like
to feel contented, not excited, having had
too much of the latter in my time.

—Elinor to Mama
(November 10, 1913) (B)

Pau was a preview of what was to follow—nothing at all
happened except that Elinor sprained her ankle. It suited Elinor perfectly: "This is one of the heavenliest places, both for
looks & climate, that I ever saw. . . ." she wrote to Mama
[January 6, 1913] (B) from her rooms in the Hôtel de France.
Horace played gold every day while Elinor sat on a sofa nursing a sprained ankle. Their intended journey to St. Jean de Luz
and then into Spain, which would save them money and ensure their anonymity, was gratefully postponed. "I am awfully
glad the Spanish trip is given up," she admitted on January 30
(B), "as it would have been so tiring & dirty." Horace would
not have to "air" his Spanish, which was a blessing, and Elinor
was in no mood for exertion, having lapsed so comfortably
into lethargy. She even refused to tire herself by writing to
Mama: "It is so hard to write on your knee if you are near-
sighted. I know you will laugh at me." Instead she learned to
knit—a skill she acquired with what she considered "remarkable quickness." By the end of January, partly because they
had been spotted by acquaintances, they decided to brave St.
Jean de Luz after all. *"And* it was the most horrible, windy,
cold dreary place ever seen, except Biarritz, which was
worse," she told Mama (January 30) (B). They promptly reversed, returning to Pau and the Hôtel de France. Their arrival was like a scene out of Arnold Bennett's *The Card.* The
French staff felt a sense of justification when wayward guests
returned to the fold. Elinor and Horace "came back . . . to the
enormous delight of the whole staff of the whole hotel, who
looked upon it as a triumph over the other rival places, as

indeed it is!" Elinor returned to her knitting, her sofa, and
some reading—an endless stream of Tauchnitz novels purchased by Horace in town with Mama's Christmas money.
Horace also rewarded Elinor for being such a good patient
with a paste necklace—"very delicate & Louis Fourteenth."

By the third week in February they had left the Hôtel
de France again, much poorer and healthier, for Paris,
"not to get clothes or anything but simply to rest & get up
courage for the channel crossing" as she informed Mama
(February 19) (B) from the Hôtel Meurice, where they
stayed because "we never heard of an American staying
here." Her ankle, she went on, was made "rather tired
with so much standing around on platforms—what clean
person would dare sit down in a French railway station?"
They put up at the Meurice for a few days, Elinor with her
leg on a brocaded sofa, and peered over Paris which was
bathed in glorious clear weather. She received $300 from
Mama and continued to think up ways of transferring her
Pennsylvania Railroad stock to some name other than Mrs.
Philip Hichborn. She was afraid that "Mrs the Admiral"
would tear up the dividends, and decided to transfer the
shares to Mama, who could relay the money to "H. Waring."

By March 10 they were installed in Sheen Cottage in
Burley, not nearly so "primitive (or picturesque)" as Durmast, but somewhat larger. They took it for three months,
until the end of June. Horace retired to bed with the "grippe"
for three days which, according to Elinor's calculation, was like
two weeks for anyone else since he was such an appalling patient. His timing was superb. It was Holy Week and the church
bells thundered constantly. Elinor hobbled to church every
evening after racing up and down the stairs and in and out of
the kitchen all day. She complained to Mama that she could not
teach the cook even the basic rudiments of cooking. A sauce
for creamed chicken turned out lumpy despite the most elaborate efforts. Elinor had to push her aside and take over.

Her ankle kept her from bicycling and she was trapped
in Sheen Cottage until the new Hupmobile [car] arrived. She
continued to knit, though Mrs. Dent called and made several
disheartening comments about her efforts. "I know all these

domestic details must be dull," Elinor told Mama later that summer [June 1913] (B), "but they compose life at present & *long may they wave!"* Elinor seemed to think that a very quiet life would erase her notoriety. But Mama saw through the thin veneer of happiness. It was she, of all people, who had suggested that Elinor should live *"openly."* This alone might grant her more freedom. Elinor replied to this astonishing suggestion (March 11) (B):

... we would if we could, but what is there to do but use an assumed name? If Holly used his own, *I* couldn't could I? And if we each of us used a different one—why how could we live? I suppose we could, perhaps, in Paris, or where there are lots of "shady" relationships, but we are so different from those people, who love notoriety & all that. If we are to live peacefully & quietly how *can* we be "open".... Of course we could go, always, to Canada or Australia, but then I'd be so utterly cut off from you.... If ever I am left alone, I will be as open as you like, I will never *never* bear that horrible name [Hichborn] again.

Her fear of discovery became almost a reflex. Despite all their precautions, she and Horace were occasionally "found out." Horace noted in his diary that they had been "spotted" in Pau, hence the hasty flight to St. Jean de Luz. But Elinor never mentioned it. She was careful to keep any disruption of her unflagging domesticity from Mama.

Every aspect of her life seemed to be a reply to Mama's questions. The single relief to her unvaried routine existed in her letters. She resumed "a flourishing correspondence" with Connie, as she told Mama [January 6] (B), but "then I sent her a Victorian Book of Verse & apparently killed it dead...." What killed the correspondence was Elinor's inability to answer Connie's endless descriptions of fancy dress balls and diplomatic functions, and the fact that Connie was pregnant for the second time. The news of Alice's pregnancy had a similar effect on each sister. When Connie heard that Henry was moving out of Washington to New York, she was furious. She blamed Alice entirely. "It is a great pity that they have the absolute freedom," Connie wrote to Mama (March 3) "to choose where they will live—we haven't." Alice's belief that either Boston or New York (where they moved in the early

spring of 1913) was more suitable for their careers finally
forced Henry to desert his mother. Elinor was convinced that
Alice had turned Henry against her as well as Mama. Mama,
for her part, simply complained to her two European daughters that she was deserted, and yearned for the return of one
or the other. Alice's pregnancy forced the unwelcome decision Henry always had to make between his mother and his
wife—Mama was furious about his choice. Unhappily for Elinor, there was absolutely nothing she could do.

But all this anger about Henry masked Elinor's true feelings: clearly, the pregnancies of Connie and Alice aroused
great jealousy in her. She reacted by trying to become even
more engrossed in domestic matters. By the middle of the
summer she and Horace had left Burley for Thruxton, north
of Salisbury, where they took a house large enough to accommodate Mama and Nancy in comfort for their summer visit.
Nancy recalled the house as "a thick plaster house with a
thatched roof and one of the most amazing gardens I have ever
seen. . . ." The garden was filled with vegetables and flowers.
The country walks continued; meals became the most important feature of Elinor's days and Horace still dominated her
life.

All boldness disappeared once she left Washington. The
only dramatic thing she seemed to do was *nearly* make a decision.

In September 1913, she was twenty-eight, but longed to
be older, claiming she wanted to erase the difference in age
that separated her from Horace. Six months later she told
Mama how she would achieve this (March 9 [1914]) (B):

I very nearly decided the other day to take a great jump in age &
call myself 35 insted of 29, since I fear I look much older than the
latter age, & nobody believes me when I tell them it, . . . However,
Holly wouldnt let me. . . . The reason I wanted to make such a big
jump was that if I changed at all I might as well change it enough
to be worth while so people would say—"O you look very young
for that!"

The years in England were spent in a kind of emotional stor-
age. Elinor was incarcerated. There was a Gerhardian twist to
her actions—or lack of them. Everything she did and said was

designed to deny her real feelings. She was playing a part, and paying a high price for what she had done.

That September the couple left Hampshire for Surrey, settling at Downside Cottage, in Merrow, some two miles from Guildford. It was their fourth house in over twenty months. Elinor's health demanded the attentions only Harley Street could give: the sprained ankle proved a prelude to graver conditions. Her blood pressure soared, her eyes gave her trouble, and her leg had to be irradiated with X-rays once a week. She never explained the actual cause, but gave a full account of the treatment, which began in October. "I only have to have it once a week I have already had two goes," she wrote from Downside (October 14) (B), "& expect two more. Dont be scared—it is very weak—one fourth full strength & it would take 40 exposures of full strength to make a burn." For the entire autumn of 1913 she imitated Mama's supine posture; she could do nothing but rest, sit quietly, and knit. She managed to make her way in the Hupmobile to Burley to visit a few acquaintances. Otherwise her routine consisted of looking at the Downs and attempting some reading. "Here I lead a very pleasant lazy life, as I cant walk yet," she wrote to Mama on October 21 (B), "except about the house, I therefore haven't had to return any calls . . . the leg lets me off for some time. . . . There is very little news when things are quite peaceful like this but that is hardly to be regretted."

The servants at Downside left nothing to be desired. Elinor adored both the cook and the parlor maid. Nancy gave Elinor another cat. And Horace added a typewriter to the furnishings, which he courageously placed in front of Elinor. She complained to Mama (November 4) (B): "Horace is your greatest ally about writing—not when I have awful headaches of course but at other times he is almost a pest. . . ." Despite all the prodding and pushing from Mama and Horace, Elinor could not write; her years as Mrs. Waring were curiously hostile to any literary activity. Only when the relationship with Horace turned sour would she start to write. Then she would use her poetry as other people use diaries. But while she was living out a sort of confession, there was no need to write about it. Her life, at present, was all surface. After the presentation of the typewriter all she managed to type was a letter asking Mama to send her some of her silver.

Elinor's letters were filled with nature notes. The trees' changing colors were documented with great care. Her defense was absolute, yet a hint of discontent even with domestic matters crept in. She longed to be rid of rented accommodation and have her own house. Her savings amounted to $5,000 and she did not hesitate to ask Mama for more: "I would so love to have it now when it would be Holly's & my home," she wrote on November 4 (B), "but afterwards if anything happened to him it would be a sort of refuge & belonging. I suppose Connie & Henry will think me grasping . . . and then I feel it would be such an interest to me, particularly with the lovely gardens they have in England."

The years as Mrs. Waring had led to the absence of "a sort of refuge & belonging," and the future offered no safety. Elinor saw herself piteously alone. Inanimate objects assumed the importance people had once held. She longed to abandon loneliness in a house of her own. It would be her gift to Horace. It was a tactic she would employ again nearly a decade later for the benefit of Bill Benét. In the mathematics of her solitude she equated surroundings with people, domesticity with devotion, and owning with independence. A house was all she could think about while Connie and Alice were pregnant. She begged her mother for family news, but suffered only increased discontent once she got it.

With the prospect of a home of her own (which Mama encouraged), solicitors, architects, and estate agents entered Elinor's life. She spent hours poring over the pages of advertisements in *Country Life.* She determined to be near London; Guildford would of course be ideal, but it presented difficulties—the expense of Surrey houses was rather frightening. The sober propriety of the professional belt was just what she wanted, and just what she could not afford. Then she thought of searching for a house north of London, but ruled it out as being too wet and dreary. The pattern of her days during the search was unvaried. Horace would leave her in the morning and stride across the golf course; in the afternoon he would drive into Guildford "for a few rubbers of bridge with old retired soldiers who largely make up the population here & with whom he gets on very well," as Elinor wrote to Mama

(November 10) (B). It suited her perfectly. She could be alone to think about her house. "I have no desire to make more acquaintances. People bore me, except Holly & you & my own family, but I would love a home with all my heart & soul." The prospect kept her going, and prevented her from being too bored.

And so it went on for two months. At the beginning of December they got wind of a wonderful house near Merrow called Puttenham Grange: six bedrooms, smoking room, drawing room, dining room, servants' accommodation and "HOT WATER HEATING" (December 1) (B). Elinor was euphoric. It was perfect. The owner had two interviews with Horace, hesitated over their offer, then sold to someone else.

Throughout these fruitless negotiations, they went up to London once a week for Elinor's X-ray treatments and for a matinée. Elinor detested London. She was convinced the air was not fit to breathe. Yet the X-rays seemed to be working; at least her leg, full of boil germs, as she finally explained to Mama, got no worse. But she had been hobbling about for months, "lame." Her doctor was less pleased with the results than his patient.

On December 8 they went up to London again, this time, as Elinor gruesomely put it to Mama (December 7) (B), to "have my leg sliced up a bit." The doctor was going to India and was anxious to clear up two stubborn "bits" of her leg that refused to respond to radiation, "& so finishing it up as he hopes. I shall have an anesthetic of course, & only hope to be in bed 3 or 4 days." The operation was ghastly. Holes were dug into her leg and then cauterized with a red-hot iron. Elinor was "under ether for about an hour, & it is not so nice as good old chloroform!" she told Mama a week later (December 16) (B). The ether gave her a cold and she was forced to stay in London for a further week. She returned to Downside with a leg "now supposed to be as pure as the driven snow, & . . . rapidly healing, though it still hurts like fire [?]."

Elinor still possessed enough energy to continue to fuss about Puttenham Grange and to have a permanent wave put into her hair. She was finally allowed to get up after her operation on December 23, just in time to rush into Guildford to buy Christmas gifts for Horace and wobble home exhausted. Christmas Day exhausted her further. "We had to get up at 4:30 on Christmas morning," she complained (December 30) (B). "This was because of the bells—the church is practically in our back garden & we knew they would ring full chimes (which always gives Holly the earache) from 5 o'clock till six!" They leapt into the Hupmobile just before "pandemonium broke loose!" and drove out of striking distance. Everyone in the village, Elinor claimed, hated the wretched bells except the rector, who lived out of earshot. They came home when silence descended, crept somewhat sheepishly back into bed, rested, and then ate "a full regulation Christmas dinner that night, even to a blazing plum pudding." On Boxing Day Elinor went to bed with a severe headache. She and Horace celebrated the New Year with candy sent to them by Mama.

The two occupations of continued ill health and house hunting were not really enough to conceal the true nature of Elinor's unhappiness. There still was a great deal of talk about hyacinths, tulips, skies and trees, and the weather ranged throughout her letters. What did not figure was what was most important to her, and mortifying to Mama. She wanted to be pregnant. She wanted to have Horace's child.

Hitherto Elinor had avoided sex. She felt, like Horace, that romantic attachment was beyond (and more important than) physical possession. It simply seemed less important than a vague concept of love. Like the emotions she denied, sex was, even at the outset of her relationship with Horace, ruled out. Yet after three years, with an increasing Hoyt population around her, her resistance began to disappear. She allowed herself, almost for the first time, to act directly on what she felt. It took her three years to achieve such honesty, but her chronic denial of what she felt only made the urge stronger. And Elinor refused to admit she was an intensely erotic woman.

Underneath what was later to become her famous cool, stylized exterior blazed an unquenchable sexuality. The more she affected a surface austerity, the stronger the fire grew. They seemed to feed off one another. "She burned, but gave no warmth," her friend Louis Untermeyer confessed nearly half a century after her death. She rewrote her eroticism, in her poems, in lavishly frigid terms. Elinor's love of ice, silver, metallic gray metaphors danced around and protected her sensuality. The Puritanism she later wrote so movingly about reached deeply into her make-up. The expression of any eroticism was strictly confined to the hearth of convention. There was no promiscuity. She had a compelling sense of propriety. Because her attachment to Horace led her well out of the region of respectability, she pledged herself, almost as a penance, to chastity. This denial resulted in the string of minor ailments and illnesses, the long series of which spoke loudly both for her true feelings and for the high price she was willing to pay. That was why her blood pressure roared. That was why her headaches were unceasing. And why her leg refused to heal. She was, for too long, unfulfilled. It was an endless horror to her that she had borne Philip Hichborn's child and failed to have Horace's. She was consumed by garden life, the growth of plants, the blossoming of flowers as a form of neuter compensation. She wanted above all else, like her roses, to swell with life.

But just as Elinor constantly tried to deny this impulse in herself, so she struggled to keep it from others. Mama aided her in this conspiracy. English letters arrived at Rhode Island Avenue at weekly intervals, scrupulously collected by Mama, who weeded out the most revealing ones for the fire; a bastard was more than she dare contemplate. Yet that was all Elinor could think about. She pinned all her hopes—and her future with Horace—on a child.

Though there had been no ceremony, no visit to a church, Elinor granted herself the luxury of believing she was truly married to Horace and therefore fit to bear his child. However, she underplayed her urge for renewed motherhood to the point of rarely mentioning it, and when she did, speaking in code. The omission alone (as well as the absence of vital letters in the family archive, clearly referred to in surviving letters) is more expressive than what was said. Only in 1923 did the facts come out, when she reeled off her case history to an American doctor. Mama's obliteration of the evidence of anything sexual in her eldest daughter's nature did not

reach far enough. By 1914 Elinor was ready to join her sister
Connie* and her sister-in-law and have a baby. But the facts,
thanks to the dual conspiracy of Mama and Elinor, are very
difficult to establish.

In January 1914 she was back in London under the surgeon's knife. Her periods were becoming excessive, exhausting her and giving her longer bouts of headaches. She wrote at length about the impending operation to Mama, who destroyed the letter. The only scrap of evidence of what occurred in London the third week in January is an almost unintelligible letter (probably why it was allowed to survive) by Horace to Mama while Elinor was in hospital. He wrote from Claridge's (January 27, 1914) (B):

Elinor has had the operation of which she wrote you and is getting on all right as far as we can see. The poor girl is very brave and she has certainly needed a great deal of courage this last year. The Surgeon has had to do a little more than he expected but says that there was found quite a sufficient cause for daily headaches and he insists that the general health must now be greatly improved whereas if things had been allowed to run on a most serious state of affairs calling for a major operation would have surely arisen.

The operation was a curettage. It is not known if it was done to terminate a pregnancy or not. In any event, shortly after this she became pregnant.

All Elinor's activities, as minor as they were, were now designed to provide a safe passage for the new arrival. The house hunting assumed even greater importance. Toward the end of the first week in February, after recovering from her operation, Elinor spotted Brook Corner in Brook, near Witley, slightly further south of Guildford than Merrow. Her spirits rose again. The house was perched on a hill in five and a half acres. There was a tennis court, orchard, paddock, a coachhouse which would serve as the garage, and a conservatory outside. The garden was in fine condition. Inside the house, which consisted of two cottages knocked together, there were five bedrooms, two further bedrooms for the servants, a drawing room, dining room, and library. The plumbing

*Whose baby, Paul, died shortly after birth.

was good, and there was a porcelain bathtub. Buying the place hinged on Horace's recovery (he was ill again with his annual "grippe"), as did their flight into France for the winter. He managed to rouse himself from bed, view the house, approve, and supervise Elinor's signing of the informal agreement before they headed to Folkestone by the end of the month. They planned to stay away until the beginning of April, giving the servants a long holiday before the problems of moving set in.

They returned from France charged with plans and color schemes, ready to take possession of Brook Corner in May. Mama and the children would be their first guests. Elinor felt that the journeying was over; she had a new interest and she now had hope. All of Connie's predictions that there would be a war were ignored. Elinor's primary concern at the moment was whether or not Mama preferred blue or pink in her bedroom, and there was the difficulty of which rooms to assign to Morton and Nancy. Elinor felt a sense of permanence for the first time. The idea of war was completely unthinkable. Mama and Nancy arrived in England fresh from Naples, where they had left Constance, in the early summer of 1914. The pregnancy was advancing smoothly.

Brook Corner required far more work than Elinor rapturously outlined after she bought the place. There was endless plastering to be done, a string of minor but time-consuming alterations. So they were forced to take another house for the summer while waiting to move into Brook Corner—Lascombe, in Puttenham, near Guildford. Mama and Nancy made daily excursions to Brook Corner to inspect the progress of renovation, and to watch Elinor hesitate over the decorations with alarming constancy. She could not make up her mind who would have which bedroom. Initially she assigned the finest rooms to Nancy and Mama; but as the decorators moved through the house, her sister and mother got shunted to others, until finally they had the worst bedrooms. In the middle of all this decisionmaking, Morton arrived in Southampton.

Throughout August Nancy and Morton lounged about the garden listening to airplanes buzz overhead. Mama had ordained that there would be no war; Hoyt plans did not include such an event. Nancy was signed up to attend a con-

vent school in Brussels to be near Connie and her husband,
who had recently been posted to Belgium. Mama planned to
spend most of the next year in Europe to be near her three
daughters. Everything was arranged.

Yet nothing seemed to go according to plan. The von
Stumms' posting in Belgium proved very brief; they moved on
to The Hague, where everyone was violently anti-German
and Tumm himself left Connie and Carlo to go to Constantino-
ple. Brook Corner was taking a long time to complete. The
summer was spent at Lascombe instead. When war was inconveniently declared in the middle of such a glorious summer,
Mama had to rush up to London to locate steamer accommodation home like thousands of other marooned Americans.
She and the maid quickly packed the trunks and left with
Nancy and Morton for Bournemouth to wait for a passage
home. Then Elinor and Horace left for London, so that Elinor
could be under her doctors' supervision during the final
months of her pregnancy.

By the middle of September they were staying at the
Hyde Park Hotel, arranging for household goods for Brook
Corner and items for the nursery. "I got sweet baby things,"
Elinor wrote to Mama after speaking to her on the telephone
before they boarded the liner home (September 18), "—had
to order them specially of course to get plain enough ones of
good material . . . I am quite well though rather tired. . . ."

The stream of news about the forthcoming birth did not
transfix Mama. Fond as she was of babies, Elinor's would
provoke grave consequences. A bastard meant even more
certainly than before—over and above Elinor's other wild
exploits—that she would avoid America. Mama realized that
she had two exiled daughters now, both of whom she was
deserting. Connie, a German by marriage, was only just welcome in America. She apparently made matters worse by indulging in German propaganda. Connie's tirades against neutral and enemy countries grew to alarming proportions. She
simply could not understand all the fuss about Belgium, and
thought the English were silly to open all letters. England's
entry into the war, she explained for Mama's benefit, was out
of the "lowest motives." Her letters became anti-Ally tracts.
She extracted uncomfortable declarations from every member

of her family (those, that is, who were old enough to make one) that they were not against Germany. How could the Germans be both Huns and cowards? she asked, after reading *The Times.* She was the first to admit that the English were brave, but the Germans were braver. What infuriated her most was that Elinor refused to take any stand at all, or when she did, immediately reversed it in her next letter. Elinor did, however, worry slightly over the prospect that Horace might rush off to the front. But as he was too old to be helpful in the trenches, had bad eyesight, and was an American citizen, he could hardly be granted the right to be impetuous. Everything, the war included, was ignored. Only her baby mattered; her pregnancy gave her hope when everyone around her seemed to have given up.

What with Elinor's caution, Mama's deft destruction of her letters, and an erratic wartime post, determining when the child was born is at best haphazard. Nine years later Elinor explained that it was a full-term pregnancy. Her years of resting and quiet life almost ensured that it would be. The war did nothing to alter her happiness and her obsession with domestic trivia. Mama sat in Washington awaiting the news that she was the grandmother of a bastard. No one in Washington could be privy to the impending event. (Alice was also pregnant with her second child in New York.) Elinor managed to get letters through to Connie (in Germany) that were "cheerful," as Connie informed her mother. And like Mama, Connie refused to mention anything about the news they all longed to hear.

Elinor and Horace spent most of the autumn in London. The child, as far as one can calculate, was born in late November or early December 1914—dead. Elinor's response to the shattering event was to become temporarily blind.

CHAPTER SIX: 1915

§ *i*   *War Wounds*

The year 1915 began torturously. It was Elinor's fifth with Horace Wylie, and it was celebrated in ill health. Elinor's bid for happiness had died. Her chances of new hope seemed gone. She was childless and blind. Her blindness was merely a psychological reaction to the baby's death, helped considerably by her high blood pressure. Curiously enough, her brother Henry was also suffering from blindness in New York. But his ailment was passed off slightingly by his family while they were endlessly concerned over Elinor. Eight years later, when a friend also lost a baby, Elinor wrote to her (April 16 [1923]): "I know . . . what it means, & how apart from the sadness there is a quite peculiar bitterness of failure & frustration." When she was able, she roamed around Brook Corner, casting off nursery furniture, folding and storing the precious and unused baby things. They were pale blue. She had wanted, like her mother, to have a baby girl first in the long line of children she would give Horace. They would be her *real* children, and the fact that they would be bastards did not seem to worry her any more. She only minded that the child was dead. With hundreds dying across the Channel, more marching to their death, her loss was just another inconsequential statistic. Except that it marked the beginning of the end of her relationship with Horace. She was caught up in events she was unable to alter by her isolation. Some twelve years later she wrote to Horace (May 20, 1927) (B): "It seems to me that "our—shall we dignify it by the name of tragedy, or shall we call it failure?—or whatever it was was one of the war's cruel mishaps. . . ."

Elinor's ironies of timing had always been amazing. Just when Brook Corner was ready, war was declared. "Our house is really perfect it couldn't be nicer," she had told Mama in the fall of 1914 (B). "I do hope nobody—German or English —smashes it up. It is the fashion nowadays to be portentously gloomy . . . but I do not pretend to take less than a perfectly normal interest in my lovely house, & my approaching baby —all of which is supposed to be terribly frivolous." The hysteria that gripped England alarmed her: "I mean it makes you almost blush for humanity to see human beings so prostrated with fear." Being American she thought she was immune, but it only seemed to make things worse. Horace was pestered nonstop at the bridge tables in Guildford about American prevarication over the war. Sometimes the charges and countercharges he received, as if he were a walking State Department, nearly ended in fist-fights. Elinor's letters were opened and scanned by the censor like anyone else's. The post became increasingly erratic. Just when she was determined to settle down to a snug family life, her baby died. Just when she needed all of her strength, she fell gravely ill. Just when they needed money from America, all financial transactions were stopped. And so it went on.

Her "blurry sort of blindness" lasted for weeks. By the end of January, with the aid of her favorite tonic of iron and strychnine, which produced a "most lovely complexion," her health had returned and her blindness disappeared. Soon she was feeling well enough to make changes to her hair: "I do my hair in a new way—" she wrote to Mama (February 1) (B), "brushed off my forehead. . . . At first it looked absolutely indecent—this great bare forehead, but now I'm getting used to it, & like it. Horace says its the lowest compatible with intelligence but it looks very Shakespearean to *me.*"

The war did little more than intensify the uneventfulness of their life. They returned to domesticity with a vengeance. It was as if they had never had the prospect of escape. Elinor sat in the drawing room like a happily married woman. Horace played bridge at his club like an occupied husband. In truth they were neither of these, though any onlooker might have been convincingly fooled. Elinor began to exercise her knitting needles, drearily, for the Red Cross, making scarves for the trenches. She moved through interminable meetings for various war charities. But her interest was, at best, tepid. Having spent so many years thinking about herself, she could not easily shift to others. Her eyesight was too poor to do any sewing. And her letters to Rhode Island Avenue never altered in tone. She still rattled on about the weather, about daffodils, hyacinths, and her neighbor's rock garden. "There is absolutely no news," she said blandly to Mama (March 22 [1915]) (B), "—everything is very peaceful & pleasant here in the country, & the war seems very unreal though very terrible. If only it could end!"

But Elinor did not have to wait long for news. On April 13, 1915, the House of Commons passed the Aliens Restriction (Amendment) Order, which was an extension of the laws passed the previous September with the Aliens Restriction (Consolidation) Order, 1914. The 1914 bill contained one vital piece of legislation for the Warings: they were obliged to register with the police in their district. It did not demand that they furnish the registration officer with any legal proof of what they said. As far as they were concerned, it was an innocent piece of legislation; their true identity did not have to be revealed. The 1915 improvement on the act was far more severe. It stipulated that all aliens must, when staying at a hotel, register as such and provide proof in the form of a passport, issued at least two years earlier by their native country. Any false entry might mean arrest for the proprietor of the hotel. These laws, deemed so important for the protection of the realm, meant exposure for Elinor and Horace. By an act of Parliament, the four years of anonymity were at an end. The Warings became a different sort of casualty of the war.

§ *ii*   *Return*

Elinor and Horace sailed back to America in late spring, 1915. One of Horace's final acts before selling Brook Corner (at a considerable loss) was to buy one share of The Country Club, Guildford, Ltd., for £1. The share certificate came through on June 11, and he kept it for the rest of his life. Just as their flight from America was carried out in deepest secrecy, so too was their return. Horace noted briefly in his diary: "Summer at Brookline and at hotel top of Park Street and move into Fenway." That is the only scrap that covers this important episode in Elinor's history. Mama had no advance warning that they were returning; she merely received a cable from Boston saying that they had arrived. They had brought most of their household goods with them.

The momentum of Elinor's life, such as it was, came to an abrupt halt. All that she had struggled to create in England was gone. All that she hoped to avoid now faced her; everything she had established as Mrs. Waring was reversed in America. They had no money and nowhere to live. Horace, at the age of forty-seven, was forced to forsake the golf links and bridge table for something entirely new in his routine— a paying job.

They turned immediately to Mama. Both had always looked to her for assistance and guidance. The constant return to Rhode Island Avenue for help was essential for Elinor, who never shed her dependence on Mama. But for Horace, it was supremely humiliating.

The summer of Elinor and Horace's return, Mama was at Bar Harbor. She had taken a large, imposing, and very attractive house, owned by the Updikes, called Arbent Ruh, in Albert Meadow. The Hoyts gathered there for the season— everyone, that is but Elinor (and of course Connie). Bar Harbor was too dangerous for her. She was too well known and did not dare risk being spotted. Henry, who was there with his wife and two children, made certain that Elinor knew how unwelcome she was. Therefore she waited until the summer was all but over, and Bar Harbor virtually deserted, before she went to see Mama. Again she had the unpleasant task of facing her mother with failure—a failure brought on by her total lack of plans, her inability to guard her family against the scandal her return would arouse, and her disintegrating status as Mrs. Waring. She did not know if she could face these new problems with Horace any longer. She was very uncertain—about everything.

It was this that brought out Henry's anger. He thought that Elinor was too ready to place her difficulties on her family; that she was unwilling to think about the consequences of her action, and too quick to overlook the very considerable pain she caused. Elinor, for her part, was very tired. She had lost everything, and lacked the strength to start all over again. She

could not maintain her resistance to the infamy she had assigned herself.

In September 1915, they took an apartment at 84 The
Fenway, in Boston, overlooking the park. It was small, and not
very comfortable, at least by Brook Corner standards. The
Warings started over again. Only this time it was far more
difficult. The month they moved to The Fenway, Horace
heard a rumor that Katharine was finally beginning divorce
proceedings and braced himself for the gruesome ordeal. He
knew it would mean that he and Elinor would be back in the
newspapers. Their story would be raked over with the most
scandalous coloring imaginable. Evidence would be given,
depositions taken; everything would start all over again. Horace was weary of it, so weary that he went to bed with the most
severe case of bronchitis he had ever had.

Elinor was forced to organize the household quickly,
which she did with great efficiency. A woman came in every
morning for four hours to do the washing and polishing. The
cooking fell completely on Elinor, since Horace was too
queasy to deal with raw meat. Elinor thought everything was
turning out splendidly but Mama and Henry were uncon-
vinced. They could not understand why Elinor had returned
and were mystified by her excuses. The Aliens Restriction
(Amendment) Order did not, in their eyes, pose any great
obstacle to Elinor and Horace's having remained, rent-free, in
their own home. In America they were even more vulnerable
to gossip than they were in England. They had friends in
England and none in America. To Mama and Henry their
return was mad. Worse than that, it increased the Hoyts' own
vulnerability to scandal. As long as the Warings were safely in
England, Mama too was safe. Now no one was safe.

Elinor and Horace vainly tried to explain the horrors of
wartime England for an alien. They could not convince Mama
and Henry of the intense hostility leveled against foreigners,
the never-ending spy hunts, insults, and accusations. The English patriotism was compulsive, very unattractive, and country society suffered from a larger dose of it than Londoners.
Even after Elinor returned to America her Witley friends
wrote to her of the gossip being spread about the village, and
of the spy craze, which branded everyone. They told her how

wise she had been to leave England. Elinor forwarded these letters to Mama, trying to verify her explanation. She was definitely not happy to return to America. She was furious at the stupidity of the English during war—a stupidity that had driven her from her home, forced her from the country she loved. But it was impossible to stay in England, especially when she had so much to hide.

It was not any easier for the Warings to keep their secret in Boston. Yet Elinor became braver; this time her boredom gave her courage. She planned to go to Symphony Hall, and did not feel altogether confident about escaping unrecognized. "Nobody knows H. from Adam now—" she wrote to Mama (November 4 [1915]) (B) "& a lace veil added to my increased years ought to be sufficient disguise for me. However we have not put it to the test yet—I mean I haven't, but Horace, who has to go to Banks & things & do countless errands, has, & he is evidently unrecognizable."

It was still only a rumor that "the other party," as Elinor coyly referred to Katharine, had filed a petition for divorce. Elinor prayed that it was true, and quickly believed any story she heard about Katharine's reasons. One was that Katharine herself wanted to remarry. Elinor's reaction was, as she put it, in "very bad taste on my part to say so . . . but it is an *appalling* prospect for any man—to be married to her I mean, & of course one *must* hope he will be nice, on account of the children." The rumor was precisely that. Katharine did not remarry.* Why she did suddenly volunteer to divorce Horace remains a complete mystery. Perhaps she finally acknowledged that he would not return. In any event Horace knew that the proceedings would take time to complete; both he and Elinor were, of course, prepared to wait. He predicted that the divorce would come through during the winter at the latest; in fact, he had some nine months to wait for his freedom.

He also knew that Katharine would not let him off lightly.

*Another even more unlikely story was that her daughter begged her to divorce Horace before she had her debut. Katharine's eldest daughter was twelve years old in 1915. This story, astonishingly enough, is still widely believed and often the only reason advanced for the Wylies' unexpected divorce.

Almost certainly she would demand some sensational court appearance. He was prepared to leave the country to spare himself, and Elinor, that ordeal. When Mama wrote to him to say that Katharine had, at last, filed her petition in January 1916, Horace hurried north to Canada well out of the court's reach. "I am astounded at what you tell me," he wrote to Mama before leaving for Montreal (January 13, 1916) (B). "I fully believed the suit had been filed long since. I was so informed last August or September. . . . Also I do not see why in any event you should have the really frightful ordeal of testifying in the case." Elinor had signed over her power of attorney and neither she nor Horace would contest the case.

They endured the worst possible climate to spare themselves the trial of the case, but had to come back nearly three weeks later because Horace fell ill. They went straight to New York, staying at the Plaza, on February 8. Since they were "great friends" with the clerk there, who had once worked at Claridge's, they were permitted to sign the private register—it was imperative to avoid the newspapers and Katharine at all costs. They also had to get away to a warm climate since Horace was getting steadily worse and Elinor developed neuralgia. Inevitably, it seems, they made the worst possible decision: they returned to The Fenway. They would have gone straight from Montreal to Boston had they not closed up the apartment. As it was, they would have to stay in a hotel for a few days, before they could move back. While Elinor was in New York she saw Henry, Mama's ambassador, who was now living at 142 East 62nd Street, to learn the family opinion and try to get some reassurance. She got little of both.

It was the beginning of another bleak period in her Waring years. Her life in America was torture. The boredom was even greater than before, and any hope seemed nonexistent. "I do so dread taking him [Horace] (& my neuralgia) back into that *freezing* Boston—" she wrote to Mama (February 8, [1916]) (B) from the Plaza; "however I suppose there is no place is there dear where we could possibly go? If only there were some place where *you* could go too—that is what I really want . . . I have thought of Bermuda, but I am sure you would not want to go so far, or have me go without you, & I suppose there just *is* nowhere in America." Mama usually retreated annually to her beloved Brighton Hotel in Atlantic City, but Elinor firmly believed that since distance and travel were no problem for her, she might convince her mother to go further away than New Jersey. "As far as my health is concerned," she tried, "I could easily stand going anywhere—travelling only seems to do me good—it is just cold & high winds which kill me, as they do you too." But all this pleading only kept Mama at Rhode Island Avenue.

Elinor was so accustomed to packing and unpacking cases that it became a reflex to pack once the cold weather arrived. Horace chased after a warm climate and golf links every winter like some migrating bird, but each succeeding year the flight south became more uncertain. In 1916 they reached Augusta, Georgia, almost by accident. Augusta was not Pau, but it did have a splendid golf course (the National). Horace's winter cures depended on golf, and on a reasonable degree of comfort, which was not easy to find since they had made no advance booking. They had set out not knowing where they were going, determined only to avoid Boston. "The problem has been to find a place where Horace could play golf," Elinor admitted to Mama (March 2) (B),

& where we could *get in,* for you have no idea how extraordinarily crowded the whole South is. . . . They say Florida is packed & jammed as it never was before. I am glad we didn't go to Bermuda, as that is *terribly* congested & the getting away again might have been a problem. . . . This town, Augusta, is awfully nice, much nicer than Charleston which is damp & muggy, but the rooms we are now in are engaged for tomorrow & there is simply no place to be had anywhere.

Their Southern retreat was, in Elinor's words, "absolutely chaotic." She jumped from prospect to prospect, studied maps, and looked at guidebooks. When they settled it was not for months, as it had been in Europe, but for weeks or days. Her long-term activities only filled afternoons. Yet, she confessed, "we are both well & enjoying the change." Change was the only constant either of them enjoyed since the return to America.

After a few days in Augusta they reached Asheville, North Carolina. Although the Grove Park Hotel did not live

up to its boast of being the finest resort hotel in the world,
Elinor did find it, as she reported to Mama (March 5) (B), *"fine*
. . . so beautiful & quiet & restful—just what we wanted.
. . . Also we hope *not* to see friends, as the people here seem
mostly Southern & Western . . . for we only want to remain
unrecognized & be let alone." The weather suited them perfectly; it was cooler than Georgia, but with "such dry & pure
air that it seems warm." The same tone that had run through
her English letters returned when Elinor reached North Carolina. Her urge for isolation became stronger. What she did not
explain was why she needed it, in fact, demanded it: she was
pregnant again.

She had tried pregnancy once before as an escape from
boredom. Now her failure only heightened her desire; further, it was an attempt to hold on to Horace. America seemed
to accelerate the disintegration of their relationship. There
was no relief from their dependence on each other. There was
no recess from the fear of discovery, no routine to fall back
on. Their complacent isolation became more and more difficult to secure. The difference in their ages grew more pronounced. The years were catching up with Horace—he
needed more support himself and could give less to Elinor.
Their roles had reversed. Now Elinor took care of Horace;
she made the plans. His illnesses were no longer just confined
to the winter. He managed, however, to infect her with some
of his flamboyant optimism. He had educated her well. She
adopted his talent for patience, fairness, kindness, and
warmth. Yet they both still lived in a vacuum. A baby might,
at least, help them break out.

As in the autumn of 1914, every aspect of their lives was
streamlined to help Elinor have an uneventful pregnancy. She
had been, as Horace himself admitted, brave before; she
needed to be brave again. Her constitution was hardly strong
enough to support childbirth. The doctors had warned her to
be careful, but she paid their advice little attention. Matters of
health aside, having the baby in America was even riskier than
it had been in England. They had no home, no money, and
no security. But the risk alone fired Elinor's hope. The danger
was very exciting.

After spending the winter in the South, they returned to

Boston. Elinor's health was getting steadily worse. On May 14 it "took a bad turn," as Horace confided to Mama the following day (B). "The blood pressure rose most alarmingly & dangerously." Two specialists were called to her side, and decided that "it was a matter that could not be delayed if there was to be a chance for the baby surviving or for Elinor's health to be saved & in one hour after the consultation she was in the hospital!" Labor was induced at once. Elinor's blood pressure dropped as the doctors had predicted. "The baby was brought on successfully. He is really pretty and astonishingly well along for seven months. He is or seems quite well but of course it will be some time before one can be certain. Elinor was as brave as she is under any circumstances, no one could have more said of them." It all happened so quickly that Horace did not have a chance to cable Mama before everything was over. She arrived in Boston to see her daughter and grandson two days after the birth. Henry was sent to Rhode Island Avenue to look after Nancy and Morton. "How my heart goes out to you in your great trouble darling—" he wrote to his mother from Washington (May 18, 1916) (B), "and to poor little Elinor. Oh, I do hope everything is all right."

It wasn't. The baby died a week after he was born. It was a tragic and ominous conclusion to their first year back in America.

Finally, by July 1916, Katharine Wylie did file for divorce. On July 7 Katharine's lawyer William Dennis, and Horace and Elinor's lawyer Frank Brown, agreed to take witnesses' depositions. On July 12 Henry's statement was taken on behalf of the petitioner, Katharine. The full story of his stay at Burley was taken down. For the benefit of the court he stated what had been commonly known: "They occupied a cottage at Burley where they appeared to be living the ordinary life of married people. . . . They were occupying adjoining rooms, bed-room and dressing room with bathroom attached." It was Henry's impression that they were "sustaining to each other the ordinary relations of husband and wife." This was the proof the court required. On July 13

William Dennis took the testimony of Katharine's brother,
James Hopkins. He stated that it was a well-known rumor
that Horace Wylie deserted Katharine in order to live with
Elinor Hichborn; that Horace had not lived with his wife
since December 1910, and that the sole care of the children
fell to Katharine. Katharine, he stated, "has been a perfectly
good mother" to her children. Other witnesses were called,
like the cabin boy on the ship Elinor and Horace took to
England in 1910, but his testimony has not been preserved.
On July 27 an absolute divorce was granted to Katharine.
She was given sole care and custody of the children. The
only financial consideration she demanded from Horace was
that he be liable for all costs in the case.

Horace was free. The whole transaction he had awaited
for over five and a half years took less than three weeks. It was
swift and relatively painless. The newspapers, mercifully, had
more important news to report. The Washington *Post* ran a
very short article on July 7 saying that Katharine finally pursued divorce to substantiate her claim on the children. Neither
Horace nor the co-respondent made an appearance in court.
They were at Moosehead Lake and at Bar Harbor with Mama.
The next month they returned to Boston, and on August 7,
1916, they were married by a Justice of the Peace. Elinor was
no longer Mrs. Waring; she was the second Mrs. Horace
Wylie—Elinor Wylie.

§ *iii*   *Finish*

Marriage solved nothing: it merely formalized their relationship. Both Elinor and Horace firmly believed that it was the
single achievement which would reestablish their previous life
and dismiss them from exile. But instead of confirming that
their elopement had been guided by the highest motives,
which had not altered in over half a decade, marriage only
managed to maintain their status as victims of unconventional
desires. It could not provide them with safety. True, they did
feel less vulnerable; Society, however, maintained a different

opinion. Even members of Elinor's family still held out against her.

The Wylies began traveling again, the only response left to them. Horace had always sought a warm climate in the winter for Elinor's health; Elinor was certain it was an attempt to cut short Horace's bronchitis. They packed up their things and left Boston for the Waldorf Astoria in New York for two weeks, before going on to spend Christmas at Rhode Island Avenue on their way south. It was a brave scheme. Elinor had not seen Washington for nearly six years. She was frightened. Suddenly her eyes started to give her trouble. The danger of returning to Washington was, for both of them, extreme. After considering all possible plans, they decided, as they informed Mama (December 22 [1916]) (B), "we couldn't very well risk going to a Washington hotel under our own name, because of reporters, I decided that it was too complicated & disagreeable to go under any other name, & so we fixed on Baltimore, where we can go as our own selves. . . ." From Baltimore they would go to Mama's on Christmas Eve, and again on Christmas Day, "& if it is possible to manage— (Horace doesn't mind sleeping on a sofa for one night) you might ask us to spend one night . . . whichever you can arrange best. At any rate, I'll see you the day after tomorrow which you may be sure I'm dying to." Elinor was beginning to believe her marriage could make up for her desertion of her son and husband. She saw old friends in New York, two of whom had never turned their backs on her. One, Mrs. Helen de Selding Melcher, whom she had met at Asticou in 1908, was living at 5 East 51st Street and, in Elinor's opinion, "has been *darling.*" Mrs. Melcher was a friend of Henry's and Elinor took her kindness to be, in a way, an index of her brother's feelings. Elinor and Horace went to the theater, went to dinner, entertained friends at Sherry's, in short, did things they were too frightened to do before.

No sooner had they reached the Belvedere Hotel in Baltimore than they appreciated that any optimism they might have had was unfounded. There was a letter waiting for them from Henry, telling them that their visit to Rhode Island Avenue "would result in the most decided injury to Nancy," as Elinor wrote to Mama shortly after arriving in Maryland

(December 24) (B). She added that while she "was not prepared to agree with him at all fully in this opinion, I do not
care to create an atmosphere so tense as it would certainly
have been if we came, for Henry proposed to register his
protest against our presence by refusing to come to the house
tomorrow." They decided to return to New York immediately, and left that same evening for the St. Regis Hotel,
without seeing Mama.

Mama was astounded. She wrote to them at the St. Regis
as soon as she heard of Henry's threat: "I am heartbroken
simply heartbroken at Henry's action—He has been like that
to me for months, but I could not believe he would go over
my express command to you in Baltimore—It is simply useless
to say how bitterly I resent it. If you will come back directly
to me tomorrow I shall welcome you with open arms dear.
. . . Nancy sends you her love she is terribly upset about it."
The letter is dated Christmas Eve (Y).

Elinor did not search for any reason behind Henry's
unaccountable behavior; she accepted it easily by blaming
Alice entirely, and two months later became very angry about
it. She knew there was far more to the episode than the matter
of her appearance at Rhode Island Avenue. What she did not
know was that she was chosen as the casualty in Henry's battle
with Mama. He was furious that Mama persistently expected
him to behave like an unquestioning, devoted son while she
treated him like a servant. Her demands had been too great.
Snubbing Elinor was a convenient way of getting back at
Mama. The remarkably conventional excuse he gave was
hardly creditable.

The hint that Henry's behavior was becoming erratic was
more frightening than his insult to the Wylies. He was showing the symptoms of nervous exhaustion and collapse inherited from his father. Papa had had two nervous breakdowns
(once he was sent to New Mexico, and the other time to his
sister's cabin in Canada). Each time his moods, like Henry's
now, grew more and more pronounced, more and more severe. Connie too inherited Papa's illness, but with her there
were no warning signs. Unfortunately the observers of such
erratic and irrational tempers reacted more to the situation
than the cause; their concern was primarily for themselves.

When Horace learned of Henry's ultimatum to Elinor, he tried to persuade her to go to Mama anyway. He wanted to meet Mama and saw through Henry's feeble reason for them to stay away. Whether they eventually went to Washington is unknown. *"No one,"* Elinor finally wrote to Mama (February 23 [1917]) (B) from the Partridge Inn, Augusta, where she and Horace had gone to avoid the winter,

> ... has adopted the attitude towards me that my *own brother* has. The attitude that I am *hopelessly* déclassée without character or virtue, & with no position other than that of a criminal & crook. I dont mean "social" or "worldly" position in the sense of place in the larger scheme of life with daily conduct, mental *yes & moral* qualities, & even *personal appearance* can give. But I do not propose to let so petty & contemptible an enmity crush *me* or hold me down. Henry will find it harder to keep *this* squirrel on the ground than he knows.

"I feel terribly about your being subjected to violence from Henry again, darling," she said at the beginning of the same letter in reply to the invitation to stop in Washington on her way back to Boston,

> which I am sure you have been, if you have written about our coming to Washington. Unless indeed, he blames me alone & entirely for the idea. I never meant for a minute, dear, that you wouldn't dare to tell him you wanted me—I only meant I hated to think of the way he would go on about it. I still feel that unless he moderates his threats it is rather too much to undertake to defy him. The quarrel will be augmented & advertised by Alice, who, of course, began it all.

Elinor had more important things to think about than her relations with Henry: her health had again become a major concern. She consulted doctors in Baltimore who prescribed a special diet to improve her general health but did nothing to relieve her headaches. Horace was not at all satisfied with their treatment, while Elinor only hoped that she would soon be well enough, strong enough, to have children. She was perfectly content to "trust to time to improve my health enough to make it possible for me to have children."

Time was only one of the elements that was against them. The war was crossing the ocean, and neutrality was becoming more precarious. In November 1916 America broke off diplomatic relations with Germany. Washington was preparing for war, but Elinor refused to believe it. Yet she saw such circumstances as a very good excuse to leave Boston. "If war breaks out, we shall very likely end up in Washington, as these would be exceptional circumstances, & even Henry could not presume to prevent Horace from using his brains to help his country, as he is too old to be very effective in any other way. But I think it most unlikely that war will come."

On February 24, 1917, the Zimmermann Telegram revealed that Germany had made an attempt to consort with Mexico against America; and on April 6 President Wilson, one month after being inaugurated in his second term, declared war on Germany. "I feel so about Henry," Elinor wrote to Mama her last day in Georgia (March 1 [1917]) (B), "that I wish it were *he* & not Germany we were on the verge of war with! I wish Henry were the German & Tum the American. Only Henry's *sort* of horribleness is far more English than German."

The war gave Mama new energy; she bullied Henry off to join the Air Service, ignoring his morbid fear of heights. Fortunately he was kept on the ground, working as a photographer and censor, sending off the most spirited and enchanting letters to his family, which he neglected to censor. He was stationed in France, but never got to the front. Morton joined the Tank Corps just before the war finished, earned the rank of corporal, and never left America.

Elinor did not carry out her threat to move to Washington. She was brave, but not that brave. Her "general health" —a favorite term of her's—was not strong enough to support anything other than complete peace and quiet. She used it as an excuse to avoid any stimulation whatsoever. She protested too much that she wanted quiet; what she wanted was a child, and to be surrounded by complete uneventfulness was the only way to guarantee that that would come about. The boredom was intense. She wondered if it were not too high a price to pay.

She and Horace left Boston for Maine that summer. As the first American troops were landing at St. Nazaire, the Wylies were in Somesville (Maine) across Mt. Desert Island from Mama. They had rented a white neo-Greek cottage that overlooked the Sound.* As in Burley, the church was nearby. The house was not large and was very easy to run. The kitchen and dining room were spacious; the drawing room was dominated by an enormous chimney-breast that hid a smugglers' cupboard. The eaves on the top floor plunged at a rake that was disastrous for Horace.

They set about making minor improvements. They slapped on new paint: the dining room was the color of butter. Books were stored in the dining room hearth, long since disused as an area for cooking. Wallpaper was hung in the bedrooms, and Elinor started poking around the garden. She adored the place. It was like her years in the New Forest. Somesville was even smaller than Burley, and just as primitive.

The Hoyt invasion began again. The family frequently crossed the island to see Elinor. With Henry in France, she more than adequately made up for her Christmas absence. Nancy often visited them, and brought with her Elinor's son. Elinor had not seen Philip for six years, but seven months earlier she had declared her attitude toward him. On November 15, 1916, she made her will in Boston. In it she stipulated: "I intend to make no provision for my son, Philip Hitchborn [sic] of Washington . . . a son by a former marriage, as I have relinquished and conveyed all my interest in the estate of my former husband with the intention that my said son should be provided thereby." Horace was named as her sole heir.

Philip was a walking disaster area. The first day he arrived at Mama's he broke the player piano. He later went on to dislocate a water pump in the forest and nearly ruin the car. At the age of eleven he was, Nancy later wrote, exactly like Penrod. Elinor had good reason to be wary of him, though his visits to his mother were much quieter, since he only came for picnics and the occasional weekend. Elinor never reported any destruction after these visits; indeed, she scarcely noted his presence at all.

*The cottage had been known at various times as Captain Somes' Cottage, after the founder of the first settlement on Mt. Desert Island; The Olde Cottage, for obvious reasons; and Willowbrook, because of the avenue of weeping willows that shielded the house from the wind that blew off the Sound. By the time Elinor and Horace lived there the willows had gone.

The strain that once drew Elinor and Horace together was
now driving them apart. In England they had taken refuge in
petty, inconsequential details of life that brought them closer
together and were incorporated into the mythology of their
English idyll. England had been their idea of complete contentment, and safety; now Elinor was beginning to resent what
she once adored.

She began to look at Horace like some piece of household furniture, associating him closely with the frustration she
was suffering. He turned too easily to domesticity. The reading, research, and lectures on philosophy that once so
monopolized his mind had disappeared; his repertoire had
been depleted. Elinor was no longer prepared to remain his
student once he stopped teaching. She had matured—while he
had grown into an old man. He leaned on her, made demands
on her. Fatherhood, Elinor thought once again, might rescue
him and save her.

The Wylies stayed in Somesville well into the winter of
1917. It was cheaper than moving back to Boston or going
south. Yet it was too cold to stay in Captain Somes' Cottage;
the wind came straight through the window frames, and no
amount of heating could keep out the damp. It was far too cold
for much exercise. The isolation without any comforts became
unbearable. They moved across the island to a small apartment
in Bar Harbor.

It was their first winter without any escape from the cold,
and it took its toll on Horace's health—at least that was the
story Elinor told when she left Mt. Desert Island for New
York. The truth was too disturbing: the islanders took against
her. They started saying the same things about Elinor the
newspapers had always said. Shopkeepers boycotted her, and
she could buy no food. People began to turn away from her
in the street. They were ignored in the worst possible way.
The fears of discovery had become a reality just when Elinor
honestly believed she had nothing to fear. They packed their
few belongings and went to New York.

They arrived late one night on Mrs. Melcher's doorstep.
Elinor was shivering from the cold and Horace was coughing
continuously. They had no money and presented a pathetic
sight. Mrs. Melcher took them in immediately.

They could not afford to go any further south than New York. Money, like housekeeping before, became the major topic of Elinor's letters to Mama. They were forced to find rooms they could manage on their own, and afford. Elinor's shares were yielding 60 percent less money than they had the year before. Horace tried to scrape together some cash, yet he was too ill to be of much use to their finances. In fact, he was a positive drain on the little money they did have, for his doctors' bills were becoming enormous. By the spring of 1918 they had reached their lowest point ever. While Elinor was extremely worried about Horace, and about their finances, he remained coolly optimistic. He never admitted how severe the situation was, even if he realized it himself. Elinor explained it all to Mama, months later (September 23 [1918]) (B), by saying, "we were swamped." She asked Mama for a loan of $1000, since she dreaded touching capital. So, it turned out, did Mama. And yet during the spring and summer of 1918 the Wylies behaved precisely as if nothing were the matter. They had a car, they held on to their house in Somesville, they went away for the summer as usual. "Had he explained it then," Elinor told Mama, "I would have made him sell the motor & stay in New York, but he was very ill & I have no doubt his judgement, never very practical, was seriously affected."

Horace's calm disregard of practicality was one of the things Elinor had adored about him. Now it was joining the list of issues that would register their "tragedy, or shall we call it failure?" as Elinor assessed it in 1927.

It appeared unlikely that Horace would ever get a job. "Horace will try to get a bank clerkship but will probably not succeed as he has no pull. I do not want him to enlist as I cannot see how it would help matters, & can easily see how it would make them worse." They ruled out the civil service, largely because it meant that they would have to move to Washington. And, it seemed, they ruled out the possibility of doing anything except moving yet again. They took the major step of moving from their rooms at 55 West 55th Street to an apartment at 19 East 56th Street in the fall of 1918. The apartment, Elinor pointed out to Mama, was new, with a southern exposure, but had no elevator. The rent was

high—$75 a month—but Elinor calculated: "To move to any
other city would have certainly cost several hundred dollars."

The precariousness of their finances was matched only by
Elinor's emotional state. Once again she yearned for a child.
It was her only response to their predicament. She even stum-
bled back to poetry to express it. According to Horace's dat-
ing, she wrote "The Room" on November 25, 1918, in their
East 56th Street apartment:

> Somewhere, I know, there is a room
> In this world or in Heaven
> The light where litten [sic] shadows loom
> The hour may be seven
> Will flames leap on the fire side
> To burn away the hours?
> Or will the windows open wide
> On sleeping Summer flowers?
> In that lost hour and hidden land
> A father and a mother
> We two shall sit there hand in hand
> And there with us Another
> If great the room or small and low
> To hug the precious minute
> I cannot tell, but this I know
> We shall be happy in it.
> And if the night is wet and wild
> Or calm moon-colored weather
> I know that [?] we shall have our child
> With three of us together

Motherhood had evaded Elinor twice, but she was undaunted,
even though they were less well suited to have a baby now
than ever before. It was a last grasp at happiness, born out of
desperation. Elinor saw the future as nothing more than an
escape from the present. Her health could not support pregnancy but the doctors' warnings were brushed aside. She was
thirty-two and Horace would soon be fifty. "Another" was
meant only for Elinor, not Horace. A child would spell her
separation, in part, from him.

By February 1919, Elinor was pregnant, according to the
history she reported four years later. The pattern of her

confinement was the same as before: she rested. They went to Bar Harbor for the summer. Elinor's only activities were praying and writing poetry. Just as she relied on hope in November 1918 for a successful pregnancy, she now resorted to God to help her along. She typed "Prayer":

> To him, O Lord,
> Unborn as yet,
> I pray Thee afford
> An hour to forget.
> His father's son.
> Will his heart not leap
> At a brave deed done,
> Though he hear it in sleep?
> If blood can bind,
> Will his heart not break
> When the brave and kind
> Die for his sake?
> Oh! keep the child
> Aloof, afar,
> Free from the wild
> Sorrow of war
> Lest he be born
> (Alas as Thou)
> With scratches of thorn
> On his little brow.

Her prayer was not answered. She miscarried after five months. It was her third failure to secure the status she longed for, and the last attempt she would make with Horace.

From that moment on their marriage declined steadily. Elinor was taking him for granted and that was the most dangerous sign in her vocabulary of love. She was no longer prepared to fight to save the relationship—one that had always flourished best by fighting. The enemies now were uninteresting and simple, and all romance had escaped. Horace, irritatingly, refused to take Elinor for granted. He needed her now, just as she had needed him nine years ago. His claims on her were no greater than the ones she once made on him. But Elinor did not suffer from generosity when it was expected, indeed, demanded. Her generosity was a spontaneous thing. She recoiled from him. In a way

she had been broken by the years of battle, isolation, and
total dependence on him. Now she was becoming hard, re-
silient, and independent. Yet nothing about the expression
of her feelings was direct. She waited for a year before pronouncing her new strength. He had sacrificed everything for
her. Out of respect to that and for the love she once felt for
him, she stayed with him even after that love had disappeared. *She* was being courteous now.

And there was no one else she could turn to. They stayed
in Maine for the summer of 1919. It was the cheapest solution
to a summer holiday, no matter how unaccommodating the
islanders were. Their Studebaker was gone in an attempt to
economize. Horace noted in his diary (B) tersely: "Somesville:
no car." Horace's diary was a wonder of monosyllables; he
used it as a basic chronology that was to form the skeleton of
a larger work he never got around to. He wrote various
incidents out at length, not so much as his own form of confession, but as an explanation for various letters and poems Elinor
sent to him. Because of his cryptic notes and Mama's urge for
secrecy, the final years that traced the disintegration of Elinor's
marriage to Horace remain mysterious. Mama hated change:
if she ignored it it might go away, and if she destroyed all
proof she would be as safe as Elinor. But despite all her efforts,
Mama's life was crowded with the most radical alterations, and
she was moving into a decade of blistering change for every
member of her family.

Nothing, however, seemed to change, at least on the
surface, for Elinor. The final months of 1919 she elected to
stay in Maine, again for reasons of economy. Outwardly she
was hibernating; she was stalling. Both she and Horace were
waiting to move into one of Mama's Washington properties
in the early part of the New Year. This was Elinor's form of
kindness to Horace. Mama knew that Elinor's attitude toward
him had altered. "I am sure you will understand what I said
about my attitude to Holly in my last letter"* Elinor wrote to
Mama from Mt. Desert Island (December 3 [1919]) (B). "I
want to help him, in every way possible, & I am sure re-
proaches never help."

*This letter was destroyed.

The only thing that helped was poetry. She was able to express her frustration in a way that was not wounding to Horace, returning to poetry with a confidence that grew out of her shattered affection for him. And it was the source of her confidence that formed the core of her work:

> I would for you that I were decked
> In Honor and the world's respect.
> Before God's mercy we must all
> Stand naked, and so stand or fall.
> Before His gaze that glittering cloak
> Dries like mist, dissolves like smoke.
> I would that mantle I might wear
> Without a stain, without a tear—
> Bright like silver, white like milk
> Lined with sackcloth and with silk
> I would for you I wore that dress
> Girt round my heart with happiness
> To make a happier resting-place
> For your own heart, of my embrace.
> Then how shall I your heart enfold
> Against the night, against the cold?
> With love, and little else beside;
> Woven with a thread of pride,
> Bound with courage, clasped with trust,
> Wet with tears and white with dust—
> White like the moon, bright like the sun
> And warm with my devotion. (B)

Horace dated the poem 1919, adding tellingly: "Our last summer there [Somesville]." Elinor seemed to draw together the frayed strands of her life in poetry. She gave expression to something she had ignored for years, and she started to speak with her own voice. Above the grocery store in Bar Harbor that winter she wrote the poems that laid the foundation to her career, and hinted at her leaving Horace.

Elinor sent the poems to Rhode Island Avenue. She sent, among others, what were to become some of her most famous verses: "Velvet Shoes," "Sea Lullaby," "Winter," and "Fire and Sleet and Candlelight." Mama was very pleased. What she had hoped Elinor would achieve seven years before now lay before her. Early in December she handed the poems to Wil-

liam Rose Benét, who was becoming a steady visitor to her
house. He wrote to his brother Stephen Vincent Benét (December 6, 1919) (Y), "I was allowed to read some of Eleanor
Wiley's [sic] poetry which she sent to her Mother. It is *very*
good."

Book Three

1920-1928

*I think you are the bravest mortal before
whom I ever bowed my own cowardly heart.*
—Elinor to William Rose Benét
[June 24, 1923] (Y)

*Went to a terrible studio party where I met a
man named Van Vechten, novelist, a horrible
woman named Elinor Wylie, who is all the go
now—she writes novels and poetry—and her
husband Will Benét—I hated them so that I
managed to insult them all before the evening
was over.*
—Thomas Wolfe to his sister
(March 26, 1927)

*"I cannot help making fables and bitter fairy
tales out of life . . ."*
—Elinor to Helen Young
[November 5, 1927] (B)

147

CHAPTER SEVEN: 1920

§*i*   *"It was Horace who made a poet and scholar of me."*

"I do not admire myself," Elinor wrote to Horace (May 20, 1927) (B),

for having fallen in love with the idea of freedom, & poetry, & New York, & any individual among them: the misery of Washington, of anonymous letters, of this & that—your memory will supply the rest —spoiled what must always seem to me the happiest part of my life —my life with you. It is not your fault in any way, and mine only in my inability to stand the terrible alterations in that life which Washington made.

If we had stayed in England? You will say impossible. If we had stayed in Bar Harbour? You will say I would have died—in some bad way I doubt it, in both instances. But this is because I wish we had never parted.

Just as Horace once regarded Elinor, unflatteringly, as luggage to be stored in the right compartment in his life, by 1920 Elinor felt that Horace was a dead weight on her life. In her 1927 letter she spells out a sobering catalogue of reasons for her drift away from him. She put it down to geography. It was far more than that, but geography played a very important part.

For a decade she had hidden from Washington; it housed the fatal reminders of Phil and Beeyup, and was the bastion of her enemies. Marriage had not mollified them. She was as unwelcome as Mrs. Wylie as she had been as the widowed Mrs. Hichborn. Only poverty forced her return to Washington, and that hastened the breakup of her marriage.

By January 1920, with the war over and the makeshift camps that had congested the parks and malls of Washington's spacious avenues dismantled, Elinor and Horace moved south from Maine to take possession of Mama's generous offer of 2153 Florida Avenue—a house Horace appraised as a "noble ruin." "It was a tiny duplicate," he described it years later for 149 the benefit of his third wife, "in shape, of the Flatiron building in New York." The similarity ended there. The roof leaked, the furnace refused to give out any heat, and the gas range spat water. The place was a shambles. Its only attraction was that it cost them nothing to live there: an essential fact that even Horace could not ignore because "My total funds amounted to twenty-five dollars but I owed fifteen that I felt I must pay to a man in New York." Horace was so disconcerted by the house that he placed it at 2122 Florida Avenue.

Horace's sister-in-law, Nancy Hoyt, gave a different version:

My mother found them a little house on Florida Avenue, and Elinor's same household gods were set up there. The eighteenth-century Sheffield mirror, with candlesticks and clusters of silver grapes, the fruit and flower still-life, the Wedgwood lamps, the blue velveteen sofa, the strictly Palladian simplicity of her eighteenth-century chairs and the hot sunlight pouring in the windows transformed the little triangular-shaped room into an attractive sanctuary.

And with a different sort of transfusion from the past, Horace's health (he was suffering from influenza again) and spirits improved. One day in January he managed to get out of bed and make his way, "with some difficulty on foot, through the snow," to the Riggs bank for the $15 bank draft he needed to send to New York. The cashier led him into the vault where the inactive account ledgers were stored and showed him that a dividend for $1,000 had been paid into the account he closed in 1910. "I could feel my temperature drop as my spirits rose. I thought I had better explore further. In the old days I carried an account in each of the three banks at the corners of 15th St. and Pennsylvania Avenue and New York Avenue." He went to another bank and discovered that his account there had amassed $18.75. Then he sauntered over to the National Trust Co. "I know I left five cents in my account here, this from a sentimental motive. Has the interest accumulated?" he asked the cashier. It had, and some Trinidad real estate notes had finally paid off to the sum of $800. Horace took a taxi home.

The return of money did not result in a return of harmony. Elinor's confidence was rising, feeding off Horace's

doubt. She was fired with ambition, anxious to get started.
Horace was driven simply to survive—to him the future
loomed dark. For Elinor he remained the sole source of her
continued isolation and was, so she believed, unfairly holding
her back. Elinor was willful enough to get what she wanted,
but not strong enough to secure it, or manage it, alone. She
was trapped by her femininity, even while she employed it to
full advantage.

Yet even Horace had to face the sobering reality—his
account ledgers demanded it. Not only was he growing very
old in Elinor's eyes, but he was running out of money. As soon
as he was well enough he took the civil service examinations.
Later he would complain to his third wife that he turned finally
to the civil service out of desperation. Katharine Wylie, he
insisted, by means of some extraordinary power, blocked
every position proffered to him by his old Washington friends.
He was offered the post of Paris correspondent to the Washington *Post;* when he accepted, it was mysteriously withdrawn.
He pointed to a long list of disappearing jobs—a conjuring
trick performed by Katharine's hand. He passed the civil service examination with perfect marks in all subjects save handwriting. He was then given a position with the United States
Railway Administration as an office accountant and began
work on May 24, 1920. All day he sat diligently, straining his
already bad eyesight, as a comptometer operator—a job described by his employer in 1926 as "a clerical position at a
nominal salary." For this inspiring work he received $100 a
month. Within two years he would rise to assistant chief accountant. During the intervening period, he had the task of
supervising the field accountants with audits of various railway
systems.

Employment did not interfere with Horace's real voca-
tions, however. In the summer he would wake at five o'clock,
go to the public golf course at Potomac Park for a round of
golf, come home for breakfast, and be in front of his comptometer by eight. In the late afternoon he would come home,
and, as he inaccurately explained many years later, cook dinner since "Elinor never learned to cook," then go out again
to play a rubber of bridge or two.

A curious sense of competition arose between the Wylies.

Elinor refused to be outdone by Horace: if he could work, for the first time since she had known him, then so could she. In fact, there was no other outlet. There was no garden to occupy her and Florida Avenue was not much of a household to monopolize her thoughts. She needed very little prodding to return to poetry. She simply got down to writing with the same discipline that took Horace to the office every day.

Elinor built her love for Horace into a form of mythology. This love—which was the only love she ever enjoyed and suffered from in her entire life—was now seen by her as a remarkable architectural feat: a vast structure that housed nothing. Her failure to have children only buttressed the exterior. Its sole function was protection, which she no longer wanted. She wanted to leave, and her poetry helped her to do so.

The total claustrophobia of Washington also helped. It was a dreary place. Florida Avenue, despite Nancy Hoyt's adolescent memories, was more than a sanctuary, it was another prison. Uncomfortable inside, it was just as unaccommodating outside. The mail brought anonymous threatening letters. Horace would hide in the shrubbery outside his old Thomas Circle house trying to catch a glimpse of his children. He tried to stop his former servants in the street just to get some news of his family. These servants were threatened, so the story goes, with immediate dismissal if Katharine learned that they ever spoke to Horace. Elinor did not attempt to see her son. Unlike Horace, she did not try to reclaim anything from the past. There were very few friends, and even fewer diversions. Elinor was like a Hawthorne heroine, branded and subjected to insults. Her circle contained only Hoyts. Heads still turned as she passed in the street, no longer riveted by her beauty but transfixed by her reputation. Morbid curiosity replaced the interest she once attracted in Washington. And Washington only accentuated what she herself was feeling toward Horace—a mixture of boredom, mild contempt and anger that was a considerable factor in the emergence of her career as a writer.

She also wanted to see some financial reward for her work. In November 1919, she braved the Chicago magazine *Poetry,* sending off from Bar Harbor some of the poems that

Morton McMichael
(Courtesy of Constance Hoyt Easton)

Ellen Thomas McMichael
(Courtesy of Constance Hoyt Easton)

Anne McMichael Hoyt. Portrait by Henry M. Hoyt Jr.
(Courtesy of Constance Hoyt Easton)

Henry Martyn Hoyt. Portrait by Carroll Tyson.
(Courtesy of Constance Hoyt Easton)

Henry Martyn Hoyt Jr., May 21, 1918
(Courtesy of Constance Hoyt Easton)

Henry Martyn Hoyt Jr. Self Portrait.
(Courtesy of Constance Hoyt Easton)

Constance Hoyt (von Stumm)
(Courtesy of Constance Hoyt Easton)

"Carlo" and "Nora" (Elinor) von Stumm
(Courtesy of Constance Hoyt Easton)

Henry Martyn Hoyt in his late thirties
(Courtesy of Constance Hoyt Easton)

Anne McMichael Hoyt with Nancy Hoyt, 1915
(Courtesy of Mr. and Mrs. Sydney Schiffer)

Elinor, age nine
(Courtesy of Gertrude Clayton Collection,
University of Virginia Library)

Baldwin School, 1896. Elinor is in the fourth row, fifth
from left.
(Courtesy of The Baldwin School)

Elinor Wylie as a young woman
(Courtesy of Henry W. and Albert A. Berg Collection,
The New York Public Library, Astor, Lenox, and Tilden
Foundations, and Mr. and Mrs. Sydney Schiffer)

Elinor Wylie
(Courtesy of Collection of American Literature, Beinecke
Rare Book and Manuscript Library, Yale University)

Horace Wylie
(Courtesy of Henry W. and Albert A.
Berg Collection, The New York Public
Library, Astor, Lenox, and Tilden
Foundations)

Morton Hoyt
(Courtesy of Mr. and Mrs. Sydney
Schiffer)

Henry M. Hoyt
(Courtesy of Mr. Henry M. Hoyt)

Movie still of Elinor Wylie
(Courtesy of Mr. Alfred A. Knopf)

William Rose Benét. Etching by Henry Hoyt.
(Courtesy of Clifton Waller Barrett Library,
University of Virginia Library)

Elinor and Bill Benét at Burley
(Courtesy of Laura Benét)

Elinor and Bill's Christmas card
(Courtesy of Collection of American Literature, Beinecke
Rare Book and Manuscript Library, Yale University)

Cecil Beaton, Sacheverell Sitwell, Rosamond Lehmann,
Elinor Wylie, Georgia Sitwell, and Lady Gray at Wils-
ford Manor
(Courtesy of Collection of American Literature, Beinecke
Rare Book and Manuscript Library, Yale University)

Elinor Wylie.
Peter Arno Drawing. (© 1927, 1955 The New Yorker
Magazine, Inc.)

Formosa
(Courtesy of Mrs. Robert Mathew)

Sketch of Elinor Wylie done by Katherine Anne Porter.
(Courtesy of Collection of American Literature, Beinecke
Rare Book and Manuscript Library, Yale University)

Elinor Wylie, 1926
(Courtesy of Collection of American Literature, Beinecke
Rare Book and Manuscript Library, Yale University)

went into *Incidental Numbers* and a few more recent ones. They were quickly rejected, but not without some promising encouragement. An associate editor, Elinor wrote in a letter to *Poetry* (November 28 [1919]) "was kind enough to write some words of praise" for "Sea Lullaby," and added "a suggestion that I should send you more. I do this with hesitation, as I do not consider most of my work modern enough for 'Poetry.' . . . I have never published anything—never tried to, until the last few weeks." During the last weeks of November she sent to *Contemporary Verse* "Les Lauriers Sont Coupés," which had appeared in *Incidental Numbers.* It was accepted and published, finally, in May 1920; the inertia was overcome. Mama's and Horace's words of praise were less interesting than disinterested comments.

The editor of *Poetry* was the first to lead the chorus of praise for Elinor's work, and Harriet Monroe was certainly worth listening to. It took her nearly two months to answer Elinor's protestations that her work was not modern enough for publication. She wrote to Elinor (January 20, 1920) (Y), "I find your poems quite 'modern' enough for *Poetry*—in fact, they interest me so much that I would like to see more so that the best you have may appear as a group." Harriet Monroe accepted "Atavism," "Fire and Sleet and Candlelight," "Velvet Shoes," and "Silver Filigree," and told Elinor she was holding them for publication at an unspecified date. She would pay $25 on publication of these four poems.*

The polish and sophistication of these early poems was astonishing. When Elinor's first volume of poetry appeared a year later, Louis Untermeyer's one reservation was "that it was a little *too* brilliant. . . ." Her poems had a dazzling quality

---

*They were published eventually in the April 1920 number of *Poetry*, pp. 18–21, under the title "Still Colors." Harriet Monroe (1860–1936) began her career as art critic for the Chicago *Tribune* and later expanded from art to poetry. She founded *Poetry, A Magazine of Verse* in October 1912. The magazine supported the Imagist movement, appointing Ezra Pound as foreign correspondent, and had a prestigious record of contributors, among them T. S. Eliot in 1915. Harriet Monroe supervised *Poetry* until her death, and is better known for that work than for her own volumes of poetry. Her autobiography, *A Poet's Life, Seventy Years in a Changing World,* appeared in 1938.

about them. Everyone who read them in 1920 thought so. And no one was louder in his admiration than William Rose Benét.

§ *ii*   *Old Bill Benét, Old Bill Benét,*
         Born in a Fort on Ground-Hog Day.
                                        —Christopher Morley

Nearly a decade after leaving her first husband, to the year, Elinor turned from her second. Horace was consigned, as Philip Hichborn had been in 1910, to the past. He was tiresome and boring; he was no help to her at all. Just as Horace had been used to help Elinor leave Phil, so now another man was assisting her desertion of Horace. His appeal initially was not love exactly, but a professional interest in her poetry.

Like Horace Wylie, Bill Benét needed women, but his need was the exact reverse of Horace's. Horace constructed an elaborate romantic myth about any woman before he met her. Bill started out cruelly realistic about the women he loved, then turned them into mythical images. Yet emotionally and practically he was even more dependent on women than Horace. He worked better when he was married: he required them for what he called "inspiration."

Energy and emotion rode tandem through Benét's nature, both with considerable force, but the course was determined and governed by a hearty domestic urge. He had a gift for friendship—a quality that knew no bounds. He could be astonishingly charming in public, and unbridledly maudlin in private. As long as he was married, the schism was not so pronounced. He looked to a wife for security and to help him define himself. He was always single-mindedly professional about his work: his novel, his poetry, and his long verse autobiography attest to his applied energy. His string of wives prove his desire to be married.

Bill Benét was a person made for caricature; Louis Untermeyer has compared him to E. A. Robinson. In many ways he

looked like a sleeker version of Noel Coward. He possessed
the same finely drawn head and features that wore an expression at once of surprise and chronic equanimity. His eyes were
small, topped by almost imperceptible eyebrows. His nose, as
one uncharitable observer put it, "looks as though it had been
gently pushed by somebody and had not sprung back into
place." His neck was short, his ears large, and his body rather
tall. He was lean, with legs made for spirited tennis playing
and extremely elegant hands, with long tapering fingers. He
was, despite the ferocity of his attack, an intelligent but gentle
critic. He possessed remarkable patience, and succeeded at all
times in seeing the other man's point of view. There was not
a shred of bitterness in his nature, save that he was an ardent
anti-Prohibitionist. His favorite meal was spaghetti; his favorite flower was the spring onion. Above all, his qualities were
enviably human. As an artist, however, he had more energy
than talent. He replaced strength with stamina, in the best
Amy Lowell tradition. His poems display the quick wit of
robust balladry. What he lacked in profundity, he made up for
in high spirits. He was a lyricist with a talent for light verse.
And he was fired with an almost deifying belief in inspiration:
women were his muse. His best poems were inspired by the
women he loved—and lost.

Like the Hichborns, the Benéts had a naval tradition.
Bill's great-great-grandfather, Esteban, distinguished himself
in the Spanish Merchant Marine and left his native Catalonia
to settle in St. Augustine in 1785. In 1812 he sailed away from
his home and wife, and was never seen again. Esteban's
brother had an even more dramatic story. While a post captain
of the Spanish Navy in Cuba, he managed to get himself
assassinated.*

Subsequent generations anchored themselves in the
Army. When Bill's grandfather Stephen Vincent Benét en-
tered West Point in 1845, the family lost another tradition.
The pronunciation of the surname altered. "The accent was

---

*Henry Hoyt portrayed Bill in a fine etching, heavily cloaked and hatted,
as a Spaniard. The portrait is now at the University of Virginia. See also
Elinor's poem "Castilian" (in *Black Armour*) which is perhaps about Henry
portraying Bill as a Spaniard.

presumed to be French," Bill wrote. An accent was affixed and the original Catalonian pronunciation "Ba-na-te" abandoned forever. This same grandfather advanced rapidly through the Army, achieving the rank of Brigadier General. He also started the family's literary tradition in the form of endless papers on logistics and ordnance. Bill's father, James Walker Benét (1857–1928), made the same sweep through West Point and the Army, rising to the rank of Colonel on a talent for ordnance because it was the least aggressively military branch. He hated the Army and begged his father not to make him go to West Point (his brother, on the other hand, wanted to go into the Army and was not allowed). James Walker Benét's literary interests were far more sophisticated and broad than his father's. Leonard Bacon,* who was a guest of the Benéts the summer of 1909 while they were stationed at the Benicia Arsenal, California, observed: "to know the Colonel, for a man of my tastes, was like a delightful electric shock ... he differed in one respect from all soldiers. He knew more about English poetry than most poets and all professors, and had the Elizabethan poets by heart."

Bill's mother Frances Neill Rose (1860–1940) was a woman of more silent accomplishment. She lived entirely for her family and was thoroughly conventional. She lavished almost excessive amounts of affection on her family, drawing them together and preventing them from developing a sense of independence. Her attitudes about family life were steadfastly antediluvian. She felt they had to be, for the family moved as guests of the Army from one arsenal to another. These transitions she managed with ease, building a nest wherever they went. Any friend of her children was absorbed into the family. Like Mama, she could not completely hide her possessiveness, but she was more direct and open; unlike

*Leonard Bacon (1887–1954) was himself a poet, awarded the Pulitzer prize in 1941 for *Sunderland Capture*. In 1910, after attending Yale, he became an instructor of English at the University of California. Thirteen years later he retired from the classroom to devote himself entirely to writing and travel, eventually settling down in Peace Dale, Rhode Island. A man of considerable knowledge, charm, and talent, he always managed to bring out the worst in Elinor. His autobiography is *Semi-Centennial* (1939).

Mama, Mrs. Benét always wanted to play an active role in her
children's lives.

William Rose Benét was born on February 2, 1886, at
Fort Hamilton, New York Harbor, the middle child. His
sister Laura was born in 1884, and his brother, another Stephen Vincent Benét, in 1898. The family drift from the sea
to ordnance came to an abrupt halt with this generation of
Benéts. Kathleen Norris, Bill's sister-in-law, said in her autobiography, *Family Gathering,* that "Billy was the first of eight
generations [of Benéts] ever to vote." All three children were
poets, to which Laura added biography and autobiography,
Stephen libretti, novels, and short stories, and Bill one novel
—*First Person Singular* (1921)—as well as anthologies and autobiography.*

Yet Bill had several brushes with a military career. He
was educated at the military Albany Academy, and was graduated in 1904. While waiting for an appointment to West Point
that never materialized, he enrolled in the Sheffield Scientific
School at Yale (Class of 1907), where he earned a B. Phil.
Then when war came he joined the Air Corps and was stationed, as he wrote to Louis Untermeyer, "non-flying and
. . . practically non-combatant," in Florida and Texas. After
that he gave up all hope of defending the nation, save for some
propaganda work during World War II.

Yale was the turning point in Bill's life. Never before had
he fallen in with so many sympathetic people. There he
formed the friendships he would keep for the rest of his life.
Never before had he been able to combine his jovial high
spirits with his passion for work. He was given the post of
editor of the *Courant* after Sinclair Lewis declined the offer in
1905, and proved superb at literary administration. He was
able to display his natural generosity to his friends, finding
them a place in print. Like John Middleton Murry's, Bill's
robust intelligence was highly vulnerable to suggestion,
whim, and fashion—indeed, he was willingly led by the people he revered. Unlike Murry, Benét's fascination with others
never led him to blind idolatry, but it led him all the same. He

---

The Dust Which Is God (1941), an autobiographical poem of over 550
pages that won the Pulitzer prize for poetry.

was uncertain of his gifts, doubtful of his talents; he was excited by everything and anything.

At Yale he met Henry Hoyt. They were both on the
editorial board of the Yale *Record.* "From the very first/his
vividness pleased," Bill wrote in his autobiography. "Yes," he
wrote earlier in the preface to Henry's posthumous book, *Dry
Points; Studies in Black and White* (1921),

I loved my friend. I loved him better than any man I have ever
known. . . . In five minutes of his energetic talk I found more
genuine amusement and authentic inspiration than in nine out of any
ten books I read.

We enjoyed many glorious evenings. And we were always talking Keats, Kipling or Browning. It was to Henry that I owed my
perseverance into the intricacies of Browning. . . . We sat up late
reciting favorite poetry and discussing all the people we didn't like.
We sat up late questioning the universe and planning great futures.
We were together as much as possible. . . . We strove occasionally,
in fantastic ways, to annoy others.

His complete independence of attitude and the individuality
with which he did or said anything marked him out immediately
from among all the other men I knew. He observed life around him
keenly. His comments were usually unexpected and always pungent.
. . . He was always witty and instinctively on the side of the underdog.

"Vividness" was the aspect about Henry that most startled Bill. The facility with which he applied a brush or a pen,
understood a poem or the complexities of politics, saw a painting—indeed even spoke, was enough to make Bill a willing
follower. Their letters during the first decade of the century
are fired with a desire to change the course of thought and art.
They conspired to set the world alight with their poems and
drawings. Henry's letters are radiant examples of optimism,
soaring out of control; Bill's are weighted with touches of
reality. Henry would dart forward, and Bill would pull him
back. At one moment Henry was ready to pack his bags and
sail to Japan. After all, he pointed out to Bill, if Sinclair Lewis,
who "does look like an ill nourished tomato," could work his
way to Europe with almost no money, the Pacific should prove
no obstacle. "Talk about Beloved Vagabond—" Henry wrote
to Bill [February? 1908] (Y), "that fellows experiences for the

last year would make a great novel. He's just back from Pan-
ama for one thing, wither he had beaten his way 'just to see
what it was like.' I am vastly interested in him Bill 'cause you
see he's just done what we want to try, and he knows all about
it." Henry got as far as California.

If Bill was unqualified in his praise for Henry, Bill's
friends were equally unanimous in their high opinion of Bill.
He seemed incapable of arousing any enemies. "Kindness
was," Louis Untermeyer recalled, "perhaps, Bill's chief characteristic. He may have had enemies (although, knowing Bill,
this seems highly improbable), but he never spoke ill of them.
He never spoke ill of anyone . . . no one even casually acquainted with him could fail to perceive that here was a man
of generosity and ungrudging good will. . . . Every prospect
pleased, every new project aroused him." So full was his character of endearing qualities that he fell into the bland category
of being a "nice guy," as more than one observer appraised
him. Even whiskey, which he downed with gusto at speakeasies, could not dislodge him from this status. When he had
too much to drink, which he often did, he merely became
more convivial, more talkative.

But his steady kindness actually stemmed from a misplaced sense of humility. It was a defense. Benét lacked
confidence, and responded to opposition with generosity—
it drew him out of his dissatisfaction. He inflated himself
with chronic self-deprecation to arouse affection from his
lovers. It worked very well. Women loved him for display-
ing his adolescent uncertainty to them while putting on a
brave face to his friends. It was this subtle imbalance in his
nature that made him an extraordinarily good friend and
an even better husband. His respect for his friends and
wives was enormous, even though he lacked any for himself.

Bill's first wife was Teresa Thompson, whom he married
in New York on September 6, 1911. Her major ambition in
life was to withdraw and become a nun, but she was frustrated
by an indomitable sense of independence. Years before she
married Bill she joined a Carmelite convent in London and
toiled away as an ardent novice, longing to serve Christ. But
the longing that drove her to the convent was not enough to

keep her there; she infuriated her superiors by her want of meek acceptance.*

Bill had first met Teresa Thompson many years before the Carmelite excursion, in San Francisco when she was working in Paul Elder's bookshop. Her sister, the robust and prolific novelist Kathleen Norris, called Teresa a "small intellectual." In fact she possessed a first-class, lively mind. Her command and knowledge of poetry was remarkable; she could leaf through any anthology of poetry and date and recite almost every author. Her sister-in-law Laura Benét was more generous, claiming that Teresa was a "saint."

The marriage to Bill was idyllic. They lived in a tiny house in Port Washington on Long Island, not far from the Norrises', which they filled with their children. James was born in 1914, Rosemary in 1915, and Kathleen Ann, two years later, in 1917.† Bill commuted to New York to assist the assistant editor of *The Century* magazine, and later became assistant editor himself. When he joined the Air Corps, which overlooked his bad eyesight, Teresa and the children went south to Augusta, Georgia, where Colonel Benét was presiding over the Augusta Arsenal. They stayed on in Georgia after the war while Bill sought to reestablish his prewar career. In January 1919, Bill received a wire that Teresa was suffering, like thousands of others, from the influenza epidemic that swept America. Later that month she died.

Bill's eight years with her were documented by a flurry of poems. Many years later he claimed that some of his best verse was inspired by her. Whatever the inspiration, he managed to produce a great deal. In 1913 he published *Merchants from Cathay;* the next year *The Falconer of God;* in 1916 *The Great White Wall. The Burglar of the Zodiac* appeared in 1918, and the year after Teresa's death he brought out *Moons*

---

*Once when told that a card in front of a statue of St. Joseph was upside down, she asked: "But he can read upside down, can't he, Mother?" Another time she asked if she might spill milk again over the refectory floor in order to wipe it up properly the second time.

†In his autobiography Bill disguised his son's real name, giving him the name he ascribed to Henry Hoyt—"Gavin." Teresa is Nora Raferty. Rosemary is Frances, and Kathleen is Janet. Bill called himself Raymond. The Norrises are the Grosvenors. His brother Steve is Peter, his sister Laura, Louise. Elinor is Sylvia.

of Grandeur (1920). The myth of inspiration gave a romantic
gloss to his work. He worshipped what he thought was his
muse—and Teresa was, in part, ambassadress of that muse.
She was an ideal wife to Bill and, (so one observer said), a
perfect mother to his children.

With his children safely looked after in Augusta by
Laura and Mrs. Benét, Bill installed himself in a New York
boardinghouse by night, and pursued his literary career in
a cubicle in an advertising agency by day. There he wrote
two of his most famous lines. One was for Mennen's Tal-
cum Powder: "The petal texture of baby's skin"; and the
other for Murphy's Varnish: "Your house under glass."
Such skill kept him in advertising for six months. In the
fall of 1919 he joined the staff of the Chamber of Com-
merce's magazine *The Nation's Business* and went to work
in Washington, staying at the National Press Club. He was
in Hoyt territory.

"At 1701 Rhode Island Avenue," Bill wrote his mother
(October 30, 1919) (Y),

I feel as if I were Rip Van Winkle, as I had hardly seen the place
since that Easter vacation in 1906. . . . Mrs. Hoyt is remarkably
bright, with an occasional imitation of somebody, in the course of
conversation that is surprisingly animated only so well done that you
find it perfectly natural. As a young girl she must have been very
vivacious. Her face looks very worn but her eyes are bright, and she
seems to me altogether a splendid kind of person.

Aside from the unchanging Hoyt household, there were
two friends in Washington who seemed to make the last decade disappear. It was Yale all over again. Henry came down
for visits from his studio in New York, and he and Sinclair
Lewis together revitalized Bill after Teresa's death. "It was
funny today," he wrote in the same letter,

We three—the old three mosquitoes—lunched together at the Food
Administration—"Red," Henry and I. "Red" talks so fast he is like
an electric message. . . . Henry and "Red" together do amuse me
so, though they are my best friends. But they are so funny together,
if you observe. "Red" amuses Henry but Henry has no chance to
get a word in edgewise when that torrent of small-talk is loosed. It
has helped me, this meeting old friends, and finding that, after all,
we are all fond of each other still.

The Yale refugees met several times at the Rhode Island Avenue dining table. Nancy and Morton were there, chattering constantly and hilariously to the collected guests. Elinor and Horace rounded out the "immense charm and individuality," as Bill remarked, of the Hoyt family. Completing the circle was Sinclair Lewis's wife Grace Heggar, a woman Bill was somewhat hesitant about. "I think it will be amusing to see Mrs. Wylie and Grace together," he wrote to his mother [January or February, 1920] (Y), "because Mrs. Wylie is so genuine and has such a sense of humor* and Grace is apt to be—you know. So there will be a certain element of richness." Part of the "you know" about Grace Lewis was provided by her belief that she was contracting anemia again, brought on by the desertion of her servants.†

The Hoyts, the Lewises, and the Wylies formed the nucleus of Bill's Washington society. He admired Horace, describing him (disguised as Sheldon Chantry in his autobiography) as "quite a classical scholar." But he believed that Horace's single asset was his brain: a subtle mechanism that was able to take in, digest, and interpret other people's thoughts. Bill even came close to adopting Horace's title for his new book of poetry—"suggested by Mr. Wylie's description of the way they struck him, of 'Figures on Tapestry.' Is that a good title?" he asked his brother Steve (February 15,

---

*Three years later Elinor went on record, somewhat sarcastically, disagreeing with Bill's contention. In a symposium sponsored by *Vanity Fair* for authors to list ten of the dullest authors they could think of, Elinor wrote on the top of her list "William Shakespeare as a Comic Writer. Because I am sadly deficient in humor." Others on her list were "George Eliot. Because her dark brown binding got into her style." "Henry James. Because of Mrs. Wharton and Mrs. Gerould." "Gertrude Stein. Because . . ."
†Another part was that Elinor believed, and told her so, that she knew nothing about poetry. Grace Lewis for her part thought Elinor's voice was "at variance with . . . her lovely face." See Grace Lewis, *With Love from Gracie: Sinclair Lewis: 1912–1915* (New York: 1951).
Further "you know" was Grace's advanced sense of silliness and conceit. Seventeen years after her Washington meetings with Elinor she recalled, ungraciously, "I don't think I ever deeply liked Elinor—very few women did—but I was her good and loyal friend until 1926. If I write truthfully about her it will not be an overly flattering picture. But she was a gallant person." Letter from Grace Hegger Casanova to Nancy Hale (July 12, 1937) (Hale papers).

1920) (Y). But Horace was incapable of any further creativity,
and this was the one thing Bill held vitally important. That was
why he admired Henry, and why he soon came to admire
Elinor.

His response to Elinor was, flatteringly, as a poet. He
took her very seriously. Though Elinor's beauty attracted him,
her talent transfixed him. In his autobiography he remembered the stunning effect her appearance made: "the bronze
mane of a little lion . . . she was tall . . . with wrists and ankles/
reminding him of the fragile china deer. . . ." And he recalled
her use of these features: "the remote fastidiousness the shy
almost sacred/ aloofness . . . followed/ by some impulsive
gesture of affection/ or phrase of scimitar with inviolate/ and
beautiful with eyes that changed expression/ from a falcon's
to a kitten's hazel eyes/ large strange and full of valour." His
affection for her came from calm, neutral worship. "You and
Henry," Bill wrote to Elinor (May 15, 1920) (Y), "both have
great & genuine ability. No one Knows it better than I. No
one really wants more to see it fully recognised as it should
be." Much later, some seven years after Elinor's death, he
appraised her talent as nothing less than genius.

As a published poet, Bill volunteered to speed up what
Elinor had begun in Maine. On behalf of the "Bennay Literary
Agency Inc." he collected most of Elinor's recent poems,
typed them, and wrote to his client (February 4, 1920) (Y),
"This ms. we think of very highly and will gladly submit to
all first-class publishers with no extra charge." The MS was
entitled *Fire and Sleet and Candlelight.* * The standard questions
about publication fascinated Elinor, though she had no grand
ambition about her work as a poet. Bill, however, did, and his
move to New York gave Elinor more confidence in the Bennay Literary Agency Inc. In March Bill left *The Nation's Business* to help Henry Seidel Canby† edit the new literary section

*Bill wrote more enthusiastically about Elinor's collection of poems to his
brother (February 15, 1920) (Y): "I also typed Mrs. Wylie's book and sent
it to Knopf. She thinks he won't take it. I myself think it is full of exquisite
things and the craftmanship all through is perfect. She is very fine—just as
fine as steel." Elinor was right; Knopf refused the book.
†Dr. Henry Seidel Canby (1878–1961) taught English literature to fresh-
men at Sheffield Scientific School while Bill was there. He produced an
endless string of critical books and a biography of Thoreau (1939). After

of the *New York Evening Post*. The *Literary Review*, as it was called, quickly made a name for itself, Bill told his brother, with the appearance of Christopher Morley's "Bowling Green."

Bill's encouragement never faltered, and Elinor was becoming more receptive. "I am quite weak with envy of both poems," he wrote to her after Morley had accepted "South of the Potomac" and another poem for his "Bowling Green" column [Spring 1920] (Y). "You are so *certain* a workman. No ragged edges."* He continued to circulate her volume of poems among the publishers. Roland Holt's reaction was, quite simply, that it was too short.

Any concessions the Wylies had made to economy before were nothing compared to the drastic cuts they were now forced to try. Elinor decided to train as a stenographer and get a job at some government office. She instantly put the plan to Bill who replied, just as quickly, that he thought it absurd. He advised (May 15, 1920) (Y): "what I see as the biggest thing you can do, and also the thing that will give you a larger income in the end, is writing." He pointed to the unedifying example of his sister-in-law Kathleen Norris, who managed to turn a minor talent into a major source of income. Since Elinor's poems were not making much money, he suggested that she write some essays and some short stories—both far better paid than poetry: "just start & write one. Most short story writers' brains would rattle in your head," he told her. She could, at all times, count on his typing skills and his agent's ability to place them, though by the late spring of 1920 he was

---

returning from Europe where he did war work with the British Committee of Information, he was asked to form the *Literary Review* of the *New York Evening Post*, which in turn became, in 1924, *The Saturday Review*. He remained editor until 1936. He was chairman of the board of judges for The-Book-of-the-Month and an ardent member of P.E.N. Elinor believed he never shed enough of his Quaker attitudes. He loved work almost as much as Bill.

*"South of the Potomac" was originally entitled "Ctesiphon." It was published by Morley on July 1, 1920. Perhaps the other poem he accepted was "The Child on the Curbstone," which appeared September 28, 1920—the only poem Grace Heggar Lewis thought she understood. Both poems were anthologized in Morley's *The Bowling Green: An Anthology of Verse* (1924) and were included in Elinor's *Last Poems* (1943).

feeling rather like a "weak reed" in the latter department.
By May 21, the Bennay Literary Agency could announce
great strides forward on behalf of one of its two clients (Henry
was the other one). *The Century* took "The Fairy Goldsmith"
and "Madman's Song," while rejecting the sonnet "Nancy."
Three days later Bill wrote to Elinor on "Auspicious Monday"
(May 24) (Y), "You see—& you see! Bugles in the empyrean
& horsemen on the skyline. A six-rayed meteor hangs over
Rome.

"In other words, the long cheer with six Elinor Wylies on
the end!" It was the first letter he sent to Elinor signed "Bill"
rather than William Rose Benét.

While Bill was advancing Elinor's career, he spent a great deal
of time with her brother Henry. In fact, he had moved into
Henry's studio in New York at 37 West 10th Street after
Henry had given up living in the suburbs and Alice had given
up living with him. Alice had taken the children south, obliging Henry to give up the house in Orange, New Jersey. He
now stayed at his New York studio full time. The change
happened to suit both Bill and Henry perfectly. When Bill left
the solitary Press Club in Washington, he moved directly into
the 10th Street studio with Henry, sleeping on the sofa.
Twenty-five years after moving in, Bill recalled the third-floor
studio. The living room was bathed in a favorable north light,
which appeared to be the major decorative feature. The place
was streamlined for work. There was a solitary easel, etching
press, lithographic stone; brushes and tubes of paint littered
the windowsill. There was nothing else on the floor to get in
the way. The studio consisted of a bedroom and a bathroom
that doubled as the kitchen. The rent was as attractive as the
bohemianism of the place: $60 a month, which they halved.
Bill's excitement was intense. "We are good for each
other & for each others work," he wrote to his parents just
before leaving Washington [c.March 1920] (Y). "We have all
sorts of stunts we're going to put over in spare time. . . . I am
selling some of his poems to the magazines. He is on the crest
of a creative wave with all sorts of ideas & his enthusiasm gives
me a lot more feeling that maybe life *is* worth living after

all—." Henry was full of nervous energy, dividing his "crea- tive wave" between poetry and art. He wrote a "one act play about Socrates' meeting with Alexander. It is really a corker," Bill enthused. "We hope he can get it produced by the Prov- incetown Players." Henry had also ingeniously devised a sten- cil which could be quickly reproduced for commercial decora- tive purposes. And on and on the list went.

Henry's enthusiasm and excitement did not last. By the early summer he was suffering from chronic depression. His work was the first victim of these terrible moods: " 'Can't seem to work/Too many things on my mind,' " Bill remem- bered him explaining. He was painting and drawing less and less, spending more time writing and then promptly tearing it up. Alice's desertion haunted him. His balance, so precarious most of the time, moved suddenly and dangerously from buoyant, almost too high spirits to debilitating depression. In July 1920 he suffered a complete nervous breakdown and entered a sanatorium. "I can't help feeling worried," Bill wrote to Elinor (July 16, 1920) (Y), "but that does no good I know. I wrote your mother fully all I thought after talking to a specialist. He is recovering from a mental illness & it is just as important a convalescence as that from a physical illness would be. Funny we expect the mind to bear up under any shock when we don't expect it from the body. Lord, I love that boy!"

By the third week in August Henry was well enough to join the Hoyts (among them Connie and her two children),* who had gathered at Bar Harbor to witness Morton's mar- riage to Eugenia Bankhead—for the second time. Morton was the only one of Elinor's brothers and sisters to escape the Hoyts' somber broodiness. He was free of both ego- mania and depression. However, he did not escape excess altogether, being a victim of unbridled high spirits and im- petuosity. He had an inordinate love of drink and, Eugenia remembered, possessed the most beautiful legs in the family. He was very tall, very handsome, and very eligible. His only drawback seemed to be his inability to manage any form of employment other than acting as his mother's chauffeur.

*Connie's second child, a daughter, Elinor (Norah), was born in 1916.

Mama did not mind this limitation; in fact, she encouraged it.

Morton's first marriage to Eugenia Bankhead had been brief, and secret. He first saw her when she was seventeen in Washington at Keith's Review. For three Mondays in succession he managed to get the seat next to her in the front row. While she was mesmerized by the stage, he was mesmerized by her; finally, in June 1918, he blurted out, "I'm tired of waiting for an introduction to you, so I'll introduce myself!" This introduction led to a drive to Rockville, Maryland, that same day, where they were married. When the couple returned to Washington that night Congressman Bankhead kicked Morton out of the house, and with Mama's help the marriage was speedily annulled. Morton then left to join the Tank Corps.

Slightly less lean than her sister Tallulah, Eugenia was stunningly beautiful and had an electrifying sense of humor and intelligence. Her energy was alarming. Elinor said of her in 1926, "one can't help rather loving" her. Mama called her "the little steam roller," and did not in the least welcome her return to the family. But Jeanne, as she was called, was not intimidated by Mama.*

On August 18, 1920, Morton and Jeanne were married again in Bar Harbor. Elinor and Horace came up from Washington—their single escape from Florida Avenue that summer—and Horace's only note in his diary was: "drive Buick back to Washington." Henry was best man. It was a riotous affair. Morton distinguished himself by eating the bridesmaids' gardenias, which had been purchased at very great expense, then, as was his custom, got stone drunk. There was a lot of laughing and everyone weaved home. Mr. and Mrs. Morton Hoyt spent their honeymoon at the Old Forge, New York, stopping over in New York City on the way.

Henry went back to his studio shortly after the wedding.

---

*Only once did the couple break the curfew Mama imposed on them. One night shortly after they opened the front door of the house in Mt. Desert Mama appeared at the top of the stairs, glowering down at them. Morton cringed as Mama accused: "You want to kill me. I will live to bury you all!" (a threat she narrowly missed carrying out). Jeanne concluded that Mama's "iron grey hair did not stop with her hair. She had iron all the way through."

The morning of August 25 was bright and sunny. That day Elinor's sonnet "August" was published in *The New Republic* and Henry received a letter in the morning mail saying that *The Bookman* accepted his poem "The Spell." Bill and Henry had breakfast at their usual place and then parted, Bill explaining he would be out that evening to play cards. Henry said, before mounting the Sixth Avenue Elevated stairs, "Well, I'll see you—later."

That night, as Bill climbed the stairs to the studio he heard the telephone ringing. The door was locked and he went to get the key from the caretaker in the basement. When it was flung open there was a terrible smell of gas. The caretaker shouted. Henry's dead body was spread on the floor not far from a rubber tube attached to the gaslight fixture. The studio was in immaculate order; Henry had spent the day tidying up his papers.

The following morning Morton and Jeanne read the news in the papers and Morton rushed back to New York to see about the cremation. Five days after Henry's death, Bill wrote to his brother (August 30, 1920) (Y):

He could not get his energy back and he felt, that being so, that he was best out of the way of others. I *know* that was so. He seemed to have tried to take the way that would make it easiest for all—as easy as such things can ever be. I do not mean to say that he was normal mentally when he went. No one is. Pain is there such as the fortunate can never understand. And he had borne that pain within him for a long, long time. No one except Alice, after all is said & done, could ever have cured that pain.

As an observer of crisis, Elinor was mute. She was incapable of responding to Henry's suicide. Like Mama, she said nothing. But she did not forget that they had never regained the warmth of their childhood since 1910. Mama kept so silent that Bill had to write to her again nearly two months after Henry's death in order to find out what she wanted to do about Henry's ashes. In Elinor's case the response was distilled years later in poetry. Many of her poems recall the feeling of loss and grief. She drew on Henry's death in such poems as "Heroics," later published in 1923 in *Black Armour,* and "With a Bare Bodkin," which was never published.

Over the following months Bill sifted through Henry's
papers. He asked Elinor to look around Rhode Island Avenue
for any poems Henry might have left there. Mama, on Bill's
prompting, agreed to a posthumous volume of his works. In
1921 Bill edited and wrote an introduction to *Dry Points;*
Studies in Black and White. In January 1921, the Folsome Galleries in New York mounted a memorial exhibition of
Henry's paintings. Elinor's reaction to Papa's death in 1910
had been her departure from Washington; it appeared that her
reaction to her brother's death was yet another departure.
This time it was less hasty, and for no further than New York.

§ *iii*   *"(more or less) one of them"*

Elinor's debut as a poet was not stunning, merely surprising.
At the age of thirty-five she could hardly be considered a
prodigy. To editors she was an unknown quantity.* Though
the polish of her work was remarkable, she could in no way
be considered in the vanguard of poetry. She demanded and
produced elegance, striding back to the eighteenth and early
nineteenth centuries with the same determination with which
Edna St. Vincent Millay broke into the twentieth. She was not
concerned with being fashionable; it meant very little to her.
She lacked the pristine sweetness of her other great contemporary, Sara Teasdale, who was very popular. She cared about
style almost as much as she cared about herself. She gave way
to sophistication, and in the eyes of her detractors, to superficial sophistication. Above all, she yearned for a career. It was

*The biographical sketch she sent to Harriet Monroe when her poems were
accepted by *Poetry* is a marvel of uninformativeness. "I lived in the country
near Philadelphia until I was twelve years old, & then came to Washington
to live. Since then I have lived in Washington, in England, & during more
summers than I care to remember, in Maine. I have published nothing as
yet" (January 1920). University of Chicago. Harriet Monroe's published
description surpassed Elinor's: "Elinor Wylie (Mrs. Horace Wylie), who
lives in Washington, D.C., has contributed to other periodicals." Elinor's
name was on the cover of the April 1920 issue of *Poetry.*

something new, to be worked at—and it meant that she would have to move to New York.

In the last seven months of 1920 Elinor published some ten poems. She worked extremely hard. In October she completed a vast poem of 608 lines called "Lonesome Rose," which dealt, in tedious fashion, with unrequited love. Bill adored it. "Rose is perfectly lovely," he wrote to her (November 2) (Y). "Great fineness. I have the feeling about your things that I am almost afraid to touch them. I do not mean they are not powerful but they seem so beautifully fragile." Bill wanted it to become the central poem in the new collection of her poems he was getting ready to send off to Holt. The original title for the collection was discarded as they rearranged the selection and added to it. Elinor toyed with the possibility of calling the book *Wild Honey. Nets to Catch the Wind,* cribbed from Webster, Bill also applauded. In fact, he supported every amateur suggestion Elinor made about the volume with lavish praise and professional advice. He went so far as to cite Elinor as his favorite female poet in the *Who's Who* entry he composed for Louis Untermeyer as early as October 1920, overlooking the fact that she was scarcely known.

Bill prodded Elinor constantly with a subtle combination of excessive encouragement and tutorial ambition. He bravely suggested, again, that she desert poetry for prose as he himself was doing. He believed that his energy was contagious. He pointed to the one lure that might encourage her to shift—money. Elinor's approach to money was, despite all her talk to the opposite, somewhat cavalier. Instead of applying her first payment for a published poem to the unglamorous necessity of household bills, she bought two hats, one of which became the source for the poem "Green Hair." Yet at other times she could be intensely practical.

Washington boasted a slender literary contingent, led by Sinclair Lewis who, now in the midst of writing *Main Street,* played Pied Piper to an assortment of women and men, leading them down to the basement on H Street that housed the Wayfarer's Bookshop—a newly opened establishment which had been the idea of three formidable ladies: Mrs. Gibson Gardner, Mrs. Charles Edward Russell, and Mrs. George

Odell. Not content with improving Washington minds with de la Mare and Brooke, they branched out into a purely social venture called the Penguin Club, a place that filled the vacancy of the Metropolitan Club in Horace's life. The Lewises took the Wylies under their wing. Sinclair Lewis continued to like Horace even after Elinor made it clear that she no longer loved him. He respected him and took considerable interest in the fortunes of a man he assessed six years later (November 22, 1926) to Alfred Harcourt as "one of the most pathetic cases I know of in the world." Lewis warmed to Horace's considerable affection for books and complete lack of bitterness about the loss of both money and wives.

Horace's appearance at the Wayfarer's was unimpressive: "At that time he was—dumpy is the only word for it. . . . Horace did not seem to fit his popular reputation," said one observer who would later become less impartial as the third Mrs. Horace Wylie. As for Elinor, her reputation was more exciting even than her appearance. Everyone expected a *femme fatale*. What they saw was a glacially cool woman. She seemed almost too good to be true. She was too careful in the details of her dress; that alone should have given her away. The frightening confidence only disguised a deep shyness, the perfect manners hid her fear. She had lost the charming freshness that had captured Horace ten years before. Her eyes were firmly set, very determined and dark, her mouth more precisely chiseled. Her leanness and tightly drawn skin were at once elegant and worrying; she seemed too frail. The magnificent head floated on a neck that no one failed to admire. Her detractors pointed to the one feature that disrupted the picture —the hint of a mustache. She presented a picture that was far from her popular reputation.

With the help of the Lewises, the Wylies made one disastrous return to the society of Washington that now ignored her and longed to forget her. A party had been organized in the Lewises' box at the Belasco Theater. As Elinor and Horace stepped into the box, necks craned and eyes stared. The audience could not believe what they were seeing. "Isn't it odd," Elinor said, "that everyone seems to be looking at us?" Horace answered, "They *are* looking at Elinor and me. They haven't seen us for a long time!" New York was steadily becoming more attractive; there, she would no longer receive unwelcome attention as the infamous Mrs. Hichborn turned Wylie. She would merely be Elinor Wylie. To Bill, however, she was becoming a great deal more.

Bill confessed to Mama (October 13, 1920) (Y) that "I admire deeply" Elinor's "courage and character." Three months later he told Elinor precisely why he was working so hard on behalf of the Hoyts. "As to love," he wrote (January 5, 1921), "My idea is its [sic] wanting to do things for someone, to do everything." That is why he was doing so much for Henry's reputation, and for Elinor's career. Being with Elinor was, in a way, a resuscitation of his friendship for Henry. "Well its this" he told Elinor [?1921](Y):

Henry's mind & temperament used to be so fascinating to me that when I was young I used always to be thinking of him & writing him even when I wasn't with him. I know there are extremely few friendships such as ours was back in 1908–9–10. It gave life a glamour. Well, when you & I are together now, its the same thing. I miss that. Then sometimes as we are man & woman, I miss most horribly —and will to eternity—the thing that never can be. That's only the truth. When I'm strong I simply curse myself out of it, when I'm weak I want to cry, and rest utterly and forever in your arms . . . I'm always longing for something.

Elinor's urge to come to New York involved no such complicated emotions, only a desire to be associated with the people she had been reading about in Washington, other writers. "I have so little chance to meet other poets here in Washington," she complained to the writer and educator Martha Foote Crow (January 3, 1921).* Bill easily misinterpreted her motives. He thought she was in love with him. "You want the truth," he declared to her in one passionate outburst. "Have it. I fell in love with you. If you think I don't know what that means it's you that are stupid. Being 'not quite a gentleman'

*Martha Foote Crow (1856?–1924), author, anthologist, and educator. She attended Syracuse University, receiving her Ph.D. in 1885, and later taught at various schools and universities, among them the University of Chicago and Northwestern University, where she was also Dean of Women. Her publications include biographies of Lafayette, Harriet Beecher Stowe, and Elizabeth Barrett Browning. She edited anthologies of Elizabethan sonnets and poems about Christ. Her papers are now at Syracuse University.

I could not quite keep it out of my letters. As for you having
anything to do with it, except by being yourself, that is nonsense." Elinor's exact feelings about Bill remained undeclared. She did not suffer from the same directness. To make
matters worse, her letters to Bill at about this time do not
survive, so that Bill's prompt replies are the only index to what
she might have been thinking.*

Elinor was quite shocked by this outburst. She cautioned
Bill that she could not offer him any encouragement, that far
from giving her pleasure by such statements, he was giving
pain. No matter what she might feel about Horace, she owed
him, above all else, loyalty. She instructed Bill never to write
such a letter again. If he could not, she would not write to him.
And, she imposed a further rule on their correspondence: they
would write to one another less often. Bill broke the rule
frequently—with apologies.

Bill's declaration of love altered what was otherwise a
new and very pleasant relationship for Elinor. He was her first
confidant outside her family for over a decade. He was her first
correspondent who received letters on a mutually enjoyed
subject other than love. He was, practically, her first friend.
And for these reasons she inadvertently fostered an emotion
she found very uncomfortable. But her desire to get out of
Washington helped her to ignore the problems going to New
York would most certainly entail.

After a great deal of hesitation and juggling of finances,
Elinor decided to attend a meeting of the Poetry Society in
New York the first week in December 1920. She alerted Bill
of her imminent arrival, and she wrote to another admirer,
Martha Foote Crow (December 3, 1920): "I shall ask for you
at once, and if you see a tall person in a black fur coat, you
might rush to protect her, as it will probably be I, scared to
death." Mrs. Crow had written to Elinor in November praising her published poems and suggesting that she come to New
York and join the Poetry Society. Elinor wrote back that the
idea of coming fitted into her scheme, modest as it was, of
merging quietly and unobtrusively with other writers: "It

*Since this book has gone to press these letters have been discovered and
sold to the University of Virginia.

would be very wonderful to me to know the younger women who are doing such beautiful works these days," she replied (November 27, 1920), "and to feel I was (more or less) one of them." Mrs. Crow's attention was flattering. She asked Elinor to send her some poems that she might pass on to Putnams for possible publication; and she invited her to the annual Poetry Society dinner to be held in January.

Elinor's brief stay was precisely what she had hoped it would be, with one reservation: Bill continued to make unwelcome over-affectionate remarks. "You can never come to the city too often to please me. Which is an out-of-order thing to say, I suppose, but you already know it is true." He had tea with her at her hotel, the Netherlands, and brought along a friend of Henry's who was reminded of Henry by the sight of Elinor and broke down in tears.

Elinor left New York with plans for an immediate return. There was both the dinner and Henry's memorial exhibition to look forward to. But Bill was taking too custodial an interest in each of these activities. He sneered at the prospect of the Poetry Society dinner: "Come to the feast of the Crowes. You will be a fire-bird among vultures. They can't spoil you. I only meant that you are the *real* thing & so many of them are paste & their society reverberates with so much twaddle." He was too ready to give advice, too quick to issue an opinion. Horace could not be ignored, and in her oblique way, that was what Elinor had been attempting to tell him. Somehow, Mama managed to find her way into the center of this tangle of emotions: unerringly, though often quite accidentally, she became the catalyst for important episodes in her daughter's life.

When Bill began negotiations with Mama over Henry's book and exhibition, Elinor naturally became a topic in a good deal of the correspondence. Mama was totally unaware of Bill's growing affection for Elinor, and mistakenly denigrated Horace to Bill. "She & Horace are at outs—" Bill passed on to Elinor [late autumn, 1920] (Y), "not his fault, certainly not intentionally as I see it. . . . Talking of you sometimes starts criticism of him on her part. . . . But in that I can't & won't join. It would be rotten. . . . Don't think *I* don't think he's acting like a perfect *brick*. I do. But that's the trouble." And so it came out. Mama never really forgave Elinor for becom-

ing Mrs. Waring and later Mrs. Wylie. Her opinion of Horace
had not altered. She managed to overlook it but could not
forget it. However carefully Mama hid this from her daughter,
she readily volunteered to expose her attitude to Bill, who had
not even asked. And for Elinor it proved a fatal revelation. It
encouraged Bill to press his affections more and more. He
could afford to ignore Elinor's protestations; he could easily
brush aside her tepid assertions of loyalty to Horace.

She also could not deny the fact that she was taking the
first step toward separation, when she declared in January
1921 that she was moving to New York—alone. With no firm
plan in mind, she confessed as much to Bill the night of the
opening of Henry's memorial exhibition. On Tuesday, January 11, Elinor came up to New York for the occasion, and
according to Bill's autobiography, found that she was unable
to go in: " 'I can't go in' " Elinor said. . . . 'I know it now I
came But I can't go in/ Where are you going?' " she asked
Bill, himself fleeing from the Folsome Galleries. She was extremely pale, alarmingly so. She was trembling, petrified by
the prospect of seeing Henry's paintings. They both walked
over to a speakeasy and had a martini, and Elinor whispered
to Bill: " 'I'm coming to New York . . . I'm going to live/
alone.' " Then she went on to recite the very reasons she
related to Horace nearly seven years later: money, longing for
independence, and dwindling affection for him.

Whether such a statement made over a cocktail was as
simple and direct as Bill conveniently remembered decades
later is unverifiable. As an autobiographer, Bill is not altogether reliable. But the finish to Florida Avenue was uncomplicated and abrupt.

There was nothing uncomplicated about Elinor's forthcoming week in New York, which focused on her appearance
at the Poetry Society's dinner. She did not have a suitable
evening dress; her wardrobe included a great many tweeds,
serviceable day frocks, and a few formal tea gowns. She had
no need for evening dresses. Now she pestered her mother
and Nancy constantly about what she should do. Bill pointed
out that the name Elinor meant " 'the lesser Helen . . . And
like another Helen fired another Troy' (N.Y.)!!' " So Elinor
found a seamstress, "who made up a classic white crepe de

Chine tunic tied with a gold cord around her waist." She topped this creation with gold leaves dotted strategically in her hair.

Matters of dress aside—and they were never unimportant to Elinor—she had other preparations to make. She booked a room at the Hotel Netherlands again. She alerted Mrs. Crow that she wanted to sit at her table on Thursday at the dinner, and asked her how she should pay for the ticket. There were conferences with Bill about her own book (still resting with Roland Holt, who seemed inclined neither to reject nor accept it), and about Henry's.

The dinner in January was an enormous success. Mrs. Edwin Markham asked Elinor for some poems that might be read at a meeting later in the month. She met Jessie B. Rittenhouse, recently appointed secretary of the Poetry Society of America. It was all that she had waited for. "I shall never forget the kindness & encouragement I received from everybody," she wrote afterwards to Mrs. Crow [February, 1921]. "If I feel a little like Cinderella now it is because the ball (Poetry Society Dinner!) was so splendid . . . it was all so exciting, so new, & so lovely." Friday came and she left for Florida Avenue.

Holt, like Knopf, eventually turned down her poems. Sinclair Lewis suggested that the Bennay Literary Agency dispatch the book to his publisher Alfred Harcourt. By late February or early March 1921, *Nets to Catch the Wind* was accepted, in principle, by Harcourt. Elinor started to waver over the new poems she wanted to add, the order, and other details. Sheets flew back and forth between New York and Washington, Bill suggesting, Elinor typing, Bill agreeing, Elinor arguing. Additions to the manuscript had to be made. Elinor thought new poems that had not been published before would be best. Bill disagreed. "The ape Harcourt—" he wrote to Elinor [c. March 17, 1921] (Y), ". . . shall be apprised of much of this absolutely edible work having appeared in Sundry periodicals of the period." Thus, published poems were sent to Bill for inclusion. Of the thirty-one poems that compose *Nets to Catch the Wind*, nineteen had appeared before the book was published.

In the spring of 1921 another novel by Elinor is men-

tioned which has become as mysterious as her first one. From
the oblique hints in Bill's letters, it seems that Elinor was
writing a fancy on Bill's private name for Henry—"Dmitri,"
a name he applied to Elinor as well. The other characters were
skimmed from life: there was "Dmitri, the younger, the famous depressionist," Dmitri the elder (who was Bill), Helen
and Mary (both Elinor)—all members of the Petrie family.
"You are so *wonderful* about that family!" Bill wrote to Elinor
[April, 1921] (Y), "I begin to see them all . . . it's so lovely
& glorious I scream & shout & roll on the floor. I love it. Keep
it up. It's great stuff." The novel was abandoned when Elinor
packed her bags for New York. Bill's comments on it, though
enthusiastic, were brief. Elinor was pleased with her efforts,
and Bill, being the good agent, managed to use the MS to
advantage. "Listen," he cautioned her, [April 29?] (Y), "I
have told Harcourt you have started a novel & if he inquires
about it don't be too willing to promise it him. Let him nibble
—because I am positive I can place it for you when it's finished
& you just be a little pleasantly noncommittal . . . maybe he'll
get so interested he'll offer you an advance or something."
Added to this, Bill claimed to have enough of Elinor's poems
for another volume, which could quickly follow the appearance of *Nets to Catch the Wind.*

Unlike Elinor, Bill found writing extremely hard work.
He too was in the middle of a novel, which he moaned was
not a pleasant place to be. He did not possess Elinor's apparent
fluency. "This novel is harder to write than digging subways,"
he sighed (May 9, 1921) (Y). Some critics later found the
reading of it as difficult. Fortitude alone pulled him through.
He was also working hard for the *Literary Review* and acting
as a clearinghouse for Elinor's poems, which arrived by mail
somewhat too frequently. The office of the Bennay Literary
Agency was littered with her work. Sometimes it aroused his
jealousy; more often it gave him an opportunity to employ his
concept of love, "doing things for people." Elinor tried to
placate the jealousy by telling him her "h.b.p." (high blood
pressure) was acting up. This only gave Bill another cause for
worry: "Be careful about that h.b.p. & don't excite yourself.
. . . If anything happens to you it's 'curtains.' Now *do* keep
alive, because—well, if only to be kind to me by simply exist-

ing" [April 29?] (Y). Elinor's curious form of consolation alarmed him by suggesting another potential victim. She believed that if she could match complaints with him, she would relieve his guilt; all she did was to increase his displays of affection and worry.

Elinor's success advanced pronouncedly in the first five months of 1921. She published eleven poems—six in *The New Republic,* one in *The Nation,* and four collected, finally, in the April number of *Poetry.* She also published her first prose work in the February number of *The Bookman,* an essay called *The Wickedness of Books.* The "wickedness" referred to is sarcastic; more significant than the reprehensible content in some books is the fact that the cost has denied her woolen stockings, fur-lined gloves, hot-water bag, Horace his Jaeger underwear, and both of them an electric heater. It is not a good essay, but it is in the best tradition of self-indulgence. Like all of her prose works it lacks the cohesion and sharpness that marks her poetry. She believed that the new form, being much more expansive than poetry, required an equal method. It was a theory she would carry over into reviewing, with unfortunate results.

Her published achievements were enough to fetch her from Washington. The brief stays expanded, and became more frequent. At the end of May she went to New York for a week. She dined with Leonora Speyer, a friend of Bill's she had met at her first appearance at the Poetry Society of America. Born in 1872 (in Washington), the daughter of a minor German aristocrat, she had an intensely active public career as a concert violinist with both the Boston Symphony and later the New York Philharmonic. She had been married twice, once in 1893, and again in 1902 to Edgar Speyer of the international banking family, and lived in luxurious surroundings in Norfolk, London, and Paris until 1915 when she returned to America and settled into an immensely grand house in Gramercy Park. Later she took on the very attitude of her mansion. Like Elinor, Lady Speyer had made some fatal transgressions against the society she was born into. She and Edgar were violently pro-German during the war—a belief that was enough to banish her from most dining tables. Lady Speyer was handsome; in fact, many thought her very beautiful, with

a wonderful figure and stunning Slavic eyes. She possessed a
certain not very robust talent for poetry, but her skill was
enough to convince the Pulitzer committee that she deserved
the prize in 1926, and enough to elect her president of the
Poetry Society. She wrote her elegant, empty poetry every
morning in a bed that had belonged, she claimed, to Marie
Antoinette. The elegance that surrounded her seeped into her
work in the matter of form but was destructive of anything
approaching content. She was exceedingly musical and was a
very great friend of both Elgar and Strauss.

Elinor's first meeting with Lady Speyer aroused both curiosity and fear. She worried that she might be accused of some
of the *hauteur* that so impressed New Yorkers. Bill was astonished. "Lady Speyer?" he repeated [late December, 1920]
(Y). "Not a chance. You couldn't be like *that* if you tried in
a million years. She [Lady Speyer] isn't so awful as that, only
an actress (I mean she dramatizes herself all the time) and a
parlor pagan." And yet Lady Speyer's drawing room drew
everyone. The place was, and looked, expensive. The teas
were good and the collection of guests even better. Coming
from the desert of Washington, Elinor was clearly impressed.

"Lady Speyer's supper was fine," Elinor wrote to Mama
(May 30) (B) flush from her visit to New York; ". . . everyone
takes you seriously over there—your work I mean—& appears
to like you, which is a blessing." But her visit was not all taken
up by supper parties and speakeasies. She had gone again on
business. There was the lingering question of Henry's book,
which was to be published, with financial assistance from
Mama, by Frank Shay. And there was the more taxing problem of work. If she had a job to go to it would make the move
from Florida Avenue much easier, and less wounding to Horace. She let it be known, less discreetly than she had informed
Bill four months earlier, that she was coming to New York.
She met a "perfectly splendid little Miss Kenyon," who
worked at Scribners, "but looks as if she was on Vanity Fair!
That is a great virtue in my opinion, to be able to, particularly
as she made her evening dress herself. . . . I could get a job
on Scribners through Miss Kenyon if I wanted or so she says!
. . . I saw their offices—it is *so* nice & literary. Of course I
would only try it out, mean while sharing her place with her."

Elinor knew that Mama responded more to enthusiasm than anything else. She thought she might get a post in London, or after such training as one got at Scribners, she might move on to any position that came along, "if you're clever."

"Horace's job won't last forever," she pointed out in the same letter; "he could then perhaps get one in New York or London. I will always stick to him, but the question is should I pass up the chance to earn my own living: I would then need to take only $1200 from you. . . . You write more not less when you have a regular literary job. . . . I should certainly like to earn my living—Gosh, *how I would love it.* But if you say so, that settles it."

Her idea of "sticking" to Horace was a unique one—she would leave him. In a curious reading she believed that leaving him was essential if they were to stay together. The grand design fell apart the moment she left Florida Avenue. Elinor was fascinated by New York. She tried to hide the appalling inconsistencies in her logic by seeking Mama's approval.

Horace, who could always be counted on for some mono-syllabic summary of events, recorded for the summer of 1921 simply: "Alone." While he was sweltering in Florida Avenue, Elinor went to New York in either late July or early August to share an apartment with Bernice Lesbia Kenyon, at 108 East 82nd Street.

Miss Kenyon, later Mrs. Gilkyson, added poetry to her office talents at Scribners. She was an elegant creature: tall, thin, pale, and blond. She had an extremely high opinion of herself and executed some spectacularly pretentious poems, later collected in volumes entitled *Meridian* and *Songs of Unrest.* She came from a well-to-do Long Island family who never managed to give her enough money to keep her in the style she believed essential, and was thus forced to share apartments throughout her life. She slinked around as a *femme fatale* and she scoured town for the most socially acceptable to people her set. On the whole she made a great many enemies. But she possessed one useful quality: she liked Elinor. It was not a difficult achievement; Elinor set out to please. She was shy, extremely careful, and very industrious. She read manuscripts for publishers throughout the summer. Winifred Welles, whom she met at Lady Speyer's, later claimed that the Elinor who appeared in New York in 1921 was unrecognizable as the woman who later moved to Greenwich Village and created such a sensation. She was like the new girl at school, eager to learn. And Miss Kenyon was more than eager to teach.

Between reading manuscripts Elinor continued to write poetry. What she did not give to Bill she handed over to Miss Kenyon, who tried to sell them. She was lucky with a work entitled "Casual Sonnet," later renamed "Nadir." It was bought by the editor of a magazine called *The Sonnet*. In her covering letter to the purchaser, Mahlon L. Fisher, Miss Kenyon skillfully pointed out (August 16, 1921): "It's new—just written." He bought the sonnet; before it could be printed, the magazine folded.*

Elinor was more fortunate with other magazines. *The Bookman* published another essay; *The Smart Set* added her to its list of contributing poets; and *The New Republic,* largely through Bill's efforts, continued to buy a great many poems. The poetry editor of *The New Republic* first saw Elinor's work in September 1920. When the seven or eight poems were submitted, Ridgely Torrence remembered seventeen years later, "I instantly accepted all of them" and asked Bill for more. He was then living in Ohio and did not return to New York for nearly a year; but because of his "wholesale purchases of her poetry," Elinor wrote to him immediately. When he came to New York he finally met her. Like Winifred Welles, he was surprised by the poet whose work so impressed him. "Perhaps I expected to find the veneer of a sophisticated woman of the world. But she hadn't that kind of surface. Actually, she was child-like, eager, sincere, self-concentrated and often really rather shy. Her art was of course supremely important to her." When Elinor was preparing to leave East 82nd Street after her New York summer, she wrote to Mama [August 30, 1921] (B), "I haven't written much poetry, but Ridgley [sic]—I have never seen the lovely creature—has bought all I've written."

*Fisher held on to the rights and finally published "Nadir" in a limited edition of 100 folders, advertising it as "The First Printing of a Wylie Sonnet"—incorrectly, as Bill Benét pointed out in his notes on "Nadir" included in Elinor's *Last Poems* (1943).

For the first time in years Elinor was actually optimistic. Her experiment was a triumph. Offers began to pour in. Frank Crowninshield—"the great Crownie"—offered her the job of caption writing for *Vogue*. Elinor refused, doubting her talents. She went around the stores, gazing at upholstery materials, furniture, and china. She allowed Mama to buy her a pair of "very grand shoes" for her birthday; and Mama added to her new cheerfulness by giving her some money.

"I certainly have had an interesting and instructive summer; I would not have missed it for the world," she wrote to Mama. "If I have accomplished no wonders, I have collected enough copy to last me the rest of my life if I were now forced to retire to the wilds. . . . I find my short stories degenerate into lists of tables and chairs and china, all very beautiful, but hardly as exciting to the general public as they are to me."*

She moved about seeing people, among them Morton and Jeanne, who were living in a tiny apartment at West 72nd Street, encumbered by unhouse-trained Pekes and an erratic stove. She met most of Bernice Kenyon's friends, parted "the best of friends" from her, and left for Washington "thin as a rail," certain of a hasty return.

Back in Florida Avenue she confronted Horace with the success of her time in New York. It meant that she was not returning to Florida Avenue to stay. He is reported to have said, "You better remain with me, Elinor. You are a fantastic creature and I understand you." She responded to this advice with a sustained bout of severe headaches. Bill sent her even more ardent confessions of love, as a new form of bromo-seltzer. Her headaches became so severe that she scrawled to Bill the calculation that they would only be relieved in seven years. "No, *don't say* seven years," he wrote back to her [?October, 1921] (Y), "—even if we fear it. But don't lets *say* anything about time." Only from Bill's side of their correspondence is it clear that Elinor was in a severe nervous state. She could write about her headaches, but not about their cause. Horace's understanding seemed to make everything worse—there was an atmosphere of blackmail, the emotional

*An item of furniture later became the title of one of her stories, "The Applewood Chair," published in *The Ladies' Home Companion*, May 1926.

sort, weighing on her. Their past was dredged up. She could
not forget what they had been through. Still they both knew
her departure was inevitable; it was only the strength of their
emotions they were not prepared for. Horace's coolness was
as perplexing as it had been over a decade before. And Elinor's anxiety was just as disruptive.

The practical considerations and details could not be
solved easily, either. Elinor cringed at the prospect of divorce.
She decided therefore on a trial separation, this time not just
for a month but a year. She would test herself and Horace. If
after the year she did not want a divorce, they might either
remain separated or, more unlikely, she could still return to
him. It was a vague compromise, generous only to Elinor.
Even in accepting such an astonishing proposal, Horace
proved that he did indeed understand her best. He readily
gave her time, knowing exactly what the outcome would be.
On September 18, 1922, Elinor started divorce proceedings
against him.

Against this upheaval, underplayed by the good manners
both Elinor and Horace demanded, Elinor projected an entirely different side of her character to New York. She was
soberingly realistic. She tried to calm Bill, who was becoming
far too excited about her return. He read it all as a declaration
of love, while Elinor merely saw it as an extension of the
career she had begun in the summer. She wrote to Christopher
Morley about a poem he might accept for his column, and sent
a list of names to Harcourt suggesting that copies of her book
be sent to them. With the same thoroughness she had some
chairs re-covered. She plotted which pieces of furniture she
would take to New York, which silver, and which dresses.
While she was poised for departure, Horace sat passive in his
chair. It was a sobering finish to eleven years.

CHAPTER EIGHT: 1922

§*i*   *A place in the Village*

Unlike Lord Byron and Lytton Strachey, Elinor did not wake
up one October morning in 1921 to find herself famous. The
recognition she received for *Nets to Catch the Wind* was of a
more somber variety, and very long in coming. When she did
receive criticism it was as thought out and premeditated as the
words in each of her verses. But the work was awarded the
Poetry Society's prize for the best first volume of poetry: The
Julia Ellsworth Ford Prize.

The first person to offer a comment on the book was
Elinor herself. She complained to her family that Alfred Harcourt had dressed the book to look "slightly like a primer of
elementary geometry." It was a dusty brown color, closer to
mustard than any more solid hue, and thinner than her ignored *Incidental Numbers*. It lacked the elegance of typeface
and setting that Alfred and Blanche Knopf would later lavish
on her work.

The spinsterish appearance of the book belied its content.
When critics opened it, they found a great deal to arrest them.
The most captivating things were the certainty and the angular
emotions of the poems. Phrases like Louis Untermeyer's
"sparkle without burning," "frigid ecstasy," "passion frozen
at its source," became critics and readers' leitmotifs in describing her work. She seemed capable of combining stunning
craftsmanship with ethereal sentiments. She was a nimble, yet
sure, technician of almost orgiastic images, which she destroyed as decisively as she built them up. Her ability to convey lushness through austerity was startling. All the confidence that was absent in her life was distilled on the page.

From his comanding position at the *Literary Review* Bill
looked for various suitable reviewers of the book. He hesitated between "Amy the only"—Amy Lowell—and Sara Teasdale, or at least "someone who has brains." In the end he
commissioned Edna St. Vincent Millay as the most suitable

reviewer for his pages. The book was sent to her in Rome. She wrote to Elinor after reading it (November 27, 1921) (Y), "Not since I discovered Ralph Hodgson have I had such happiness in a new volume of poems." The comparison was not an altogether welcome one. Ralph Hodgson, while so startling to Edna Millay, failed to make the slightest intrusion on the history of poetry. Like Elinor he started publishing his poems when he was in his thirties and by 1917 he had stopped altogether. The most that could be said of him was that he was a "major minor poet."* And Edna Millay's review, which was published January 28, 1922, registers the qualification that her comparison implied. Like others after her, she praised *Nets to Catch the Wind* more for its status as a first book than for its contents. "The book is an important one," she stated frankly. "It is important in itself, as containing some excellent and distinguished work; and it is important because it is the first book of its author, and thus marks the opening of yet another door by which beauty may enter to the world." The poems, she calculated, "are carefully and skilfully executed works of art, done by a person to whom the creation of loveliness and not the expression of personality . . . is the important consideration." But the poems fared less well individually. The first was "the worst in the book"; the third, "Madman's Song," was "gracefully done, but even as it is being read is forgotten." Of the eight sonnets, one was rated "trivial" and another "worthless." The severe denunciation of four poems out of thirty-two was lessened by the lavish praise bestowed on others. Two were quoted in full, and the critic generously threw in an appraisal of Elinor's talent: "The author . . . has the fine equipment of intelligence, skill, discrimination, reserve, and the full powers of sorcery. . . . There is no proof or even evidence in this first book of something which she cannot do."

Of all Elinor's critics, Edna Millay spoke most fully. It is curious that she should accuse Elinor of the one thing criti-

*Born in Yorkshire in 1871, Ralph Hodgson moved to New York where he worked, for a brief time, on a newspaper. His first volume of poems, *The Last Blackbird and Other Poems*, appeared in 1907; four more volumes appeared in 1913, and in 1917 his *Poems* heralded his silence for four and a half decades. Critics have remarked that he was, unlike Elinor, the most unselfconscious of poets. He died in 1962.

cized in her own verse—unevenness. If nothing else marked Elinor's short career, it was her consistency. Other critics were unqualified in their praise and unable to explain why. Louis Untermeyer fell on "too brilliant" as an explanation; Alfred Kreymborg pointed to "aristocratic scorn"; Harriet Monroe stipulated that the work was "austere" and "immaculate," and blandly summarized the volume as "An unusually interesting first book." Edmund Wilson, writing in *The Bookman* (February 1922), said her verse strode between tenderness and bitterness. But more important, he wrote, this book proved, yet again, that women wrote the best modern poetry. Elinor Wylie's style "never falls down or turns bad. Its accuracy never misses; its colors are always right—two qualities exceedingly rare in contemporary American verse. The 'new poetry' has been, among other things, a carnival of literary bad-taste. . . . Now Mrs. Wylie's tone (it is a vague word, perhaps, but I can't think of anything better) is always certain and pure."

Edna Millay noticed that Elinor's influences sometimes "outvoiced" her own; others spotted this as well. *The Dial* compared her to Emily Dickinson. Rica Brenner found a too pronounced echo of Blake in her lines. Herbert Gorman bravely compared her to Donne.

But all these doubts were minor compared to Amy Lowell's reservations, which she was careful not to communicate to Elinor but rather to Louis Untermeyer. To Elinor she explained the delay that had kept her from reading the book Elinor sent to her as a gift: her entire Brookline household was laid low with illness—Mrs. Russell, her companion whom Bill liked enormously, had tonsillitis; then one of her maids "threatened mastoiditis." Next, "Amy the only" launched herself on another lecture tour. It was not until the end of February 1922 that the Archpriestess of Imagism pronounced on *Nets to Catch the Wind*. "My admiration for your poetry is only deepened by reading it again. I have been over many of these poems several times, and the neatness and the deftness of your touch is something very remarkable," she wrote (February 28, 1922). Among her favorites were "Bronze Trumpets and Sea Water" and "A Proud Lady." The poems Amy Lowell liked least were the very poems Edna Millay liked most.

There was little praise in her comments to Louis Untermeyer, however. Amy Lowell merely misplaced yet another
poet. Her capacity for misjudging poetry and its place in posterity is surely unequaled in the history of criticism. She was
quite unerring in her misjudgment and completely unhesitant
in offering her verdicts. "I admire it," she wrote of Elinor's
poetry to Louis Untermeyer,

but it is a fact that it is not as good as her prototype, Emily Dickinson's. . . . I do not feel at all certain as to Eleanor [sic] Wylie's future.
She is thirty-six years old, I understand, if not more, and this is her
first book. Now I am the last person to quarrel with an author
beginning late in life. . . . But the thing that makes a reputation in
the end, the thing that really makes a poet, is not the first book, but
the last book, and all the books in between. . . . A minor poet may
throw off an excellent poem or two, an excellent thirty poems, as
Eleanor Wylie has done. . . . Now Eleanor Wylie's work is at the
moment static. These little poems of hers are all built to a pattern.
She has learned her pattern perfectly, but I see no reason to suppose
she can ever vary it.

Had Amy Lowell lived longer, she might have retracted this
judgment; her life spanned only one more volume of Elinor's
poetry.

The great hodge-podge of criticism, both public and private, reveals one important fact: people did not know what to
make of Elinor's poetry. The technical precision was widely
admired, indeed, accused of being *too* fluent. The content left
readers decidedly uncertain: it was not unique, new, or unselfconscious. Elinor's imagery was startling, and then again just
as startling was the unrelieved confidence that ran through the
book. It was staggeringly precise for a first book. This is the
single detail which caught every one of her readers.

As if to emphasize the ambivalence of this new poetry,
there was the poet herself, who had not yet learned to fit the
image of her own work. It all contributed to create a mystery.
Elinor had fallen on New York an unknown quantity. She was
shy, uncertain, almost withdrawn. Her success, qualified
though it appeared, surprised no one more than Elinor. Of
course her infamous past was dredged up again, for no other
reason than to heighten her social currency and accent her
curiosity value. It became all the more important because

Elinor did not fit into the part. People were more tantalized than ever, and she was learning how easy it was to turn a long-standing embarrassment into an asset. She was not altogether opposed to executing some clever embroidery on the tale—by the end of her life she had become a genius at this. But what people saw and what they heard was, and remained for a long time, hard to believe. Carl Van Vechten confessed, as late as 1933, that the woman he met and the history that preceded her made a very odd combination: "This character apparently contradicted at every turn the evidence of her semi-public actions."

To celebrate her new status as a recognized poet, Elinor deserted the Upper East Side and Bernice Kenyon for good. On March 3, 1922, she moved into apartment no. 2, 1 University Place, in Greenwich Village, next to Washington Square.* Her rent was $100 a month for a large room on the entrance floor. It was spacious and unusually elegant to a degree unknown to the "brainy coves" of Greenwich Village. Her "household gods" were brought up from Washington and placed, as always, with meticulous care. Edmund Wilson sniffed at her pictures and furniture, saying "although rather grand, [they] were a little bleak, but they gave her a civilized setting which in the Village was rather rare." The ceiling was unexpectedly high; the room had originally been designed as the drawing room, and Elinor went to great pains to maintain its once elegant atmosphere. It was dominated by large windows that overlooked the street. Near the windows was her divan, which could be converted, with a few adjustments of pillows, into her bed. The sideboard, with her silver candlesticks planted on top, was on the left as one entered, and above it her fruit still-life. Her Sheffield mirror hung atop the fireplace. The books and upright eighteenth-century chairs were as meticulously arranged as the papers on her desk. Each week Mrs. Damrosch, her maid, came in to polish everything to mirror-like brilliance. "My room grows more comfortable day by day," Elinor informed Mama [November 2, 1922] (B),

*Winifred and Harold Welles also lived in the same house. After Elinor moved out to Gramercy Park in October 1923, Edmund Wilson moved into the building. It has now been destroyed.

"... it is definitely a winter room, and is now well-warmed and charming; everyone likes it."

In the first room she had exclusively to herself in some fifteen years, Elinor created an atmosphere that was, as her sister said, "a mixture of Horace Walpole, Lady Wortley Montague and Miss Austen." So stripped was it of any clutter that it appeared "suitable as one of a lady's twenty rooms but seemed slightly ridiculous and almost unbelievable as the only dwelling-place of a human being." Elinor's dressing-table equipment was stored, with precision, in the bathroom, as was her minute cooking outfit. That one room encapsulated Elinor's fanatical meticulousness and her frank elegance. It was not a warm or hospitable place. Some people complained of its lack of comfort, but it was so individual that no one could doubt it was Elinor's.

Elinor's life was led with the same precision, caution, and complete want of abandon. She was not spontaneous. She set about at once to be apart, and yet in the center, of Greenwich Village life. She did not rush to the Provincetown Players or Bill's favorite speakeasy haunts. Her pleasures were more subdued and certainly a great deal more refined than her brother Morton's. Yet she was not abstemious: she loved wine and brandy (but, unlike Bill, loathed whiskey). She shared Horace's love of tea. Her favorite foods were the simplest and the most delicious: spring lamb, asparagus, artichokes, new potatoes, and scones. She and Bill would frequent Marta's, a crowded Italian restaurant not far from University Place, at Washington Place. But Elinor preferred the Brevoort House, rebuilt since her mother and father ate there some forty years before, or the Lafayette Hotel. She felt most comfortable in the cold formality of anonymous large rooms. It was as if she had spent too long trying to convince herself she liked coziness, the miniature warmth of Brook Corner.

The year 1922 was not an eventful one in Elinor's life. After the reviews of *Nets to Catch the Wind* appeared, she made one appearance in Washington. The occasion was her younger sister Nancy's "Black and White Party"—the second celebration to mark her debutante status. Elinor refused to attend the first dinner and dance for Nancy, knowing how far back Washington memories reached. There had not been a Hoyt invitation since 1910, and Elinor knew that if she attended it would be apparent there was no need to issue any again. But the second invitation was a less starchy event; it was to be a fancy dress party on the theme of black and white. Mama even switched from her favorite gray to a "transformation" in black. Elinor bent the rules slightly by arriving alone in a concoction of silver and black with shiny patent-leather leaves shaped like a coronet in her hair. She gave out the excuse that her husband was on the West Coast. Her escort, John Peale Bishop,* went one better: he arrived an hour late in an assortment of eighteenth-century ruffles with a peruke and a black ribbon on his hair. He was not called on to escort Elinor again. Nancy presided in a wig that was a confection of white curls. The party passed off without any unpleasant references to Nancy's infamous sister. In fact, Elinor received a great deal of attention for her startling appearance. She seemed to brush aside the decade and a half that separated her from the rest of the guests. She was mistaken for Nancy's younger sister, and she was indeed striking. Her reputation as a beauty preceded her wherever she went. Edmund Wilson thought that her thinness—"almost skeletally thin"—detracted as much as her voice, which reminded him of a peacock, from the beauty she clearly once boasted. Others did not seem to notice any fading. For someone with such a lurid past, her atmosphere of cool chastity and "puritan-patrician" bearing was somewhat disconcerting, at least to Louis Untermeyer. In what is proba-

---

*John Peale Bishop (1892–1944) poet and novelist. He was extremely presentable, with the high qualifications of a good brain and good behavior. It was widely rumored, so Edmund Wilson wrote in his diary, that Bishop would marry Elinor. Fifteen years later Bishop himself remembered little of this deep intimacy. The surviving letters he wrote to Elinor never touch on the subject.

He was born in West Virginia and was educated at Princeton where he met Edmund Wilson, who conducted him safely into the pages of *Vanity Fair*. The same year Bishop graduated from university he published his first volume of poetry, *Green Fruit* (1917). Five years later he collaborated with Edmund Wilson on *The Undertaker's Garland* (1922). Aside from poetry, he published one novel, *Act of Darkness* (1935), and a volume of short stories, *Many Thousands Gone* (1931). After sharing Edna Millay with Edmund Wilson, he moved on to matrimony (with Margaret Hutchins) and Europe.

bly the best description of her features, he compared her to
Queen Nefertiti:

Here were the same imperious brows; the high cheekbones and the
scooped-out cheeks; the proud and narrow nose; the small taut
mouth; the carved and resolute chin; the long smooth column of the
throat. . . . The eyes were bright and a hypnotic hazel—witch hazel,
it seemed to me. To offset the stare and the general effect of stiffness,
her hair was loose and lively.

Elinor herself described her hair as "lion-colored." Five years
later, in an unequaled moment of honesty, she wrote her own
verse portrait in *The New Yorker:*

> She gives the false impression that she's pretty
> Because she has a soft, deceptive skin
> Saved from her childhood; yet it seems a pity
> That she should be as vain of this as sin;
> Her mind might bloom, she might reform the world
> In those lost hours while her hair is curled.

Though stories about her vanity are legion, Elinor's
friends agreed that she had a great deal to be vain about. But
she could not decide which she preferred people to admire:
her intellect or her beauty. She had a considerable talent for
misreading compliments. In 1924, after she had been in the
hospital, Louis Untermeyer said to her: "You look particularly
lovely tonight." It was, as it sounds, meant as a compliment.
Elinor disagreed, firing back, "Have you ever seen me looking any other way?" Untermeyer thought she was joking, but
Elinor never joked about her appearance. Though distinctly
more confident about her poetry, she bridled at the slightest
hint of unfavorable criticism. She was angry at Louis Untermeyer for suggesting that her poems were *too* brilliant, despite
the elaborate praise that prefaced this judgment. He had to
wait over a year to be forgiven.

Louis Untermeyer survived the turbulent initial meeting
with Elinor to become one of her best friends. Born in New
York City the same year as Elinor, Untermeyer was, in his
words, "an inept student," who failed to complete high school
and neglected to get accepted to Columbia. He read haphaz-
ardly but voraciously, and decided to become either a composer or a pianist. Meanwhile he worked in the shipping de-

partment of his father's jewelry firm, Keller and Untermeyer; later, he progressed to the display department and then became a traveling salesman. He wooed his first wife, Jean Starr, by thundering out piano renditions of MacDowell and Wagner. He was married at the age of twenty-one and it seemed that matrimony and fatherhood were enough to shunt him over to poetry. His first poems were published in F.P.A.'s (Franklin P. Adams) column* and his first book, *First Love*— "a conglomeration of echoes from Herrick, Heine, Housman, Hardy, and Horace . . . it managed to draw a long sigh through seventy-two lyrics plus a sweetly swooning envoy"— appeared in 1911.

Untermeyer became contributing editor for *The Masses* (founded in 1911 and given to news, commentary, and hearty left-wing social criticism). But his most memorable contribution was in the pages of the Chicago *Evening Post,* where he noted that the only good line in Amy Lowell's first volume of poetry, *A Dome of Many-Colored Glass* (1912), was the title, and that was borrowed from Shelley. Two years later he established himself with the publication of *Challenge,* a volume of "high-pitched" protest. He went on to devote himself to parody and refused to consider the jewelry trade. From this circuitous entry into poetry Untermeyer became one of the most intelligent and open-minded appreciators of modern verse. Apparently indefatigable, he managed to produce some ninety books, among them the most authoratative anthologies on modern American and English poetry. He combined critical skill with one of the driest senses of humor sported by any critic. This humor, alas, was somewhat wasted on Elinor; but not on Bill, who was his friend long before Elinor arrived in New York.

While Louis Untermeyer had to overcome his criticism of

*Franklin Pierce Adams (1881–1960), columnist, radio performer, and humorist. He began his career in journalism in Chicago, then moved to New York, where he worked first on the *Evening Mail.* In 1913 he moved to the *Tribune,* and his famous column "The Conning Tower" appeared there until 1921 when he transferred to the *World.* His taste in poetry remained uniformly high and open-minded, and he boasted contributions from the most eminent writers of the day, to which he added his own "salty" and sane comments.

Elinor's poetry to become her friend, Edmund Wilson succeeded much more easily. He had a safer passage than most.
He was unqualified in his published appreciation of her—
always a good start. He was beginning an obviously distinguished career, and Elinor fully appreciated this fact. His
perch at *Vanity Fair*, which was offered to him when the offices
were ventilated of Dorothy Parker's perfume, gave him the
sort of command post for Princetonians that Bill's place on the
Literary Review afforded Yale graduates. Seventeen years later,
writing to Nancy Hale, Wilson claimed that he could not
remember when he met Elinor. He "first got to know" her
before she moved to Greenwich Village.

Like Elinor, he was born in New Jersey, in 1895; unlike
Elinor, he never sought to deny the fact. He sailed through
Hill School with his mother's pet name for him, Bunny, which
stayed with him for life. After Princeton (Class of 1916) and
the war, he landed up in New York. He was of medium
height, sporting reddish brown hair, scrupulously parted and
frictioned, and later exposing more scalp than he would have
wished. His brown eyes narrowed as he grew older and his
other moderately remarkable features spread out as he put on
age and weight. He was somehow neither unattractive nor
handsome. He was timid and shy; he almost grew into his
nickname. Prone to stuttering when excited, he claimed to be
absent-minded. He was, without question, dazzlingly intelligent, though he never managed to conquer the complexities
of mathematics. This ineptitude dogged him through his entire life, and spilled over into rudimentary mechanics. When
he bought a motorcycle and attempted to ride it, he wrecked
it immediately and then was arrested for "operating" it without a license.

Edmund Wilson himself was like an extraordinary mental
automobile, rambling ahead at great speed, kicking up a considerable amount of dust, and stopping temporarily for an
erotic interlude. Elinor soon learned that intimacy with Wilson was a distant thing. "Bunny is funny," she told Mama
[November 3, 1922] (B), "I can't tell you what he is ever
thinking. . . ." His mother had been isolated by deafness, and
his father was removed by forbidding respectability. Wilson
had learned to fear and distrust closeness: lasting affection

seemed to have the seal of propriety and that was enough to
revolt him. Love was for him a covert operation involving
dance-hall girls. Somehow his daytime affections never quite
managed to become nighttime love. He felt unequal to the
transition from respect to love. So did Edna Vincent Millay,
with whom he had a disastrous affair.

Elinor fared far better. Not even the slightest erotic
flutter prefaced their friendship, which was chaste and cerebral. To some men Elinor managed to put on the air of sullied
virginity, and yet there was far more to mesmerize Edmund
Wilson about her than her essentially feminine and forbidding
air. Her talent as a poet, which he classified as that of a "brilliant amateur" when they first met, surpassed his. As a critic,
however, Elinor was decisively outclassed. And Wilson was
not uncritical of her work: he was one of the few to survive
this breach of her etiquette. There was mutual admiration at
work. His was a studied, rehearsed, sometimes ornate, and
oftentimes boisterous admiration. In inventive ways he never
ceased to give her attention: he dispatched parodies of her
poems, wrote the most outrageous anonymous letters of
praise, and plotted florid practical jokes—which is probably
the major reason for his lasting status as a friend. He admired
her scholarship and her love of the esoteric, her ability to show
interest in the oddest things, and her fascination with witchcraft. And his admiration assumed a more useful form. As
editor of *Vanity Fair* he introduced Elinor's poems to its pages,
and Elinor to its offices. Her poem "Love Song" was published in the August 1922 issue, and over the following eighteen months she continued to contribute to its pages.

No one, however, was more useful to Elinor than Bill
Benét. He had tried to make himself indispensable to her
simply by depending on her, even before she got to New
York. While Elinor's idea of lovemaking through the post had
altered a great deal in thirteen years, Bill's remained strikingly
consistent. His letters are a staple crop of harvested self-deprecation, resolutions, and ripe declarations of love. He recorded
his unsifted emotions. When he attempted self-analysis, he
contradicted himself; when he tried understanding, he
managed only to get confused. As 1922 progressed so did the
amount of ink he used on each letter. He wrote to Elinor of

her letters: "they are so lovely they make me miss you *far*
worse than any toothache." When the business nature of their
early letters was stripped away, a core of inarticulate emotion-
alism became visible. He was more feminine than Elinor in
this respect. Unlike Horace, he allowed Elinor to take the lead
in their courtship. She was less uninhibited. Certainly she was
more articulate, if equally impractical. And she *appeared* more
confident; she had to be, for as in her romance with Horace,
there were a great many obstacles and people to be overcome.

One of the major impediments Elinor easily dismissed—
she ignored the inconvenient fact that she was still Mrs. Horace Wylie. Bill, for his part, could not brush aside his own
mother's evident dislike for Elinor. He tried to overcome this
by reading her extracts from Elinor's letters, planting poems
under her nose, and by bringing Elinor herself out to Overhill
Road in Scarsdale. Bill's mother and sister both tried to like
Elinor, but they saw in her the usurper of their position as
custodians of Bill's three children. Bill calmly believed that his
mother's opposition could be overcome simply with time. His
father was more adamant; his dislike for Elinor was intense.
He pointed out that she had "no rudder but her own will and
desire," and said he could ignore her well-advertised past,
"had she repented." His reading of Elinor seemed to be accurate, and it was made less flattering by his warm memories of
Teresa.

Elinor's decision to "repent" took an exceedingly unattractive form. Every time she recalled to Mrs. Benét her miscarriages and still-born children, tears flowed and sobs were
heard all over the house. The fact that Elinor referred to each
dead child by special and new names, while rarely mentioning
the one who survived, lent these scenes an air of melodrama.
She managed to get round Mrs. Benét, leaving her very sympathetic and forgiving. Stephen Vincent Benét wrote to his
fiancée, Rosemary Carr:

Mother had lunch with Elinor today followed by an hour or so of
hysterics on Elinor's part. It must have been pretty ghastly from
Mother's description—apparently she poured out the whole story of
her life, interjecting "But of course, you don't believe me—you
think I'm ruining Bill—a hard, crafty designing woman" from time

to time, together with floods of tears. This sounds like a heartless description but I discussed the whole thing with Laura coming back on the train last night, a little with Bill, after lunch, and a great deal with Mother this evening and must laugh or frazzle myself to pieces about it. However it made Mother feel very sorry indeed for E.— which may help things a bit. Not that she wasn't before—but she told her about her children—oh the whole things too frightful and I won't bother you about it. She told her that her Mother, Mrs. Hoyt wishes her to be celibate for the rest of her life—which moves me to laughter akin to weeping. Her first husband seems to have been entirely crazy, at least he used to call her pet names such as "bitch". . . .* (Y)

Elinor was nothing if not a master of tactics. She used Bill's family in precisely the same way as she had used Horace's before their affair became public. The opposition was very exciting and it always played a vital role in her romances. She saw it as the key to Bill; indeed, the family dislike of her made him more attractive. He was essentially a family man and if she could win over his family she might cement their relationship. Bill's own plan of making himself indispensable had worked; Elinor began to believe that she could not live without him.

The fear of celibacy certainly did not force Elinor into Bill's arms. When her sister Nancy broke off a five-month engagement the day before the wedding, on May 15, 1923, it was Elinor who prompted the decision with one very simple question: "Why get married if you don't want to?" Then, when Nancy sighed with relief, Elinor "gave me an oblique look and said, 'But people can't be *celibate*!' " Elinor needed men, not for sex alone but as a means of satisfying her myth of romance. Love, physical love, played a very small part in her desire to marry, though it was an urge apparent enough to prompt an elaborate denial. Six years after the scenes with Mrs. Benét, she wrote to Bill from Edith Olivier's house in

---

*When Rosemary Carr Benét finally met Elinor, she wrote about her to Bill, as Bill, in turn, relayed to Elinor: "She reminds me so curiously of someone I adored all my little girl days but who grew up to be quite different . . . leaving me a disappointed feeling that she had vanished. Mrs. Wylie is exactly what she should have been like. . . . I *did* like her so much." The feeling was mutual.

England (September 14, 1928) (Y), "I certainly don't Think you very sensual—we are neither of us so. We are affectionate & fairly demonstrative, but like all artists slightly aloof as to spirit. 'The ghost that never is, & never will be however[?] by me' applies to both of us, as it doubtless applies to Vincent [Edna St. Vincent Millay], Padraic [Colum], or any other actual poet, or even Thornton [Wilder] if he ever dared to worry. . . ." Bill was obsessed by Elinor; Elinor never came close to returning the compliment. She looked on the idea of their marriage as a social necessity, and another escape from the past.

Everything about their romantic involvement was much easier than Elinor's affair had been with Horace: she avoided secrecy, ignored her husband's feelings, and made it obvious that Bill was her intended fiancé. Everyone believed that they would, eventually, marry; but it was not until the late summer of 1922 that a formal proposal was made. Elinor had not even bothered to take the most tentative steps toward divorce from Horace when she accepted. And the decision was kept secret for a very long time. Mama's response was more courteous than elated: "If you and Elinor are satisfied," she wrote to Bill (August 23, 1922) (Y), "I don't see why I should feel otherwise—I trust you will be very happy together. As you say she is remarkably gifted. And you are fitted to give her companionship in more ways than one—She has always had a will to enjoy life."

The Benéts were less courteous than Mama. Mrs. Benét never really warmed to Elinor; she was more tolerant of her than anything else. After they married, she sighed to her daughter that Bill had become "supernumerary to that woman." Other people shared her opinion, and even when Bill himself began to realize that his mother was correct, he did not mind. His obsession with Elinor would far outlast his marriage to her.*

*His two subsequent wives were made to live in her shadow. Her photographs cluttered his study and living room. At a dinner to celebrate his forthcoming marriage to Marjorie Flack, Bill rose to answer the toasts by praising Elinor. After his death, a vast amount of Elinor memorabilia—everything from paperweights to underwear—was discovered.

While Benét opposition helped to speed along their affection, separation seemed to help even more. Elinor left New York for the summer of 1922 out of the best possible motive: to get some work done. She readily accepted an invitation to the MacDowell Colony to work on the novel she had begun earlier in the year. In 1920 Laura Benét had been to the Colony, and the summer of 1921 Bill himself had gone; both returned full of praise for the place. Elinor left New York for Peterborough, New Hampshire, in July.

Elinor found the MacDowell Colony somewhat obscured by a welter of creative activity surrounded by airless torpidity. Situated in the foothills of a minor mountain range which only served to restrain the movement of air, the colonists were treated to prospects of unbroken land which had been tampered with to make room for studios and altered only by sprouts of young saplings. There were some refuges of shade and no escape from the isolation.

The MacDowell Colony had been founded in 1896, when the composer Edward MacDowell and his wife Marion Nevins were looking for a country home to get them away from New York and to help MacDowell work. They bought a tract of land in Peterborough, New Hampshire, a house— Hillcrest—to which they added a music room, and built a primitive work room in the grounds which he called a studio. During the last year of his life, 1908, he founded the Edward MacDowell Memorial Association, which incorporated the New Hampshire property and $30,000 to establish a living tribute to his work. The desire set a bad precedent, since it fired a great many wealthy people with the idea that in death they might be vicariously credited with creativity.

When MacDowell died at the age of forty-six, he left behind an energetic widow who turned his plans into reality. Her real work began with his death. For thirty-nine years she was director of the Association. Trained as a pianist, she rarely stopped her work at the keyboard in order to raise money for the Colony. She was only creative when performing or raising money. Her energy was astonishing and her longevity amazing. She grew in importance yearly and lived three months short of a century.

On an expanded Bayreuth principle, the MacDowell Col-

ony threw open its doors to eager writers, composers, and
artists for four months in the summer. Colonists were there by
invitation only. "The qualification for admission to the Colony
is talent," stated the directors. "A prospective colonist must
either have some fine achievement to his credit, or be possessed of a talent for which two recognized artists in his field
can vouch." By the twenties MacDowell Colony invitations
were as hallowed in reality as Mrs. MacDowell believed them
to be in spirit.

The colonists were billeted, unhappily for some, according to gender. From these clean but somewhat bleak accom-
modations the artists fanned out to their assigned studios,
designated for daylight use only: "One may not use one's
studio after six," Elinor wrote to Horace (July 20 [1922]) (B),
"'tis said for fear of fire, but methinks 'tis a far other variety
of fire than our ancestor Prometheus ravished with such difficulty . . . that causes this rule to be imposed upon the company
of excellent old maids and worthy bachelors to be found
within our walls halls and screened porches."

The heat was annoying and the uncompromising simplicity of the place somewhat tedious. "Nevertheless for actual
hard grind, it is a good idea," Elinor continued, "for from
breakfast to supper your whole day is undisturbed save by a
lunch-basket . . . the fare is plain but excellent. . . ." Elinor's
self-imposed "hard grind" was a thousand words a day on her
novel, which she referred to as "Gerald," after the hero Gerald Poynyard (it became *Jennifer Lorn*). When not actually
writing, she was reading an extraordinary mixture of sources:
the encyclopedia, *Candide,* Lytton Strachey, William Hickey,
Hajji Baba, and *Vathek.* Elinor's form of research was closer
to cramming than anything else. She was priming herself,
preparing her brief. Two years later, when she was working
on another historical novel, *The Venetian Glass Nephew,* Margaret Widdemer saw her at work and concluded that it was work
that could only be done by someone with the mind of a lawyer.
She sat a long table with about two-thirds of the *Encyclopaedia
Britannica* spilled out in front of her, harvesting facts. She kept
the volumes out of the library for a long time—too long for
some colonists. Once when the poet Virginia Moore extracted
Volume T from her, Elinor made a modest but surprising

request: "she begged me not to tell anyone she'd had it; someone might think she got her novel out of it. I said I wouldn't. But she kept repeating the request in a rising voice. I had never seen anyone 'take on' so much over so little. . . ." The request was made even more absurd by the fact that everyone knew she had the volume. But her tantrum was probably the result of fatigue. Elinor drove herself very hard at the MacDowell Colony. During the summer of 1922 she reported to Bill with clinical accuracy every detail of her throbbing headaches and exhausted eyes. The heat, added to an unrelenting work régime, which she later compared to the progress of a steamer, clearly overtaxed her. Her blood pressure was never permitted to subside and her approach to the medical advice she sought became more and more cavalier. Doctors urged equanimity; her activities encouraged the exact opposite.

Horace thought the whole idea of the Colony absurd. Bill heartily endorsed anything that helped one work. Elinor, for her part, shared both points of view. The pious atmosphere at MacDowell was slightly ridiculous, and she was able to concentrate almost anywhere. There were marvelously petty intrigues to keep her going, stirred up by Mrs. MacDowell's intricate network of old maids. As there was supposed to be no talking between colonists during the working day, anyone seen entering someone else's studio was immediately suspected of ulterior motives. The evenings' events were far from rollicking. After supper, as Elinor related for Horace's benefit, "one walks to the village with the Colums* for exercise, or sits and watches Mr. [E. A.] Robinson and a horrid old composer

*Mary Maguire Colum (188?–1957) educated in Holland and Ireland, came to America in 1914 with her husband. Bill Benét termed her "the best woman critic in America," equal to Rebecca West in England. She contributed to most major periodicals. From 1934 to 1940 she began and edited the "Life and Literature" department of *Forum,* and was an ardent supporter of Irish writing all of her life. Her autobiography is *Life and the Dream* (1947). Padraic Colum, (1881–1971) indefatigable poet, playwright, and short story compiler, was also born in Ireland. In the early part of the century he was at the center of the Celtic revival and friends with Yeats, Synge, and Lady Gregory. He was famous for reading his own verse, and for his friendships.

called Mr. [Arthur] Nevin and a horrider young composer
called [Louis] Grunberg and the delightful Italian factotum
Emile play pool until sleep descends definitely upon one's
eyelids. . . ."

The summer at MacDowell Colony shifted the concentration from Elinor the woman to Elinor the writer—an alteration she herself had been working very hard to achieve. She published an enormous amount of work in the first half of 1922. In fact, most of the poems that make up *Black Armour* (1923) were published in periodicals beforehand. Like her headaches, her poetry offers an index to her feelings. While the letters reveal a certain degree of childlike absurdity, since she was playing up to Bill and indulging in a degree of arrogance, her poems uncover a darker, almost fatalistic submission. There she descended into the emotions that in life she tried so hard to hide, and even then she was not direct. She abstracted her emotions, moving from reality to myth, and so giving them dignity. Her imagery reversed night and day. She turned standard symbolism around, equating daylight with fantasy and night with harsh reality. Truth unfolded in blackness, while fantasy thrived in full light. This extraordinary reversal had its root in nothing more complicated than her chronic fear of her own feelings. The poem "Full Moon" (published in *The New Republic* June 28, 1922) displayed the paradox she would never let go:

> My bands of silk and miniver
> Momently grew heavier;
> The black gauze was beggarly thin;
> The ermine muffled mouth and chin;
> I could not suck the moonlight in. . . .
>
> Mortality I could not tear
> From my ribs, to leave them bare
> Ivory in silver air.
>
> There I walked, and there I raged;
> The spiritual savage caged
> Within my skeleton, raged afresh
> To feel, behind carnal mesh,
> The clean bones crying in the flesh.

She saw life as an ordeal of torture, chronic but necessary. The stronger this torture made one, the more harshly it twisted one's surface, giving further proof of pain and struggle. That gave her the excuse to lie. That gave her a reason to play to an audience—she had to react against the hardness of life. This process, outlined so well in her verse, reached its finest expression later in *The Venetian Glass Nephew;* but a tentative, and more personal, reading of it came in her "Epitaph" (published in *The New Republic,* May 24, 1922):

> For this she starred her eyes with salt
> And scooped her temples thin,
> Until her face shone pure of fault
> From the forehead to the chin.
>
> In the coldest crucibles of pain
> Her shrinking flesh was fired
> And smoothed into a finer grain
> To make it more desired.
>
> Pain left her lips more clear than glass;
> It coloured and cooled her hand.
> She lay in a field of scented grass
> Yielded as pasture land.
>
> For this her loveliness was curved
> And carved as silver is:
> For this she was brave: but she deserved
> A better grave than this.

Elinor's poetic documentation of her enthusiastic pre-matrimonial throes with Bill is equaled, curiously enough, only by Horace. Elinor wrote to Horace asking for dates and facts about the year 1772 in Paris and London. He fired back five spirited pages by return of post (July 23). He was living in Washington, indecorously in R Street rooms, and conducting his own romantic campaign in pursuit of the woman who eventually became the third Mrs. Horace Wylie, Eleanor Taylor Marsh. They dined in the extravagant splendor of the Willard Hotel, which Horace could ill afford, and rode around in taxis with Horace complimenting Eleanor Marsh on her beauty. There was no hint of complaint about Elinor in anything Horace said; he was simply moving on. It was all

wonderfully sophisticated. His confidence, unlike Bill's,
matched his assured demeanor. And his silence was commend-
able. He closed his summary of the year 1772 to Elinor by
saying [July 23, 1922] (Y): "I have no personal news. 'Happy
are the people without a history.' "

Elinor toyed with the idea of leaving New York for the
winter; she thought, without taking any legal advice, that such
a move would facilitate the divorce. Bill promised to write to
her every day if she were to flee to Charleston as she threatened; more important, he offered to consult lawyers to "Get
info." "When I get the full dope on R[hode] I[sland] I will
write fully," he promised [July 1922] (Y). "Nev[ada] seems
the only watertight legal-document way, and one could stay at
Tahoe. . . . But the season and the distance and the loneliness,
for you, it does not look so good to me. France . . . would not
demand the other party, merely someone to act for him. The
only advantage [of] the R.I. business is not having to reside,
as the decree isn't absolute until six months have elapsed."
When he returned from his summer holiday at Amagansett,
Bill proudly added [September 1922] (Y), he finally had "the
dope on RI. Only impediment, it costs $500. . . ." On Septem-
ber 18 Elinor filed for divorce in the state of Rhode Island.
All attempts to speed up the proceedings by leaving New
York got her no further than the suburbs.

Elinor celebrated her first step to freedom by motoring
out to New Canaan, Connecticut, with Burton and Hazel
Rascoe* to dine with a friend's mother. Burton Rascoe as
literary editor of the *New York Tribune* prided himself on his

*Arthur Burton Rascoe (1892–1957), journalist, was born in Kentucky. He
was trained by the newspaper in Shawnee, Oklahoma, and discharged from
the Chicago *Herald Tribune* in 1920 after an irreverent allusion to Mary
Baker Eddy—thus he possessed all the credentials required to become the
literary editor of the *New York Tribune.* In such a capacity he wrote a column
called "The Daybook of a New Yorker" which appeared weekly and was
syndicated in over 400 newspapers. For six years (1922–1928) the "Daybook" was a "causerie of literary gossip and vague philosophy," as Rascoe
himself described it. Mercifully, there was more gossip than philosophy. He
later held such posts as editor of *The Bookman* after John Farrar left. For
many years he was on the editorial board of the Literary Guild, literary
editor of *Esquire* for one year, and critic for *Newsweek.* In 1913 he married
Hazel Luke from Chicago. He is an autobiographer of forgettable talent.

talent for recognizing new writers, and writers prized him for his florid declarations of praise. He was quick to take up Elinor, not as a poet but as a critic, and then as quickly regretted it. He sent her Herbert Gorman's book *The Barcarole of James Smith and Other Poems* for review; by the first week in September she sent him her review, with a covering letter saying: "If this is too rotten, don't use it; I shan't mind a bit, for as it is my first review I know it is a compact of fault and stupidity." Rascoe agreed with Elinor and never printed it; Bill did, however, in the *Literary Review* (December 16, 1922). Rascoe made up for this unwelcome opinion by quickly passing on to Elinor's ability as a poet. On the same day they went to Connecticut he published in his column the judgment: "Elinor is, I think, one of the three or four leading woman poets in English." By the summer of 1924 he allowed Emily Dickinson, Sara Teasdale, and Edna Millay to lead his revised version. (Three months after Elinor's death, he revised his revised list and calmly rated her talents equal to genius.)

Elinor looked on Rascoe as little more than a very useful publicist. For that office alone she granted him cool cordiality. He slipped in and out of her life easily when the need arose, and Rascoe himself set out to be used. He was a representative member of the band of people who scurried about New York determined to make themselves important by appearing so. He was also one of the many men in her short career who were used and then discarded. Rascoe—like Christopher Morley before him and Carl Van Doren and Carl Van Vechten after him—was drawn to Elinor. When her adolescent timidity gave way to confidence, these men still waited on her. First they thought they were protecting her, then they learned she needed no protection. Yet they still formed a cohort around her. They were vulnerable to her femininity; they were mesmerized by her talent; and they were flattered by her acquaintance. She never failed to overlook the value of these relationships, while deliberately failing to make them more important. Elinor was not an intimate of any group. Her best friends often went for months without seeing her or getting a letter from her. Her vanity sheltered her from intimacy with people, and her health conveniently disposed of any social demands. She was liked, and she was feared. Her unpredictability was exceedingly tiresome while increasing her appeal. She always protected herself.

Waiting for the divorce demanded some more active form of protection, however. Bill's visits and his flood of confessions were becoming rather tedious. He would often call on her before he went home to Scarsdale, and generally there were minor scenes which Bill calmly reinterpreted as expressions of their heroic nature.* Elinor was far less convinced. She put no attractive reading on episodes that were very unattractive. Bill's assertions that everything would improve once they married failed to persuade her; she had heard that excuse too often. She thought her divorce would be made absolute by June, and the idea of Bill's unrefined declarations until then sent a slight shudder through her. She hatched the idea of leaving New York. She wrote to her friend Eunice Tietjens†— conveniently posted at *Poetry* in Chicago: "Listen—do you suppose I could get a small job in Chicago after January 1st? On Poetry pays nothing of course —but some little job that did—about $25.00 a week. . . . I *can't* stand the strain here of six months waiting to make it [divorce] absolute. It's simply murdering me . . . by inches. So, from January till June, I'd like to emigrate. What do you think?"

The same day as she was charting her itinerary, she wrote to Horace in mauve ink (B):

*His analysis is worth quoting: "It is like putting on armour we must wear against the world. And, through the demanding day, we take a little of that armour (strange figure!) into our souls—the iron enters, in other words. And sometimes when we first meet the iron is still there because any such effort of will is hard to relax at once in proportion as it is a great effort. And when we have only several hours together it takes us nearly that time, sometimes, to wholly relax that effort & truly show each other our hearts —and then we must part." [Fall 1922] (Y)

†Eunice Strong Tietjens (née Hammond) (1884–1944), poet and novelist. Born in Chicago, married twice, she started her career on the Chicago *Daily News* as a war correspondent in France. Later she joined Harriet Monroe's *Poetry* and did not leave for twenty-five years. An inveterate traveler, she is more known for her kindness to other writers than her own work (much like Harriet Monroe). Her excellent autobiography, *The World at My Shoulder,* was published in 1938.

You are angry with me, nor do I blame you. If you can ever be friends, you are the dearest friend in the world to me. I am the most lost creature imaginable without your friendship. If tonight we could be back in Winchester, what would I not give, almost to my soul? I mean we were once in Winchester on Halloween.

. . . I have never known anyone so generous, so kind, so warm hearted, and so comforting as you. I make this statement for fear you did not know I held this opinion. You may say you do not believe me, but you will. . . .

She added to this astonishing confession a clipping of her poem "Peregrine's Sunday Song," saying, "This is me, not you."*

Elinor's actions when compared to what she believed are frequently mysterious. She left Horace, yet with an acutely selective memory wished she were still with him. It was her way of counteracting the severity of Bill's suit, and was not a compliment to either man. Other members of her family did not suffer from such selective memories. Connie was, as ever, anxious to fall back on convention. She prized respectability like some new form of virginity. That for Elinor was singularly annoying. She calmly told Elinor that she had gone too far this time. But such accusations had ceased to have any effect on Elinor. She was too busy to care.

The only thing that seemed to affect her was the amount of work she was doing. "I have been working tremendously hard," she typed to Mama, who was in London with Nancy [November 3, 1922] (B),

and have not yet finished my novel, though I have done more than I thought would serve to complete it, but the characters are now in obstinately conversational mood, and I cannot stop them. As it will not now appear before spring [she was optimistically off by six months], it doesn't matter, only I shall be very happy upon the day that it is done. I have written a lot more poetry, and a short story

*The most telling.lines are Peregrine's own and the final ones of the poem: "The noose draws tighter;/ This is the end;/I'm a good fighter,/But a bad friend:/I've played the traitor/Over and over;/I'm a good hater,/But a bad lover." It was third poem she published in *Vanity Fair* and later included in *Black Armour* under the simplified title "Peregrine." Her two previous poems in *Vanity Fair* were "Bartholozzi Prints" (March 1922) and "Love Song" (August 1922).

Such a routine had the predictable ill-effects: her eyes "suddenly went back on me, and from working six hours a day I was all at once able to work no more than half an hour without contracting a most terrific headache," as she wrote to Mama (November 21) (B). She claimed it was the after effects of a cold, and attributed her cold to a dose of tonsillitis. "As soon as I begin to write or read—whee, it's off in either one eye or the other like a demon wood-pecker. I have almost gone crazy, but I am now going to give them a rest, and I shall never be a novelist once this book is published. It is all done, except for going over and revising, but it nearly did my eyes in forever; poetry for them, evidently, is to be the order of the day. . . ." She did, however, manage to escape the pain, "like a horse kicking at my forehead," long enough to go to the theater with Edmund Wilson to see Barrymore bestow everything "except nobility" on the part of Hamlet.

The first draft of "Gerald" had taken her less than a year to complete; the revisions would take approximately as long, with more "channel steamer" work at Peterborough. To celebrate her achievement she decided to have her Christmas party early. She bought a silver tree and decorated it with one solitary red apple. Around it she clustered small gifts bought at Woolworth's. On December 23 friends were invited to call after eight thirty—among them Steve and Rosemary Benét, Padraic and Mary Colum, and Bill. She gave Bill a small tin trumpet and he gave her, no less appropriately, Medwin's *Life of Shelley* (1847). They all drank weak toddies made from whiskey Leonora Speyer gave her—"So no one went blind," Elinor told Mama five days later (B). On Christmas Eve she went to midnight mass and fell asleep during the sermon. The following day she took the 9:30 train out to Scarsdale, "plunging into a mass of tissue paper and ribbon," and confronting a daunting collection of Benéts. She returned to New York that same evening in time to catch the remnants of John Dos Passos's own Christmas party: cold turkey and white wine. It was a family-less Christmas, and it was precisely a year since Bill told his mother "exactly how things stood," as he had written to Elinor a year before (Christmas Day [1921]) (Y), "that we hoped for a divorce next spring & to marry next fall. . . ." By the New Year of 1923, he was begging Elinor: "Do be my wife soon, soon, soon. . . ."

§ *ii* *"I don't want to be just a literary woman."*

The proposed desertion of New York while Elinor joined the ranks of Clare Boothe Luce's women got her no further west than West 44th Street. She took over Edmund Wilson's position as literary editor on *Vanity Fair: A Monthly Magazine of the Stage, Society, Sports, Fashions and the Fine Arts.* It had been two years since she threatened to take a job; at the age of thirty-seven, she was subject to her first office work. On January 8, 1923, she assumed her position; her pay was $30 a week.

The hierarchy at 19 West 44th Street began with Frank Crowninshield—"the great Crownie"—who was editor. He was forty-two when the first issue of *Vanity Fair* came out in 1914. A cautious man, he was teetotal and attributed untold horrors to the curse of tobacco. He hated fountain pens and detested the radio. He was a ruthless golfer. But as an editor, his taste outstripped his caution. His eyes were firmly set across the ocean: he spotted writers like Gertrude Stein, P. G. Wodehouse, Noel Coward, Aldous Huxley, Colette, and others before they came into clear view. Condé Nast once said of him, "Crownie discovers people before they discover themselves." He was no less adventurous about painters and paintings. (Music completely escaped him.) He was one of the organizers of the Armory Show and introduced Augustus John to New York. On home shores his offices were frequented by people like Dorothy Parker (before she changed her name), Robert Benchley, Edmund Wilson, Robert Sherwood, John Peale Bishop, Edna St. Vincent Millay, and other Algonquin refugees. He had remarkable editorial dexterity; he could get the most unlikely people to write about even more unlikely subjects, and with success. His magazine had a sophistication and a gloss that was uniquely attributed to him.

Tall, with silvering hair at the temples, impeccably turned out, he strode through the offices in a walk that has been described as "at once strutting and mincing, with the upper part of his body bent forward." He had the annoying habit of grasping one's elbow in conversation and the winning quality of being totally unpredictable. "I am not as genial as I seem," he confessed once. He smelled his mail before opening it in order to scent the sender. He could be alarmingly generous and equally mean. His pranks had the same rehearsed qualities as a bow-tie. He springs out of memoirs in a very unspontaneous manner. He was distant, individual, and perhaps the last surviving example of that breed known as "a gentleman."

Vanity Fair suited Elinor. It had a rather outspoken elegance, limbered with social acceptability, and frequent brushes with the intellectual. It plunged her, less radically than any other paper, into the harsh reality of journalism and the heady atmosphere of self-advertisement. It was exciting, and exhausting: two qualities her health could have done without. At one moment she was writing Horace [April 1923] (B), "I have a nice easy job; three days a week, ten dollars a day. All the Office Force is amiable and frivolous, so I like it." Another moment she was complaining: "But I have had a touch of flu myself, and my bp [blood pressure] is the sweet sum of 230 which any gallant man would admit was about 110 too much. I am dog-tired. . . ." All of which, she added, in the best Benét style, could be remedied by a "coupla days off" in Washington, near Horace—an extraordinary prescription for the early days of a divorce action.

But not all her attention was focused on the fashionable precincts of *Vanity Fair,* especially during the first month of her employment. On January 20 her third review appeared: "Mr. Eliot's Slug-horn." Bill asked her, his captive poet, to review Eliot's *The Waste Land,* that great watermark that divided the modern from the archaic. Elinor's position was deftly sheltered—her review came close to being unintelligible. Yet she was concerned that any word she might say would be misread. The body of Eliot criticism was already massive even before she added her few words. The first draft of her review, titled "Star Among the Ash-Cans," was more direct than her published review:

The extraordinary quality of criticism already levelled at . . . The Waste Land, transforms any word of praise into a word of defense. . . . We cannot gracefully bestow a wreath before we have repelled a rotten egg. . . . Therefore the present review must be a quarrel rather than an appreciation. . . . It must be clear to any intelligent person that an unread poem is difficult of assimilation by even a highly superior mind.

As a critic she was either extremely shrewd or too frightened to offer anything but a subjective response to the poem. The only direct comment she made centered on emotions: "this poem trembles and stammers on the very extremity of emotion. . . ." She realized that any response to it would betray one's age. The old would be annoyed by its obscurity; the young would revel in its intellectual pessimism. Elinor's standpoint made her both an enemy and an ally. The final draft of her review was neither quarrel nor appreciation. It attempted to scatter the critics and praise the poet. It was, as she intended it not to be, a defense. Yet this was Elinor's favorite line of attack:

I think Mr. Eliot conceived "The Waste Land" out of an extremity of tragic emotion and expressed it in his own voice and the voices of other unhappy men not carefully and elaborately trained in close harmony, but coming as a confused and frightening and beautiful murmur out of the bowels of the earth. . . . If it were merely a piece of virtuosity it would remain astonishing. . . . But it is far more than this; it is infused with spirit and passion and despair. . . . That he expresses the emotion of an intellectual is perfectly true, but of the intensity of that emotion there is, to my mind, no question, nor do I recognize any reason for such a question.

Elinor was not a good critic; she was a much better fiancée. Bill was ill in bed. From Scarsdale he gave energetic reports of his cough and a cold that apparently left him appetite enough to eat huge meals. He also had sufficient energy to read Great Expectations, some P. G. Wodehouse and Jane Austen, to write unconscionably long letters, and to dream of Elinor, which entailed thinking of Horace. "I am glad H[orace] has left W[ashington]," he wrote to Elinor from his bed (February 1, 1923) (Y).

It is better for him, better for you—if you do pay a visit—better all
around. I have thought & thought about H. enough first & last to
satisfy the most exacting moralist, and arrive always at the conclusion
that, first & last, he has had as much happiness as any of us & no more
sorrow. . . . I regard your attitude toward him throughout as noble,
chivalrous & affectionate. . . . He is a mixed personality. We are all
mixtures. I have considerable weaknesses, he has not. He has failings
I haven't.

Bill's illness provoked new and stronger symptoms of
self-depreciation. Between hot-water bottles and syrups, he
wrapped himself in worry. He labeled himself Elinor's "very
imperfect man." Elinor herself wrote to Mama (February 9)
(B): "Bill is still alive, but nacred, I imagine, with Scarsdale
scum. I have to go out & call on him tomorrow, with soup &
flannel petticoats, [indec.]." Her visit to him the Sunday before was nothing short of disaster. Instead of cold remedies,
she took proofs of *Black Armour* (which she dedicated to Bill),
and stories about Amy Loveman's* insults to her. Both patient
and visitor were on edge, Bill from excitement and Elinor
from exhaustion. She was overwrought after "Amy's on-
slaught," as Bill put it the next day. Elinor set out to read a
personal slight in every action. Bill's mother and Laura were
anxious to leave her alone with Bill, and Elinor saw this act
of sensitive kindness as deliberate avoidance. She thought

*Bill's assistant on the *Literary Review*. When it was transformed into the
Saturday Review on August 2, 1924, she became co-assistant editor with Bill.
She worked up to the day she died in 1955. After Bill's death she became
Poetry Editor. She was indefatigable, efficient, and painstakingly straight-
forward. She ruled over the men on the staff—Dr. Henry Canby, Christopher Morley and Bill—with affection and sternness. They were answerable
to her, somehow, if they either neglected lunch or paid too much attention
to it. She was the strength behind the scenes, as well as an able critic. She
was seventy-five when she died.

The few actual references to her in Bill's letters to Elinor were always
extremely complimentary—complimentary because she complimented Elinor: she admired Elinor's work enormously. In organizing Elinor's letters
before they eventually went to Yale, Bill clearly combed the pages of his
own letters (which Elinor had left to him) for anything that might give
offense. The mention of "Amy" that was deleted from his letter of February
4, 1923, came in subsequent letters, less well checked. What the insult might
have been is not known.

Mrs. Benét's neuralgia purely imaginary and an attempt to offend her. She disregarded the fact that they had made up the fire and brewed her favorite tea for her before they withdrew. Anything they did had the worst possible interpretation placed on it. She gathered up her proofs and stormed out of the house, leaving Bill and the others absolutely mystified. After she left, Bill wrote to her [February 4] (Y), "I feel that I failed you today without or rather against the uttermost feeling in the opposite direction. I too am inarticulate & dumb when I feel most." By the next day, after reading Elinor's letter, his apology had turned to anger. "Have you a passion for martyrdom?" he asked [February 5] (Y). "Better by the exercise of Kindness where you think I would wish you kind (even if you considered it a stooping of your pride) to seek that martyrdom, to make that sacrifice, than in dismissing me to a safety from the exigence that love is, which both would despise."

Bill's anger took her by surprise. It was the first time he had accused her of anything; he was far too accustomed to take all blame on himself. Elinor quickly backed down, retreating to a more tender mood. She continued to arrange for letters from Bill's friends, this batch signed, to cheer him up. She sent little notes of affection which served to make him uncertain about her.

Such uncertainty stemmed ultimately from Elinor's own ambivalence about sex. Bill had made some blundering attempts to get her into bed. She withdrew, angry. She was trapped by the extraordinary cross-current between her appearance and her belief. Frank Crowninshield saw it on a different level. Sixteen years after her death he remembered, "She liked to pretend that she was Bohemian, but the sham was at all times apparent, for she was too delicately bred to enact the role with anything like assurance or success." It was the same with love: as long as an affair could be conducted chastely on paper, and somewhat less chastely in gesture, she teetered on the brink of the erotic. When it dissolved into actual activity, she hastily retreated to conventionality. Bill saw her desire for propriety much as he had viewed Teresa's need for a convent; he also saw it not so much as a challenge to his impulses as an opportunity for his generosity. "And if you felt a need for something in the

Church so strong that you wanted to be in it," he wrote to
Elinor [February ?, 1923] (Y),

I would give up *gladly,* & more than gladly, any physical happiness
with you for a time—till we were actually in their eyes, married.
... You will never, never, *never* be happy really until you have your
love always with you, admittedly, in the sight of all, with children
you can freely call your own & think of as your own, &, even beyond
this . . . & beyond me—a certainty of the rightness of everything.
. . . It is what you are seeking when you turn to the Church . . . don't
you see that all you are wanting is a *home?*

While Bill was in bed, thinking about bed and Elinor's
constraining ideas, Elinor was up to high jinks at *Vanity Fair.*
Crownie would produce African masks and make the secretaries wear them. He was forever bringing in paintings, direct
from France, that he wanted to reproduce in the magazine. Or
he would lead a reenactment of "The Rape of the Sabine
Women," dragging the secretaries over their typewriters. Elinor and Edmund Wilson would rattle on about ghosts, elves,
dwarfs, and goblins. Wilson even snaked out of a ticklish
problem with their help: when Elinor lent him her apartment
at Bank Street in 1926, he said poltergeists had broken her
parchment lampshade and not he. Or, in the words of Crowninshield (Y), she would "step all over Bunny." And there
were sustained pranks with Edna Millay in the office. One day
the poet Arthur Davison Ficke* went to meet "His Lordship"
(Crowninshield) at West 44th Street. Crowninshield addressed him with avuncular warmth and introduced him to the
"Dolly Sisters." Perched beside his desk were two females
with their backs to the light and faces hidden by "two absurd
paper fans that had eyeholes in them and that represented the
most dreadfully pretty of magazine-cover-girlie faces." They

---

*Arthur Davison Ficke (1883–1945), poet, born in Iowa and educated at
Harvard under Santayana and William James and classmates with F.D.
Roosevelt. Though he always preferred poetry, he acceded to his father's
wishes, trained as a lawyer, and during his first decade in practice he produced eight books of poems and two studies of Japanese art. In 1923 he
married his second wife, Gladys Brown, a painter. Conrad Aiken said his
verse was charming, but "shapeless and ungoverned." He was remarkably
handsome and suffered from uncertain health. He was a man of great charm,
humor, and intelligence.

sat there simpering and bowing in reply to all questions, clearly impeding the interview. Finally Ficke became annoyed and asked "His Lordship" to remove his harem. "Then the females took down their fans and howled at me. One was my very old and dear friend Edna St Vincent Millay, and the other was a dark-eyed stranger, Elinor Wylie." Then they all crowded into a taxi to drop Elinor down at University Place to nurse her headache. Ficke later remembered Elinor's most annoying habit was that she "would never look at *you* but always at her thumb-nail held within six inches of her eyes."

By the first week in February Elinor was going to the office every day, which she complained to her mother was "rather hard work, after all. But it is very amusing & quite instructive. . . ." She managed to find time to have her photo taken, in a coy Katherine Mansfield pose, with hat, and *Vanity Fair* reduced it to miniature proportions in the pages of the April issue. The newspapers, however, printed her picture before *Vanity Fair*. On March 26, 1923, her divorce finally came through from Rhode Island; six months remained before it was absolute. Three days later *The New York Times* and *New York American* ran the story; the *Herald Tribune* waited one more day before they printed their version. Describing Elinor as "Mrs. Elinor Hoyt Hichborn Wylie," the *Herald Tribune* reckoned that her announced engagement to William Rose Benét "opens another page of the romantic, tragic chronicle which has been Mrs. Wylie's life for the past sixteen years. . . ." "I don't mind for myself," Elinor wrote to Eunice Tietjens about three weeks later (April 16), "& it bothers Bill only as it can hurt me—but it has made much trouble between my mother & myself, of course. However, I hope it is over now for good," she added, referring to the publicity.

The only thing that was over was the rumor that she would marry Bill. The formal declaration brought conflicting opinions. John Peale Bishop wrote from Paris [spring, 1923] (Y): "I'm glad to hear that you and Bill have definitely decided to get married. . . . You will, I know, be calmer and hence other things don't somehow seem any longer to count so desperately." Edmund Wilson was less enthusiastic: "I was somewhat shocked by this [marriage plans] and remonstrated with her about it," he wrote in his diary. "It seemed to me that from a literary point of view he was so inferior to her that it made her marrying him inappropriate. . . . When I expressed my doubts about their union, she said with her harsh and callous laugh: 'Yes, it would be a pity that a first-rate poet should be turned into a second-rate poet by marrying a third-rate poet.' " Sinclair Lewis understood the whole sequence of events as a logical conclusion of Bill's affection for Henry. "He killed himself in Bill's apartment, and Bill felt that established a claim for him to die for Elinor." Elinor improved on Sinclair Lewis's analysis, telling Margaret Widdemer, "Bill thinks I'm everything he loved best in Henry and Teresa." Nancy Hoyt wrote candidly, "I liked him, but certainly I was a little bit astonished." Mama, for her part, was calmly resigned. And the Benéts trembled at the prospect of Bill's children leaving Scarsdale to live with their new stepmother. The children themselves did not know what to think; they liked Elinor because she gave them a lot of attention. She brought them presents, she told them stories, she copied Bill's habit of drawing pictures for them. She worked very hard at being liked.

Elinor's second book appeared on May 25, 1923. George Doran, on Bill's introduction, published *Black Armour* and Elinor was pleased that, this time, her publishers dressed it in a "snappy suit of clothes"—a silver and black dustcover over black boards.

The second book did not sweep the critics with surprise; they were armed with something more fierce: expectation. Yet the critical declension was approximately the same as it had been twenty months before. There was the same outright praise mixed with uncertainty. The critics again shielded themselves with nimble comparisons. They compared Elinor with Blake, Donne, Keats, and the American triumvirate of "Tears Eliot," Amy Lowell, and Edna Millay. Louis Untermeyer said that the very titles of the poems showed the author's keen reading of the Metaphysicals.

Amy Lowell, who was again on Bill's short list as a potential reviewer, was also at the top of Henry Canby's list. She refused. She was in the middle of her massive life of Keats and wanted no interruptions. Without publishing anything she managed to review the book, this time directly to Elinor. She wrote to her, in a very telling stroke, care of her previous publishers, in such terms of praise that *Nets to Catch the Wind* was damned (May 29, 1923): "It is appealing. . . . I repeat with very sincere words of my first reaction: 'My that girl can write!' . . . Your work gives me more pleasure than almost any that is written to-day." No one disagreed with that vague and general assessment.

The critics' qualifications seemed to rest only in the future. Edmund Wilson, writing in the April *Vanity Fair,* demurred that she was in danger of nursing the interesting rather than the beautiful: "Even when her poems are not suffused with beauty, they are alive with intelligence; at worse, she can charm us with her distinguished manner and fascinate us with her literary dexterity." Mark Van Doren, reviewing for *The Nation* (June), wrote, "There is every reason to suppose that she will achieve sophistication and fineness in her own right. Her readers at present are aware chiefly of her amazing liberty at rhyme, her scrupulousness as to detail, her perfect finish, her cold fire, her hard wit."

And they saw her as essentially divided. Archibald MacLeish, in the December *New Republic,* envisioned her mind as masculine and her method as exclusively feminine—a dexterity that embraced the "impossible clean beauty" of Donne. On top of this he predicted that her work would not evolve. "It is as definitely shaped in its own image as any poetry that has ever been written." Her distinction was already great and was likely to increase. Malcolm Cowley, writing in *The Dial* (June), also saw her as divided, not on the same level of sophistication that MacLeish claimed, but like some Robert Louis Stevenson scientist let loose on poetry. She was half conservative, half modern—"Mrs. Wylie, with her double personality, is half in the movement and half outside of it." Cowley, like Edmund Wilson, placed her alongside T. S. Eliot as the representative of the happy marriage of erudition and unexpected imagery, of intense emotion tied to a deep respect for form. It was a comparison Elinor warmed to, for that was the very same line she herself assumed regarding Eliot. But Cowley's praise dipped severely when he said that her poetry

was written only for magazines. Surprisingly, Elinor agreed,
writing to Eunice Tietjens (April 16) before Cowley himself
made the comment, that *Black Armour* "contains not one single unsold pome [sic, and not exactly accurate], so it has been
profitable already." Miss Tietjens, herself a late reviewer of
the book (in the February 1924 issue of *Poetry*), reread the title
and organization of the volume: "In it she has made for herself
a breastplate of courage, a helmet of almost ruthless self-
knowledge, gauntlets of her own sophistication, and a mock-
ing plume of her very sensitiveness, her happy taut nerves."
And Bill merely reread everything (Y): "The book, which is
dedicated to me, is full of poems personal to E.W. & W.R.B."

The critics could not fall back on surprise alone as they
had done with her first book. The second book duplicated the
previous brilliance, while still striding forward. The thirty-
nine poems dated from 1921 and 1922—years complicated by
Bill and her work on *Jennifer Lorn*. She managed to sustain her
unique "voice," thought Louis Untermeyer. The echoes from
her sources, despite Edmund Wilson pointing to clear reminis-
cences of Eliot and Chesterton, were much weaker than they
had been. She had grown, standing on the same spot. And the
polish of her work was still overwhelming, even for a second
book. Elizabeth Shepley Sargeant wrote that the "most conspicuous act of her life was to emerge, as a finished artist, with
no period of fumbling or apparent preparation." Her years of
waiting, of exile and isolation, had been turned to advantage
—the advantage of extreme confidence on paper which somehow never informed the other aspects of her life. It was as if
all her attention to sophistication went first to her work and
then to the denial of her emotions. She had merely concocted
another form of carapace to climb into, to make her less vulnerable. No one could explain how she managed such an
accomplishment; Elinor herself never even tried. Like the critics she merely recorded sensation and avoided explanation.

"I dread and execrate the prospect of going to Peterborough," Elinor wrote to Horace on exercise book paper
[June 4, 1923] (B), "I am having a grand time and that will
be simply work and really no rest at all." The early summer

in New York was unusually mild. Her health was rather better than normal, save for her eyes, which she confessed to Mama were badly overtired. Her final weeks at *Vanity Fair* were a chronicle of hard work. She wrote a play, *Mary's Husband; a Farce Tragedy* (Y), which in one act paraded unboarded ships, poems found under a screaming baby, a tolerant woman, and a dubious check. It was neither farce nor tragedy. She had captions to write for the August number before she left and a *Vanity Fair* page to compose. She had four yards of British cloth from the purser of a liner and must superintend Bill's getting it made into a suit. It was light brown, and too loud for her taste, but cool enough for a New York summer. Elinor told Mama [early June] (B) the resulting suit made Bill look "a little like a gaming table on its way to the race-track." She had her bags to pack and her notes to gather up before boarding the train for New Hampshire.

She made elaborate plans to visit Amy Lowell at her house Sevenels in Brookline on the way up. On June 5 she wrote that she planned to stop in Boston, at the Hemenway Hotel near her old apartment in The Fenway, for one night before going on to the Monodnock Mountains. Mrs. Mac-Dowell was expecting her on Sunday (June 10) but Elinor thought the opportunity of dining at Sevenels was far more important. Sunday was, alas, not possible for Amy Lowell and Elinor replied to the cable that Boston also was, after all, out. She went straight to MacDowell from New York.

Elinor's approach to Amy Lowell was exclusively literary. They had sat on the same platform at poetry readings before, among them the famous one arranged at the MacDowell Club in New York where Amy, a late arrival on the program, spoke last as the audience filtered out. Her "place of honor" had been prefaced by a dancer shuffling under colored spotlights to the cadences of a spoken poem. It was not an auspicious meeting.

Amy's approach to poetry was exclusively entre-preneurial. She once told Grace Hazard Conkling that God had made her a businesswoman and she made herself a poet. "Publicity first," she cried. "Poetry will follow." She brought, for the first time, the unique American love for business into the arena of poetry. She turned a great many qualities on their side. In his stunning memoir of her (printed with her collected

poems), Louis Untermeyer recalled, "Amy Lowell had everything a poet should have except passion"; and he repeated,
"she substituted motion for emotion." She would have been
ripe for parody if she were not so interesting and generous.
She possessed great wealth (the doorknobs in her house were
sterling silver) and great weight (which she balanced on very
slim ankles). She worked at night and slept during the day. She
was a heavily armed general leading reluctant forces to battle
for Imagism, and later, free verse. She was appallingly energetic, but her battle plans were cruelly off course.

She was designed for committee work, causes, and public
service. She took these Boston Lowell qualities and placed
them at poetry's disposal. Allergic to failure, she turned herself into a one-woman institution in her own right. No two
people could have been more dissimilar than Elinor and Amy.
Elinor looked every inch a poet; Amy, with a bearing as grand
as her proportions, did not. Elinor had very little of the cru-
sader in her while Amy loved battle, causes: "she always carried with her the zest for intellectual conflict," Bill wrote in
the *Saturday Review* after her death. Elinor detested public
battle; here Amy showed strength, Elinor employed cunning.
Amy, through sheer cyclonic force, could alter the entire routine of a hotel, while Elinor, simply by appearing frail, got
what she wanted.

They never had their dinner together in Brookline. Amy
was very disappointed: "if you do not come on your way down
[from Peterborough], there will be a fuss, spelt with capitals
and every alternate letter red. I was looking forward to having
a really pleasant evening. Think of what you have deprived me
of!" Elinor missed her again on her way back to New York,
using Bill as the excuse, but said that she might be returning
to Boston in October, which she never did. They only met
twice again before Amy died, unexpectedly, in 1925.

The pleasure of the MacDowell Colony lay in its consistency. Elinor was torn between her role of what she thought
a fiancée should be and a writer. The petty intrigues kept her
very busy in New Hampshire. She helped Douglas Moore*
return to favor after he had offended Mrs. MacDowell's spy

*Douglas Moore (1893–1969), composer. Born in New York and edu-
cated at Yale, he later, after the war, went to Paris to study under Nadia
Boulanger. In 1921, while he was Director of Music at the Art Museum of

network; "the poor kid had said the most indiscreet things in criticism of several elderly and unbeautiful females," Elinor told Bill [June 25] (Y). The Colums were back again, and Elinor enlisted Padraic to lecture her on the Jesuits, while Mary was ill with an attack of appendicitis. She was pleased to see DuBose Heyward again, and not too pleased to see the Gormans (Herbert, the poet, critic, and biographer and his wife). The mosquitoes continued to be as annoying as the weather, which ranged from very hot one moment to very cold the next.

Bill complained that the heat in New York was far more unsettling. He was staying in Elinor's room, which she had decorated for his benefit with a series of billets-doux planted everywhere from the pillow to the typewriter. She arranged to make it more comfortable, and Bill was forced to carry out her plans: screens were added to the windows, chintz covers made for the furniture, and green and white awnings appeared outside the windows. She instructed him to get a fan from Liggetts at Grand Central Station and cautioned him [June 18] (Y): "remember that there are other things to eat beside frosted chocolate, quite as cool and considerably more nourishing." He put her laundry away, kept the place as neat as a pin, and hung up the dress Elinor asked him to send up.

She was assigned the Regina Watson Studio for her stay that summer, the most sought after studio at the Colony. She sat over "the old Pay to Pol—that's for Persia—volume" of the *Encyclopaedia Britannica* and wrote over 1,000 words a day. "Funny," she wrote to Bill her first week there [June 13] (Y), "but I seem to write much faster than last year, with fewer changes, but that is probably a fault, and the result of frivolous-

---

Cleveland, he studied with Ernest Bloch. He was awarded a Pulitzer Fellowship in 1925, and a Guggenheim Fellowship in 1934. He was President of the National Institute of Arts and Letters in 1946 and later became MacDowell Professor of Music at Columbia. He collaborated with Stephen Vincent Benét on several works, among them *The Devil and Daniel Webster* (1938) a one-act opera. He wrote *Giants of the Earth,* an opera (1951), for which he won a Pulitzer Prize, an opera based on *The Wings of a Dove* (1963) and five years later an opera called *Carry Nation.* He spent three summers with Elinor at the MacDowell Colony. He set her poem "Lament" to music under the title "Never Ask the End."

ness and not so much book-larning." Five years later she
changed her mind. In a letter she failed to send to Clifton
Fadiman (April 14, 1928) (Y) she wrote:

The fact that my prose appears to you and various other people a
laboured & carefully wrought thing is in no way an insult—it is a fact,
to a certain extent, an undeserved compliment, but it is completely
an error. I write with truly disgraceful speed, carried away by the
little dictionary of fireworks in my head—I am certainly whisked
along—& perhaps away—by my own exuberance. . . .

She was determined to finish her novel that summer; she
was less certain about the title. She no longer thought of it as
Gerald, preferring *The Lady Stuffed with Pistachio Nuts,* which
she also abandoned in face of wide opposition: "Everyone—
most of all the Colums—thinks that the pistachio title is too
terrible; I hate it myself," she told Bill [June 24] (Y), "with
its vague suggestion of jurgenism [a complaint against Cabell],
and its blaring, insistent quality of the grotesque. Padraic
wants me to call it Jennifer in Persepolis. . . ." As the summer
progressed, it became more and more apparent that she would
not be finished by the time she left MacDowell, which meant
that she would have to finish the novel in New York. Bill,
caught off guard by her new tenderness toward him during
her MacDowell stay, unaccountably developed the unhappy
notion that if she were to return directly to New York, *he*
would not be able to get on with his work. She assumed the
best affectionate posture:

if I worked all day and lay very quiet upon the sofa do you think you
could sometimes maybe work in the same room with me if I didn't
speak? . . . if you think I should, I'll learn to be alone, though really
it is hardly necessary, because if we were married and you were in
the next room working I shouldn't feel alone at all. All you need to
do now, my darling, is to tell me what you wish and I will obey you,
for I only want to make you happy, and if my absence makes you
happiest, then you must have it, or we will neither of us be happy.
Ours will be a strange marriage. . . .

Why Elinor wanted to marry Bill is a major clue to her
nature and one of the major paradoxes in her character. "She
always wanted people she could not count on," Rebecca West
aptly assessed nearly half a century after Elinor's death. Bill set

out to be counted on—it was his way of loving—but his family was, at least at the outset, determined not to count on Elinor. That alone provided Bill with more fascination than all his elaborate recitals of affection. And for Elinor, his family's opposition was vital: she assumed the attitude of defense, while the Benéts did not assume offense. By March 1923, there was an uneasy truce between them: "Your letter gives me hope . . ." Mrs. Benét wrote to her (March 4, 1923) (Y). "Well, let us look to the future and be patient with each other. . . . I am not at all proud of myself, with regard to much that has passed between us." She offered, almost as a token of peace, the house in Scarsdale once they were married—a move designed more for the benefit of the children than the newlyweds. Mrs. Benét was a much easier opponent than Katharine Wylie.

When Elinor had calmed, or at least silenced, the fears at Overhill Road, she began to wonder if she really loved Bill. She brushed aside his cloying attentions in favor of his uses, perceiving him more for his literary role than for himself. She placed him in a position he was happy to occupy: as her supporter. He served her, he flattered her, and he defended her —that was enough to disguise the absence of love. She saw their marriage as a form of alliance, almost a document denying her past. He led the way to her new reputation, and built it, out of proportion to its worth. She repaid his uncompromising devotion to her with an attempt at love. For this Bill was very happy.

While Elinor wavered over her decision to marry, Bill took all the steps required to establish their lives together. He searched for an apartment in New York, he looked at houses in the suburbs. He drew up a detailed account of their joint income since he could not support Elinor by his money alone. When he sent her the pencils she needed, she bought him a tie (her favorite gift for Bill). Both performed according to the strict rules they had set for themselves.

Mama's behavior was no less in tune with what she believed. In an extraordinary act of philanthropy she asked Elinor to sail with her to England for the remainder of the summer, thus avoiding New York and Bill. She hoped that the invitation would be read as an act of kindness, but underneath more serious motives were at work. She did not want Elinor to marry again. With an ocean separating them, she hoped that Elinor might appreciate that celibacy was, after all, more ap- propriate. Mama knew that Elinor's health was bad—her stay at MacDowell had resulted in migraines—and the strain of marriage, complicated by the care of three children, could only make it worse. Elinor's incredible belief that she was competent to look after children who were already so well cared for filled Mama with horror. It was as if Elinor had learned nothing in the last decade.

Elinor forwarded Mama's letter (now either lost or destroyed) on to Bill. "I'm sorry that Mama's letter gave you gooseflesh," she wrote [June 15](Y) from MacDowell,

but I know exactly what you mean, for I had a pang myself in thinking perhaps I should go after all and leave you and Katherine [unidentified, perhaps Katherine Alexander, a family friend of the Benéts] to make a match of it and please your parents. If you want that, it's not too late, but somehow it seems rather silly—even selly —to waste the ring and several other things doesn't it, old kid? Mama has undoubtedly been brought to heel; we must feel very proud of ourselves in that instance, I think; yes, we must treat her rough. Rough kindness is the dope.

Bill calmly dismissed the whole episode, writing tersely [June 18](Y): "That about Katherine that you said was just hoy, my darling." He arrived at MacDowell the last day of June and stayed on for five days before taking Elinor back to New York. His own family had dispersed—his parents and sister to Canada and his children to stay with Kathleen and Charles Norris in California. When they returned at the end of August, Elinor herself left New York. "I want to be away for a good part of September," she told her mother [August, 1923](B) who was at Manchester-on-Sea, Massachusetts. ". . . Col. Benét is sailing for France on the 12th [September], & I Think the ensuing days would be excellent ones for William to be at Scarsdale. I have therefore so advised him . . . I hope to avoid setting eyes on Mrs B or Laura until Bill & I get back the end of October."

There was a scramble to get everything arranged before the wedding, set to take place at the beginning of October.

The divorce had to be made final. The proofs for her novel, now titled *Jennifer Lorn: A Sedate Extravaganza,* had to be waded through. Decorators and builders were busy in their new apartment at 142 East 18th Street, which they had taken from August 1. University Place had to be vacated, and Bill packed off to Amagansett for a brief holiday with his family.

In the middle of this chaos, news came through from Germany that Constance had committed suicide. On August 3 *The New York Times* published a brief statement that the death of Baroness von Stumm had been announced in Murnaw, Bavaria. Elinor had not seen her sister for three years. They had never been really close since childhood. The distance between them was conveniently blamed on geography, and the mysterious circumstances of Connie's death somehow disguised the grief Mama and Elinor might have felt.* The only reference to the event in Elinor's letters comes at the end of a long letter about herself to Mama [September 2(?), 1923](B): "I had a note from Leonora [Speyer] about Connie which has certainly Sincerely moved & distressed. Poor Tum —it is heart breaking indeed."

The casualties in Elinor's life were mounting up. Constance was the third suicide in seven years of someone closely connected to her. Both Connie and Henry had survived the war only to kill themselves. The threat that Mama made to Jeanne and Morton—that she would live to see her children dead—was becoming a reality.

§ *iii*   *"Ours will be a strange sort of marriage*
. . .*"*

Elinor married Bill on Friday, October 5, 1923, at the apartment of a friend at 25 West 56th Street. They had done

---

*Constance was no less immune to outrageous stories than Elinor. Accounts of her suicide range from drowning in Holland after a disastrous love affair to shooting herself at the dinner table before the soup was served. Mama's destruction of letters went a long way to foster these stories, and it has been impossible either to verify them or to uncover the truth.

everything they could to avoid publicity; they got their license
at Scarsdale rather than City Hall. Neither the Benéts nor any
of the Hoyts attended: Colonel Benét deliberately left for
France well before the ceremony. Mama did not come up
from Washington, claiming, yet again, illness, and Nancy said
she had not been asked. The best man was Franklin P. Adams
and the maid of honor Esther Root (later Mrs. F.P.A.). Elinor
carried a cluster of orchids. Fourteen years after the wedding
Claire Mumford reported that the entire ceremony passed off
"delightfully."

Amy Lowell looked in afterwards, preceded by Mrs. Russell, who climbed the two flights of stairs carrying Amy's
sables. When Amy Lowell finally entered the apartment after
the climb, she turned to Elinor, puffed out some words of
congratulation, then added: "But if you marry again, I shall
cut you dead—and I warn you all Society will do the same.
You will be nobody."

That night the newlyweds went to Brooklyn on their way
to the Puddingston Inn, Boonton, in New Jersey: "We hear
this is pleasant, with pretty walks," Elinor wrote to Mama on
her wedding day (October 5)(Y). "After all, I was born in
New Jersey." When they got there, they discovered that it was
nothing more than rooms in a store, and quickly moved on to
The Ardsley in New Canaan, Connecticut, which proved to be
ideal. They had a very comfortable room, with delicious
meals, and enjoyed "walks in real New England autumn land-
scape. . . . How I *wish* we lived here!" Elinor said wistfully
to Mama (October 15)(B). On October 28 they returned to
New York.

They had signed a lease for fourteen months for apartment A at 142 East 18th Street, at a rent of $125 a month. It
was downstairs from Elinor's editor at Doran, Eugene Saxton,
and four floors off the ground. Elinor complained that the
building looked like a prison but assured Mama that she could
manage the stairs. The apartment had marble fireplaces, grates
for coal fires, and steam heat; it was very sunny. Elinor instructed the painters to make the walls buff color and the
woodwork cream. When they moved in, she found the walls
"dead white" and the woodwork transformed to a pale yellow
shade.

The apartment had seven rooms and a large kitchen, strung out along a vast corridor. In the front was a square, tidy drawing room; next to it was Bill's study, with bookcases covering the walls and a window-seat; then a bedroom. Opposite the front door, planted in the middle of the hall, was the dining room, which had been made over as a bedroom for Bill's daughters (Rosemary and Kathleen Ann). Toward the back was Jim's small bedroom, the maid's room, then the bathroom. The large sunny kitchen was at the very tail end of the hall.

Elinor's decorative skills were extraordinary. Her attitude toward dressing her rooms was precisely the same as toward dressing herself. (Once, she refused an invitation for a weekend in the country because she did not own a white flannel suit, which she insisted was essential for a summer day.) Every detail was considered, even to the point of assigning kitchen chairs to the children. Where her mother managed to exclude both comfort and beauty from her houses, Elinor willingly sacrificed comfort for beauty. Rosemary Benét remembered that even the blue silk cushions on the sofa, which had a Chinese shawl spread over it, "were somehow unusual and beautiful." But she gave little thought to the suitability of her choice of decoration: in the girls' room she placed an extremely fragile Chinese horse and a watercolor by herself of Eve with a coiling serpent.

Bill's children were not enthusiastic about the move to New York. They were enrolled in the Friends' Seminary around the corner—an unwelcome change from Scarsdale—and were not made comfortable by Elinor. The children were neither young enough to be shuffled away under the care of a nurse (Jim was nine years old, Rosemary eight, and Kathleen Ann nearly six), nor old enough to be of any practical help. The problems started over what they should call Elinor: she objected to any version of "Mother," which the children themselves would not like, and "Elinor" was ruled out as being too familiar. Rosemary remembered: "in the end we always called her Missy," which is how she referred to herself in letters. The strain of running the household soon told on Elinor, and her choice of combination cook-maid, Freida, was disastrous. Freida preferred her dachshund "Zeppel" to the

children and would take dolls' blankets away from the girls to
give them to the dog (when she eventually returned them,
they were not wanted). Her idea of a special treat, when
Elinor and Bill were out, was to feed the children boiled
potatoes, quickly smeared when hot with butter and jam.
When they complained she sternly told them to like their meal
as it was a delicacy in Germany. Freida's bad cooking was only
matched by her inability to help around the house. And Elinor
was as frightened of her as the children were.

Elinor tried to arrange Bill's children as if they were
furniture. She bought them clothes they did not like, she
expected perfect manners from them, and she gave them impossible instructions. She took endless care over furnishing a
dollhouse with such expensive and fragile items as a china tea
set that had to be removed before Rosemary or Kathleen Ann
could play with it. As soon as any game started, Elinor grew
furious if they moved any of the dolls' furniture she had taken
such trouble over. She simply could not understand that her
form of attention was not enough for them. Their grandmother and aunt had taken a loving and carefree approach to
them; the shift to Elinor, who did not seem to share either of
these attitudes, was traumatic. When she decided to read to
them, she took down a volume of flower poetry from the
shelves, the pages marked with sprigs of holly, rosemary, and
ivy—the names, she told them, of her children who died. She
described her son Philip, who they never saw and began to
suspect was as mythical as the other children. Since Elinor was
unable to have their love, she bid for their sympathy. Though
she had made everything look very beautiful at 18th Street,
she could not hide the tense atmosphere. "Living with Elinor," Rosemary wrote, "was like walking through a flowery
minefield."

Elinor had waited too long for children; she had outlived
the belief that they alone could provide her happiness, and
they no longer held the same importance for her. Casually, she
moved the idea of children back into the realm of fantasy,
where it had been stored when she was with Horace. Her
failure with Bill's children was not her fault, she told herself,
because they were not *her* children. No amount of effort, or
desire, could change the fact. She tried; in fact, she worked

very hard at being a good mother to them; but even she had to admit, eventually, that she had failed. For the rest of her life she kept up a whimsical approach to children. She was undeterred by reality, merely deciding to look again at her own childhood: "I've been meaning for some little time to write —when I get round to it," she confided later to Mama (October 28, 1928) (B), ". . . a reminiscence of my own childhood and, incidentally, a sort of tribute to Henry and Constance. . . . Of course the nursery would come into it, and I do remember that room with perfect distinctness and should love to write about it. Do you remember our profiles on the plaster wall before it was papered, which you drew around our shadows?"*

The only one of Bill's children who fitted into Elinor's fanciful scheme was the youngest girl, Kathleen Ann (known as K.A.), still young enough to be smothered. Every day Elinor would collect her from kindergarten and they would spend the afternoon together before the other children came home from school. Elinor taught her the ballads she had learned from Mary Ann McDonald over three decades before. She would reel off enchanting stories, and invent some fairly painful games. One afternoon Rosemary and Jim came in to find Elinor and K.A. sitting on the sofa, both crying, obviously in great pain and holding their hands up in the air. Elinor explained that they had each tied a rubber band tightly around one finger; when the finger turned purple and swelled up, the rubber band was untied and they waited for the gruesome agony as the blood rushed back.

Pain played a very important part in Elinor's expression of frustration over her failure with the children. It was her attempt to get the attention her affection failed to produce. She would beat her head against the wall with rhythmic precision until Bill stopped her. Or she would quietly slip out of the room and throw herself on her bed convulsed with crying. All the promises she had made to Bill before they were married about the home she would create for his family ended in disappointment, and worse, anger. She began to resent the children for keeping her from her work.

*She never wrote this memoir but Mama did.

Elinor's failures as a stepmother did not damage her public reputation in the least. She was admired for taking on her husband's children; observers thought it was another proof of her nobility. Less than two weeks after the move to East 18th Street came the publication of her first novel, on November 9. *Jennifer Lorn* captured a readership far greater than both her volumes of poetry put together.

Like her poetry, Elinor's novels stepped back into the eighteenth and early nineteenth centuries. She shared with Joseph Hergesheimer, Robert Nathan, James Branch Cabell, and Carl Van Vechten a deft talent for escapism. She felt more at home in the world she read about in William Hickey. And she produced a novel that Max Beerbohm claimed (in a letter dated November 1923, but never sent): "I feel I should like to have written myself."

Dedicated to her mother, written almost under the eye of Bill, the novel is unquestionably about Horace. After the book was published, Elinor sent Horace a clipping from *The New Republic* (December 5, 1923), of her sonnet "Unwilling Admission," adding the note: "In lieu of dedication of Jennifer Lorn. Gerald protests his unworthiness." In the opinion of Dr. Evelyn Helmick, "the whole novel is . . . an allegory of her life." Horace is fashioned into Gerald Poynyard; Elinor is Jennifer; and other friends such as Louis Untermeyer, who figures as the not altogether complimentary figure of the prince, make an appearance. The whole novel hinges on the device of allegory. Five years later Elinor formulated her apologia in the essay *Symbols in Literature:* "If you call a spade a diamond some people will think you are frivolous and affected, but other people will understand how much blacker things may be said about spades by the simple trick of pretending they are diamonds." Events and characters in the novel are grotesquely exaggerated, almost to the point of obscuring what she intended to say; yet it is, mercifully, a novel without a message.

While adhering to the literary conventions of the eighteenth century, Elinor created a novel that was very weak on interest. She overcame this obstacle, she believed, by being fascinating instead: "The thinness of incident in *Jennifer Lorn* is obscured by the lush descriptive foliage; where plot may appear deficient, characterization maintains the interest," maintains Nancy Potter, who has written a thesis on Elinor. The book evolves into an inventory of detail. It was as if Elinor was unable to assimilate and transform her sources; she had done too much research.

"Of the character of Gerald, it may be said that our literature affords no more ingenious, and, at the same time, no more dreadful, illustration of the truth, that the most polished taste and the highest accomplishment may coexist with selfishness and cruelty; and the exercise of great abilities have for accompaniment the contempt of religion," Edmund Wilson commented in his published letter to Elinor nearly two years after reading the book (October 7, 1925). Nancy Potter sums up Gerald more simply as another version of Henry James's Gilbert Osmond, the "champion of amoral taste." He is at once successful and elegant, without pursuing any of the values one associates with a hero; yet he does not manage to be a villain either. He is another statement of Elinor's commitment to surprising contradictions.

Jennifer's character is less happy. There are no unexpected opposites. She is beautiful, quintessentially feminine, and really rather stupid. Her beauty achieves for her what a brain does for others. She is plagued, as one observer commented, with "puzzling pride"; she is alarmingly susceptible to flattery and beauty in any form. Her health is delicate and she possesses but one quality—admiration of, devotion for, and willing submission to her husband. She says of him at one point, "As a travelling companion, and indeed in every other relation of life he was the most superior person whom it has ever been my privilege to know." It is Elinor speaking of Horace. In every one of the four novels she wrote in as many years, Elinor displayed her preference for men to women; the men she created in fiction were the heroes she wanted in real life.

The story of *Jennifer Lorn* is uneventful. It is a romance that moves from India, where Gerald Poynyard (later Lord Camphile) has earned a fortune, to England, where he marries Jennifer, and back again. To this slim outline Elinor adds

Gothic melodrama in the latter portion of the novel: Gerald is killed—it is thought by robbers; Jennifer is imprisoned in a Persian court from which she escapes, is eventually recaptured, and dies. Upon this narrow plot Elinor weaves elaborate descriptions and florid details. Brilliant metaphors, feats of imagery, and lengthy depiction, stand in the place of events. Elinor saw the novel as an opportunity to expand the truncated skills she employed in her poetry. And if *Jennifer Lorn* is an allegory, it perhaps displays her favorite device. Defense proves the surest form of attack—the detail, the dense "foliage," and the over-ample lushness of the narrative replace action. Being, for Elinor, was more important than doing.

Jennifer Lorn was an instant success. Spontaneity, so lacking in the criticism of her poetry, now swept over the critics. "The only thing I want to talk about is 'Jennifer Lorn,'" Sinclair Lewis wrote to Elinor from London (December 29, 1923)(Y). "I wonder if there has ever been written a more distinguished first novel? I am so interested in it as an American phenomenon that I can scarce think of it in relation to you . . . for the first time America has ceased to be a Colony, has become a Power—sure, deft, serene, and 'sophisticated.' . . ." He added, judiciously, that the cultural transition was not Elinor's work exclusively; she was assisted by that triumvirate of escapist novelists: Cabell, Van Vechten, and Hergesheimer. In order to create an American novel, she had ransacked the storehouses of English social history and every known device of satire. The book is only American because that was where Elinor was born.

John Peale Bishop wrote to her from Paris (December 23, 1923) (Y) that the book "has that intelligent charm which is the rarest thing in American letters, is exquisitely written and has a delicious grace which, very pleasantly, reminds me of *Daphne and Chloe*." Readers were dazzled by the book. They were happily seduced by Elinor's recital of historical detail. Carl Van Vechten claimed that the scholarly gloss gave "credibility" to "this enchanting tale." Elinor established a smokescreen of historical detail that passed for a novel and, in turn, made her famous. Readers were more impressed than entertained.

The novel won her an exceedingly vocal readership, of

which the loudest of all was the critic-novelist-photographer Carl Van Vechten. Though he failed to achieve his grandmother's prediction that he would live to be hanged, some people believed that his fate was worse. He was educated at the University of Chicago and later became society columnist for the Chicago *American*. After two years he went to New York to work for the *Times*, which, in turn, shipped him further east to Paris in 1908 for another two years, thus completing his education in the *avant-garde*. His élitism began early in life when he grew to the height of six feet long before any of his classmates. He made himself more obvious by quickly adopting sophisticated manners and a form of dress that could only be described as Midwestern Wilde. As a music critic he lent staunch support to *Salome* after its single performance at the Metropolitan Opera. He took on Gertrude Stein as another of his causes, and saw himself as the leader of the campaign for the modern movement. Van Vechten united the extremes of eccentricity with a redoubtable wit. He always used ink to match his letterhead, the colors ranging through yellow to mauve to pastel blue or pink. And he always made certain some celebrity witnessed his signature on contracts.

Leonard Woolf has said that a man should change his job after seven years. Van Vechten expanded this theory: at the age of forty he announced that his "intellectual arteries" had hardened, and he was therefore turning his dilapidated faculties from criticism to the novel. He tossed off a string of amusing, sophisticated, delicate—what Elinor called "wit & glitter"—novels: *Peter Whiffle, The Tattooed Countess, The Blind Bow-Boy, Firecrackers, Parties,* and his most famous (or infamous), *Nigger Heaven* (1926). In the middle of this phase, Elinor wrote: "Carl Van Vechten's career as a novelist has been truly aeronautic in its swift ascension, but behind it lies a multi-colored background, a mental pattern reaching from music to mysticism, and back again, by way perhaps of Babylon, to cats and composers . . . it is safe to hazard the statement that Carl Van Vechten is a diabolically clever young man."

His apartment was around the corner from Elinor and Bill's; its decoration ranged from modern to inflated Victorian. It was a place full of surprises and even more astonishing people. One was as likely to meet an acrobat as a jazz pianist

—the most famous and the most obscure. His collection of
paintings was just as unexpected, and his rooms were crowded
with books and manuscripts; invariably a cat would have to be
shoved aside to read one.

Ernest Boyd once described someone's face as all light
and no shade; nothing could be more accurate regarding Carl
Van Vechten. As his years increased, his features billowed out,
his hair turned an angelic color of fleece and his clothes became more outrageous.

He produced his books with a speed that rivaled Elinor's.
His success was spectacular. For all his generosity, kindness,
and hilarity, Van Vechten had a great many enemies: he possessed easy facility and an apparent lack of seriousness that was
despised by people like Thomas Wolfe.* Those who knew
him, however, could imagine no more congenial couple than
he and his second wife, Fania Marinoff. When he had finished
with novels, he picked up the camera and became famous all
over again.

Carl Van Vechten met Elinor in the late summer of 1923,
with the best introduction possible—the praise of his friend
Hugh Walpole. Two months later he provided a higher
recommendation with lavish, almost outrageously favorable
praise for *Jennifer Lorn,* published in *The Dial.* His enthusiasm
for the book did not stop on the page; he organized a torch-
light parade through Manhattan streets to commemorate the
publication of the book. Elinor's response was in a lower key:
"I bless you for thinking she is *funny,*" she wrote (November
28, 1923) (Y), "instead of piling the responsibilities of an
historical novel upon her porcelain shoulders. . . . I knew all
along that I was writing the book for very few people, but you
have almost made me believe that I wrote it for *you.*" A week
later (December 3) (Y) she added, "in the opinion of a mere
author, you are the only person, except myself, who under-
stands the book." After receiving this message, Van Vechten
quickly wrote to Hugh Walpole (December 10) (B): "Jennifer Lorn . . . is absolute perfection, a masterpiece of beauty,
humour, & satire." Elinor's gratitude was unbounded; she
scarcely knew how to express her appreciation. In the end,

*Who pilloried Van Vechten, as well as Elinor, in *The Web and the Rock.*

after cajoling her publishers and pestering their salesmen, she
found one of the misprinted first copies of the first edition and
sent it off to her admirer, belatedly, for Christmas with the
inscription: "But for whom this book would never have been
read."

Van Vechten's enthusiasm for the book never waned.
When the novel was reprinted in the collected edition of
Elinor's prose in 1933, Bill asked him, as the most obvious
choice, to write the preface.* What he had said in *The Dial*,
he expanded in his preface. "My enthusiasm has mounted in
ten years rather than ebbed. I am confirmed in the belief that
Jennifer Lorn is the only sustained satire in English with which
I am acquainted.... Elinor Wylie... apparently... cherished
a delightful perverse profusion of aims, lifting *Jennifer* thereby
out of a class of pastiches into a niche in literature quite its
own."

The book soon became the major object of interest in
New York. Dinners were arranged on the themes suggested
in it. The sales surpassed the publishers' wildest dreams.
Doran's edition was beautifully produced—buff-colored mar-
bled-paper boards with wonderfully delicate designs—to look
like an eighteenth-century book. While her poetry had earned
critical esteem, her novel succeeded in winning over the critics
as well as the public.

Elinor might have enjoyed her surprising success more if
she had not been "incarcerated" in her apartment. Kathleen
Ann was seriously ill with diphtheria. The other children were
shipped back to their grandmother and Aunt Laura during the
worst stages of the infection. Elinor used the child's illness as
the excuse for her late Christmas gift to Carl Van Vechten,
writing (January 13, 1924) (Y): "the fact that the youngest
and prettiest of my step-children elected that holiday season
in which to have diphtheria accounts for the delay.... I have
been completely immured from the world for the past four
weeks." She sat by K.A.'s bedside day and night. Bill later

---

*Yet four years later, in 1937, when the Elinor Wylie Poetry Fellowship was
organized, he was overlooked as a choice for the committee. The Fellowship
committee realized their mistake later that year, in June, and asked him to
join, but he refused.

recalled that the quarantine that was placed on the apartment petrified Elinor. She was tireless, helpful, and very worried throughout the course of the illness.

Mama was neither sympathetic nor understanding. She wanted some of the attention Elinor lavished exclusively, it seemed to her, on someone else's children. Elinor had not come to see her either for Christmas or New Year, and Mama, in her New Year's letter, reminded her that she had her own son to think about: "Philip was perfectly fine—So gay & good hearted & good looking. . . . He is a remarkably good dancer" (Y). A year later Mama would be less restrained, writing to Elinor (December 26, 1924) (Y): "I am so fond of Philip—You must arrange to come down when he is here—Why not soon, while the children are out at school—Wouldn't you let Laura look after them? I do think it is MY turn."

The children continued to be at the eye of a storm that raged around them between "Miss Fanny" (Bill's mother), Laura, their aunt Kathleen Norris, and Elinor. Kathleen Norris, who eventually became their guardian, said bitterly in a letter to Elinor (November 27, 1923) (Y) that "to have us all gathering about them like vultures is at least an improvement upon the Fordham Orphanage." Each of the three women had something to say against the suitability of the children's present guardian. Kathleen Norris pointed out that as the sister of their mother, her claim on them was very strong. The Benéts played on their generosity, reluctant though it might have been, in letting the children leave Scarsdale. Kathleen Norris explained their action as courageous, while Laura and "Miss Fanny" clearly saw it only as a grave mistake. While Elinor tolerated Kathleen Norris, she despised the Benét females. The fact that she was never home when either Laura or "Miss Fanny" visited the children was too obvious to be coincidence.

Elinor answered the unfortunate accusations implied in Kathleen Norris's letter with an extended and studied account of her stepchildren, thus inferring that all three of the relations were wrong. Kathleen Norris wrote back (January 1924) (Y): "The analysis of our mutual Jim, Rosa, and Kit—the delicate and humorous comprehension of the three—went straight to a fond aunt's heart. It is not only that I rejoice that you can love Tee's [Teresa's] children so—I am grateful to you for letting me *know* just how deep it had gone. No I did not send the letter to Miss Fanny. . . ."

Mama was also convinced that Elinor was sincere when she spoke about the children, and sometimes even managed to reverse her own jealousy of their claim on her daughter. She complimented Elinor (January 9, 1924) (Y), saying that she had been wonderful to nurse K.A. with such devotion. "All the same you were imprudent to use up all your strength which isn't unlimited. . . . I am inordinately proud of your performance—Both Jennifer and this standing proxy for the mother of those three nice children . . . let Bill take care of you—I know he wants to, and am *not* picking on him." Elinor had become oversensitive to any accusation; she started to interpret the mildest comments as insults. The struggle over Bill's children was drawn out, just as her status as stepmother to them was questioned, for no other reason on her part than revenge. She fought Bill's mother, father, and sister through his children. She held on to them long after she recognized her own failure, enjoying this variety of victory and disregarding the unfortunate effect it had on the children.

The success of *Jennifer Lorn* afforded her a more natural form of enjoyment. She was invited to Richmond, Virginia, by Emily Clark, founder and editor of *The Reviewer,* * to celebrate the appearance of the novel. Carl Van Vechten, who suggested the invitation, was also asked, along with Alfred and Blanche Knopf. Elinor stopped in Washington on the way down to Richmond to rest, and was well enough by April 2, the day she reached Virginia, to proceed through the strenuous round of parties that had been planned—"almost like a convention," Carl Van Vechten wrote to Hugh Walpole (April 9, 1924) (B). She was met at the train by Joseph Hergesheimer, who was greatly admired by the porter, and then went on to the Jefferson Hotel. "I dashed upstairs for a quick bath

---

*Emily Clark, with the help of Hunter Stagg, was determined to start a small literary magazine—appearing fortnightly as a book review. The first issue appeared in February 1921, and was projected to run for six months; it ran for five years. James Branch Cabell edited three issues between October and December 1921, and although *The Reviewer* was designed to further Southern literature, the scope broadened to include most of the major writers of the day. DuBose Heyward was an early, then unknown, contributor.

& a leap into my silver dress," she told Bill (Thursday) [April
3] (Y), "& by eight was meeting the Cabells & Carl Van
Vechten in Carl's room, & go to Emily Clark's." They had
supper, a more honored occasion in the South than dinner as
Emily Clark explained in her autobiography, *Innocence Abroad.*
"We had . . . mint julips, shad roe with bacon, Smithfield ham,
spoonbread, [indec.] biscuits not to mention trifles like tomato
salad & strawberries. For liqueurs we had apple-brandy—so
romantic! . . . I was accounted the guest of honour—so they
claimed—& everyone was most kind & lovely to me."

James Branch Cabell came up to Elinor and asked her,
with a respect new to any of the other guests, a few "shy
questions about *Jennifer*"; the book had, Emily Clark reported, "electrified" him. Like Van Vechten, Cabell ignored her poetry, and as the novels subsequent to *Jennifer
Lorn* appeared, his interest declined. In his opinion only
her first two novels classified Elinor as a "reformed and
civilised" poet. In his own rococo style, Cabell wrote in
1930: "To no other woman save only Helen of Troy and
that unaccountable person who imprudently married me
have I been indebted for more of fond delight and of
unanswerable surmise." His essay on Elinor, *Sanctuary in
Porcelain,* is a feat of quiet boasting; he merely catalogues
his previously voiced praise for Elinor to reward himself.
He said he was a "discoverer" of the novel, writing of it
as a "compact of color and legerity and glitter."

The publication of *Jennifer Lorn* marked the high point in
Cabell's friendship with Elinor. He was shy, but while the
author herself frightened him, he had no fear of what she had
written; indeed, he was captivated by her. Twenty-five years
after his first essay on Elinor, the notorious author of *Jurgen*
wrote in his autobiography, *As I Remember It* (1955): "Yes, I
admired Elinor Wylie wholly, both as an author and an actually all-beautiful woman; I cherished even a latent respect for
the mad stubbornness with which, as an obligation to perfection, she chose to live in a perpetual semi-blindness rather than
to wear glasses in public." Peering through his own famous
spectacles, Cabell could not resist adding: "You, in her company, had thus an uneasy feeling of smoking rather more than
was good for you in a gunpowder magazine." Later, Elinor's

ability to create scenes, which became notorious, sent him running.

Cabell himself enjoyed extravagant critical praise, and for a brief period popularity in university circles. He was a dedicated escapist, inhabiting the mythical land of Poictesme which he charted in his novels. He lived as if in constant hibernation, rarely leaving his house, and then only to present the picture of a Southern gentleman—all manners, and a great deal of silence. The arrival of Elinor in Richmond was enough to force him to throw open the doors of Dumbarton Grange in a gesture of unexpected hospitality. She dined there her second night and quickly reported back to Bill [April 4] (Y): "Dumbarton Grange is amazing—the very worst Victorian, so bad that it succeeds in being distinguished. And this party— for me—was the first they had had in years. Tonight they are actually coming to see me again." And she could not help telling him, "I have made a greater hit with *James* than with Joe [Hergesheimer]—not young & pretty enough for Joe, & James likes me because I like witchcraft in Western Europe, I think. Also Mrs. James . . . seems to think very highly of me."

The one person in Richmond who did not think highly of Elinor was Ellen Glasgow* a foremost Southern writer, who lived in a house in the center of town that was covered with ivy and wisteria, and protected by box hedges, magnolia, and an iron fence. Her deafness isolated her, but her hearing was acute enough for her to learn that Elinor had been married several times. Whereas stray dogs and cats were welcome and protected, Elinor Hichborn Wylie Benét was forbidden. The invitation to dine was swiftly withdrawn. Overnight Elinor was transformed from a sought-after celebrity—pursued by both local newspapers for photographs and interviews, and a rare visitor to Dumbarton Grange—into an unwanted guest. The Knopfs immediately refused to go to Ellen Glasgow's house, preferring to dine "in comfort," as Elinor told Bill, at

*Ellen Anderson Gholson Glasgow (1874–1945), novelist and author of some twenty books, which alone established her as one of the foremost writers in the South. She is famous for her realism, feminism, and vivid pictures of the South. Besides being a modest golfer, she was a staunch supporter of the Colonial Dames and President of the Richmond S.P.C.A. She won a Pulitzer prize in 1942.

the Jefferson Hotel with Elinor. Ellen Glasgow retaliated with an invitation to tea, like some sort of apology.

Altogether the journey to Richmond was a great success. Though the newspapers had altered what she said, "making it more genteel & 100% American!", Ellen Glasgow had juggled her invitations, and the pace was uncompromisingly brisk, Elinor admitted: *"Everyone has been so nice & kind—apparently eager to know me that my heart is really touched."* What touched her most, however, was the compliment she was paid on her beauty by a very handsome young man, completely ignorant of *Jennifer Lorn.* "I used to get on with men like him in Washington," she told Emily Clark, adding, "and I don't want to be just a literary woman." Before boarding the train back to New York she was pleased to inform Bill that she had not had one headache. Equally pleasing were the two poems inspired by her Richmond visit: "Miranda's Supper (Virginia, 1866)" and "Aaron Mordecai."

It was a very good sign. Although the doctors threatened the most most dire consequences, almost maintaining that she was committing suicide, Elinor became pregnant. To her it was the logical extension of marriage; it would conceal her failure with Teresa's children's and fulfill the urge that still plagued her. Mama had had children when she was in her late thirties; Elinor would be thirty-nine years old in September. But as if living out her fantasy, she remained obstinately confident.

Ten days after she returned from Richmond, Bill's children were sent to the Norrises in California in an attempt to safeguard Elinor's strength. She did little other than rest, and wait. Horace witnessed this sequence of events three times. Bill, like Horace before him, watched, hoped, and waited. He was endlessly attentive and patient. But neither of them had long to wait: toward the end of May Elinor suffered a miscarriage and was rushed to Madison Avenue Hospital.

"The poor child has had an awfully tough time," Bill wrote to Louis Untermeyer (June 5, 1924). "She has had a miscarriage, which is a terrible disappointment to her & has gone through agonizing physical pain as well. As for me, I have been scared all colours of the rainbow. But now—thank God!—she is recovering finely. She will remain in the hospital

... about a week longer. Today she is able to be read to & the worst is well past."

The excitement of New York had worn off; the spring, like the previous fall, slipped by with almost no work accomplished. And in September 1924, Elinor and Bill would have to look for another apartment since their lease expired at the end of the month. Elinor wanted to move to the country. She blithely waved aside Bill's objections over money; his chronic worry about money was too reminiscent of Horace.* In a grand gesture, Elinor decided that she would buy the house in the country on a mortgage. If the first poems she sold could buy two hats, then her first novel's royalties could be stretched to buy a house.

They found a small cottage in New Canaan, at 151 Park Street, costing $12,000. It was like Somesville, moved south, all over again. The tiny white Colonial-style house (now destroyed) was perched on the crest of a small grassy hill that sheltered a vast horse chestnut tree. The ground floor was composed of an incongruously long drawing room—focusing on a massive fireplace flanked by two comfortable armchairs —a small dining room, and a kitchen. There were four bedrooms upstairs into which were squeezed the three children, Elinor and Bill, Freida and "Zeppel," who refused to sleep in his kennel outside. Elinor's only fear was whether or not Freida would like the house. The one comment the cook made was that she had friends who lived in greater comfort. She immediately set to work mismanaging the kitchen and the household, without appearing to notice that she had left New York.

The autumn in New Canaan was just as Elinor remembered it from her honeymoon a year before. Bill got out his gardening tools and set to work; they planted a kitchen gar-

*Bill's concern was not unfounded. In his autobiography he says that he alone paid the rent for "that great railroad flat" at East 18th Street (which is not strictly true—Elinor contributed some money). Added to that were school fees and the medical bills for both K.A. and Elinor. It had been a very expensive year.

den, raked leaves, and went for long walks. No sooner had they established themselves in New Canaan on October 1 than the problems began to pile up. As the packing crates were emptied bills started pouring in, and Elinor assumed all the responsibility for them. It was designed as a house for Bill and his children; it, like Brook Corner, was her gift to him. She submitted any saleable poems she could find to editors. Carl Van Doren, editor of *The Century,* was a new entry on her list.

Van Doren had all the qualities required to join Elinor's small but growing band of devotees: he enjoyed all the views she believed essential. He addressed her at length on her beauty; he was convinced she was a "pure yet troubled genius"; and he was in a position to be of use to her. He wrote about her in the most respectful, deferential, indeed almost sycophantic tones in his autobiography, *Three Worlds.* He boasts of having had the privilege of knowing her. As a member of the management committee of the *Dictionary of American Biography* (for the ten years 1926–36), he nominated himself to write the entry on Elinor.

Van Doren traveled the well-worn circuit from the Midwest to New York; whereas Rascoe and Van Vechten moved by way of journalism, Van Doren stayed steadily within academic channels, advancing from the University of Illinois to Columbia, where he did his Ph.D. on Thomas Love Peacock, and stayed on for five further years as a lecturer. He appears to be a man difficult to have strong feelings about, though his earnestness ran close to obnoxiousness. "By nature I was a scholar of the ranging kind," he confessed in his autobiography, "erudite when excited, but always incurably passionate . . . I saw most of the past in the light of literary history, and most of the present in its shadow." He never swung clear of an undergraduate mentality—passion always replaced profundity. Literature was his God and his friends were acolytes at the shrine. He considered himself honored to be included in the collection of worshippers, but eligible for a front pew.

After lecturing at Columbia, he became headmaster of a girls' school, Brearly, in New York, which—fortunately for him—the daughter of the owner of *The Nation* attended. After his three-year contract at Brearly elapsed, he was offered the post of literary editor on *The Nation.* He quickly got his brother Mark appointed poetry editor. In 1922 he joined *The Century* and three years later retired, determined to dedicate himself to writing; but that was short-lived. He was asked to become editor of the Literary Guild.*

Van Doren's greatest asset was his wife, Irita Bradford, whom he married in 1912. She made a very comfortable home for herself, and their three daughters. Appointed editor of the Books section of the Sunday *New York Herald,* Rebecca West described her as "an extremely competent editor," combining generosity and adventurousness to make it one of the most important critical papers in the twenties. She gave work to unlikely, and in many cases unknown, candidates, and never lowered the standards of the supplement. Unlike her husband, she had a contagious sense of humor and fun. She left Carl Van Doren—a fact he neglects to mention in his autobiography— and it was widely rumored that she was the mistress of Wendell Willkie. While Carl invited Elinor to serialize *The Venetian Glass Nephew* in *Century,* Irita asked her to contribute reviews to Books with increasing frequency, and appointed her "Visiting Critic" during the month of February 1927—the first person to hold the post after Rebecca West.

Elinor first met Carl Van Doren late in 1922 when, significantly, he was chairman of the MacDowell Club reading in New York. The summer before their move out of New York, Elinor and Bill eagerly accepted every invitation to the country: they visited the Canbys at Yelping Hill and they went to the Van Dorens' house at Wickwire, where Elinor impressed Carl by perversely refusing to wear a coat in the cold wind and forcing herself to swim too far out to the float. Such displays pleased him; they were appropriate for a poet.

As were her urgent requests for money. "I find I have unexpectedly to pay the *interest,* as well as the *paying off,* on the mortgage," Elinor wrote to Van Doren (October 3, 1924), as he quotes in his autobiography; and again, in a varying form earlier: "P.S. Of course I hope you can manage this advance,

---

*This various other posts read like some literary furlong: managing editor of the *Cambridge History of American Literature,* 1917–21; editor of *The Borzoi Reader,* 1936; editor of *Modern American Prose,* 1934; editor of *Anthology of World Prose,* 1935; and a Pulitzer prize winner for his life of Franklin, 1938.

but if you can't, don't picture me suicidal in consequence. It is my reprehensible nature to welcome excitement & change, & the idea of being melodramatically foreclosed & forced to find another—& of course better—place to live is in itself attractive to my mind. But one must do one's duty, hence this letter."

Elinor did not merely "welcome" excitement and change, she actively sought it. Only one-third of *The Venetian Glass Nephew* was written when she issued this request (she had worked on the novel in September at MacDowell, thus skillfully avoiding the problems of moving to Connecticut), and she had but one copy of the draft—a technique she shared with James Branch Cabell. She had no hesitation about sending the only copy to the printers, entrusting her work to the mails. To keep up the fast tempo of excitement, serialization began long before the novel was completed. "She liked the risk," Van Doren said. "Although I was troubled by the danger that the manuscript might be lost, I could not refuse to share a hazard which was so much more hers than mine. To her the risk was tonic, I think it kept her waywardly excited to realize that her sharp and shining prose had to take its chances in the mail. . . ."

She was also forced to keep going by the fact that her progress was well behind schedule. She was not being as swift as she had predicted. "My book advances under difficulties," she told James Branch Cabell (October 3, 1924), "but I hope to finish it in November. Expect it to begin in January Century. . . . It should be out in February, & you shall have one of the first copies, since you are kind enough to want it." As usual, Elinor was optimistic: *The Venetian Glass Nephew* was eventually serialized in the March, April, and May numbers, and Doran published it September 11, 1925. The novel took exactly one year from start to finish.

Elinor's original plans were abridged drastically by the demands, yet again, made on her by the household. The furnace collapsed in the dead of winter. The children suffered from a series of colds. Freida had to be begged and coaxed not to burn every meal, and not to give notice. Elinor came down with severe headaches, largely brought on by trying to balance complicated account books and by a series of fights with Bill, one over the fact that she bought books with the housekeeping money. There were tears, scenes, and most unpleasantly, a tantrum that culminated in Elinor bashing her head against the wall. The children scattered the moment any such episode threatened, or were willingly banished to a neighbor's house. Elinor struggled to make them wear the fine coats they hated. Yet everything had settled down again by Thanksgiving, when Stephen and Rosemary Benét visited them,*and again for Christmas, when Elinor made her last attempt to win over the children.

*Elinor wrote a long poem to Stephen Vincent Benét that Thanksgiving, 1924, called "Love to Stephen," which she eventually published in 1927. It was reprinted after Stephen's death in 1943 and again in her own *Last Poems*.

CHAPTER NINE: 1925

§ *Elinor Wylie, Elinor Wylie, What do I hear*
you say?
"I wish it were Shelley astride my belly instead
of poor Bill Benét."
—*Sara Teasdale*

Elinor Wylie's reputation was at its peak by the middle of the decade, and it would not vary for many years after her death. Her fame rested not simply on her talent, but on her beauty. She had made herself into a sensation that endeavored to give the lie to her past infamy. No party was complete without her: she brought a form of elegance into every room she entered that became the envy of office girls for years. The Elinor Wylie style was aped and parodied all over town. Her wardrobe and her hair style—meticulously parted down the middle and tumbling in precisely waved rows to the top of her neck—managed to receive as much comment as her poetry and novels. In her fortieth year she succeeded in looking years, perhaps even a decade, younger by her skillful use of make-up. She continued to lie about her age, and no one doubted her. And she continued to work at a pace that astonished greedy editors—a pace which Edmund Wilson put down to her steady high blood pressure.

Her fascination lay in her complexity. The closer people got, the more shadowy she became, and yet from a distance observers thought they understood her. She was classified as vain, egocentric, and temperamental, and she was all of these; but they were little more than an insulation, a veneer that completely hid anything underneath. Mary Colum noted that Elinor was puzzled by the outside world and groomed herself to the core of her personality simply for protection. There was a rehearsed air about her, and there was a reversed nature to her attitudes. She cared about her work in private and her person in public. She saw herself as one of her own well- 245 planned creations and thus virtually invited criticism. She received it in the most aggressive form, appearing in a blistering string of portraits.

Thomas Wolfe drew her as Rosalind Bailey in *The Web and the Rock* (1939):

> There was no doubt at all who she was. Her cold beauty was celebrated, her picture was well known, and, in justice to her, it must be said that she was one author who fully lived up to her photographs. Although she was past forty, her appearance was astonishingly youthful. The impression she gave was virginal and girlish. . . . Anyone who ever saw her would retain the memory of her lovely, slender girlishness, her proud carriage, the level straightness of her glance, and a quality of combined childishness and maturity, of passion and of ice.
>
> Immediately, however, she began to misbehave in a strange manner. Taking no notice of the newcomers, she swept through the doorway and then stood there . . . with a proud and outraged look.

Wolfe went on to point out that she was at the center of "a precious coterie—a group of privileged personalities who had won for themselves an intoxicating position in the life of the city. They had formed themselves into a clique, which at that moment was supreme, and at the head of that clique, crown jewel of its reverence, object of its idolatry, was the poetess, Rosalind Bailey."

To Thomas Wolfe, Elinor was like a statue of a pagan goddess, magnificent to behold but totally repellent when she turned into living mortal flesh. She stood in the middle of a swirling orbit of sycophantic admirers, headed by Carl Van Vechten, and followed by a multitude of lesser stars. Wolfe's hatred of her was intense—not only for her person, but for what she represented: the whole band of simpering, self-advertising, self-congratulating minor talents whose collected force counterfeited true greatness. The opinion Elinor held of herself, Thomas Wolfe believed, was only surpassed by the opinion often voiced by her "cultists." She and they were revolting.

Elinor emerged only slightly better in other pictures. Kathleen Coyle wrote of her as Victoria Beresford Rising in *Immortal Ease* (1941): "They say . . . that you are ravishingly beautiful and . . . that you are made of stone." And later on the character Robert Ilion, who represents Horace, says: "I begin to believe. . . . That you are ice cold. Any heat that comes from you is the heat that comes from intense cold." In 1928 Anne Parrish published *All Kneeling,* which she hotly denied, for legal reasons, was based on Elinor. But all the signs of a strict *roman à clef* are there, even down to the color of the pale blue writing paper used by Christabel Caine, the Elinor figure. Anne Parrish says of Christabel: "She wanted to be adored. She wanted to prove almost too much for men. . . ." Christabel herself utters the well-known lament of Elinor: "Oh . . . If only I had a child! You don't know, you can't imagine, the sorrow of childlessness!" Such were the words, almost syllable-perfect, Elinor wrote to Bill at the end of her life. Christabel Caine is the most sympathetic portrait of Elinor in fiction. Anne Parrish, like other observers, was hypnotized by Elinor's most superficial qualities, and yet she somehow fashioned them into a sympathetic likeness. She equated her heroine to a sea anemone, beautiful, protected, and distant.

All these pictures of Elinor only demonstrate her imbroglio. Margaret Widdemer assessed her as essentially childlike—"she couldn't believe in consequences." Mary Colum admired her professionalism: "what really stood to her was her industry at her work and the discipline that came with it. . . . What disturbed me far more than her neuroticism was her vanity. . . . If she was not overtly considered the most important and beautiful person in every gathering, she suffered and showed her suffering openly." Beatrice Kaufman, a victim of Elinor's extreme willfulness, put her down as being a "half-woman, half-child kind of person." Elinor attended a party given by Miss Kaufman at her house and spied an ivory Italian crucifix which she instantly wanted to own herself. Elinor asked if she could buy it, paying double the price her hostess had paid. Miss Kaufman refused, and the next day noticed that the crucifix had gone. A few days later she received a check from Elinor for the price she had offered, which was torn up. Yet nine years after Elinor's death Beatrice Kaufman said of the thief, "She was very loyal in her friendships and very generous in her admiration for other women. I never knew her to do an unkind thing or to be petty in any way."

Men were kinder to Elinor. Carl Van Doren's memory ran close to hagiography, and his behavior toward her in life was no different. He asked her to join the staff of the Literary Guild as soon as he held the top post. He helped organize "The Poet's Club," which was designed almost entirely for Elinor-worship and very short-lived. Carl Van Vechten never shed his consuming admiration for her. And Edmund Wilson, for all his intelligence, was quite unable to explain his total captivation.

It was as if Elinor had three lives: that of childhood, shy, timorous, and fairly sheltered; followed by the second, which was passed buried alive; and the third, the shortest of all, as a very famous writer and woman. This period spanned eight years and she acted as if she knew it would be short.

The Venetian Glass Nephew was finished the third week in January 1925, written at a wild pace under more difficult conditions than any other novel. She did not make anything easier by depending on *Century* to send proofs as quickly as possible so she herself would have a working copy before she handed it over to Doran. Even before Doran published the book, Elinor was entering into negotiations with Alfred and Blanche Knopf for their firm to take over her future books. Secrecy was, of course, essential, for if George Doran sensed desertion, he "will leave him [*Nephew*] lie & let him die on their hands," as Elinor wrote to Blanche Knopf (January 19). Elinor was not an easy author for publishers; she kept a highly critical eye on publicity and advertisements, and though she lacked Amy Lowell's boisterous approach, she was never at a loss for some sharp comment on her publisher's selling policies.

Blanche Knopf (1894–1966) first entered Elinor's life on a strictly business basis. A remarkable woman, many people have credited her with the real intellectual force behind the firm founded by Alfred Knopf in 1915, whom she married a year later. She threw open his list to European and Latin American writers, while her husband imprinted the characteristic elegant Knopf style on his books. Thin as a rail, Blanche Knopf seemed to suffer from a lifelong case of *anorexia nervosa*. "For lunch she would have a lettuce leaf," Rebecca West recalled, "and then in the evening she would break out and have a lettuce leaf with dressing." Her aversion to food was well known. Writers often refused to dine with her because the meal simply failed to appear. At a luncheon (of all things) to honor her in 1940, Thomas Mann stood up and said, "It seems rather paradoxical to honor with an excellent luncheon the merits of a lady who notoriously eats nothing." She was a strikingly beautiful woman, her face composed along Slavic and well-defined lines: the heavily hooded eyes were there, her nose protruded to create an impressive profile and her lips were full and pursed—the very features celebrated by the post-Impressionists. Like Elinor, Blanche was strikingly beautiful and always wonderfully turned out. But she was not an exclusively urban creature. She played golf, rode to hounds, adored dogs, and it was her Borzoi that was sported on the spine of Knopf books. Her energy was positively alarming. "Blanche always looked frail," Hammond Innes remembered, "but her enormous reserves of vital energy, which she poured out so unselfishly, made one forget this as soon as she began talking." She had but one consuming interest—books.

Elinor's letters to Blanche are like literary balance sheets, each entry a notation about work and print. Sometimes Elinor would recklessly refer to some personal problem, but these additions were rare and brought out only in relation to her writing. Speaking of her *Venetian Nephew* Elinor confided to Blanche, from the Algonquin where she had gone after a brief visit to Mama (January 23): "Now that the book is actually done, I wish very much that you & Alfred were going to publish it, as you'll have my books in the future. . . . Well, at least it's a vast relief to have the thing finished, & I hope it's all right—as a piece of Venetian glass."

Most of the first six months of 1925 Elinor spent trying to avoid New Canaan. She snatched at every invitation that brought her into New York, and invariably found some excuse to stay overnight. On April 4, 1925, she and Bill went up to Boston to attend a "Complimentary Dinner in Honour of Miss Amy Lowell" held in the ballroom of the Somerset Hotel. The collection of editors and poets was vast. Elinor was asked to say a few words—"Nobody will be allowed to talk more than five minutes," Amy warned her (March 23, 1925); "personally I wish you would stretch your time." Elinor's platform appearances were not impressive. Her voice was unexpectedly harsh, "rather like a peacock." Aside from the deep, rough quality of the voice, it did not carry well. The look in her eyes was disconcerting, enhanced by her aversion to spectacles. Once when Bill and she were asked to join Louis Untermeyer at the theater, Bill took the precaution of warning their host (March 4, 1925): "Could I whisper in your ear that my talented helpmeet . . . is really so blind, despite her orient gaze, that unless she is almost down among the saxophones she can't see what I humorously speak of as the actors on the stage." Yet, like everything else in her life, Elinor turned the extraordinarily vacant look in her eyes into an advantage; when she stood up to recite her poems, the audience was entranced. Her posture, always stiffly upright, and her poise, more than made up for her other limitations as a speaker. She detested formal readings; the traveling to get there was annoying or the dinners were invariably bad and boring; but she adored any attention given to her. The few times she accepted invitations to speak, she usually found some excuse for canceling again. Nancy Hoyt reports that when she returned from a lecture tour that included Chicago (of which there is no record), she was reduced to "shudders" of loathing.

The dinner for Amy Lowell was an entirely different matter. Like a series of literary jack-in-the-boxes, poet after poet after editor leapt up, uttered a few ardent words of respect or devotion, then promptly sat down. Robert Frost and Louis Untermeyer had the added distinction of staying at Sevenels with Amy Lowell. S. Foster Damon (later to become Amy's indefatigable biographer), John Farrar, Dr. Canby, and others, among them Amy herself, all popped up to say a few words. The dinner was a year late; Amy had been asked to preside in a similar manner behind her orchids over a celebration for her fiftieth birthday, but had refused. Instead, the honor was moved to 1925 to commemorate the two-volume biography of Keats she was about to launch in Europe. As it turned out, the dinner was a farewell of a different sort. Amy Lowell died on May 12, 1925.

Despite Elinor's growing antipathy to New Canaan life, she had moments of considerable pleasure there. Mary and Padraic Colum lived in a house conveniently close down the road (it later became the scene, after the Colums moved out, of a notorious murder). The children were sent off to the

Benéts, or anyone else, with increased frequency and Bill and
Elinor were able to have an occasional house party. When
Bill's own best man married Elinor's maid of honor in Greenwich in May, some of the guests moved on from the wedding
to Park Street for the night—Edna St. Vincent Millay and her
husband Eugen Boissevain, Arthur and Gladys Ficke, and
Dorothy Parker. They accepted more from convenience than
desire. Arthur Ficke said nine years after Elinor's death: "I do
not think I have ever known an equally beautiful woman who
was so little affected [by] what one calls one's heart. I just
couldn't imagine how it would be possible to become intimate
with Elinor. She frightened me a little. . . . It did not seem
possible that she could ever be influenced in any way by what
one said or did to her. . . ."

The party got off to a wonderful start with a "terrific"
battle with the taxi driver, who having agreed on a fixed price
for the journey from Greenwich to New Canaan, promptly
decided to charge them "some fancy amount." The guests
then weaved into the dining room for some supper and more
to drink. Afterwards everyone save Elinor, Dorothy Parker,
and Arthur Ficke squeezed into their bedrooms upstairs. The
remaining trio stayed downstairs in the long drawing room
and Elinor quickly urged Dorothy Parker to recite her poetry,
which Ficke as quickly volunteered to criticize. After this poetry tutorial, Dorothy Parker went off to bed, leaving Elinor
and Arthur talking: "I think we talked very seriously," he
recalled,

about such simple things as life and death and the nature of man
. . . I cannot recall a word of it just now.

After a while we went upstairs—and, God alone knows, went
into Dotty's bed-room and waked [sic] her up. Elinor showed me
the scars on Dotty's wrists where she tried to cut her blood-vessels
a year ago. . . . Then we comforted Dotty, and I think Dotty cried
—maybe out of weariness with Elinor and me. . . .

The next day was perfectly terrible. Everybody a little on edge,
everybody trying to conceal his own edginess. Sometime about noon
the party broke up, with love and kisses.

The serialization of *The Venetian Glass Nephew* in the
Century was finished by May. It is Elinor's most exquisite and

famous prose creation, and indeed that is precisely what the *Nephew* was—a creation, spun from glass into the shape of an heir to satisfy the vanity of Cardinal Peter Innocent Bon, who actually descends into the pagan underworld to retrieve his nephew. The entire novel is a battle between opposites. It is constructed almost like a frieze of undigested research, across which dance like light and shade the permutations of the basic theme: reason struggling against emotion, and lust opposing chastity. White and black play an important part in the story. Virginio is introduced, as one might expect with glass, in a portrait drawn in white. His lover, Rosalba Berni, "better known among the Arcadians of Italy as Sappho the Younger, or . . . the Infant Sappho," enters swathed in black.

Her hand was warm and vibrating with life; Virginio's hand was cold and thin, and as she clasped it, an ominous cracking startled her with strangeness, she felt as if his fingers were so many brittle icicles. . . . Although, in her brilliance, she was fire to Virginio's ice . . . the essential substance of that element is delicate and tender and more malleable than the very air, whereas ice is denser even than water, and often hard as stone . . . it was Rosalba's spirit that must inevitably be wounded in this unnatural warfare, however brittle Virginio's bone's might prove.

The victim of "this unnatural warfare"—the combat between the warm vulnerability of emotions and the frozen invulnerability not so much of reason as the absence of emotions—is Rosalba. She is the one who crosses over in a journey that takes her from life to porcelain. Rosalba was burned in the furnace of Sèvres to make her a suitable wife for Virginio:

The faces of the lovers are most beautiful and pure; the gentle and elegiac quality of their love appears unmarred by longing. Having forgotten fear and the requirements of pity, their tenderness becomes a placid looking-glass in which each beholds the other; the mercurial wildness which no longer moves them is fixed behind this transparent screen, lending brightness to the mirrored images.

Elinor's *Nephew* is the most acute documentation of her affection for reversal. The lifeless, bloodless qualities of glass and silver heaved with animation in her mind. The exigencies of the flesh were ripe for distress. Life was, for her, a subtle progression of denial, a steep advance on the Puritan; pleasure is born in denial and happiness is the result only of pain. Every sensation has its root in the destruction of sensation. Elinor understood standard values by turning them around; and if one viewed the entire *Venetian Glass Nephew* in a mirror, its reversed image would be an appropriate nursery fable. Such transitions gave Elinor's work their strength, and Elinor herself her endurance. It is a deceptively simple tale, complicated by the simple device she explained in her essay *Symbols in Literature.*

Once again the symphony of opposites is clad in the richest clothing from the wardrobe of eighteenth-century Venice, and, as in *Jennifer Lorn,* Elinor comes close to suffocating her story. She dazzled her readers, who stood back, admiring the force of her erudition (so hastily and briefly acquired) and her supple prose. "For this," James Branch Cabell wrote, five years after the book was published, "we know, is but a make-believe land of animated figurines, wherein not lust nor death, not poverty nor bankrupt love, but the cool joys of virtuosity, and of finesse, and of each tiny triumph in phrase-making, are the sole serious matters." Edmund Wilson was less impressed, writing to her that her research had not come up to the standard set in her previous novel. "I must object further that you have mingled the fictitious with the real in a manner hardly allowable. . . . As for style . . . I fear that the imagery has here become so copious as somewhat to impede the progress of the action. . . . Of the fable itself, it can hardly be said that, if it is to be taken literally, it is absurd; and if allegorically, licentious."

Of all her novels the *Nephew* is the one Elinor wrote most swiftly, the one she cared the least about, and the best. After her death it was turned, unsuccessfully, into an opera. It would have been better suited for transformation by Madame de Pompadour into a stage production at Versailles. It possessed all the qualities of a minutely traced dance, designed entirely for entertainment. It is the easiest to read of all her prose works, and her shortest novel.

The breathless, almost frenetic pace of her life seemed to accelerate by the summer of 1925. Elinor was driven by financial problems, ill health, and her past. Her history loomed up at the most inconvenient times to plague her.

Toward the end of May the Attorney-General of Rhode Island began to investigate the fraudulent divorces granted in his state and Elinor's was one of the most famous cases on a long list. The newspapers were quick to pick up the story that she had not been, as she stated on a legal document, a resident of the State of Rhode Island and was therefore illegally divorced from Horace. The District Court had no right to hand down a decree.

It was the kind of publicity Elinor was desperate to avoid. She left for Washington and then headed up to the MacDowell Colony. No sooner had she arrived in Peterborough than she fell ill. Her headaches thundered and her blood pressure soared. She was also exhausted. "I wasted two weeks," she told Bill (August 4) (Y). She recovered sufficiently to spend the first weekend in August with the Van Dorens.

When she returned to MacDowell on August 3, after getting the last seat on the Pullman out of Hartford, she began her work in earnest. The Colony was crawling with writers and mosquitoes that summer. In a curious form of memorial to a composer, writers outnumbered musicians almost three to one in 1925. And Elinor was anxious to be considered, like the other standard MacDowell fixture E. A. Robinson, the doyenne of the colonists. When the poet Virginia Moore arrived, she was instantly introduced to Elinor. "I was introduced as a 'poet,' and to my surprise and embarrassment [Elinor] said as she took my hand, 'You *look* like a poet'— whatever that means—leaning impulsively to kiss my forehead."

Throughout her stay in New Hampshire Elinor performed in the finest prima donna manner: story after story of her extraordinary behavior accumulated about her. When she went swimming with Louis Untermeyer one morning she overtired herself on the swim out to the float, and by the time she had to swim back to shore, she asked him if she might rest her hand on his shoulder part of the way. Flattered by the request, he agreed, but soon he too began to feel exhausted and asked her to let go. She became very angry and said, "Posterity will remember me as the more important poet of us," clearly implying that it was his duty to help her. "Only

Elinor," Louis Untermeyer added, "could have said that and meant it."

Her behavior toward Bill was scarcely more attractive. She sent him into town one day to buy a pair of shoes she admired in a store window. He returned not with the shoes, but an excuse: "I'm sorry, Elinor . . . but they only carry the one shoe—you can order your size from it." She was furious with this explanation, and accused Bill of making a fool of her in front of the other colonists. Everyone in the dining room heard the scene.

Her letters to Bill before he arrived at MacDowell that summer were of a much more affectionate tone. They had to be since she had endless errands for him to run—she wanted a blouse from Franklin Simon, then when he bought it, she changed her mind and asked him to exchange it for a neat, inexpensive dress from Bloomingdale's instead. There were overdue books (on witches) she needed returned to the library. There were endless problems over Park Street, which she left to him to sort out. Freida had finally made good her threat to hand in her notice, and cleared off leaving two cats in her place and Bill to arrange cleaners and his own cooking. He was forced to investigate the possibilities of renting the place out, or selling it, because Elinor had told him she no longer wanted it. And, most important, she wanted him to place a story for her with *Woman's Home Companion.*

"I cannot afford to have my mind distracted by constant worry about money. SO," she complained to him (August 4) (Y), "with an exceedingly bitter cry, I shall begin the damn story this afternoon. . . ." Four days and 6,000 words later, "The Applewood Chair" was complete. It is a story that deals, unconvincingly, with the problems of marriage while focusing on the insensitive use of the wife's (Monica's) favorite, yet fragile, chair. Monica is Elinor—she has bronze-colored hair, a silver dress, tiny wrists and ankles, and an acute sense of detail. Her husband, Ernest, is Bill—he insists on tying up his boots while balancing, much to his wife's anger, on her applewood chair. The autobiographical interest is as slim as the story.

Unlike Logan Pearsall Smith, Elinor had no prejudices about writing for glossy magazines; she simply had to pay her

bill at Wanamakers. Although she did go on record as de-
nouncing *The Saturday Evening Post* to Emily Clark—"I can't
bear the look or the feel or the *smell* of it," she said, instructing
her to remove it from the room—she could not overlook the
uses of magazines that paid very well. She was paid $750 for
"The Applewood Chair." Her stories for *Woman's Home Companion* ("The Applewood Chair," "King's Pity," and "Ninety-nine Cream Bottles") and *Harper's Bazaar* ("A Birthday
Cake for Lionel") demonstrate that even with her remarkable
facility for writing, Elinor could not produce memorable
works simply for money.

Such writing for money kept her from the work she was
anxious to get to, reduced her to a frenzy, and made her very
angry. It absorbed desperately needed time, which was to her
more important than money, no matter how pressing her
debts. And with each day she took off from novel writing for
short story work, her temper got blacker and blacker. The
scene related in Eunice Tietjens's autobiography, which probably occurred the previous summer, indicates the hysterical
reactions Elinor was subject to. The Regina Watson Studio
was the only studio at MacDowell equipped with electricity
and a grand piano, and once a month colonists met there for
readings or recitals. The summer of 1924 it was Elinor's studio, and Eunice Tietjens entered with the others, for an evening. "I noticed that Elinor, who sat at a little distance from
me, was sitting in a peculiarly rigid manner, tense and white.
. . . When in the course of the proceedings she was asked to
recite a poem, she started violently, and I almost expected her
to refuse." She quickly composed herself, recited a poem
wonderfully, then relapsed into her tense silence again. Everyone save the Gormans and Miss Tietjens filed out of the studio, whereupon Elinor promptly burst out:

"Did you see how they hate me, how they all hate me? . . . They
are trying to down me, to injure me, to keep me from working. But
I won't be downed! I have a typewriter and a better brain than any
of them, and they won't succeed. I'll beat them all yet! Did you see
how they asked me to recite so they could laugh at me? . . . And did
you see how they left the door open on purpose so the mosquitoes
would get in and bite me tomorrow when I am trying to write? The
mosquitoes! I tell you they will stop at nothing!"

In the summer of 1925 Elinor moved between two
women, Tennessee Anderson and Grace Hazard Conkling,
both of whom were devoted to her but not each other.* "I
find it difficult to be nice to her [Grace] without neglecting
Tennessee, who looks to me for company," Elinor reported
to Bill (August 4) (Y), "the more so inasmuch as the two are
not particularly taken with each other, I fear." Elinor kept Bill
informed of the new arrivals as well: "A pretty prissy rather
Zona Galeish person called Janet Ramsey [a novelist] has
arrived . . . she is too formal to live. . . ." The day after Bill
read this report, Elinor changed her mind, saying (August 6)
(Y), "The joke is that the super-refined Janet Ramsey is a far
better mixer. . . . She is so pretty, in a ladylike way, that she
is a pleasure to see, and really she is very nice too." The
colonists idolized Elinor, doing favors, bowing and scraping.
When Elinor missed breakfast one morning, Tennessee appeared with prunes. Grace fell from favor momentarily until
Elinor received an invitation to visit her studio. Elinor sat, in
regal oblivion, for Tennessee that summer, but the bust modeled of her, if finished, is lost. And Elinor sat at her long work
table broadcasting requests for books: from Bill she wanted
Lady Blessington's memoirs, Trelawny's letters, William
Hickey's diary, Hogg's biography of Shelley, Wyatt's poetry,
Captains Courageous, and *Shelley and the Unromantics,* and from
Carl Van Doren an endless stream of Americana.

"I would give my eyes to get to Shelley," Elinor wrote
to Bill on August 5, referring to the novel she wanted to write
next. She discarded the idea of doing a book on witches and
her relative who was hanged at the Salem witch trials; she
would get to it later, she told herself. She wanted to concentrate on Shelley. Her fascination with him had been of very
long standing; it was notorious, and an obsession. All the

*Tennessee Anderson, sculptor and writer, was the second wife of Sher-
wood Anderson from 1916 to 1924. Margaret Widemer remembered her
as "a big, lithe, handsome sorrel-haired woman," given to resting on sofas
a great deal. She died a year after Elinor. Grace Hazard Conkling (1878–
1958), the mother of Hilda Conkling and professor of English at Smith
College. She was a poet of considerable talent, relying on nature for her
material, and a woman of memorable generosity. She liked Elinor very
much, and briefly.

trappings of excess accompanied her adoration. She thought she saw Shelley's face peering through a window once when she visited Emily Clark at Half Moon Street. She easily distorted history to accommodate her feelings, denigrating Shelley's wives as totally unsuitable for him (implying that she herself would have been a more likely candidate). She spent vast sums of money to buy first editions and a letter and check in his handwriting. Observers began to wince when the subject of Shelley was brought up, and Elinor invariably steered most conversations in his direction. She alone was the great authority on him, she was certain. In fact, she did know his work and the studies of him extremely well. She studied, memorized, read, and researched every detail about him. She took pages of notes on his manner of speech, his appearance, his idiosyncrasies, and anything else that brought her knowledge closer to him.

"Elinor was quite dotty, not just crazy, but dotty about Shelley," Rebecca West recalled. "I remember her telling me that she had heard Shelley come into the next room that afternoon and then saw him press his face up to the door. She was quite serious!" Elinor's neurotic fascination with Shelley went straight to the core of her talent for fantasy. One can nurse, as Elinor herself did, the similarities between the arch-Romantic poet and his cultist; Elinor quite happily disregarded perspective and proportion when she analyzed his life and hers. They both shared ill health, a distaste for obligation, a casual brutality to first spouses, a string of dead children, a fascination with water and with the country—and they were both poets. Elinor waved aside the sex difference and several times expressed the belief that she actually *was* Shelley. But the facts cannot be brushed aside. What Shelley rebelled against, Elinor accepted, easily and passionately; and what Shelley cared about, Elinor ignored. She paid no attention to politics, humanity, or disrupting conventional attitudes, merely pointing to a shared (but in her case undeveloped) interest in mysticism and the occult as yet another similarity between them. Shelley was made for hero-worship, and Elinor had left room in her life for a hero—a constant, changeless and intensely romantic figure that filled the gaps in her marriages. He became the object of the love she denied her husbands;

he supplied her with a steady object for devotion and in her way, service. Her obsession grew until it completely dismissed the fact that he had been dead for over a century.

Elinor's infatuation with her image of Shelley reveals her own character more clearly even than the actual facts of her life. His appeal lay in her ability to bring him back from the dead, her talent to re-create him; he was her excuse for the emotions she tried to deny and claimed to detest. She loaded her Shelley-language with precisely the same emotional excess she damned in others. Because her emotions were buried so deeply within her, they never changed; they remained stubbornly adolescent and therefore only appeared either in a highly stylized form or wildly uncontrollable. Her silences after the suicides of Philip Hichborn, her brother, and her sister demonstrate more than a ruthless lack of feeling—they reveal a morbid fear of spontaneity and a distrust of her own truly-felt responses. Her egomania made her immune to other people. Her tantrums and self-absorption crowded out the people she tried to love. The ice imagery in her poetry had a firm foundation in her character because she forced it to, making it stand in place of warmth.

This alarming aggregate of inhuman qualities was counteracted by her speedy development as a writer. Her career started when she appreciated that her capacity as a woman and a mother (and they were linked to one another) would never be fulfilled or satisfied. As each child died, she moved closer to the ultimate denial of her vulnerability. She turned herself into a writer when she discarded the idea, and hope, of being simply a woman. While one side of her character remained submerged, another developed. Elinor's talent as a writer seemed to rise out of the ashes of human feelings. And poised between these opposing forces was her idea of Shelley. He was the bridge between the denied and recognized; it was an uneasy and fragile construction.

Shelley's importance had been established early in Elinor's life when she withdrew Trelawny's recollections of the poet from her father's bookshelves at the age of eleven. Horace continued to nurture her early intoxication with him. She found in Shelley all the elements suited for obsession—an early, tragic, and mysterious death, a life of unbridled activity and considerable fame as a member of that exotic breed known as poet. It was a picture she retained throughout her life, and firmly refused to alter. And he became a safety valve for her. She distrusted romanticism, just as she distrusted her eroticism; yet around Shelley she wove both romance and sex in a manner, hidden in scholarship, that was instantly acceptable to her. She attributed to him, in a respectable academic process, all that she hid from herself.

Into Shelley she sank the affection, care, and devotion she withheld from her three husbands. Into him she deposited the love she only flirted with regarding Horace and Bill. While her letters to Horace in 1909 and 1910 are flourishes of romanticism that she eventually grew out of and later even mocked, she never shed this element in relation to Shelley. He was her private preserve, safely seated in her intellect. To him she pledged unswerving affection, largely because he was of her own making and because he would never hear it. He was her Venetian glass nephew—fantasy composed mainly of facts. Unlike Edith Olivier's "love child," Shelley was a safe and admired object for such attentions; but he was also obliged to perform exactly the same purpose—to fill the region in Elinor's character that had been made lonely. The contradictions in his own character and the unreliability of his biographers and friends at once provided Shelley with enough interest to support all of Elinor's efforts. She slandered Harriet Westbrook, swore at Sir Timothy Shelley, and accused Mary Godwin of falling out of love with her husband, long after they were out of earshot. "I am far sillier about Shelley than you ever were about Jane Carlyle," she would confess to Horace (June 12, 1927) (B) when she noticed that Shelley's Marlow house was for sale. There was an element of crusading on behalf of her hero, but she never undertook the logical enterprise, as Amy Lowell had done for Keats, of biography. Elinor's approach was, as it had been in her previous two novels, to marry her idea of Shelley and history—to join her imagination and fact.

Her novel *The Orphan Angel* was designed to retrieve Shelley from his premature death in the Gulf of Spezia on July 8, 1822, by having him found and resuscitated by the crew of an American clipper ship, *Witch of the West*. Thereafter Shelley was bound on a progress that stretched the breadth of America, once the vessel docked in Boston, accompanied by a sort of primitive travel agent, David Butternut, who saved him from drowning. Elinor's portrait of Shelley (renamed Shiloh, which she borrowed from Byron) is a mixture of accuracy and awe:

> He looked very tall . . . very slim . . . with preposterous elegance, his romantic grace, and the aristocratic attenuation of his frame. At the same time, he wore the indubitable air of an athlete. . . . His face was bronzed, save where the exceeding whiteness of the forehead betrayed itself under the tumbled hair, whose dark eccentric exuberance was flecked with silver.

And her story makes heavy strides through well-researched scenes, episodes, and terrain. Her devotion to Shelley obliged her to pause too long and too often in the course of her narrative. She was hopelessly impeded by her passionate regard for her subject—a dependence that was lacking in her previous two novels.

The idea for the novel was inspired. In her Shelley/Shiloh character she merely, so she told herself, took over where history left off. To her the belief that Shelley might have been fished out of Leghorn Harbor was not so preposterous; she had been envisaging it for years. It was an extremely clever device by which she could mingle the real with the imagined. But the execution of the novel was not inspired, largely because she sensed potential opposition from her readers (a detail she rarely thought about while writing her other books) and retreated further than ever behind the protection of her researches into nineteenth-century America—a location and period she found herself as uncertain in dealing with as in her earlier excursions into eighteenth-century Venice, England, India, and Persia. Instead of enticing her readers by her irrepressible enthusiasm for Shelley, she would leave them dazed and impressed simply by the weight of her work. Paradoxically, *The Orphan Angel* cost her the most care, the most worry, and the most work of all her books. It was the only one that would split the critics decisively between ardent admiration and utter loathing.

"I am working myself deaf dumb blind and lumbagoishly

lame, but am otherwise well & contented," Elinor wrote to Carl Van Doren (August 12, 1925). Such was the pace she kept up throughout the summer of 1925, only taking time off to spend a weekend with the Van Dorens at the end of August, and even then she brought her manuscript with her to show her host. She wanted to remain at the MacDowell Colony until October 15, and obtained Mrs. MacDowell's permission to stay on for three weeks after the Colony officially closed on September 22, but complained to Blanche Knopf (September 12), "the children are the problem. They return [from California] on the twenty-sixth of this month, & I feel they will simply make a sandwich of me & my darling characters & devour us. But I am trying to find a way." Two days later she was delighted to tell Blanche that she had indeed found "a way," writing (September 14): "I know you'll be glad to learn that I've arranged it with the Norrises about the children . . . I shall have a chance to work." Elinor's arrangement with the childrens' aunt and uncle was simple; the Norrises would take over all responsibility for them. These plans came as no surprise to Kathleen Norris, who had had some particularly heart-rending scenes with her nephew Jim. Once when she called at Park Street, she went upstairs to see Jim who was ill in bed with a cold and he begged her to take him away with her. Kathleen Norris responded meekly that Elinor and Bill were his parents and she could not look after him. The children were dismissed easily, and for Elinor with no difficulty whatsoever. She did not even go from New York to New Canaan to say goodbye to them. Her egomania had discarded husbands; now her career left no room for children. Bill was deeply upset by this turn of events, and tried to hide it from Elinor. But the children were not unhappy to leave.

Elinor left MacDowell toward the end of September, with 40,000 words of her Shelley novel completed. After seeing Bill off to New York, she went to Northampton, Massachusetts, to stay a few days with Grace Hazard Conkling. There she staged one of her most famous scenes. One night the conversation moved, surprisingly enough, to the subject of poetry, and one of the guests ventured the opinion that Edna St. Vincent Millay was the "greatest lyric woman poet." Elinor immediately shot out of the room and up to her bedroom and started tossing her clothes into a suitcase. When her hostess caught up with her, Elinor cried out: "I was insulted! . . . They said Edna was our greatest woman poet. And everyone knows I am!" To confirm this judgment Elinor sent Grace Hazard Conkling quotations from her poem "Wild Peaches" as her thank-you note when she reached New York, staying at the Commodore Hotel rather than returning straight to Park Street.

Nothing had been resolved about the house and it looked as if all her plans made in August for selling it had simply evaporated. When she reached Park Street at the end of September, Elinor was appalled at the condition of the place. "Things are about as bad as they could be out here," she wrote to Blanche (October 3), like some dispatch from the battlefield. Again, "Things have gone from bad to worse," she informed Grace Hazard Conkling (October 8):

I have had no servant whatever, & at the end of a fortnight I am somewhat weary. Now all is about to be changed; my mother says I must go abroad & drop all responsibility like a heavy hotcake, & I see now [no] other way of escape. If the original plan had been followed out, & I could have been alone with Bill for one winter, I think it would have been better for everyone—it was *his moderate, his sensible,* his kindly plan—This is thought excessive, but is now rendered unavoidable by the desperation of the circumstances. And, when all is said & done, I have not seen England for ten years, & it is the cradle of Shelley. I am going all alone, in about a month I suppose.

She also told Edmund Wilson that she was going abroad, either "the end of October or the beginning of November." Bill heartily endorsed the proposed voyage. He wrote to Elinor in New York (October 12) (Y) while she was making her bookings: "Don't worry about anything. All will be plain sailing now and you'll have a lot of fun in England." A day later he added (Y): "So just dismiss all worry of every kind and make your plans for your trip with the assurance that everyone wants you to have a perfectly grand time . . . I certainly shall help in every way I possibly can." Elinor never sailed to England or anywhere else in 1925; either her plans fell through or she used them to get what she wanted out of Bill—release both from his children and the house in New Canaan. Once Bill handed the children over to the Norrises on October 12, she pointed out that there was no need at all to hold on to the house, and no need to "escape."

"Did we not make a fine mistake in our youth," she asked Carl Van Doren at the height of her frustration (October 6),

—which was so nearly contemporaneous [he was born three days after Elinor]—in becoming what the Miss Sinclair & the Peterboro servants call *creators?* . . . But our present trouble—if your impeccable admirableness will accept the word—springs from our stubborn attempts to utilize our wretched minds, to make unpleasant greyish convolutions work for us instead of trained & agile fingertips & the beautiful rhythmic strength of habit. "How lovely is benign stupidity!"

This is as close as Elinor ever got to an actual complaint about work. She habitually boasted about her work, and now as before, when she was kept from it, she was furious.

Exhaustion ranged throughout her letters in the autumn of 1925. Even the pleasure she expressed to her critical bodyguard limped with fatigue. Almost verifying Thomas Wolfe's contention (voiced nearly a decade later) that a "clique" formed around Elinor, both Carl Van Doren and Carl Van Vechten published lavish recommendations for *The Venetian Glass Nephew,* which was published on September 11, 1925. Elinor complained to Carl Van Vechten (October 3) (Y) that the book lacked "vitality. That is because I wrote it under difficulties, & when I was tired." Her tiredness even permitted Edmund Wilson's unfavorable comments in *The New Republic* to pass. Wilson was not only against the book but very much against the cheering duet of praise sung so loudly by Van Doren and Van Vechten.* "I very much enjoyed your witty & amusing skit," Elinor wrote to Wilson (October 8) about

---

*Van Vechten, he would later write, "is of so particular a taste as to render him insensible to the beauties of many works, and those among the greatest; so that whatever falls in with his humour obtains the suffrage of his judgment." And Van Doren, Wilson added, is "like the sun of tropical latitudes, which shed its warmth all the year round, diffuses his mild benignance upon the excellent and the unworthy alike, until, by its uniformity, it causes us to long for the asperities of more inclement climates." See *The Shores of Light,* pp. 259–60.

his review, which was couched in the form of a letter to her
from Samuel Johnson; "when I found it was the only review
printed in the New Republic which dealt with the V.G.N. I
admit I was sorry. It is hardly a review—its very charm pre-
cludes the possibility of its being read as a serious comment
upon a serious, however faulty, book."

"I suppose," she addressed the final member of the di-
minishing band of "Wylieites," Carl Van Doren [October 5],

I ought to be afraid—from the point of view of royalties—to be
called erudite, but I adore it in reality. . . . I am heartily disgusted
with the—really you must forgive me, it is the only possible term—
gutless Virginio now that I have him between dull commonplace
blue cloth covers. . . . Thus it is to write a book under bad conditions
& when one is tired—the lack of vitality is all too apparent in the tale.
But what is one to do—sell matches?

Her solution in the final part of the year was leave
New York for Washington to stay with Mama. New Ca-
naan was left to Bill to sort out. On November 29 she and
Bill both read their poetry at St. Mark's-in-the-Bouwerie,
by which time they were resettled in "the Villudge," as
Bill called it, at 68 Bank Street, down the street from
Willa Cather (whom Elinor never met). The novel on Shel-
ley was put aside, briefly, while Elinor wrote her first con-
tribution to the new *New Yorker:* "The Useful Gift—Why
Not?" which appeared just in time for Christmas on the
December 19, 1925, issue. The trip to Europe was post-
poned for eight months.

§*ii*   *Come, let us fill the lively chalice*
         With one delicious draught of malice!
                              —Elinor Wylie,
                         "Vale atque Ave"

Elinor eventually got to Europe at the end of May 1926. She
waited until *The Orphan Angel* was complete before boarding
the liner. It was a very close finish. A week before she sailed,
she sat for publicity photos at Nicholas Muray's studio. The

very night before sailing she stayed up writing the final pages, finishing at six thirty in the morning. "I send you this book with a mixture of feelings," she typed to Blanche the day she sailed (May 21, 1926),

of which the chief one is sadness that it should be over. It is not really a book at all, and sometimes I believe no-one will ever care to read it but myself. It is a life which I have made for myself as I wrote, but now that it is finished I cannot possibly remain in it, and as a book I daresay it is very much too long indeed, and rambling and discursive in the extreme.*

On Thursday, May 21, Elinor and Bill piled themselves and their luggage into cabin C 58 on the Red Star Line's SS *Pennland*—"seen at first," Elinor wrote to Mama (May 23) (B), "it is frankly a shock, to eyes used to even the smaller English boats with their chintz curtains & slight air of country houses." Stephen Vincent Benét—who, along with Marc Connelly, F.P.A., Mr. and Mrs. John Peale Bishop, and Edmund Wilson—made up the going-away party that tried to squeeze themselves into the cabin, had a different opinion. "I sent them a dozen yellow roses," he wrote to his wife (Y), ". . . and saw them off at the boat. It looks a nice boat though not terribly large and they have a very nice cabin. . . . Bill seems a trifle dozed and not quite sure even yet that he was sailing." More daunting than his "dozed" state was Bill's constricting fear: "he won't ask for *anything* himself," Elinor complained to her mother. "From baths to Sherry-&-bitters I have to demand all the necessities of life. After Horace it is excruciating, because he went too far the other way."

It had been fifteen years since Elinor crossed the Atlantic to England, and this crossing was like none other. She com-

*At least one aspect about the book was happily resolved: the title. "I have thought of only three that I really like," Elinor told Blanche at the height of her indecision (March 5, 1926), "& each of those there is some objection, more or less vital. First *Mortal Image.* . . . The *West Wind*—too much like *South Wind* I am afraid. . . . Last—& this would be the ideal title if it were not too much of a steal from M. Maurois—*Ariel Unbound.*" By the end of March she was forced to discard *Mortal Image,* at least on the American side of the Atlantic, because Willa Cather's *My Mortal Enemy* was being published and the titles were dangerously alike. In the end, Elinor selected one of her choices and Carl Van Doren's favorite of the three, *The Orphan Angel.*

pared it not to her 1910 and 1911 crossings, but to the one in 1903 with Dada and Connie. Just as Bill replaced Horace, her desire for anonymity gave way to increased celebrity. Her novels had a following in England. Two years before (on May 29, 1924) Grant Richards had published *Jennifer Lorn* and the *Times Literary Supplement* had praised its "delicate artistry and humour. . . . It is a pleasant relaxation from conventional fiction, and in spite of its fantastic setting it maintains a real interest by the analysis of character." By April 1926, she had switched to Heinemann, who brought out *The Venetian Glass Nephew*. It aroused considerably more comment than her first book. John Rothenstein was lyrical in his anonymous review (which he could not keep secret, especially from Elinor) in the *TLS,* saying (April 22, 1926): "It's an arabesque, so well conceived and executed as to make it almost without flaw within its limits. . . . The story's theme is entirely fantastic, its chief merit being that it never once descends to solid earth." George Doran circulated the novel among the other authors on his list; he sent a copy to Aldous Huxley, who replied directly to Elinor from Benares (January 6, 1926), "your *Venetian Glass Nephew* has been as a friend from home." "English reviews of the Nephew," Elinor summarized for Mama from the *Pennland* before she landed, ". . . have I hear been marvellous."

The very intensity of Elinor's urge for hibernation in 1910 seemed now to be focused on the social events of this crossing. She accepted every invitation and appeared actively to pursue everyone there was the slimmest opportunity to meet. It was one of the rare periods of her life when every moment of her days could be accounted for. No sooner had they docked and hastened to their modest hotel, The Dysart, in Henrietta Street (located north of Oxford Street, which was mocked by Elinor's sister as being slightly too déclassé to be stylish) than they found a pile of invitations waiting for them. The Lynds* asked them to dine in Hampstead. Alyse Gregory

*Robert Lynd (1879–1949) was literary editor of the *News Chronicle,* "Y.Y." in the *New Statesman and Nation,* a prolific writer and fine essayist. Sylvia Lynd (1888–1952), née Dryhurst, married Robert Lynd in 1909. She was a novelist and poet of considerable popularity during her lifetime. She was ravishingly beautiful and a memorable hostess. Their house in Keats

Elinor
Wylie

(Mrs. Llewelyn Powys) asked them to Dorset for the weekend. Edith Sitwell invited them to tea. May Dent was still in the New Forest and begged to see her old friend. The Rothensteins invited Elinor to tea—"Curse their tea invitations—" Elinor complained to Bill (July 4) (Y) "don't you think? The poor boy [John Rothenstein] told them to ask me to dinner." John Drinkwater turned up with an invitation to a party. The Knopfs turned up with proofs of *The Orphan Angel*. Even when Elinor went out for a quiet dinner, she found herself sitting next to Rebecca West and H. G. Wells. Aldous Huxley caught up with her, finally, and Elinor caught up with Mama and Nancy in Paris, dragging Bill behind her.

In the middle of June they crossed the Channel for two weeks in France. Bill, in the best Anita Loos fashion, was mad about "the Tweelerees Gardens." The steady stream of cocktails (which he certainly preferred to tea) and the food, impressed him just as much. But crossing the bridge from their hotel in the rue du Bac (the Pont Royal) to Mama and Nancy at the Continental impressed him least of all. Nancy was on a shopping spree and convinced Elinor that the real pleasures of Paris were not the sights but the stores. She and Elinor made a determined assault on Saint-Germain and the salons of Paul Poiret. The staff instantly adored Elinor—their idea of the perfect client. "Madame Hélène at Poirets," Stephen Vincent Benét informed his brother later that summer (Y), ". . . wanted to know . . . when Elinor was coming back to see the new collection—always a pleasure to see Madame Benét wear the gowns she so exquisitely becomes or something like that"—a compliment offered when the bill was offered. Elinor's selections, Nancy remembered, were two "metallic cuirass dresses and a wrap of deep vivid blue-green with a Kolinsky collar."*

Grove was made famous not only by them, but by the people they attracted there. Rebecca West dedicated *Harriet Hume* to them. Elinor dined with them in Keats Grove on June 11th.

*The dresses had been anticipated the previous month in Elinor's short story "My Silver Dress" in *The New Yorker* (May 8, 1926). In the story Elinor, as the narrator, fails to wear her silver dress and then flies off in self-deprecation: "this week of all weeks of course Mr. Talloh wouldn't wave my hair; Fanny never makes it look the same; cinnamon bear-cub color; I

By the time Elinor returned to England—without Bill,
who sailed home from Le Havre on the *Olympic*—she was
armed with her Poiret clothes and made the best impression,
reminiscent of Madame Merle's entrances, when she wore
them at Wilsford Manor. Her regal descent of the staircase
that angled upward from the entry hall was remembered for
a long time by Edith Olivier. "The upper part of the staircase
beside me was in shadow, but I heard a movement, and
turned, to see Elinor coming down. I didn't know who she
was. How finely she held herself, making a picture which
remains in my mind," Edith Olivier wrote after Elinor's death.
". . . She was wearing a dress made of stiff shiny silk, and it
looked like frozen green water." It was the dress Elinor was
buried in.

The Wilsford Manor weekend was the high point of
Elinor's ever-extended English summer. The house itself
might have been a creation by Elinor herself—there was
something deliberate about it, with its comfortable but very
well planned casualness. It was situated in a dip of the
Wylye Valley that went on to a sweep of parkland behind,
yielding superb views from inside. Sturdy, somber, of the
best Cotswold stone, the house was scarcely fifteen years
old. From the outside, as one approached it from Salisbury,
it was impressive but not beautiful. Inside, everything was
impressive: the rooms were larger than life and the furniture positively massive. Lady Grey, Elinor's hostess, treated
sofas like armchairs, chaise-longues like footstools, and Venetian gilt side tables like ashtrays—the rooms were
crammed with things. There was a Mediterranean aspect
about Wilsford: sand replaced lawn, lizards doubled for
cats, palm trees were dotted about the garden, and the
round greenhouse was stocked with tropical plants. Inside
the house was the garden statuary, bowls of flowers, and
stacks of books. Wilsford seemed more like a stage set than
a house. Elinor was dazzled, and ultimately disdainful:
"This is a lovely place—beautiful, peaceful—not too grand
—but just too calm and easy—it would kill the soul. It

---

have always hated my nose but if I had worn my silver dress I might have
been more reconciled to it. . . ." (p. 17).

comforts me that darling Shelley avoided this over-easefulness. . . ." she wrote to Bill from there (July 18, 1926) (Y).

The other performers at Wilsford that weekend were
the famous Jungman sisters, Zita and Baby—famous alike for
their beauty and their portraits by another guest, Cecil Beaton. Rex Whistler, Rosamond Lehmann, Steven Runciman,
Sacheverell and Georgia Sitwell (whose clothes, annoyingly,
were just as impressive as Elinor's), and Elinor Brougham
(former lady-in-waiting to the Queen of Spain turned anthologist of English and Scottish poetry) were the other
guests of Elinor's host, Stephen Tennant, who had met Elinor earlier that summer in London and was mesmerized by
The Venetian Glass Nephew. The youngest son of Lord Glen-
conner and Lady Grey of Falloden, Stephen Tennant
managed to transform himself into the most interesting feature of the house. He was an ardent admirer of Willa Cather
(he wrote a brilliant preface to her essays collected in *On
Writing*) and of Elinor. He was raised as an invalid and
poured any energy he had into thickly lined drawings (which
illustrated his mother's poems), and even more thickly lined
poems—and into an astonishing wardrobe. Cecil Beaton's
first glimpse of him was perched atop a papier-mâché horse
on a roundabout, wearing a cloak of black leather and chin-
chilla, and blowing kisses to a gallery of beauties. He was
tall, slender, and very handsome, with stunning blond hair.
His conversation was electrifying and his tastes exotic. He
never ceased to fascinate people, first by his appearance, and
then by his lively mind and dedicated devotion to gossip.
Navajo Indian culture, jewels, reptiles, and make-up were
some of his interests, but people always remained the chief
one. No matter how full the house became with guests,
there was always room for a few more to be fitted in. While
Elinor stayed there, Sir Arthur and Lady Colefax, Lord Berners, and Edith Olivier looked in for dinner before Elinor
and her hostess settled down to reciting poetry in the garden.

Almost from the moment she arrived, Elinor made it
clear that she thought she was not getting enough attention.
She changed her clothes as often as she shifted the conversation to herself or Shelley. The other guests thought her very

tiresome; everyone that is except Stephen Tennant and Rosamond Lehmann,* the novelist, who fell for Elinor's bid for pity when admiration failed. As a result Rosamond heard long recitals of Elinor's history, tales of dead babies and of the ceaseless hardships she had endured. No one had warned Rosamond Lehmann there would be such a performance and her generous pity quickly turned into disgust. When Elinor went upstairs to her room to dress for dinner, her fellow guests collected downstairs and hatched a plan to treat Elinor with the respect and deference she was convinced was her right. That night they all drove over to Stonehenge, lifted Elinor up onto one of the fallen stones, and pranced about in the most awestruck manner deserved by any goddess. Then they knelt and prayed to her. By the time the story of this incident got across the Atlantic it was changed to include Elinor dancing nude in the moonlight.

When Elinor returned to London, Aldous Huxley informed her that he had sufficiently unwrapped himself from his aunts' affection—"I have a whole Swarm of Termites, or Great White Aunts," as he told her (July 7)—to take Elinor to dine with Leonard and Virginia Woolf, on Monday, July 12. Elinor's descent on Bloomsbury was a catastrophe. It began with Virginia Woolf volunteering that she had not read any of Elinor's books: "the authoress said severely 'Really! Not read any of my books!' "† Virginia Woolf later passed on her versions of the evening to Vita Sackville-West [July 15, 1926]:

Oh what an evening! I expected a ravishing and diaphanous dragonfly, a woman who had spirited away 4 husbands, and wooed from buggery the most obstinate of his adherents: a siren; a green and sweetvoiced nymph—that was what I expected, and came a tiptoe in the room to find—a solid hunk: a hatchet minded, cadaverous, acid

*Rosamond Lehmann (1901–), born in London and educated at Cambridge, had not yet published her first novel, *Dusty Answer* (1927), which instantly established her as a remarkable novelist. Her first husband, Leslie, was the brother of Steven Runciman, her sister is the actress Beatrix Lehmann and her brother is John the author. Like the other guests at Wilsford, she combined beauty with talent, which for their host was an instant recommendation.

†There is no evidence Elinor ever picked up one of Virginia Woolf's.

voiced, bareboned, spavined, patriotic nasal, thick legged American. All the evening she proclaimed unimpeachable truths; and discussed our sales: hers are 3 times better than mine, naturally; till thank God, she began heaving on her chair and made a move as if to go, gracefully yielded to, but not, I beg you to believe, solicited on our parts. Figure my woe, on the stairs, when she murmured, "It's the *other* thing I want. Comes of trying to have children. May I go in there?" So she retired to the W.C., emerged refreshed; sent away her cab, and stayed another hour, hacking us to pieces. But I must read her book.

Elinor set a quick tempo in trying to win over the distinguished. She fought with Edward Garnett, who begged her not to publish *The Orphan Angel.* "If the true honesty of your nature," Elinor wrote to him (July 13, 1926), "which in spite of your mistakes I fully recognise, does not admit the worth of what I have written, then I will admit that my taste & my talent have been at fault. Of the honesty of my purpose I cannot seriously believe that I need speak to you. If you see me descending, it must be that our heavens are set in opposite directions."*

She found Llewelyn Powys "a bit scary," looking as if he suffered from a "slight fit of lunacy" while retaining the more attractive air of "wild shepherds & shepherdesses in the Old Testament" when she stayed at his cottage—"modern & ugly," in Dorset the middle of July. Though she had a tepid "very nice" for Osbert Sitwell, she called his brother Sacheverell and his wife likable "in moderation." She played a spirited game of rummy with John Drinkwater. And she could

*Edward Garnett (1868–1937) was adviser to various publishing firms, one of them Heinemann. It was in this capacity that he was in the vanguard of opposition to Elinor's Shelley novel, which he had read in Knopf's proofs. Like Charles Evans, the managing director of Heinemann, he heartily believed that the book would be attacked by all the critics. Later in the summer Elinor complained to Bill that one reader of the book, as she referred to Evans, "had not one word of praise for the book, & he objected to dozens of specific phrases, such as 'milk & melted butter & honey' . . . all my 19th century colour is to be washed away in his prejudice. I think he is one of the most contemptible worms. . . ." (August 16, 1926) (Y). Garnett's dislike, added to Evans's, which in turn was augmented by Mama's that summer, caused Elinor seriously to consider withdrawing it from English publication.

not find much praise for J. C. Squire and his wife, especially as their house was "no more than a mile or two from my old house at Brook," as she told Bill (August 8) (Y). "I cursed rather when I saw it, I admit. *I* never wanted to leave it. . . . Yet if I'd stayed I'd not have had you, so thus it is." She found Tallulah Bankhead, both on stage and at the Eiffel Tower Restaurant in Percy Street, "very dull," later adding, "very pretty but a great bore." Tallulah asked Elinor, calmly and directly, "You've had lots of lovers, haven't you?" Elinor, with the same composure, replied, "I've had no lovers at all, Tallulah—that's why I had three husbands. When I've fallen in love, I have married. That is just three times."*

Just as Elinor had spent the previous summers concentrating on her work, the same concentration was employed in 1926 in avoiding it. There were evenings at the theater and Russian ballet, and days spent shopping or going to Ascot. But she could not avoid Mama and Nancy, who were in England and had gone to the south coast for a rest. "The only disagreeable incident was the night I spent with Mama," Elinor informed Bill (July 29) (Y); "she became very cross & most absurdly accused me of 'harping' on the fact that the Pennland was a second-class boat, I having merely said that it was so nice that it seemed ridiculous for the company to call it so." Then there was Nancy's annoying indecision over when she would get married. "I have to be in England," Elinor wrote to Rosemary and Stephen Benét (August 3) (Y), "on the slim chance that it really happens this time. We all doubt it—but I can't go rushing off to Paris, I'm afraid, until it's definitely settled. . . . Really, isn't this thing getting to be, not a coincidence or a miracle, but a habit?" And Elinor used Nancy's extreme indecision, which she saw, somehow, as Mama's work, "who, quite unconsciously, overturns all these apple-carts of poor Nancy" (as she interpreted for Rosemary Benét), in order to postpone sailing home. First she could not find any accommo-

*Elinor added to Emily Clark, who overheard this exchange (later widely publicized), "You are probably the only young woman of my acquaintance who would consider three times amazingly often to have fallen in love!" Elinor also said to her on observing an elegant young female lunching alone, "It is said that she lives with women for pleasure and with men for profit. . . . A full life, isn't it?" See *Innocence Abroad*, p. 176.

dation, she claimed; then she decided to wait until September 25 and sail with Rebecca West; then she reconsidered, thinking the 25th too late. This decision reached, she changed her plans again and found a berth in a cabin after all, but refused to entertain the idea of sharing it and promptly canceled once again, leaving her itinerary to be settled by Nancy's final choice for the day of her marriage.

"London at last begins to get on my nerves," she complained to Bill over two months after leaving New York (August 8, 1926) (Y). She had no idea what she would do while waiting to leave. She hesitated over returning to the New Forest and then moving on for various weekends in Dorset and Wiltshire, but realized that she had nothing to do there, or indeed anywhere. In the end she accepted an invitation to stay in Cookham, at the Cliveden Reach Hotel, on the Thames, some four miles from Marlow. "I am here for ten days & it is all very romantic—" she wrote to her sister-in-law Rosemary Benét (August 17, 1926) (Y), "a beautiful old Regency house owned by the most enchanting people who have lost all their money & turned it into a hotel, inadvertently turning themselves into socialists although they are themselves aristocrats—not Regency but exquisite Georgian or Queen Anne! I am staying here & paying for my room, but lucky enough to be allowed to be one of them."

George and Helen Young turned their house, Formosa Place, into a hotel for two years; George Young's transition from diplomat to academician lasted far longer. He held a maze of diplomatic posts, among them attaché in Washington where three of his children were born: George Peregrine in 1908, Joan in 1910, and Virginia in 1911. (Courtenay was born in England in 1914.) It was in Washington, too, where he and his wife originally met both Elinor and Horace. "Imagine being *great friends* with the Youngs as we knew Them!" Elinor exclaimed to Horace (June 12, 1927) (B). "George & Helen—can you remember them? Now they have grown poor & Liberal & completely lovable, & they have the four nicest children on earth—" George Young moved from diplomacy to Berlin correspondent for the *Daily News* to Professor of Portuguese, examiner in Ottoman Law at the University of London, and Labour candidate for Parliament in 1923, 1924, and 1929. It was his influence that caused Elinor to record her only vaguely political comment (other than complaining about the coal strike in 1912): "By the way," she absurdly wrote to Bill in America (August 21, 1926) (Y), "don't you think we ought to vote Labour this year? Find out about it, will you?"

The atmosphere of Formosa Place and its adjacent Formosa Fishery (where the third Baronet lived until 1930) was intoxicating in itself; but Elinor was also totally captivated by the kindness of Helen Young.* In many ways Formosa Place was like a ship, laid to rest yet appearing to be still adrift. (When George Young took over his father's house he installed paneling from the *Mauretania* after she was broken up. The house is now destroyed.) One approached it through near-wilderness, traveling down a lane obscured by trees and plants rising from the riverbank. Then it appeared, rising almost unexpectedly behind willow trees that dipped into the river, towering, massive, and magnificent as a shadow of its former elegance. It was a complete world, divorced from the outside, quiet and yet full of life. Like Wilsford Manor, Elinor saw it as being closer to an elaborate stage set than anything else:

> . . . all Formosa's stairways leap
> On arches curved and faultless;
> Its flying steps are never steep;
> Its bread is sweetly saltless.

Earlier she wrote to Bill (August 21) (Y), "coming here was the best day's work I've done for many a day. It really is incredibly lovely—the old & melancholy house, the river running dark & green beneath green & golden banks, the enchanting breed of blue-eyed children native to the scene like fauns & dryads." Elinor was absorbed into the place, into the family; she was completely free of the urge to demand respect and create scenes when she was with the Youngs. She was hypnotized by them, and appreciated at once that her tantrums would be sorely out of place. Helen Young did not need to

*Jessie Helen Young (1880–1942), née Ilbert, was the sister of the novelist Olive Heseltine, who wrote about their childhood in *Three Daughters* (1930) under her nom de plume, Jane Dashwood. Helen married in 1904.

be won over, nor did she need any reminders who Elinor was; she knew everything about her. The children were deferential to her, but not obsequious, and most important of all, not dependent on her. Elinor managed to display a side of her character to the Youngs she denied everyone else—calmness.

The news that her son had turned up unexpectedly at Bournemouth, an event instantly relayed to Elinor at Cookham by Mama, was not welcome. On August 22, Elinor and Gerry Young (aged eighteen) got into his dilapidated Citroën to drive up to London, "& I am to see *Philip,* if you please," she wrote to Bill the day before. The meeting between mother and son, so urgently requested by Mama, passed off without record. A malicious story circulated after the event was that when Elinor entered Mama's hotel suite, she did not recognize her own son.

One effect Philip Hichborn had on Elinor was that, by way of Nancy, he provided the inspiration for Elinor's short story "Sundae School," which appeared in *The New Yorker,* February 20, 1926. The month before the story was published, Nancy wrote to Elinor and Bill (January 4, 1926) (Y) that Philip "leads a life of luxury at Harvard and describes cocktails made of equal parts gin and vanilla ice-cream which is a ghastly thought." Elinor was tantalized by these extraordinary concoctions and listed, in "Sundae School," her son's recipe, as well as "the wonderful possibilities of raspberry ice and Scotch . . . maple-nut Martinis and banana-Bronx splits." The heroine disappoints her friends by drinking an Old-Fashioned whiskey cocktail.

The last weekend in August Elinor accepted Edith Olivier's invitation to the Daye House in Wiltshire, not far from Wilsford. Edith Olivier was one of ten children born to Canon Dacres Olivier, at the rectory at Wilton on a date she resolutely refused to divulge: "I am horrified to discover how much older I am than most writers. I seem completely out of date," she once confessed. (It was calculated that she might have been born six years before Elinor, in 1879.) Apart from sharing this reluctance to confessing her age with Elinor, Edith Olivier inhabited, in her fiction, a well-charted region of fantasy. Her father was an inflexible autocrat, ruling his parish and his family alike with little leniency. Edith Olivier did not

survive by means of education, though she had received one
from her mother and Oxford (which was even more idiosyn-
cratic than the tutoring she had at home), but by escapism.
Her first novel, *The Love Child* (1927), is similar to Elinor's
The Venetian Glass Nephew, though not buried under the
weight of history. Her second, *As Far As Jane's Grandmother's,*
which appeared the following year, is a more extensive documentation of her airless and lonely childhood. Duty, both to
God and the Canon, was made the exclusive occupation of her
early life. But she did escape, finally. Her novels are written
with a light and delicate touch. She is far easier to read than
Elinor, and an extremely competent storyteller; though more
romantic and less cynical, there is no question that Elinor
influenced her greatly.*

With her sister Mildred, Edith had set up the Daye House
as a less raucous annex to Wilsford Manor, sharing many of
the same guests with Lady Grey and her son. Edith was an
ideal hostess, with something of Lady Ottoline Morrell's consuming interest in her friends, but herself able to offer a great
deal more than mere eccentricity.

Daye House was the dairy house on the estate of the Earl
of Pembroke that was the work both of Holbein and, later, of
Inigo Jones. Edith's house was in the heart of the bird sanctuary on the estate, and she remarked in her autobiography that
the noise of squawking birds began annoyingly early every
morning. Elinor arrived the last Saturday in August, slightly
too early. "She looked very exquisite," Edith remarked in her
diary (August 28, 1926) "—a little carved pointed Venetian
glass face, rather coppery hair, with the American simplicity,
obviously expecting to be lionised." Elinor's expectations
were not satisfied. The only other non-family guest was Brian
Howard, who had arrived with precisely the same intention
but without his dinner suit.

The next day the guests wandered through Fonthill, the
ruins of William Beckford's estate, and listened to Lady Pem-

*Apart from producing fiction similar to that of Sylvia Townsend Warner
and David Garnett, she was passionately interested in Wiltshire, writing
Secrets of Some Wiltshire Housewives (1927), *Country Moods and Tenses* (1941),
and the official Wiltshire guidebook.

broke's talk of ghosts over tea, before moving on to dinner and Elinor's poetry recital. "Miss W's poetry is marvellously sure—her language very good, vocabulary large and living, and her rhymes are brilliant. . . . She is sure of her work and herself." Then Brian Howard read, with considerably more trepidation. The following day there was more sightseeing, more poetry from Brian Howard, and more lecturing on Wilton House, also from Brian Howard. Elinor "moves serenely through it," commented Edith, "sure that she contains within herself more perfect loveliness" than Wilton. Luncheon, before she left for London, was an ordeal of Oliviers who did not appear to appreciate their fortune in being allowed to be with Elinor.

While Elinor liked Edith Olivier, with her air of devotion and respect, she did her best to ignore Brian Howard, who went almost unmentioned in her letters. Unfortunately for Elinor, he considered himself just as much a beauty as she and the two vied constantly for attention. Howard had drawn an admiring circle around him, transfixed by his outrageous behavior and convinced that he possessed great, if dormant, talent. He was precisely the same sort of person as Elinor, lacking only the ability to concentrate on his work. Energy alone pulled him through while his band of friends waited, with an inordinate supply of patience, for the masterpiece he was certain to produce. As Elinor could not a score a victory over him, she ignored him.

Elinor returned to London, stopping briefly at Walter de la Mare's house in Taplow to listen to his appreciation of her poetry, and to visit the famous Shelley scholar and editor Roger Ingpen, at the beginning of September. The date for Nancy's wedding had, at last, been set: September 7, 1926, Elinor's forty-first birthday. "I was not very bridal," Nancy later reported, standing in St. George's, Hanover Square, with a throbbing toothache. Her husband—Elinor informed Rosemary Benét—was a handsome but penniless old Etonian, Gerald Wynne-Wynne. Four days after the wedding, on September 11, Elinor boarded the *Savoie* and docked in New York eight days later. She had been gone nearly four months, carefully avoiding the worst of the move from Bank Street to her new apartment at 36 West 9th Street, which Bill had been sent back to find.

Mama and Papa had lived across the street at Fifth Avenue and 10th Street before she was born; Henry's studio was at 37 West 10th Street. Elinor completed the tradition of Hoyt residences. The outside bell to their second-floor apartment was labeled in their joint names: Benét/ Wylie; but once inside it was strictly Elinor's taste that presided, everywhere except Bill's study off the sitting room. There, two walls were lined with white bookshelves, jumbled with his vast collection of books. On his desk was a small framed photograph of Elinor, aged eleven.

Outside Bill's study one returned to the meticulous neatness Elinor insisted upon. The sitting room and dining room, which faced West 9th Street, were full of Elinor's well-traveled furniture, arranged for reading. Down the small passage, passing the bathroom Elinor ordained was for Bill and guests, was the bedroom, stripped of all unnecessary items and furnished simply with two maple beds (brought up from Washington) dressed in blue chintz, with an applewood dressing table and the rush-seated chair Elinor had written about. There was no attempt to disguise its age, only to conceal the fact that it was ever used. The room was always ruthlessly tidy, with Elinor's looking glass and powder, scent, make-up, and jewelry lined up with military exactness. The same sort of fastidiousness invaded her private bathroom. No jar of cream or box of rouge ever looked disturbed, there were no wrinkles on the towels, and no one was allowed in except Elinor.

Elinor's own study was reached through the two open arches, on each side of the fireplace, that led from the bedroom. Two windows faced south, shedding light on her scrubbed deal table piled, more often than not, with sheets of pale blue paper, a collection of books, and a Chinese porcelain bowl lined in a rich mulberry-pink glaze that contained clips and erasers. One wall was loaded with her books lined up neatly from one end to the other: each book had been slid into its proper place. Americana competed with antique guidebooks, leather-bound poetry jostled with memoirs for the best position. Angled in front of the books, with its back to the windows, was the one comfortable armchair Elinor permitted herself, upholstered in flowered material. There was a less comfortable, delicate chaise-longue, which Elinor used more often, along the other wall. Impersonal flower prints and small landscapes completed the decorations, the former on the wall above the fireplace. At the side of Elinor's table was a door leading to the tiny kitchen and another unused rear room. Elinor paid no attention to the deliberate inconvenience of this arrangement and she quickly stamped the same aloofness on West 9th Street as she had on her previous homes. The only difference was that the neatness had advanced to nearly unlivable proportions. Nothing was permitted to stray from its place. The only disturbance allowed came from the maid, Marjorie, who spent half of every day cleaning at Elinor and Bill's, and the other half at the Gormans'.

"I suppose all this moving & fixing houses is enough to startle an ox," Elinor wrote to Mama once everything was settled (November 22) (B), "not to mention you or me." Elinor's "startle" came in the least welcome manifestation— her headaches returned. She had been free of them for about a year: "it was too awful—what is known—you know them— as hemicranial or migraine, never going away day or night for two weeks, & hopping from one side of the head to another every six hours. I almost went out of my mind." She put it all down to the strain of moving, while her friends, less charitably, said she was too frightened to begin a new novel.

Dorothy Parker arrived at eleven o'clock one morning "saying she was going to kill herself that night, & as she'd already made two attempts—wrists & veronal—it was not very soothing to the nerves." Elinor tried to reach Bill at his office and he finally got back to West 9th Street at three thirty. They both subjected Dorothy to a sustained harangue in an energetic attempt to dissuade her. She withstood the joint attack for an hour and a half, then went home for a quiet evening, saying, "she had given it up for the present." Elinor added after she left, "We were queer ones for her to come to, in a way. I suppose she thinks we are experts on the subject!"

Elinor considered herself an expert on only one subject —Shelley. The responses to *The Orphan Angel*, published on October 29, by Knopf,* proved her correct. It was selected as the December Book-of-the-Month and the sales were impressive.

The people who knew Elinor best loved the novel. Carl

*And in England, as *The Mortal Image*, by Heinemann in January 1927.

Van Doren, predictably, cheered, believing himself to be some sort of midwife to the story. He applauded the audacity, the originality, and the lengthy period touches. Bill was, as usual, incapable of finding a single fault in the course of the hundreds of pages. His brother Stephen Vincent Benét, who wrote the preface to its republication in 1933, said the novel showed that Elinor's devotion to Shelley "was entirely sincere . . . also entirely mature." He was, however, quick to point out that the tone of the book was a "little exaggerated." Louis Untermeyer said that "Elinor wrote her finest work under the guiding principle of Shelley's subtle spirit," thinking perhaps more of her sonnet sequence dedicated to him, "A Red Carpet for Shelley," than of *The Orphan Angel.*

Other readers were less happy about this alliance of invention and history. It appeared to many readers that her use of historical detail, which had hitherto been employed to give credibility to extended fantasy, had overgrown its intention; it *was* the novel, rather than a device supporting the story. This shift in technique aroused considerable opposition. The loudest complaint came from James Branch Cabell. *"The Orphan Angel* really did appear a most inane wasting of wood-pulp . . ."* he wrote in 1930.

I declared, as I still think, that the writing of *The Orphan Angel* was one of the most gloomy errors in literary history. . . . One cannot wholly put out of mind how very, very freely . . . Elinor Wylie had shown fatal gifts for being ineffectively humorous, and for confounding with the quaint that which to the candid seems unmistakably dull, and for reaching flat bathos where her avowed aim was seraphic beauty—and all this too in connection with an unbridled incapacity for self-criticism. Elinor Wylie honestly believed, as but too many of her friends learned at the cost of friendship, that *The Orphan Angel* was an excellent fantasy made up of her finest endeavors.

Cabell's most severe charge remained, however, that after six attempts he still put the book down unfinished.*

*Sinclair Lewis agreed with Cabell, but waited until Cabell published his irreverent comments in *Some of Us* to add: "there [are] cliques of Wylieites to whom every word she wrote was perfect, while, of course you are so right about her terrible *Orphan Angel.* It wasn't merely an orphan; it was a bastard. . . ." The letter is published in *Between Friends; Letters of James Branch Cabell,* edited by Padraic Colum and Margaret Freeman Cabell (New York: 1962), p. 282.

If *The Orphan Angel* was a "gloomy error" and a lapse of taste, Cabell was mercifully spared a further excursion into Elinor's obsession. She failed to complete another novel dedicated to Shelley—*April, April* (undated), of which only two full chapters survive (now at Yale). It is even less subtle than *The Orphan Angel.* Shelley and his complete panoply of Godwins, Hogg, and Trelawny are transported to twentieth-century New York and there made to behave precisely as if they were still in nineteenth-century Europe. In a stunning form of conceit, Elinor portrays herself as Clare [Clair], Shelley's ideal companion. If *April, April* predates *The Orphan Angel* (as it may), the latter can only be called an improvement.

The response from England to *The Orphan Angel,* which she had feared, was enthusiastic. Aldous Huxley wrote to her on Christmas Day, 1926: "It has something of the quality of Shelley's own poems. . . . I congratulate you on the way in which you have made your orphan angel live." The *TLS* was no less complimentary, calling the book "the oddest mixture of seriousness and humour. . . . She succeeds—sometimes brilliantly—in giving vivid interest to her pages, but she does not escape repeating herself. . . . Mrs Wylie has made an interesting experiment." The curse of Edward Garnett had not been fulfilled; the *TLS* assured her she was right to publish the novel.

Elinor continued to parade before the public her absorption with Shelley. The second week in January 1927, "A Red Carpet for Shelley" was published in *The New Republic*:

> But this is nothing; an eccentric joke,
> The legendary patchwork of a year
> Flung into muddiness, like Raleigh's cloak,
> To ask the honour of your step, my dear.

And as "Visiting Critic" in "Books" of the *New York Herald Tribune,* she published as her final contribution for the month of February a review of the Julian Edition of Shelley, edited by Roger Ingpen and Walter Peck in ten volumes.* Entitled

---

*The other books she reviewed for Irita Van Doren that month were *Murder at Smutty Nose* by Edmund Pearson and *Famous Poison Mysteries* by Fredrick Smith, under the title "Orpiment and the Axe" (February 6th); *Reveries Over Childhood and Youth, The Trembling of the Veil* by W. B. Yeats, under the title

"Excess of Charity," the piece is more confession than review, reaffirming what she had suggested in *The Orphan Angel*—that she believed Shelley was goaded by circumstance into being wrong, occasionally, rather than by any deficiency of character. "The theory that Shelley was completely unaware of his own defects seems to me especially preposterous. By the circumstances of his life he was caught up into a situation where any loud bewailing of the past, any open self-reproaches or laments would have cut a living woman to the heart and left a dead one none the better for her revenge."

Elinor was highly reluctant to let the subject of Shelley rest. Not content with making him stride across America she wrote about him again, in another fictional portrait, "A Birthday Cake for Lionel," as a hermit in Maine. In March she was trying to adjust the extreme imbalance between objectivity and passion, fostered at length by her fixation, in an essay entitled *Mr. Shelley Speaking** in which she tried to explain her method of portraiture. "I have attempted, in 'The Orphan Angel,' to reproduce the essential quality of Shelley's speech; to balance my patent adoration I have faintly caricatured his dear and ridiculous mannerisms." She addressed her critics sternly, emphasizing the long list of her sources and ordering them to read as she had done. "When you've done this, and particularly if you've been doing it since you were seven years old, you are certain to adore Mr. Shelley; his voice will be ringing in your ears, and you may even go so far as to write a book about him. I, for one, will never blame you."

Elinor's obsession with Shelley brought out the worst in her, destroyed her own finely drawn lines of professionalism, and violated Papa's edict, "Don't justify yourself." When not

---

"Path of the Chameleon" (February 13th); a review of the libretto for Deems Taylor's "The King's Henchman" by Edna St. Vincent Millay, under the same title (February 20th); and the Shelley review "Excess of Charity" (February 27th). Bill later included "Path of the Chameleon" and "Excess of Charity" in Elinor's *Collected Prose.* On April 10th she returned to "Books," publishing "Three Folk Songs." Three years earlier, on October 5, 1924 she reviewed Forster's *Passage to India* for "Books." In the autumn of 1926 she was appointed contributing editor of *The New Republic,* and she was asked to join The Literary Guild.

* *The Bookman,* pp. 29–33.

indulging herself, she was trying to explain the overblown manifestations of that indulgence. Shelley threw her off balance, obscured her sense of judgment, and inspired her worst writing.

Yet, in the middle of this period of Shelley preoccupation, Elinor wrote "Portrait," a seventy-eight-line marvel that sliced straight through her character:

> "She gives herself;" a poetic thought;
> She gives you comfort sturdy as a reed;
> She gives you fifty things you might have bought,
> And half a hundred that you'll never need;
> She gives you friendship, but it's such a bother
> You'd fancy influenza from another.
>
> . . .
>
> She gives the false impression that she's pretty
>
> . . .
>
> She gives the vague impression that she's lazy,
> But when she writes she grows intense and thorough;
> Gone quietly and ecstatically crazy
> Among the sea-blue hills of Peterboro;
> She'll work in her cool, conventional flat
> As self-sufficient as a Persian cat.
>
> And she can live on aspirin and Scotch
>
> . . .
>
> She gives you nothing worth consideration;
> The effervescence of enthusiasm
> Is trivial stuff; she'll give you adoration
> If you belong to her peculiar schism;
> As, that a certain English man of letters
> Need never call the Trinity his betters.
>
> Sometimes she gives her heart; sometimes instead
> Her tongue's sharp side.
>
> . . .

She asked *The New Yorker* to publish the poem anonymously, but it was eventually signed with the initials E.W. Four days after Burton Rascoe finally exploded the myth of authorship in his "Daybook," Elinor wrote to him (April 12, 1927), "the piece was *unsigned,* save by initials, & then only at the extreme insistence of 'The New Yorker' . . . so many people are telling me that Bunny [Edmund Wilson] wrote the piece that I be-

lieve even Edith Wharton must be held responsible in some
quarters."

The poem became a major topic of conversation. Elinor's
friends' opinions were divided between her accuracy and her
questionable taste. Rascoe quoted the poem at length in his
column just in case someone might have missed it in *The New
Yorker* (March 19, 1927). And Elinor instructed him to make
capital use of the fact that the initials were misleading. Peter
Arno's heavy line drawing of Elinor was just as radical. He
drew Elinor's reflected image in a mirror. When Nancy Hoyt
asked him how he managed such an amazing likeness,

He told me that he felt rather frightened of the appointment with
my sister. . . . She had asked him to wait a moment while she fixed
herself up, and then she walked over to a mirror and started primp-
ing. . . . In a few minutes, while she stood at the mirror, he did the
sketch. . . . My mother and I think it more like her than any of her
later photographs. Of course, it is exaggerated, but so was Elinor.

The tempest that brewed up around her "Portrait,"
which even brought in a letter from a Yale professor recom-
mending that Elinor take libel action against the imprudent
author of the poem, was nothing compared to the furor that
followed two weeks later. On March 30 Elinor was asked to
be one of the "Honor Guests" with, among others, Edna St.
Vincent Millay, at the Authors' Breakfast of the League of
American Pen Women in Washington, set for Saturday, April
16. Elinor read it as a sign that her past was no longer held
against her. She took it as a compliment, and a honor. But she
was not to be that lucky.

"An awful thing has happened," began a letter written by
Mrs. Hoisington on behalf of the hostesses for the breakfast
(April 6, 1927) (Y).

Something that never occurred to Mrs. Seton or to me. Washington,
it seems, is still provincial enough to object to you! I might as well
tell you the truth. . . . It is the limit. The powers that rule the L.A.P.
down in Washington have countermanded our asking you for the
Authors Breakfast and that is the flat incredible fact. I choose to talk
straight to you and not "wiggle out." Do not think that either Mrs.
Seton or I were in ignorance in our invitation . . . but we thought
it of no consequence to anybody, anymore than it would be with a

man. But the invincible bourgeois mind has conquered. I cannot get over it.

Elinor stood back, furious, hurt, and pledged to silence. There was nothing she could do. Edna St. Vincent Millay was not obliged to keep quiet. Her anger was intense. After Elinor spent a weekend with her at Steepletop and told her of the League's behavior, Edna fired off her own letter, sending it to them by way of Elinor. "Please read the letter," she instructed Elinor [April 18, 1927], "then post it at once.—Be a good girl, & do as I tell you, & post it at once."

"It is not in the power of an organisation which has insulted Elinor Wylie, to honour me," the letter declared.

"And indeed I should feel it unbecoming on my part, to sit as Guest of Honour in a gathering of writers, where honour is tendered not so much for the excellence of one's literary accomplishments as for the circumspection of one's personal life."

The expression of the affection between the two poets was, for Elinor, preserved in silence, and for Edna Millay in lines formulated of well-controlled enthusiasm.

The friendship between Elinor and Edna Millay, more than any other in Elinor's life, was a sustained enigma. It appeared that as Elinor's energy increased in the last eight years of her life, her emotions, always guarded, became completely submerged. What she felt was controlled by what she did. Respect is the single feeling that emerges in Elinor's attitude to "Vincent," as she grew to refer to her. They met one another a few times and corresponded with the same frequency.* When they did write, their letters were confined largely to the subject of their work. Edna Millay was less cautious in her attitude toward Elinor, though relying on poetry to express it. Eleven years after Elinor's death, she collected six poems dating from 1927 to 1938 that encapsulated her feelings about Elinor in *Huntsman, What Quarry?* (1939),

---

*In the preface to her sister's letters (published in 1952), Norma Millay wrote that many of these letters were destroyed in a fire. Judging from the very few letters from Edna St. Vincent Millay to Elinor (preserved first by Elinor, then by Bill, and now by the Beinecke Library at Yale), the two women wrote very infrequently.

Oh, she was beautiful in every part!—
The auburn hair that bound the subtle brain;
The lovely mouth cut clear by wit and pain,
Uttering oaths and nonsense, uttering art
In casual speech and curving at the smart
On startled ears of excellence too plain
For early morning!—*Obit*. Death from strain;
The soaring mind outstripped the tethered heart.

Yet here was one who had no need to die
To be remembered. Every word she said
The lively malice of the hazel eye
Scanning the thumb-nail close—oh, dazzling dead,
How like a comet through the darkening sky
You raced! . . . would your return were heralded.

Elinor came into Edna Millay's life as a poet at the end of 1921, and only after several years began to be more. As soon as the transition had been made, Elinor died. Yet, for Edna Millay the two—poet and person—merged wonderfully well. Elinor was every inch a poet, dedicated, professional, and mysterious, while sustaining the image of a very beautiful woman. The poet came first, and Elinor's closest friends learned that after trying to peel away the facade that protected her both as woman and writer, it was impossible to probe further. Elinor used her reputation as a writer as a defense, joining it to the copious resistance already established in her character in the form of vanity. "She is a *good* companion," Dr. Canby said of her to Edith Olivier at dinner the end of July 1927, *"better* as a writer, and as a character rather bad. Unflinchingly egoiste." When Stephen Tennant and Edith Olivier got together to discuss Elinor, they agreed only on one point—that she had streaks of real madness in her. No one managed to get past the obstacles she placed in their way. Her friendships grew only through the safety of distance. Her affection warmed when thousands of miles separated her from its object. Edna Millay refused to be caught in this lifeless equation, but death separated her from Elinor when she made her confession. Edna Millay's side of her friendship remains stylized and expressive, in glaring contrast to Elinor's silence.

Elinor's frenetic social activity was just another form of protection and isolation. For the eight months she stayed in New York she was astonishingly busy; she rarely refused an invitation. She saw more people in a few months than she had formerly encountered in five years. She enjoyed her fame, but she soon became too exhausted for any pleasure. No longer capable of the stamina that would once have successfully dismissed insults like that of the League of American Pen Women, her tiredness made her vulnerable. On April 22, 1927, she sailed on the *Minnetonka* for England, alone.

The tension that had mounted over the past eight months in New York relaxed the moment she stepped on board. "I've been very sensible," she boasted to Bill as she was nearing Cherbourg (May 2) (Y), "rested, walked, breakfasted in bed, sat out on deck all day. All in all it's been the most delightful nine days." She was less sensible once she reached land. She rented a house in Chelsea, then headed straight to Paris, getting drenched on the Channel crossing, to visit Mama, Nancy, Morton, and Jeanne (who gave a party in their new flat on the Île St. Louis), and Bill's brother. When she returned to London a week later, she had a cold and a severe case of loneliness. She had taken the Chelsea house until the middle of August, but said she would be ready to leave a month earlier in order to go with Bill to California.

Cheltenham Terrace, near Sloane Square, connects the King's Road and St. Leonard's Terrace (where Logan Pearsall Smith was, when Elinor moved in, staging his last ditch campaign against bad writing, and where Lady Ottoline Morrell had been strictly forbidden to live when she gave up Garsington).

No. 9, Cheltenham Terrace, faced the Duke of York's Headquarters, off the King's Road, with its weeping brass lettering addressed across the Palladian capitol and its vast sweep of parade ground that rolls out the length of the terrace. Like the other houses, it looked deceptively small from the outside; inside, it was a classic example of a stair-infested, late Georgian terrace house. Facing east, it trapped the sun all day. At the very top was a miniature bathroom; a few steps below

the master bedroom in front, and a small square second bedroom in back. One floor down was the sitting room, exactly
the same size as the master bedroom, and dominated by two
floor-to-ceiling windows. The sitting room was connected to
a smaller room at the back by massive doors. On the ground
floor was the dining room, with one window peering over the
tops of the railings that guarded the house from the street; a
study reached through another door in the long entry hall. At
the back was a postage-stamp-size garden, overlooked by the
backs of Walpole Street houses.

In the basement Elinor took over, along with furniture
and decoration, the maid, Edith Baldry. From below Edith
ruled the house with a passion for cleanliness that was only
rivaled by Elinor's own. The two women got along very well
together, and after only a few weeks at Cheltenham Terrace
it was clear that Edith was more friend than maid.

Such a relationship helped; Elinor's disorganization was
profound. When she went off to the New Forest for the second time in late August, she forgot to bring a bottle of whiskey
for Bill and Edith was forced to go through the complicated
procedure of sending it on to her. She forgot to pay for the
repair on her typewriter and it was left to Edith to scratch up
the money. Elinor believed she simplified the menus, but
often forgot to tell Edith how many people would be dining
or who might call for tea. And when Madeleine Boyd (novelist wife of Ernest Boyd, the critic) asked if she could stay for
a few nights before she sailed back to New York, Elinor
allowed her to postpone her departure continually. These
lapses in the domestic arrangements were easily overlooked in
the basement. Edith's job was to look after the house as well
as the tenants, and after Elinor left, Edith wished that she had
stayed on. On the whole Elinor was extremely kind to Edith,
and very quiet. When Elinor moved on to Henley from Chelsea the following year, Edith went with her.

The pace of Elinor's life had caught up with her and left
her depressed. She was alone, miserable, and subject to recurring thoughts about Horace. After the attack of acute self-
awareness that produced "Portrait" in late February of 1927,
she wrote to Horace and asked him if he minded her continued and publicized use of his name, Wylie. He quickly fired

back (March 1, 1927) (Y), "How the dickens was I to know that your nom de plume was your nom de vie? Of course I dont mind your being Elinor Wylie & you know it darned well. . . . I am sort of glad I goaded you." Solitary and unoccupied, Elinor's mind did not return to the more accessible past, but reached back nearly fifteen years, to the time when she and Horace were together in England. She wrote him (May 20, 1927) (B) the most moving letter of her life, asking him to destroy it.*

"Dearest Horace," she addressed him from Cheltenham Terrace

A strange thing is going to happen to you, for that thing is going to come true which undoubtedly you once desired, & for which you will now not care a straw. I am going to admit to you that I wish with all my heart I had never left you. I don't want you to keep this letter, & I hope—& trust—that you will tell no one, but although the admission may afford us both a certain pain, it is founded upon such deep principles of truth & affection that I feel it should be made.

You must not tell this, because the knowledge of it would give pain to Bill, who is one of the best people who ever lived & with whom I expect to pass the remainder of my days. But you & I know that that remainder is not long, & the entire past—which is so much longer—makes me wish to tell you the truth.

I love you Horace, with an unchanged love which is far more than friendship, & which will persist until my death. It is impossible for me to tell your present sentiments towards me, but it can hardly be a matter for regret that your former devotion should have bred a devotion in me which nothing could destroy.

In Paris I was constantly reminded of you, & although even if we had been together we should have been no longer young, no longer, perhaps, lovers, nevertheless I wished we were together. In England the same thing is true—you are constantly in my thoughts, & remembered with an affection which is undoubtedly the strongest I shall ever feel. . . .

Well, my dear, do not think I am divorcing Bill or something like that. He is the best boy imaginable. I suppose it is, in a way, devilish to write this. But I loved you first, I loved you more, I loved him afterwards, but now, that I love you both, I love you best. Surely, you must, in some way, be glad to know this.

*Fortunately he ignored this request.

If you ever want me, I will come back openly. I have never
cheated any one, you know. But I don't suppose you do want it, &
I think it is much better as it is. Only—well, if you had been me, you
would have written this letter from this little house in Chelsea.
Answer it.

Painful as such a letter had been for its author to write,
it provoked as much pain in Horace. Elinor believed she had
been guided out of the highest impulses. Her loneliness and
the intuition that she would soon die gave her the right to
make a final bid for peace of mind, both for herself and Horace. After nearly six years of neglect, she returned to Horace,
giving him a form of attention that managed to revive many
unpleasant memories. She was incapable of dealing with these
emotions, new and unknown. Her immediate response was to
pity herself; then she pitied Horace. This letter, extraordinary
as it seems, was Elinor's attempt to express regret.

Horace's answer was consummately courteous and brief.
He wrote to her from his rooms in the De Sales Chambers in
Washington (June 1) (Y):

I wish I could answer your letter & convey what I feel. For that I
should have to be a great artist and have always lacked even the
ordinary power of expression. But you have been able by your letter
to make right many of the things that went wrong with me. You
know well that I have never, to you or to others, blamed you for
leaving me. The situation was too much for your flesh & blood. That
through the fault of neither one of us.

In your old phrase, which always touched me, "be friends." We
should be, the best of whose life was spent together in friendship and
in love.

Elinor was released. The renewed correspondence with
Horace refreshed her. And by reviving her second marriage
her third husband missed, consistently, the letters that Elinor
vowed to write every week. He grew increasingly worried
until hurriedly scrawled accounts of her engagements started
pouring in toward the end of June.

George Young invited her up to Oxford for Eights
Week, to have lunch with a band of her admirers and to
witness the antics of his "anti-Shelley club . . . where we burn
one of his poems at every meeting." He added that if this were

not sufficient temptation to draw her from London there was a performance of Gilbert and Sullivan's *Pirates of Penzance* on the 25th which she might fancy more. Anne Sackville-West* invited her down to Knole, in Kent, where she met Vita Sackville-West, Harold Nicolson, and Hugh Walpole—all of whom escaped Elinor's comment. For the Whitsun holiday she spent a miserable weekend in Rye with a band of ladies from the *Minnetonka*. A week later she was back in the New Forest with May Dent, which is where she received Horace's letter. "Was it not by a very strange chance that your letter was forwarded to me while I was at Burley?" she wrote him (June 12) (B).

I go back to Chelsea tomorrow, but today I am here in the Forest, & yesterday—truly—I picked the holly to send you. . . . There are fewer ponies & more motors: otherwise it is much the same. . . . I wish with all my heart you were here. . . . I saw your old house in Rye [The Old Hospital, where Horace stayed with Katharine and his children in 1910] last week where I went for a house party. . . . I hear a motor-horn at the Corner & I wish it were yours.
Thank you for your noble and generous reply. The apparent frivolity of this is only my volatile nature & the hurry of things I had to tell you. In a way I am very sad when I think of it, but I would not forget you & me together at Burley for all the rest of the world.

The report of "the hurry of things" she saved for Bill. She ran into his employer, "the little Fiend"—as she referred to Henry Canby—at the Sitwells', and managed to extract a promise from him that he would permit Bill two extra weeks off so he could come to England to celebrate Elinor's birthday. As if this were not inducement enough for Bill to cross the ocean, Elinor even offered him first-class passage back, instead of his customary "student third" accommodation. He planned to travel the usual way, arriving on September 5.

*Anne Sackville-West, a New Yorker by birth, married Charles Sackville-West in 1924 and eventually became Lady Sackville in 1928, hence hostess at Knole. Nigel Nicolson writes that she played the uncompelling part of a complaining lady: the servants were troublesome, the house uncomfortable, and she became the source of a great deal of disharmony in her husband's family. Her idea of a great social event was a bridge party. Elinor, who had known her in New York, found her very amusing; her niece by marriage, Vita Sackville-West, did not.

The "hurry of things" was indeed rapid—Sylvia Lynd asked Elinor to lunch. Roger Ingpen invited her to dine. She was asked to attend the Russian Ballet, again, and Edith Olivier came up to town. Before Edith's arrival at Cheltenham Terrace, Elinor went to the Ivy with "the chinless poet" Brian Howard for dinner. When Edith arrived, her constellation of friends attended her in Chelsea: Rex Whistler, Cecil Beaton, Steven Runciman, Sacheverell and Georgia Sitwell, Zita Jungman, and Frankie Birrell, who alone among this collection insisted upon drinking whiskey. Elinor's weekends were no less full; first there was Wilsford, which promised to be grand and silly with another moonlit ceremony at Stonehenge and Stephen Tennant parading the newly administered finger-waves in his hair for everyone to admire. Then came a few days in Rochester in Kent with a woman Elinor had met during Eights Week who cried at the height of the festivities and lived in the house Dickens used in *Great Expectations* as Mrs. Haversham's. From Rochester she went on to Llewelyn Powys's coastguard cottage in Dorset, where she encountered appalling weather, and then pressed on, near the end of July, to the Daye House where Edith Olivier's cousin, Lord Olivier, promised to show off his white top hat.

Elinor exercised the patience and tolerance of the Oliviers and their guests almost beyond endurance, but the one who gave way under the strain was Elinor herself. She staged her annoying campaigns across the dining table, starting the moment she arrived at luncheon on Saturday when the talk moved to Lord Olivier's "great subject" and, as the hostess noted in her diary (July 23), Elinor "got very worked up over a discussion about black and coloured races . . . and took personally to her nation a remark . . . that civilised cruelty was worse than a savage's." Elinor claimed that the comment was clearly directed at her, "and *she* would never be so brutal to a stranger within her gates."

At dinner Elinor revived her feud with Edward Garnett, saying that he had told her to kill herself after the "outrage" of *The Orphan Angel,* overlooking the obvious fact that Edward Garnett was not there and the whole matter was laid to rest over a year ago. But Lord Olivier happened to be a friend of Garnett's and "tried vainly to make her treat it lightly," which incensed her further. That day Elinor progressed from "touch-iness itself" to "a stormy petrel," never straying from either herself or her writing as topics of conversation. On Sunday, mercifully for the other guests, Elinor stayed in her room resting, no doubt storing up strength to read aloud several of her short stories about Shelley that evening, which her hostess found "very good indeed in themselves, but I think its a vein which should not be worked too hard. . . . I doubt their cumulative effect."

On Monday, before Elinor boarded the 12:30 train from Salisbury to London, her hostess had a "Talk with Elinor—about her face, neck, nose and other features. She is absorbed in every detail of herself." Even after she left, she remained the sole topic of interest. At lunch the verdict on her was that she was "meretricious," and at tea the conclusion was that she had "streaks of real madness in her."

From Cheltenham Terrace Elinor wrote to the people who were busily judging her: "Your cousin," she remarked to Edith Olivier [July 27, 1927](Y), "is not only an interesting but a truly noble person." She had had "the loveliest week-end."

At Cookham with the Youngs she went much further than she had at Wiltshire, adding jealousy to her other well-developed social weapons. For some reason she instantly took against another friend of the Youngs', believing he had a pernicious effect on the family she adored. Metford Watkins, known alternatively as "Watson," was at that time manager of the Odney Club in Cookham, and later bought Formosa Place from the Youngs, where he moved in mid-March 1928.* He and Elinor were having a quiet cup of tea on the terrace with the Youngs when the conversation turned, mildly but predict-

---

*Metford Watkins, later Sir Metford Watkins (1900–1950), was called both Watson and "The Commander." He was educated at Cambridge and became Mathematics Master at Westminster School before joining John Lewis and Company, where he rose to Deputy Chairman. He married Elizabeth Umfreville in 1928. He held such varying posts as Chairman of the Council, Royal College of Art, Member of the Board of Trade, Director-General of Civilian Clothing, and Chairman of the General Purposes Committee of Retail Distributors Association. In short, his transition from the academic to trade was absolute.

ably, to Shelley. Watson did not subscribe to any of Elinor's views on the poet, and with her nimble powers of distortion, she read every one of his comments as heretical. An enormous fight ensued, Elinor accusing Watson of being outrageously inhuman. Her anger mounted steadily, but she managed to control herself sufficiently to thank her host and hostess before she stormed away.

Helen Young was astonished by Elinor's reprehensible behavior, but knew that there was no point in disregarding her tantrums. She stood up to Elinor, and upbraided her, kindly. "How beastly to be feeling so wretched & how vile of us to have given you even a minute's unhappiness when you have been such an angel of generosity to us," she wrote in a note (July 28) (Y). "But you know your imagination & one-skin-short sensitiveness has most to do with it. Everything is hideous underneath a magnifying glass. . . . We've shared too many experiences not to understand one another." By her tact and generosity, Helen succeeded in cementing their friendship still further. Of all Elinor's friends, she understood her best.

Elinor called upon this exact scene in her novel *Mr. Hodge and Mr. Hazard,* though she changed Shelley's name to Milton. She showed such acute interpretive skill that Watson himself was impressed, so impressed that he ignored his antipathy for Elinor and wrote to her eight months later (March 17, 1928) (Y):

I have also been allowed to read Mr. Hazard. I admire immensely your psychology & your uncanny power of penetration, & still more your self control that you can be so aware of things & yet make so little fuss as you do. But I never thought my simple nature would ever survive to suggest a suitable villain to a book, & I think you're quite wrong to have twisted things that way. . . . I'm longing to see you again & argue it out with you, if your delicate fancies were ever born for argument. . . . You poets do so distort the truth for your own trifling purposes.

Elinor's behavior was becoming increasingly unrestrained. Being in England brought out the worst in her, while she steadily professed to prefer it to New York. It might have been the result of panic over her health. "I've the blood pressure of a parrot," she once boasted to Steven Runciman. She complained of a persistent case of flu both to her mother and to Alfred Knopf when she asked for an advance on her new novel. Hostesses were cringing at the prospect of her society. For all her effort to counteract the infamy that accompanied her reputation in America, she was creating a new variety in England, and it was happening very quickly.

As a result she discarded Society and went back to work. "No novel but reams & reams of poetry," she announced to Bill [late July](Y). "I write a poem every morning before I get up. Honest Injun. Novel is all written in my head but not on paper yet." Though her last novel was slow to find its way onto paper, once begun it was finished rapidly. "The novel of Mr. Hodge and Mr. Hazard is," she commented in her brief preface, "an everyday fable; its historical trappings are slight, and it must remain not a disguised biography but a brief symbolic romance of the mind." It was, in fact, closer to disguised autobiography; she spun the fable straight out of her own everyday life. In writing about Mr. Hazard, she was writing about herself:

He was evidently the victim of an excessive sensibility which the high order of his talents failed to stiffen into character. With gifts and natural abilities far above the common, he nevertheless lacked the power of self-discipline to a regrettable degree, and therefore fell an easy prey to morbid introspection and the disapproval of Mr. Hodge.

Elinor was adjusting the picture she presented at the Daye House and Formosa, addressing her patient friends and proving that she could always be counted on, with a talent she had only recently acquired, to make a more scathing indictment of her own character than anyone else. She was leveling the opposition by getting in the first blow. Unfortunately this skill was reserved exclusively for mental dexterity and writing, never active employment in life. When the novel was nearing completion in November 1927, she hotly protested that Hazard was not her. She wrote to Helen Young, to whom she dedicated the novel (November 5)(B),

You will see that Clara is not you, though to my mind she is adorable, which is like you, nor is poor Mr Hazard me, but far nicer, nor is anyone anyone exactly, not even Mr Hodge, but everything is changed and no more the story of us than the Venetian Glass Nephew was the story of Bill and me. I cannot help making fables and bitter fairy tales out of life, and this little romance is so very metaphysical and transcendental that it is no more like us than meringue is like bread and butter.

Yet when the novel appeared, the characters were quickly recognized by their real-life antecedents: Helen Young saw herself as Clara, one of her daughters and her son saw themselves as Rosa and Allegra, Watson spotted himself unmistakably as the detestable Hodge, and the setting, Lyonnesse, is, without question, Formosa. Elinor had a talent, as E. F. Benson once expressed it, for smudging the truth. She blurred reality, and in *Mr. Hodge and Mr. Hazard* she ran her hand over a nineteenth-century English canvas that depicted scenes introduced from her life in the twentieth century. She reproduced in her books, and especially in this one, a somewhat more satisfactory version of actual scenes. "I say it is meringue," she added to Helen Young, "but you will see it is really meringue flavoured with strychnine rather than vanilla-bean. This is my only *metier;* to take a *memento mori* and trim it with rosebuds and *point d'esprit. . . .*"

In four months Elinor produced her most mature, and for many of her readers, her best novel. It lacks the outright fantasy of *The Venetian Glass Nephew,* but it at once encompasses the imagination that made *Jennifer Lorn* so attractive and the cynicism that comes from frank awareness. It has a maturity that all her cramming had buried so well before. She is more comfortable with her characters and her narrative. In a device that Carl Van Vechten used to such advantage, characters from her previous novels crop up. Lady Clara Hunting is the daughter of Gerald Poynyard, who himself had met, at one time, Rosalba Berni before she turned into porcelain. Just as Elinor had grown older, so her characters receded further and more easily into the history she created for them. The narrative moves more gracefully, more gently, and yet there is as little incident as in the three earlier novels. Elinor saved drama for her life.

The blurring of fact and fiction starts with the character of Mr. Hazard. As soon as he comes into clear focus as Shelley

—older, unflinchingly romantic, slightly absurd, and not dead —he melts back into a fog, only to emerge once again, this time more like Elinor, frail, tired, and failed in his ambitions: "Whatever might have been one's opinion of Mr. Hazard in his twentieth year, at forty he looked invulnerable and coldly withdrawn. This frigid demeanour was a deliberately contrived effect; this was his armour." He was a victim of "thin-skinned and fastidious taste." Elinor moved all her travel-scarred Shelley luggage into the plot: in London, arriving after an absence of fifteen years, in February 1833, Hazard falls under the unwelcome hospitality of the Hartleighs (Leigh Hunts) and a three-month attack of influenza. Bird and Piggott—Peacock and Hogg—flutter in his memory. Isabel Paterson said, in her preface to the 1933 republication of this novel, that it was a supplement to *The Orphan Angel*. When Hazard retreats to Lyonnesse, on the Thames, he is caught up with something far worse than influenza: he meets Mr. Hodge, who had been private secretary to Gerald Poynyard and is now a tutor. On learning that Hazard is toiling away in nearby Gravelow (Marlow) on a sonnet to Milton, Hodge says tersely: "Poor Milton."

Mr. Hodge's words inflicted a severer wound; the three heavy syllables were pointed with hatred. Mr. Hazard knew hatred when he heard it, and the knowledge wrought no good in him. . . . He translated Mr. Hodge's two words with acute skill; they informed him that he was an appalling person, unfit to associate with the innocent and the noble, that his appearance was odd, his principles outrageous, and his opinions contemptible.

It was Elinor receiving the judgment of Watson. These two words, once uttered, kill the comfort of Lyonnesse, the society of the Huntings, and the confidence of his work. Hodge unleashes the very fear Hazard had bottled and stored away. Everything is ruined by this contemptible man, who had imposed himself on the life at Lyonnesse with only two words. Hazard flees.

Mr. Hodge and Mr. Hazard is a simple tale, almost deceptively simple. Its thin story does not crack under the weight of the overwriting and florid imagery that detracted from her other novels. It has at once a freshness and depth that was denied Shiloh, Jennifer, and her Venetian characters. Some of the touches are arrestingly clever. When Hazard is suffering from influenza, he refuses to go to sleep, preferring to sit up reading Tennyson: "Presently he could read no longer. While the chill shook his bones asunder, like breakable dice in a black dice-box, he lay staring out of the window into the impenetrable emptiness of the fog, wishing that the exaltation and valour of his mind had not been shrivelled up into scorched peas and rusty needles." The little that passed for plot was made up for in effect. It was her simplest and most successful prose achievement, less successful in terms of sales than *The Orphan Angel,* but a far more sustained, subtle work. It was her fourth, and final, novel. Knopf published *Mr. Hodge and Mr. Hazard* on March 16, 1928, and a month later Heinemann brought it out in England. Thereafter Elinor turned back to poetry.

She stayed on in England longer than anticipated. Bill caught up with her the first week in September, coming over from New York on the *Berengaria.* When the lease on Cheltenham Terrace expired, she took a miniature house in Burley —Atkin's Plot—which she explained to Rosemary Benét (August 30)(Y) was "the size of a dog kennel." From there she and Bill crossed over to May Dent's house to celebrate Elinor's forty-second birthday, then went on to the Daye House. They returned to Southampton on September 17 to sail back to New York.

§*iii*   *"Is that all it is?"*

"Anyone can have two tries," Elinor declared in 1909 after toying with a burning matchstick. Her second try then ended in a burnt fingernail. Nearly two decades later she again permitted herself a second try, attempting to relive the happiness she thought she had enjoyed with Horace in the New Forest. She returned to New York only, it seemed, to prepare herself for England again. But this second attempt at life, so blithely enacted and so calmly accepted, was designed for Elinor alone—and it was mortally isolating.

The final year of her life was less turbulent. She was bedridden for longer stretches than ever before. Her face recorded the increasing strain: the features turned harder, the eyes ringed with lines of pain, the mouth more pinched, and the posture, once so graceful and majestic, stiffer. She could no longer keep up the myth that she was young. The brightness had faded; she was tired.

Yet her ability to work despite any obstacle seemed to contradict her physical state. She wrote poetry with uncompromising speed, and thought that her publishers, ever anxious for any novel she might produce, were ignoring the fact. "As you know," she pointed out to Blanche Knopf (October 20, 1927), "my reputation was founded upon verse: *Jennifer Lorn* would never have received so kind a hearing had not my two books of poetry preceded it." She considered herself primarily a poet, and could not accept the fact that the Knopfs did not share her view. They were doing nothing with the poems she had collected for the volume eventually called *Trivial Breath*. "I gave the firm a very imperfect form of this book last spring," she wrote in the same letter to Blanche, "& perhaps it was unnecessary to comment upon the quality of the work. In this instance, however, when I deliver to you a strict & highly wrought selection from my best poetry of the past four years, I look for an interest to meet it. . . . Surely the question is natural: what do you think of it?" But there was nothing either Blanche or Alfred Knopf could say; they had seen the poems before. Every poem save one that was collected in *Trivial Breath*, Elinor's shortest volume of poetry, had already been published. Blanche replied to Elinor's letter by return; her firm's publication of the book was more lethargic. Though *Trivial Breath* was delivered before *Mr. Hodge and Mr. Hazard*, it was published three months later, in June 1928.*

Trivial Breath, taken as a whole, was a tidying-up exercise. After disposing of the burden of Shelley, Elinor moved straight on to herself as the main subject matter for her poems. The material in these poems is entirely different from that

---

*First as a Limited Edition, which was available in the middle of June.

encountered in her first two books: the Elinor here has grown weary of paradox, distrustful of striking imagery, and indeed, disdainful of her own excessive frigidity. Less antagonistic, less brittle, less harsh, she seems finally to have crossed over into the region of more human feelings—a journey she had been making steadily in her poetry since 1923, but had only recently achieved in her novels. She appeared to retire from the battle waged heroically with herself. The transition was swift and undramatic, but it is difficult to read the collection of poetry in any light other than autobiographical. The relationship with Bill is lightly touched upon in "Peter and John"; her success in Richmond is remembered in "Miranda's Supper"; and her visit to the Powyses (where she stayed in a nearby cottage that had been owned by a man who had recently drowned) is celebrated in "The Coast Guard's Cottage." Rather than looking back, the sonnets that open the third section of the book hint at the "One Person" sonnets that signaled her farewell. Other poems, like " 'As I Went Down by Havre de Grace . . .' "—which sings a *ritornello* on her entire life, looking far back to her father's grave at Forty Fort, Pennsylvania—and "A Strange Song," stand among the finest she ever wrote. The bitterness of her poetry six years before has been sweetened, not by greater strength or mere cleverness, but by resignation. The current of transition is strong in these poems.

At the beginning of 1928 Elinor was invited to Philadelphia for a party given by Emily Clark. When she accepted Emily's invitation, she hoped Philadelphians would be more conscious of what she had become.* As the guests filed into the Walnut Street sitting room they proved even less fastidious than Mama could have imagined. They did not leave Elinor's side until early morning. All night a blizzard was brewing outside and the theatricality of the entire scene increased Elinor's pleasure. She was safely armored in her Poiret silver dress, stationed in a comfortable armchair by the fire from which she did not stir the entire evening.

*"After all," Mama had pointed out to Elinor (January 1, 1924) (Y), "in an old & established community like Philadelphia they still care who you are."

When she got back to New York she wrote a glowing report of the event to Mama. Elinor's unexpected success in her hometown made Mama unexpectedly generous: "I will give you a present of the rent of the London house, if you take it again for three months—so you can count on that, over and above your allowance. I do approve of the rest & recreation you enjoy there," she wrote (February 3, 1928) (Y). Mama herself wanted to return to Philadelphia and Elinor's success there encouraged her still further. She complained of the loneliness and expense of 1701 Rhode Island Avenue—all of her children had left and it was far too large for her. She planned to buy back the McMichael family house in Spruce Street and completely renovate the interior; but when the estimates came in, she decided to stay in Washington. Elinor yearned to return to England.

In April she submitted an application for a Guggenheim Fellowship. The tone of her proposal cut directly across her feelings of sustained gloom; it is curiously optimistic because it had to be—she wanted the money very badly. She took seven years off her age: "The writer," her proposal states, "at the age of thirty-five, feels that she is now entering upon a period of her fullest powers and contemplates work of greater scope, involving the necessity for broader horizons and more detached perspective even in regard to her own country toward which she feels the greatest devotion." The novel she was planning was to be about European witchcraft, obliging her to live in Italy, France, and England in order to ransack the national libraries. While she mentioned Europe to the selection committee, she spoke only of American witchcraft to her friends. Her plans for her poetry were equally vague, though no less financially demanding: "She desires to increase the range and depth of her poetry through more comprehensive study." The Guggenheim Foundation turned her down.

It was Bill who had urged her to apply, as he was always far more worried about money than Elinor. His chronic juggling of their finances made her dizzy, and occasionally as worried as he. Yet Elinor was never held back by lack of money; she merely sporadically denied herself the expensive luxuries she so adored.

Neither Bill nor her publishers were too unhappy to see

her board the *Minnewaska* on Saturday, April 21. She was
forever rearranging the order of the poems in *Trivial Breath*,
debating whether or not to include a new one or exclude an
old one. Even as late as March she was still sending new work
to Knopf. "It would be worthwhile to postpone publication
for a week in order to include this," she instructed her publishers (March 5, 1928) referring probably to " 'As I Went Down
by Havre de Grace . . .,' " which she believed to be one of
the best poems she had ever written, "as I may not have
another volume of poetry for five years. . . ." Bill was totally
preoccupied with the affairs of his family. On March 30, Colonel Benét died in Westown, Pennsylvania. His death affected
Elinor only in that it took Bill away from West 9th Street more
and more often. Remembering the Colonel's intense dislike of
her, Elinor concluded that the best place for her was well out
of sight. And news of his death came through, inconveniently,
in time to spoil her and Bill's weekend at Steepletop with Edna
St. Vincent Millay and her husband. Elinor was usually un-
helpful in an emergency, and she realized she would be more
use by going to England, leaving Bill to spend all his spare
time with "Miss Fanny."

During the crossing she drew up a formidable list of
excuses for deserting New York so quickly after Colonel
Benét's death and just over seven months after she had returned. She wrote to Rosemary Benét, who was in Calvados,
as the *Minnewaska* was nearing the Irish coast (April 28, 1928)
(Y),

it has been an infernal winter, with a fit ending in that sorrowful
calamity [Col. Benét's death] . . . after two months finishing poor
darling Mr Hazard I had two months being ill. . . . The expense of
living in New York is appalling beyond words. Do not come home
on any account if you can possibly avoid it. For us all to live in Paris,
including Mrs Benét & Laura is so far as I can see the only ultimate
solution. This way is ruinous beyond words—rent alone is a moderate income.

But the journey itself was just what she needed to get
over the "infernal winter" and to remove herself from financial worry. "I have been quite well," she wrote to Bill the
same day, "—the sea agrees with me admirably, except that

it is so stimulating that I don't sleep very soundly at night. But it will take a week or two to get really rested." She missed the " 'tonka,' " as she called the Atlantic Transport Line's sister ship *Minnetonka,* since the " 'waska' " was inordinately stodgy, both in atmosphere and passengers. The pint of wine she split between luncheon and dinner helped her overlook the slowness of the voyage (nearly twice as long as it took the *Majestic, Mauretania,* or *Berengaria* to cross.)

The confusion when Elinor reached Cheltenham Terrace was considerable. Landing at a "cruelly early hour" and going straight from Waterloo Station to Chelsea, she found Mrs. Boswell (the owner) still in residence, obviously having ignored the Marconigram sent from the ship. Elinor was nearly reduced to tears. Instead she got back into a taxi and went over to her bank to draw out £66 for the rent. At the bank she found that Knopf had forwarded her money in the name of Elinor Wylie, and only after a great deal of persuading was she able to convince the manager that Mrs. William Rose Benét and Elinor Wylie were one and the same. Then she got another taxi and returned to Cheltenham Terrace, where she found that not only had Mrs. Boswell mercifully vanished, but so had her typewriter, until she realized that she had left it on the dock. She was always leaving the machine somewhere—one summer Stephen Vincent Benét had to send it to her by airmail from Paris where she had left it. After a good deal of telephoning, it was found. Then she could fall into Edith's arms, home at last.

Elinor's engagements piled up quickly. There was a stack of letters awaiting her. Her first evening in London she went up to Hampstead for dinner. Before her bags were unpacked, two weekend visits were settled—first to Edith Olivier and then to May Dent. She went to Formosa for a day, which she claimed was "exquisite in decay," and Helen Young stayed for two nights with her in Chelsea before going to Norfolk to help her husband campaign for a parliamentary seat.* But

*He was not successful, despite discarding one of his more comic political predictions: the previous summer, after Lindbergh successfully flew across the Atlantic, Young declared that the pilot should become President of the United States.

there was one weekend invitation she did not tell Bill she had
accepted. She waited until she was actually at Rockylane Farm,
Rotherfield Greys, in Oxfordshire, to announce (May 5,
1928) (Y): "I am here for the weekend with Becky Woodhouse who as you know is one of my great friends. She has a
nice husband & two dear children, of which the boy, Paddy,
is really much my favourite. Queer, because I generally prefer
girls."

Elinor had first met Becky Woodhouse at May Dent's
house in the New Forest in August 1926, and they liked
one another instantly. Elinor told her she was looking for a
house to buy, and their conversation turned exclusively to
that. Becky Woodhouse volunteered to act as Elinor's
agent; her letters to New York were full of details about
houses. When Elinor returned to England the following
summer, she visited the "Woodlice," as Bill later referred
to them, at their house near Henley and renewed the
agent relationship. The Woodhouses fitted into Elinor's
scheme of English life wonderfully. She was quite easily absorbed into their family life. There was nothing complicated about them, or their friends, and nothing intellectual
either: Elinor was a celebrity among them. She visualized
the arrangement at Rotherfield Greys as everything she believed she valued, wanted, but had failed to achieve. The
pleasures of house and family she so longed to have herself
were enjoyed vicariously through them.

Just as she had foisted herself onto the Youngs, so now
she latched onto the Woodhouses, who were on the whole less
capable of withstanding her attentions. It was an exercise that
was only moderately successful, because her advance on Rotherfield Greys was directed out of panic. They willingly
granted her the respect she wanted, but she made it impossible
for them to show affection. Elinor grasped at her friendships,
squeezing them dry almost before they had a chance to de-
velop. She was too frightened of loneliness to take a calmer
approach, and in the end, when she had drained all hope of
love through sheer exhaustion, she invented the love she had
not won. The myth stood for the fact. But Elinor was always
able to dress her intrusions, her endless demands for attention,
her ceaseless requests, in a manner that could easily be misread

as generosity. She would often send gifts, for no special occasion. Frequently her appreciation was as excessive as her appeals. She manipulated the people around her through a curious mixture of implied obligation and vulnerability, and the Woodhouses were helpless victims of her suffocating attentions. Becky Woodhouse had never surfaced from domesticity to meet anyone like Elinor. And her husband, Henry deClifford Woodhouse, soon wished she never would again. Elinor succeeded in intruding herself and so disrupting the family she claimed to admire that she herself turned from an object of admiration into an enemy. Her departure revived the love Becky initially had for her. But only her death reversed the Woodhouses' hatred back into affection. They were a vulnerable target, and they learned it too late.* Elinor stalked into their lives like a spider advancing on the dinner in his web, and she had spun a fantastic web to entice her victims.

From Rotherfield Greys, Elinor went directly to the Daye House. There, over tea, she confessed to Edith Olivier "of a sudden love affair which has swept her off her feet. She is *possessed* by it. I know not where it will lead," Edith noted in her diary on May 8. That night in Edith's bedroom Elinor went on "to rhapsodise once more. The thunderbolt fell during this weekend and she is more like a girl of 18 over it. Poor Bill!"

The next day Elinor's condition over "Cliff" Woodhouse became worse. "Elinor is in a strangely emotional state—" Edith Olivier observed,

---

*And they are mysterious. All attempts to discover more about them have drawn a blank. Bill's pruning of Elinor's letters certainly helped a great deal, but he failed to obliterate completely all reference. And Nancy Hoyt refers to them helpfully as "the X—s". The identity of the Woodhouses was first discovered by John D. Gordan of the Berg Collection when researching his biography of Elinor Wylie, and later revealed in his article, "A Legend Revisited: Elinor Wylie," published in *The American Scholar* (vol. 38, 1968–9). Gordan went to visit the Woodhouses, who had moved to the West Indies, and spoke to them about Elinor only after Mrs. Woodhouse's considerable resistance had been overcome. Even as late as the 1960s Becky Woodhouse requested that any reference to their relations with Elinor should not be made; she has, in part, succeeded.

speaks of this affair as one that must last forever. She and "Cliff"
"lovers for life," though determined not to hurt their husband and
wife. As it only began three days ago I can hardly feel it is bound
to be so permanent. She is very young. . . . In all spare moments we
talk of her affaire, and she ended the day sobbing in my bedroom
at 11 o'c and being revived by a hot whisky.

The following day (Thursday, May 10) Elinor's passion
assumed a quieter form—she wrote three sonnets in quick
succession about her "love affair." Everything else was
brushed aside. Having complained to Bill about money, he
had sent her a book to review for the *Saturday Review*. Now
she tossed it over to Edith Olivier and went so far as to suggest
to Bill that he add $10 or $15 to her payment, and she would
reimburse him. Even the house she was planning to buy now
had to be a convenient distance from Rockylane Farm. Edith
Olivier took her to see two houses: one in Chilmark (Whitehall Cottage) and one in Tisbury, both very close to the Daye
House, and some fifty miles from Rotherfield Greys. While
everything about the Tisbury house made it more suitable,
Elinor preferred Whitehall Cottage and left a deposit of £250
for it. A month later, by which time she was even more consumed by her passion, she declared that fifty miles was, after
all, much too far away and she no longer wanted Whitehall
Cottage, which meant forfeiting her deposit.

What Elinor said and and what she did were entirely at
variance. Money, which had been her main excuse for leaving
New York, was now of no consequence. In fact, she was
willing to throw it away. As she drew closer to Woodhouse,
she declared greater affection for Bill, which was not, as it
seems, an attempt to blunt his potential suspicion. The list of
inconsistencies increased steadily.

"I'm still ecstatically happy—" she had written to Bill
(May 16, 1928) (Y), "the change from Hell to Heaven is
really dazzling." But she hid the source of her unexpected and
sustained ecstasy from him and almost everyone else. It had
even given her the strength to ignore her failed reconciliation
with Watson. She wrote to him and asked him to be friends,
if for no other reason than to avoid any scenes at Formosa. He
showed little inclination to reconciliation, writing to Elinor
from the Odney Club in Cookham (May 10)(Y):

And whether to be friends or not is still a problem to be faced.
I am too tired to face it. Hazard has had his winter off duty, & worked off his troubles in tears. . . . Surely when I meet you I will be so kind & polite to you that no one would ever guess. But not friends. We are too far apart, too different, and not complimentary but antithetic. . . . I would not be friends with you because we both love Helen [Young], any more than you would be friends with me because we both love Shelley.
Your dear & everlasting enemy, Watson

When Elinor called at Formosa, Watson behaved very well, too well in fact, so that the atmosphere became "very highly charged," as one observer remarked long after the incident. Both Elinor and Watson seemed to be waiting for the other to make a move. Robert Stopford, a cousin of the Youngs, offered to drive Elinor over to Marlow, and she jumped at the opportunity to escape. Just as they were preparing to set off, Watson thrust his reply to Elinor's letter through the window at her. He had had it waiting for three days, unable to decide whether or not to send it. As Elinor read it, tears welled up in her eyes and she was forced to tell Stopford what had happened. He asked her candidly why Watson should dislike her so much: "she replied that there were two reasons: firstly, that he knew that she was a closer friend of Helen Young's than he was: and, secondly, that she was more of a re-incarnation of Shelley than he was." Elinor had chosen her model for Hodge too well, and was paying for her inability to let the matter rest. She had made a grave mistake in writing to Watson.*

After that, Elinor avoided the Youngs and the Woodhouses for a while. She went to Cambridge to be shown around by Steven Runciman, who was a great admirer of her poems; she, for her part, admired his cigarettes—Zakaznija, number 10. But her determination, aided by Steven Runciman's companionship, was not enough to keep her from Henley for long.
A roundabout way of traveling to Henley arose through

---

*She treated Stopford more carefully. As a reward for allowing her to cry on his shoulder she gave a dinner on May 17 at Cheltenham Terrace where he, his cousin Joan Young, and Steven Runciman watched her spray the room with champagne.

her work, gratifying alike her romantic fascination with Woodhouse and her need for money. She manufactured a case against Knopf, based on the royalties she thought that she deserved and their inefficiency had lost her. In a letter to Bill (May 29) (Y) she accused her publishers of letting

> poor darling Mr Hazard crash to the ground, & I'm only to have about two thousand dollars . . . from the book in October. Isn't it *filthy* of them? I suppose they suspected I was [?perhaps] leaving [the] firm, but I do think they cut off their great Jewish noses to spite their faces, don't you? Now, as a matter of fact, I shall never write a single other novel except Mary Tamberlaine. . . .*

She asked Bill to forward a copy of her long poem "Lonesome Rose," which she had discarded before *Nets to Catch the Wind* appeared and now wanted to rework and sell. A copy arrived in time for her to read it to Edith Olivier at the Daye House the second weekend in June. She also read some of the new poems she had written—"the best poetry of my life," she told Bill (June 2) (Y). "Strange but true." These poems were the early drafts of the sonnets she wrote, dedicated to her infatuation with Woodhouse. When not writing about Woodhouse, she was talking about him. Edith Olivier was astonished by the strength of her affection for him, founded as she saw it on so little evidence and expressed in the most incoherent terms. "She suddenly says she won't buy Chilmark and will forfeit her £250 to get out of it," Edith Olivier wrote in her diary (June 10). "She is so madly in love that she can't make up her mind to settle anywhere more than an hour's journey from the beloved one. It *must* end in disaster. They are both already married, and Elinor insists on taking all the risks. She is really demented." When Edith and Elinor went together to consult

---

*Elinor mentioned little more about this novel, designed to satisfy her contractual obligation with Knopf. She calculated it might take her as long as four or five years to write, thanks to the Guggenheim's lack of confidence in her, and her own preference for writing poetry first. She told both Knopf and Heinemann that *Mary Tamberlaine* would be her next novel, and she told her friends that it would be more "modern" than her previous work —that is to say, late nineteenth century. A page of this letter is missing.

The Knopfs in fact had good reason to think Elinor was deserting them; Liveright made her an offer which she seriously entertained, but did not pursue.

the solicitor dealing with the sale of Whitehall Cottage, the latter informed Elinor that she had signed a contract and the owners of Whitehall Cottage had already bought another house. She could not get out of it. "She now begins to think she *may* keep it after all," Edith Olivier noted, adding that Elinor was impossible as a businesswoman and infuriating about Woodhouse.

As to "taking all the risks," as Elinor boldly explained her activities, she had taken very few. She had not seen Woodhouse for nearly a month since the time she had fallen in love with him. If they corresponded, these letters have not survived. Neither Bill nor Becky had the slightest hint of what was going on in Elinor's mind; they could not, because there was no evidence or activity to support her recitals at the Daye House. When, a few days before her death, she showed a photograph of Woodhouse to Mary Colum, she compared him with Horace. Woodhouse had evolved in her mind as an embodiment of the fantasy she retained about her life with Horace in the New Forest, the happiness she had fought for and lost. Mary Colum wrote in her autobiography: "it seemed to me the old life she had once told me about, relived again almost as a dream. That she was really in love with this man I believed to be true and real as far as romantic love was concerned. . . . As she spoke to me of it, it seemed a simple and pathetic relationship. . . ."

Woodhouse admitted to Bill Benét in February 1929: "I . . . know that she attributed to me qualities which I don't possess and only wish that I had. Her imagination, I think, ran away with her. . . ." Sometimes reality caught up with her. Casting aside her initial prudence and discretion, she burst out to Carl Van Doren, who managed to be in London during the height of the infatuation, "I don't want much. I don't expect it. I could be satisfied if I could know that sometime, maybe when we are very old, we could spend the same night under one roof. It would not have to be together. Only under the same roof, peacefully. Is that too much to expect? Don't you think I could dare hope for that?"

This was her unwitting declaration that "love" was to her a mere gesture; her affection was little more than a chess game. Sex remained beyond reach and intimacy or, more precisely, closeness was the same as consummation. Woodhouse, who

was elevated to the very center of all her thoughts and activities, hopes and desires, was afforded no greater intimacy than being locked outside her bedroom door.

The victory over circumstance and inhibition was easily achieved; Elinor dreamed it and acted as if it were real. By the second week in September she was convinced she was pregnant. The natural questions as to how this came about are impossible to answer. Elinor's health was so frail that pregnancy was out of the question. Yet she was convinced it was real. She told Edith Olivier all about it. "Elinor thinks she is going to have a baby," Edith Olivier noted in her diary for Wednesday, September 12, "and is afraid to move lest she should stop it. She wants one dreadfully, but I believe she never *can* have one." The following day Elinor's anxiety grew to violent proportions; she appeared to be suffering from some sort of breakdown. Her hostess thought she was going mad. In 1924 the doctors who attended the miscarriage of Bill's child had told her firmly and gravely that any further attempt to have children would end in certain death—she would kill herself. But she confessed to Edith Olivier, four years later, that it would be "the best of deaths." By Friday she had settled into a ghostly calmness. She came downstairs from her room after breakfast and said her "hopes were over—and she is less despairing than I feared." Edith Olivier was as startled by this new mood as she had been by Elinor's mad ravings. It had all been a fantastic mental exercise, even by Elinor's standards.

The last fortnight in June was a welter of social engagements. She entertained Carl Van Doren, who failed to turn up in his evening clothes but did manage to get a broken waterpipe repaired; the novelist Robert Nathan, who understood Elinor better than was good for him; and Edith Olivier. She dined with Steven Runciman. And she went to Rotherfield Greys.

Rockylane Farm had the unfortunate effect, especially in 1928, of making its inhabitants ill. Scarcely six months before, Becky wrote to Elinor (February 28, 1928) (Y), her maid "got into trouble and nearly died." Then one unsuspecting guest dislocated her right shoulder and "needed long and careful nursing." But Elinor was too overjoyed, too pleased to be in the same house with Woodhouse, to pay any attention to these stories.

On Sunday the 24th, as Elinor was coming down the fifteenth-century staircase to join Becky and her husband in the garden for tea, she felt faint, lost her footing, and fell down seven steps. When she regained consciousness a few moments later, she looked around to see if anyone might have heard or seen the accident. The time, she remembered precisely, and later wrote to Horace (December 16, 1928) (B), was "seven minutes to six o'clock, when she was so happy that life seemed too heavenly to be true . . . I . . . shot through the air & downwards because those friends of mine, being so proud of this staircase, leave it uncarpeted & polish it with best butter." She then picked herself up off the floor, smoothed her dress and tidied her hair, and made her way, with great difficulty, into the garden. She went through the motions of the tea as if by reflex; but the pain in her back became so intense her face turned white, and it was obvious that she could no longer conceal her accident from her hosts. When she did tell them, she spoke about it in such terms that they were not alarmed.

Elinor kept to her original plans, staying over until Monday, because she suspected the extent of her injury and wanted to be in her own home before consulting a doctor. She did not sleep at all Sunday night, and on Monday morning she climbed into a third-class carriage on the train back to London. The journey seemed endless. "Elinor," Nancy Hoyt wrote in her biography, "alone, hung onto the upholstered strap and wept. She was too weak to stand and could not lean back or sit except sideways. Every jolt pierced her. Finally, only half conscious, she reached home. . . ." Edith helped her up the stairs to her bedroom and into bed, then rushed to get the doctor. He ordered an X-ray, which revealed an injured vertebra half way down the spine and a hairline fracture across the sacrum. She was badly bruised but there was nothing that could be done. He told her that she must stay in bed for at least a month. This was the only form of cure he could advise.

"I had the damned idiocy to fall & fracture my spine," Elinor wrote to Rosemary Benét (July 18, 1928) (Y). "Well it has been unadulterated hell. . . ." It was the hottest July in England for thirty years and all the heat seemed to collect in

her small, airless bedroom at the top of the house. She had
difficulty eating, she could not sleep, nor could she write. She
managed through sheer force of will to get off one letter to
her sister Nancy in Paris, congratulating her on the birth of
her daughter Edwina. The letter reached Nancy ten days after
the telegram announcing the birth had been sent, in itself a
delay sufficient to arouse suspicion that something might be
wrong. On top of that Elinor's handwriting, never very legi-
ble, looked pitifully labored and strained. Then Elinor told
her mother—who was also in Paris, standing in for Nancy's
husband who had stayed in New York—what had happened.
But Mama could not leave Nancy, who was not recovering
quickly from her confinement. When Blanche Knopf, who
was in London at the time, heard of Elinor's accident, she
rushed to see her and reproached Mama for her cruel neglect.
So did Elinor. "Mama has been a brute to me—" she told
Rosemary Benét, "Two lines on a bit of notepaper & my
allowance *tout simple. . . ."*

Mama, in fact, was torn between all three of her children,
all of whom were giving her cause for concern. Morton, who
had been divorced from Jeanne since April, threatened to kill
himself if she would not remarry him, and he made good his
promise—he jumped off the *Rochambeau* mid-Atlantic but was
somehow miraculously saved. His rescue cost Mama a very
substantial contribution to a seamen's charity.* "The bad boy
Morton is petted," Elinor complained to her sister-in-law,
"while I who try to be brave get plain kicks for it."

Elinor did not write to Bill about her accident; she swore
everyone to secrecy. He was planning to sail to England at the
end of July, and Elinor was convinced she would have recovered by then. In complete ignorance, Bill sent Elinor all the
news about Morton's leap, which, in a way, saved her the

*The exact cause of the leap, which Morton himself never revealed, has
been given many explanations. One was that he bet that sound waves could
carry a great distance, and with the help of an enormous number of cocktails
tested his theory. Another, given enormous coverage in American newspapers at the time—the first part of July—was that it was the culmination of
an unsatisfactory shipboard romance. His threat to his estranged wife was
the most likely reason, but the amount of alcohol he consumed doubtless
contributed.

urgency of confessing to him. Morton occupied all interest. "I hope you haven't been unnecessarily worried about Morton," Bill wrote to her (July 11, 1928) (Y). "... We have naturally been worried in retrospect. In fact it nearly knocked me off my pins when I first read of it, but thank God he was safe." There was a great deal of unwelcome publicity. Cameramen and reporters lined the pier when the *Rochambeau* docked, desperately trying to get some statement from Morton, but he managed to disembark by the crew's gangplank and escape. After the worry subsided, the excitement of his rescue still lingered.

On the other side of the Atlantic there was considerably more worry about Elinor. "I can only say over and over again how sorry I am—" Becky Woodhouse wrote (Thursday [?July 5]) (Y) in reply to Elinor's letter. "I am really so worried and unhappy about it that there is no room in my mind for anything else—and not the least part of my unhappiness is the thought that any harm should have come to you in this house —Also the thought that Rockylane, having permitted such a thing to happen, ought to find some means of putting it right. ... There must surely be something that I could do." Helen Young sent a list of nurses' addresses. Sylvia Lynd wrote to her. Llewelyn Powys wrote from Dorchester (July) (Y), "I would have thought the very [?] spiders in the crevices of that ancient staircase would have cried out a warning. And you who step always so lightly and always with such grace should have had so untoward a chance seems to me a most treacherous evil."

Elinor said nothing, and for that alone she wanted great praise. "Isn't it lucky that ... I had the wit & courage to conceal it from him [Bill]," she wrote to Rosemary Benét (July 18) (Y), "so he need not waste his whole blessed (& so well deserved) holiday in Chelsea, fetching & carrying for me with a broken back? *Aren't* you pleased with me—won't even Steve stop tapping the old foot now & praise me?" To Bill she spoke only of royalties, publishers, the prospects of his new job with Macmillan (which he did not get), her reviews for *Trivial Breath,* and their holiday in the country later on in the summer, deftly avoiding the most important topic in her mind.

Her decision to remain silent only fanned the sensationalism when news of the accident was eventually reported. By

August, American newspapers, having just recovered from their hysteria over Morton's escapade, ran the story that Elinor was dying. The stories made gruesome reading, saying at one point that Elinor had thrown herself down the stairs, and at another that she was languishing "Near Death" in London. They were made more painful by the fact that Elinor had, by then, recovered. "We have certainly spent two days of great anxiety," Bill's mother wrote to him (August 9) (Y) after he had reached England and heard Elinor's own account, "& unhappiness—A long column & a half appeared in an evening newspaper, telling of a terrible accident to Elinor . . . I cabled you at once, but received no answer. That frightened me still more—Laura could get no other news until Amy [Loveman] cabled & got an answer." Letters shuttled back and forth across the Atlantic—some people were even convinced that Elinor was dead.

Later, when Bill returned to New York in September, he wrote a spirited letter to the *Evening Post,* which had been the author of the original rumor. "Lovers of cheap sensationalism," he wrote, at the end of his own account of Elinor's fall (September 7, 1928), "implying an appalling lack of consideration both for a distinguished writer and for all those who love her, may, it seems, turn to the columns of the *New York Evening Post.* But this is an aberration from the high tradition of editing that I cannot bring myself to believe is anything but an aberration." A week later the *Saturday Review* ran its own correction of the *Post*'s story. When Elinor heard about the newspapers' performance, she fired off her own trenchant comment: "To the Gentlemen of the Press":

> The wish is father to the thought;
> But—here appears the deadlock—
> Your wishes, which have come to nought,
> Were all born out of wedlock.
>
> . . .
>
> Go soak your heads, my merry men all,
> In gingerbread and water!
>
> . . .
>
> God rest you gentlemen, for His sake
> For whom this cross the sign is,

And, if you have backbones to break,
God mend them straight as mine is!

Bill had arrived in Southampton the beginning of August, and spent two nights at Cheltenham Terrace (the Boswells allowed Elinor to stay on after her lease expired on July 30), helping prepare for the move to the house Elinor had taken in Henley: Riverslea. Before he arrived, Woodhouse came up to town to visit Elinor—a courtesy that was made much of by the convalescent patient. While Bill was in England Woodhouse was banished, although not entirely. Bill and Elinor went off to Burley together. They went to see Edith Olivier at the Daye House. They went to look over Whitehall Cottage, which was now Elinor's; Bill played tennis, they had picnics together by the river, and paddled in a canoe. They called on the Woodhouses, briefly and uneventfully. It was their last burst of pleasure together. Elinor recovered sufficiently to plunge into a profoundly reflective mood.

"I have suffered so much this summer that I am a changed spirit," she wrote to the poet Anna Hempstead Branch (August 28, 1928) (B), in reply to her compliments on *Trivial Breath*; "but I have had an extraordinary reward in a new spring of poetry within me, & I have written thirty-odd poems which I trust & pray you will approve." These poems, of which her sonnets to Woodhouse comprise the largest portion, were later collected. They form the largest portion of work included in her last volume, *Angels and Earthly Creatures*.

Elinor was correct—she had changed. She was more subdued, withdrawn. The pendulum was back to where it had been at the beginning of the year. Her select "hand-picked" friends, as she once categorized them for Bill, intruded less frequently; she no longer pursued the social obligations that had monopolized her time in April. The tone of her letters slowly coasted downward. She placed bravery before anything else. She disguised any fears she might have had from Bill— indeed, she hid a great many things from him, even the fact that she understood she might soon die. It had become her habit to exclude him from her thoughts. From the moment she confessed to Horace that she loved him more than Bill, she began to ignore her husband. She never lied to him; she

merely concealed the truth and failed to tell him things. He
was, in her eyes, no longer her husband but a companion. This
drift in her attitude allowed Woodhouse to rise to an importance out of all proportion to the facts. It was impossible for
Bill not to notice the shift in his status. Elinor had now told
him about her feelings for Woodhouse. She made it clear, yet
every aspect of her outward behavior to him was precisely the
same as ever.

They were installed in Riverslea, a red brick Victorian
house situated in Mill Lane, off the Reading Road, leading out
of the center of Henley. From the top floor one could see the
river and Marsh Lock, which was at the end of the lane. It was
not a big house, it was not very comfortable, but it was a
manageable size with several small rooms. The sitting room,
dominated by a vast brick hearth on one wall, faced the back
garden. A dining room, small study, and Edith's territory
comprised the ground floor, which was elevated well above
ground level in order to counteract the Thames, which had an
unfortunate tendency to seize up and flood. The situation was
superb in the summer and lethal in the winter, when the
coolness generated from the river turned to frosty dampness.
Its major asset was that it was very quiet. Bill passed his holiday there. When he left at the end of August, Elinor stayed
on, debating what she would do with Chilmark.

Bill was not pleased that she elected to stay in such a
place, so close to Rotherfield Greys, and so far away from him.
About the latter he was resigned, and accepted Elinor's
wishes. "I do not think—aside from the theme of the sonnets
—that the proximity of the W[oodhouse]s can never be anything to you but painful & somewhat poisonous," he wrote to
her as his ship, the *Homeric,* was nearing New York (September 4, 1928) (Y).

Their situation contains those two p's [painful and poisonous] & is
both depressing & boring. As I look back they seem like something
queer in a book. . . . I like the man as a casual acquaintance. He is
not the type that stirs me to any great friendship—aside from the
present situation. Frankly viewed, our companionship for five years
has not brought you particular happiness. . . . As to children, you
know exactly what I have felt & how your health has been. If you
hold that against me, it does not seem quite just to me. I am, of

course, far more sensual than you, and have tried to be unusually considerate because I have great respect concerning you & because of the past.

. . . One thing remains to me as just one of the perfectly incomprehensible things in life. During my whole stay neither one of those people expressing [sic] to me one single, solitary regret concerning your accident. To tell anyone else that such was the case would simply be unbelieved. I shall never forget as long as I live.

I had a feeling of essentially false friendship toward me on their part that remains a bit sickening . . . they are an experience I do not desire to repeat. . . . Still I have to thank you deeply for having been perfectly frank about it & told me everything. I always hope I shall be one of your very best friends.

As Bill was sailing home, Elinor's thoughts were evolving in precisely the same direction as his. She answered every point he raised in his letter before she had seen it. She started to look at the Woodhouses more critically, more severely. She had arranged a party on the river with their children, Paddy and Gwyneth: "all went happily & gaily," she told Bill (September 1, 1928) (Y). "But the parents, fetching [them] at ten-thirty, were a pair of heavy cotten blankets soaked in bilge-water." She agreed with Bill that Henley, and Riverslea, were not the ideal solution to where she might live; but London was strictly beyond her finances, now that most of her money was being syphoned off to the builders working at Whitehall Cottage.

But the most dispiriting aspect of her life was, she told Bill, that she was not a mother. She perceived this desolate status, incorrectly, as one casualty of her career, believing she had exchanged motherhood for being a writer. Her mind surveyed the facts and cruelly misread them. "It is quite evident to me," she wrote in the same letter to Bill, "that I am happier with children than my contemporaries. [Indec.] *It is, & always will be, the greatest tragedy & complete frustration of my life that I am childless.*" It was a lament Elinor had sung often, but always before she had hope and a desire to go on trying to have children. Now it was displaced only by remorse. While Elinor blamed her failure with Bill on her failure to have children, Bill blamed himself and his excessive consideration as the real source of the trouble.

He knew their marriage was over. He told Elinor as
much, yet she would not accept the cold facts that she herself
had supplied him with. They reached an unstated agreement
that they would stay married in word only. But when released,
Elinor got frightened: her letters became more ardent and
more loving. Yet she did not cross the ocean herself.

Elinor's depression, which Bill had noticed while he was
at Riverslea, was alarming, and various things she wrote in her
letters kept the fear alive. "I am, of course," she said in the
first letter he read at West 9th Street, "a complete failure, but
one mustn't mind that I suppose, since so many of our best
people are failures. I suppose the only way to avoid it is by
dying young, or living to be so old that one's age in itself
. . . becomes a sort of accomplishment." She pointed to a string
of reminders that had provoked such an idea. First the Woodhouses forbade all future picnics with their children, "as if the
picnics had been mass-murder plans," Elinor later added (September 10) (Y). Then Mama, Nancy, and the infant Edwina
arrived in Bournemouth; Elinor was excited by the baby, and
bought her outrageously expensive baby clothes, almost as if
she could not deny that the very sight of her niece aroused an
intense longing that she had been hers. Then the clippings
arrived from American newspapers about her accident, exag-
gerating the truth and reviving all the old myths of 1910. It
was like reading her own obituary, which omitted her achievements as a writer but included all the scandal she had struggled
to outlive. Failing to point out that she herself had asked Bill
to forward as many accounts as he could lay his hands on,
Elinor wrote to Mama [September, 1928] (B) that Bill very
foolishly

—he is a darling but not very tactful, you know—sent me a mass of
clippings about how I was dying of having fallen *four flights of stairs*
—how it was a suicide attempt, & even bringing in the lie about
Corsica & the Corsican children [first printed in 1911]! . . . It was
as usual a piece of evident malice—the wish that I *was* dying was
father to the thought, & its inaccuracy went so far as to say that dear
Phil was especially devoted to his wife, that Horace—poor devil!—
deserted me. . . . I wish to Heaven I never see New York again
. . . the damnfool letters I get from New York! . . . Vincent Millay,
shouting her silly head off over Sacco & Vanzetti, & then writing to

me, timidly & sweetly, as if she were afraid I'd been mixed up in a badger game or a lot of second story work! Swine is the only word for it, in your presence, though I really think one or two others might be more exact.

Her Guggenheim rejection was another indication of "failure." Then Bill's letter from the *Homeric* (September 4) arrived, and reading that he was as downcast as she, her answer (September 14) (Y) served as a justification, as tepid as her attempts to comfort him: "Of course I was thoroughly smashed up by the accident—a fall downstairs & over a cliff during one summer is enough to shake the most iron nerve a bit."

As the days grew colder, Riverslea became increasingly uncomfortable. With the windows closed, the smell of gas was nauseating. Edith and Elinor arranged for one room to be kept warm, where Elinor read, wrote, and had her meals, avoiding the dining room at all costs. Her favorite meals were cutlets or steak, fresh cauliflower or marrow, and half a bottle of Pommard. Eleanor Chilton,* who had stayed with Elinor in Chelsea after the accident, volunteered to brave the house to see her. Elinor used Edith Baldry's annual holiday to vacate the place herself for two weeks, and went straight to the Daye House. From there she went down to Eleanor Chilton's cottage in Sussex and toyed with the idea of following her hostess back to London. One party that pulled her from her one-room existence at Riverslea to London was given by Stephen Tennant at his mother's home, Mulberry House in Smith Square. It was a very grand occasion. Stephen Tennant decorated his bedroom in pure Elinor style: the walls were lacquered silver, the ceiling was midnight blue and the carpet jet black. The furniture had been painted silver and the curtains were silver, lined in white silk. In order to fit into these surroundings, Elinor spent an entire afternoon at Cyclax's beauty salon, one

*Eleanor Chilton (1898–1949), novelist, wrote most of her novel *Shadows Waiting* (1928) while she was supposed to be helping Edith look after Elinor. Her other works are *Nelly's Work* and *Follow the Furies.* In 1933 she married Herbert Agar. She was, as one observer remarked twenty-five years after her death, "Someone I always avoided." She prided herself, so she told Elinor, on not worrying about most people.

of her favorite haunts. She had warned her host that she could not stand for any length of time, and he placed a bed, with a silver counterpane, in a strategic position for her. She hobbled in, and as Rebecca West recalled, "lay down on the wide bed . . . with her head on a silver pillow. Her face looked gray." When she saw Rebecca West, she struggled to her feet again and went to talk to her about the newspaper reports of her fall. Then she made her way over to the lacquered walls, where their host had commanded that all of his guests, among them Paul Robeson, should brush their signature in black ink. Elinor moved round the room in great excitement and admired all the signatures before she herself signed. Then she stopped, clung to a wall for support, "looking up wistfully and crying, 'Oh, that is beautiful! I shan't be able to do it half so well.' The terrible and absurd despair in her voice was so intense that it staggered one. 'How is it possible,' one asked oneself, 'that a woman who feels little things so acutely as that can go on living for a week?' "

By the time Elinor was ready to leave Riverslea, she detested the house. "This," she told her mother [September 1928] (B), "was never anything but a gimcrack cardboard box, but it's done very well, & gave Bill a grand holiday." From Mill Lane she moved closer in to Henley, in fact into the very center, taking the Old Cottage, New Street, which was owned by friends of hers who had gone off to Italy until the following June. Her lease ran from the end of October until they returned, despite the fact that she promised Bill she would sail back to New York at the end of November or the beginning of December. She also got Bill to promise that he would sell her poems for her.

His skill as an agent left a lot to be desired; he had left her manuscript behind at Riverslea, even though he assured Elinor it was the most important article in his luggage. In New York he was not doing any better, and Elinor decided that she would not be impeded by editors' reluctance, or any other obstacle. She arranged with a local printer in Henley, George Blows of The Borough Press, to have her sonnets privately published. The small paper-covered edition of *Sonnets* was promised for delivery the end of October. The order of the sonnets, as she arranged them for this edition, varies slightly, as does the text, from the final version she prepared for Knopf as the first section of *Angels and Earthly Creatures.*

Elinor's "One Person" sonnets are, perhaps, her finest achievement. They are her testimony to the power of her emotions, distilled and purified. It is appropriate that she should have chosen the form of Petrarch, which was so suited to and famous for love. The love in these poems is not a private love, not a variety of confession, but an abstracted one, free of the protection of subjectivity. And although her expression is clear throughout, she does not ignore the pain that affection arouses; she does not, as she had done in her actual relationship with Woodhouse, misinterpret, overbalance, or spill into excess. The nineteen sonnets are paced with strength, energy and undeniable feeling, sustained as a group by shifting through the complexities and vicissitudes of love. And the confidence that had been born in doubt is impressive.

On paper, Elinor did not waver when she thought about Woodhouse. She strode beyond the transient quality of the affection she had contrived, outpacing the manufactured nature of the love she forced on him and that caused her so much anguish. These poems are the natural progression of the movement away from herself that began with *Trivial Breath.*

Yet they are threaded through with her own experience and nimbly expanded to redress any individual quality. The spontaneity is evident; they are not overworked. Caught on a wave of euphoria—tempered, perforce, by deferred fulfillment—Elinor stopped herself in the middle of the sequence of progression of her mood to explore its very nature, rather than sailing on to the consummation. She demanded that Woodhouse play a part in her life sufficient to keep her on the crest of her investigation. His courtesy alone provided her with just enough fuel, just enough assistance, to avoid sadness, anger or frustration. It was as if she set out to use him, knowing that any manifestation of their love would be a dividend. She was content with the emotion alone, content to play both sides of their affair.

The most impressive aspect of these sonnets is that Elinor showed she realized every intricate detail of her emotion. She knew exactly what she was feeling. She never had to depend on imagination for any sensation, which proved that the strik-

ing imagery of her earlier poetry had not merely been a device
but her form of perspective, her only manner of interpreting
herself. Even her picture of herself was refined:

> The little beauty that I was allowed—
> The lips new-cut and coloured by my sire,
> The polished hair, the eye's perceptive fire—
> Has never been enough to make me proud:
> For I have moved companioned by a cloud,
> And lived indifferent to the blood's desire
> Of temporal loveliness in vain attire:
> My flesh was but a fresh-embroidered shroud.
>
> Now do I grow indignant to that fate
> Which made me so imperfect to compare
> With your degree of noble and of fair;
> Our elements are the farthest skies apart;
> And I enjoin you, ere it is too late,
> To stamp your superscription on my heart.
> —Sonnet V

While the sonnets are themselves Elinor's monument to
Woodhouse, they do not commemorate something that has
eluded her grasp. By the nature of this love affair, there was
no conclusion, only an optimistic beginning. Thus she excluded any potential adversity—fear, pain, regret, or the other
residues that follow the end of an affair. She left herself with
the lexicon of pure emotion to explore. And Woodhouse left
her with an enormous amount of pleasure, only by failing to
deviate from courtesy. His absence inspired her to forget her
egomania and forced her to discard self-indulgence as a means
of perspective. Yet through this very self-indulgence she
found the key that unleashed her perception. It was a wonderful marriage, safely encapsulated within Elinor alone.

But the "One Person" sonnets did claim a victim. Elinor
quenched any remaining glimmer of Bill's affection for her by
proving that he could not inspire her poetry. He had looked
to his family, always, for his own inspiration, and could put
only the most brutal interpretation on his wife's performance.
Elinor knew that she had failed him in his family network, and
again by not providing him with their own family. Since Colonel Benét's death Bill had been drawn with increasing

strength back to his mother, brother, and sister. He became protective of his mother, not his wife. "I do appreciate you," Elinor confessed to him on September 10, "& I do love you, darling. Only you see you have other responsibilities which come first (naturally enough, since they are to people supposedly more helpless than I) & as I must fend for myself I must use my own judgement as well as my own actual manual & intellectual (?) labour." Two months later she worded her sentiments about Bill's disaffection for her more strongly to her own mother: "I really like Bill, if only he were not such a weak-minded idiot. I have no intention of being ever otherwise than married to him for the rest of our lives, but I won't be married to Mrs Benet and Laura and The Saturday Review of Literature. . . ." The very same qualities she had admired eight years before, she now detested. She noticed that Bill had remained annoyingly consistent, while she had changed. She was blacking him with the same brush that had blacked Horace.

Bill's resigned acceptance of Elinor's attachment to Woodhouse swung back to jealousy once he returned to New York. He tried to hide it but did not succeed, and Elinor used it as yet another excuse to avoid New York. Her "own judgement" meant that she should stay at the Old Cottage—a ramshackle house perched on the corner of two well-traveled roads, with large, low-ceilinged rooms, easy to keep warm and built in romantic stucco and timber. There was no garden worth mentioning, but Elinor was close to the countryside where she was taking long walks, as much as ten miles a day. When she told Bill of this achievement, he instantly concluded that these walks led straight over to Rotherfield Greys, but Elinor assured him she was completely solitary. What she did not tell him was that her reason for the exercise was to make herself more attractive to Woodhouse—to build up her legs. She confessed to Mary Colum that Woodhouse "had referred to the legs of American women as contrasted to the sturdy ones of his countrywomen as 'spindleshanks.' She [Elinor] exhibited her legs to me. 'Look how they have filled out!' she said. 'That is from walking; I have walked and walked.' She joined with me in laughter over this because she used to be so proud of her slim legs and ankles." Elinor justified her new,

Hazard-like régime—as she referred to it—because "I want to be extremely well & calm before I face New York" (October === 26) (Y), adding that she expected to return about December 10, having postponed her sailing yet again.

Her life was following the course she had plotted for Mr. Hazard. Outwardly, she led an extremely quiet existence. She explained to Harriet Monroe (November 4, 1928)—the day after reading a cable announcing that she had been awarded *Poetry* magazine's Helen Haire Levinson Prize—that she was torn between alternating feelings of martyrdom and pride:

When I tell you that after actually breaking my pelvis straight across the back—I will not stoop to say by accident, since it was at a moment of great joy & beauty; at six o'clock on a June afternoon, I mended it again, & in the process, being unable to write novels, I wrote some forty poems of a certain merit. So do you really think it was an *"unfortunate* accident" or are you not convinced for the thousandth time of the beauty & strangeness of life?

Elinor transferred every unfortunate incident to the growing list of symbols that supported her neurotic obsession with Woodhouse. Since there was so little actual proof of love, she invented her own evidence. It kept her in the Old Cottage, solitary and content.

Her friends appeared less often. Steven Runciman and Eleanor Chilton were elevated to the highest favor—"These are my only friends, & the only ones I really like," she told Bill (October 26, 1928) (Y)—alongside the Youngs, May Dent who had gone to Italy, and Edith Olivier who had left for Ireland. But none of them were invited to Henley. Even when Elinor made plans to go to London, she longed to return to solitude; she forced herself to leave for a few days in order to give Edith Baldry an excuse to visit her sisters in Hounslow. "I stripped off my beloved mackintosh and my squashy hat," she wrote to Bill (October 31) (Y),

and dressed myself in a complete disguise of a *mondaine,* in elegant melancholy black, with a pathetic and expensive black hat even two green orchids pinned to my lapel, and went up to London carrying a shiny black suit case with my best me-coloured evening dress in it . . . went to the bank and had my hair washed and was to arrive at the Cavendenofiniquity [Cavendish Hotel] at cocktail time, and became a complete wild beast trapped in the city.

She had her hairdresser ring up Rosa Lewis, saying Mrs. Benét had a cold and could not come. Then Elinor "cut and run" back to Henley, got a neighbor's charlady to light the fires and struggled (unsuccessfully) with the Ideal Boiler herself. She thought it wonderfully funny, and better still to be alone.

Such pranks did not occur again—her joke on Edith had disastrous consequences. On the train back from London she caught a chill. Days later she woke up afflicted by Bell's Paralysis, which, she wrote to Mama about two weeks after the attack [c. November 20, 1928] (B), "comes from an earache which comes from a nerve in the ear being pressed upon and squeezed in the bone behind the ear . . . and . . . I found that one side of my face really was completely—though temporarily—paralyzed, and therefore I was asymmetrical, and could hardly taste any taste. . . ." She sent out for Dr. Wainwright,* a local doctor who was very sympathetic and understood Elinor's fear of publicity. He cautioned her that she might take weeks or even months to recover; it was impossible to tell. He strongly urged her to cancel her plans to sail back to New York.

Elinor tried to make light of the illness. She waited some days before writing to Bill [?November 8, 1928] (Y) saying that it might even take years for her to recover completely,

and while it is lasting one's face is simply utterly paralyzed on one side darling and there's no use scotching the fact. "The deformity" as darling Wainwright calls it. . . . After the goddamned earache goes —in a fortnight—I can have electric batteries trained to my face, which will help, and meanwhile I am supposed to but don't wear a hook in one corner of my mouth. It is very funny and would not be too annoying save for the earache and the total destruction or rather metamorphosis of one's sense of taste, which suddenly becomes a collection of poisons such as strychnine and bichloride of mercury —I mean ordinary food tastes like that, not that it is. . . . You ought to taste an egg, to experience real horror! . . . And the queerest part is that I, the vain girl, the foolish female who cared about her looks, simply don't give a damn except that it complicates our Christmas plans.

*He was married to Edith Cavell's sister.

The revised plan was simple, at least to Elinor: Bill would
come to England. As soon as she was convinced that she would
not be able to travel, she cabled him (November 13) (Y):

COULD YOU POSSIBLY MAKE LONDON OR PARIS FOR CHRISTMAS
SLIGHT FACIAL OR BELLS PARALYSIS FROM COLD MAY LAST SEV-
ERAL MONTHS WAINWRIGHT ADVISES AGAINST VOYAGE BUT CAN
COME IF NECESSARY DONT WORRY.

It was impossible for Bill not to worry—he became frantic. He
cabled Wainwright directly, thinking that Elinor was again
shielding him from the severity of her illness, and then cabled
Elinor herself (November 14) (Y):

FRIGHTFULLY WORRIED ABOUT YOU IS PAIN SEVERE CERTAINLY
DO NOT SAIL IF DANGEROUS WILL MAKE CHRISTMAS IF POSSIBLY
CAN.

Wainwright showed Elinor Bill's cable and she became furious, firing back the same day (November 14) (Y)

STOP CABLING WAINWRIGHT IT HUMILIATES ME QUITE ABLE TO
COME IF YOU CANNOT NO DANGER ONLY DISCOMFORT. . . .

Bill sent his third telegram in reply that same day (November
14) (Y):

SORRY DARLING BUT WAS CONCERNED DO NOT SEE HOW CHRIST-
MAS TRIP POSSIBLE IN PRESENT STATE OF FINANCES . . .

Wainwright's own reply to Bill crossed Elinor's saying she
would travel after all, sailing December 1 on the "tonka."
Wainwright's message only clarified Elinor's first, telling
Bill that her condition was not dangerous but the paralysis
might last for months. When Bill read Elinor's third telegram he sighed with relief that he did not have to cross to
England.

Elinor was furious with him, not just for the flurry of
cables but for his excuses not to come to her. "As you know,"
he wrote in his letter of November 14,

I always sail rather close to the wind, and while all is well here
financially I am not so affluent that, if you are in no danger, I can
really afford to cross back and forth at this time of year. . . . If you
really need me I shall come anyway. But here I can do at least one
thing for you, market your work. . . . Say the word, and I will scrape

the money together by hook or crook and get the time by the same means to spend Christmas with you in England.

Bill simply took Elinor at her word; she had said that she was well enough to go to Paris, and not critically ill. She never once said precisely what she really wanted—she never once told him to come. Every excuse he found increased her anger, but still did not force her to tell him the truth.

She was horrified by the prospect of New York, even more so now that her face was disfigured. The idea of reporters, cameramen, and publicity tormented her, yet her vanity did not permit her to admit that she was not well enough to travel. Wainwright only cautioned her against the voyage, he did not order her to cancel it.

Bill's obvious hesitation was compounded by Becky Woodhouse's evident relief that Elinor would, after all, be going. She even said as much to Elinor, "and I think," Elinor added in her report to Bill [?November 8] (Y), "devoid of any other emotion. Still, I am fond of her, you know." Her husband, however, was "very much concerned," while he himself hesitated about coming to the Old Cottage. He shared, in part, his wife's own feelings.

Elinor accepted that she would have to go, though she never accepted Bill's attitude, telling him (?November 15) (Y),

I now very much regret that you were ever told anything about it, but of course there's this to be said; that you will now be prepared to see me with an asymmetrical face and will also, I hope, be warned that I wish to avoid the reporters and my friends ??????? as much as possible, but this I am sure you can manage better than you can manage Herr Seidel-Canby.

She saved her savage attack on Bill's insensitivity for Mama [?November 20], saying:

when Dr Wainwright . . . told me that it would be ridiculous to go, and that it might be well in six weeks with common sense and care and might last six months if I braved the Atlantic gales and the reporters and all that, and when I considered that my looks were—temporarily—ruined and that my ear never stopped aching, and that I was after all—or biologically—the woman and Bill the man, and that he knew I'd pay his passage, and also that my back had been broken and mended since June, I really—though foolishly—thought I had a good excuse not to go. The doctor thought of course I wouldn't go; he now says, liking me, though, and not liking Bill so much, that I'm weak-minded and that the thing's absurd. He says "Is this a case of a weak woman or a weaker man?" knowing which it is naturally.

Bill in his letter (November 14) (Y) had outlined the real excuse that kept him anchored in New York—the practical considerations. "It is simply that taking three weeks off at Christmas and spending three hundred dollars, while it could be done, doesn't seem sensible if you are really comfortable enough." Such cool reasoning outraged Elinor. She replied (November 23) (Y):

So now you have no cause to worry, and even if you had, I'd come, but "sensible"; no, I am not being sensible, nor insensible either. . . . I will be very hard-up in NY, and it might as well be faced now as later. It would have been more restful, for me I mean, and much more economical, if I had paid your passage over and back, but on the other hand I hated the idea of your being the one to take the trouble and the discomfort. . . .*

Elinor's final week in Henley before sailing was busy with preparations for the voyage. She was addressing George Blows's copy of her *Sonnets,* "which will serve as a Christmas card for our few deserving friends." Woodhouse called to say goodbye: "Poor c.," Elinor told her mother, "—for all men are idiots, only some one loves and some one doesn't—is loading me with scarfs and walking sticks and electric torches —these things being my choice rather than his, and the sort of things I like." Becky invited her to dinner on Wednesday, two days before she left Henley. Alfred Knopf came up from London to have lunch and discuss the publication of her poems, during the course of which Elinor got up several times to examine her face in the mirror. She and Edith did some packing, sorted things out, and planned the move to Whitehall Cottage in Chilmark. Edith Olivier came to lunch at the Old Cottage on November 29, Elinor's last day there, and took away with her several copies of the *Sonnets* to dispatch nearer

*Referring to the fact that Bill would travel by student-third class.

Christmas. On November 30 Elinor left Henley for London and stayed with Eleanor Chilton until she sailed. At the last moment she changed her booking from the *Minnetonka* to the *Berengaria.* She left Southampton on Wednesday, December 5.

The crossing took a week, and Elinor rarely left her cabin. She docked in New York on Tuesday morning, a bright and viciously cold day. Nancy was waiting on the quay for Elinor, who was one of the last passengers to disembark. The paralysis had scarcely left any sign on her face, but her features were tight and pinched, as if gripped by exhaustion. It had been a difficult crossing. While Elinor and Nancy stood in the Customs building, and Elinor's steward piled up the few pieces of luggage she had brought with her, she remarked happily that she would see him again in three weeks. When they were clearing Customs, Bill raced up, breathless and frantic. They got into a taxi and went straight to West 9th Street, where Marjorie was waiting to help Elinor unpack. When she saw Elinor so changed after nine months in England, looking so much older, she was shocked and gasped.

Elinor went quietly through the motions of her return and avoided her friends. She did not hurry to hear all the gossip. She only wanted to see Nancy. On Wednesday they had lunch together, after Elinor had read her some of her new poems. She went to see the baby Edwina, who tossed an entire box of aspirins across the floor like some sort of greeting. Elaborate plans were made for Nancy and Edwina's visit to Whitehall Cottage in the summer, and Elinor talked about going to Atlantic City to see Mama and give her a copy of *Sonnets* as a Christmas present.

On Thursday Elinor sat at the hairdresser's most of the afternoon before dining with Padraic and Mary Colum. After dinner she and Bill returned to the Colums' apartment and she settled down to recite, from memory, the entire "One Person" sonnet sequence. Ridgely Torrence, one of the invited guests, asked if he might have them to publish in *The New Republic.* The next morning Elinor returned to Mary Colum's apartment to discuss not only her sonnets, but Woodhouse. After taking a bromoseltzer for her headache, she gave a detailed description of her affair, drawing out a photograph of

Woodhouse to show Mary. " 'I am not taking anything on this
time,' she said, and these are her words precisely," Mary
Colum noted in her autobiography. " 'He calls to see me once
a week, and we talk and sometimes walk together.' What they
talked about she told me—a great deal about philosophy—and
he would repeat to her Scots ballads in dialect." Elinor then
left to have lunch with Blanche Knopf before going uptown
to see her doctor, Connie Guion. Her headaches were already
worse since her return to New York; she was taking aspirin
and bromoseltzer in massive doses. From Dr. Guion's, Elinor
did some last-minute Christmas shopping.

By Sunday, December 16, she had slowed up enough to
sleep later than usual, then she went into her study to catch up
on her letters. One of the first she answered was Horace's: "I
was very glad to hear from you & admit I should have been
very surprised if you had not enquired at all about my broken
back. . . . I'm going back to England on the 11th of January.
I wish I could see you before I go but I suppose no such
luck." (B)

That afternoon Morton and Jeanne called to see her.
Within a short time Bill asked them to go, seeing Elinor was
getting tired. In the early evening, after a cold supper alone
with Bill, Elinor settled into the armchair in her study. She
thumbed through the typescript of *Angels and Earthly Creatures,*
put two rubber bands around it, and laid it down on the small
table beside her, ready to hand over to Knopf on Monday. She
then picked up a volume of John Donne's sermons. Looking
up, she called out to Bill, who was in the kitchen, for a glass
of water. When he came in, she was standing in front of her
chair slowly moving toward him. Her book had slipped out of
her hands. She stopped abruptly, murmured quietly, "Is that
all it is?" and fell to the floor. Bill slid a cushion under her and
ran to the telephone to call Dr. Guion, then ran back to Elinor
carrying a glass of brandy. It was too late. She had suffered a
stroke. She was dead.

On Tuesday, two days after Elinor's death, her funeral took
place at West 9th Street. Mama asked that the service be held
privately; she wanted to avoid any further publicity. Elinor

was laid out on her bed dressed in her silver Poiret dress. Her face had been wiped clean of all pain. She looked like a marble effigy, peaceful and serene—as she had never been seen before. The Reverend Remington of St. George's Episcopal Church read the service.

Only Elinor's closest friends and family were there. Philip Hichborn came with Mama, who sat in a chair throughout the service almost as mute and immovable as her daughter. Edna St. Vincent Millay leaned over Elinor's body and placed a laurel wreath around her immaculately groomed hair.

Elinor's body was then taken up to Forty Fort Cemetery, Wilkes-Barre, Pennsylvania, where she was buried near her father. Even in death she carved two years off her life. Her tombstone reads:

Elinor Wylie (Elinor Morton Hoyt)
1887–1928
"Well done thou good and Faithful Servant"
An image of some bright eternity.
Shelley

Notes

ABBREVIATIONS

(B)—The Berg Collection, The Astor, Lenox, and Tilden Foundations, The New York Public Library. When the third Mrs. Horace Wylie died, Horace Wylie's papers went to the Berg Collection, then under the direction of the late John Gordan, himself an Elinor Wylie enthusiast. Elinor's early letters to Horace, his own memoirs, as well as Mrs. Wylie's manuscript of the joint biography of Elinor and Horace, form this major collection of Elinor's early papers. While this biography was being written, the Hoyt family's collection of her letters was sold to the Berg. All quoted sources denoted by (B) are at the Berg.

(Y)—The Beinecke Rare Book and Manuscript Library, Yale University. When William Rose Benét died, his papers, and those of his second wife (Elinor), were sent to Yale. The vast collection, largely uncatalogued, dates from Bill's first letters to Elinor, as well as Elinor's own letters to him, to the wide correspondence kept by Elinor throughout her life. Henry Hoyt's papers are also at Yale. All quotations denoted by (Y) are at the Beinecke Library, which is the largest collection of Elinor Wylie material.

Hale Papers—Nancy Hale's correspondence with Elinor's friends. In 1937, after Nancy Hoyt's biography of her sister appeared, Alfred Knopf suggested a volume of Elinor's collected letters. In the summer of that year Nancy Hale (now Mrs. Fredson Bowers) undertook the task of collecting and editing all the letters she could find, writing to everyone who knew and might have corresponded with Elinor. She gathered an enormous range of material, but with Mama's flat refusal to cooperate, the project did not succeed. Nancy Hale later deposited her notes, and the material she had amassed, at Smith College. She has generously handed over her research of forty years ago to me. All references denoted by Hale Papers are taken from the Smith College Library collection of Nancy Hale's work.

SOURCE NOTES

BOOK ONE

CHAPTER ONE
page

1 " . . . I expect to . . . dreams with romance."
   Elinor to Horace Wylie (July 20, 1923) (B).
4 "washed in pale . . . than paper." Anne McMichael
   Hoyt, "Your Father and I, or The Crow's Children;
   The Simple Annals of Our Early Years." Unpublished
   typescript (Y), pp. 4–5.
4 "was determined to . . . onions came up." Anne Hoyt,
   p. 5.
5 "small and pink . . . of a baby." *Ibid.*, p. 6.
6 "fat as a mole . . . look human." *Ibid.*, p. 11.
6 "Down to the . . . fenced with stones." Elinor Wylie,
   "Wild Peaches," from *Nets to Catch the Wind* (New
   York: 1921), later in *Collected Poems of Elinor Wylie*
   (New York: 1932), p. 12.
6 "I could kick . . . 1628," Elinor to Bill Benét (cited
   hereafter as WRB) (n.d.) [Oct. 15?, 1928] (Y).
8 "none of our name . . . the world." and
   "the title is . . . pride onto.'" D. W. Hoyt, *A
   Genealogical History of the Hoyt, Haight, and Hight
   Families* (Providence: 1871), pp. 214, 213.
13 "I simply had to . . . dusk fell." Anne Hoyt, p. 12.
13 "brick . . . and pretty." *Ibid.*, pp. 13–14.
13 "an unattractive . . . Rosemont" Interview with Mrs.
   Henry Goddard Leach, October 1974.
13 "when'a bath . . . add that." Anne Hoyt, p. 14.
13 "He was red . . . fat and rosy." *Ibid.*
14 "It out-blizzarded . . . this great storm." *Ibid.*, pp.
   13–15.
14 "A much worse . . . started up." *Ibid.*, p. 16.
14 "Henry never . . . sedately," *Ibid.*, p. 18.
15 "the real triumph . . . undisturbed possession." *Ibid.*
15 "their silver . . . more milk." *Ibid.*, p. 19.
15 "a plump . . . *their* nursery," *Ibid.*, p. 20.
15 Footnote *Ibid.*
16 "Elinor had beautiful . . . proud of it." *Ibid.*, p. 21.
17 "Well there . . . was changed." *Ibid.*, p. 29.
17–18 "a treasure . . . afraid of her." *Ibid.*, p. 24.

18–19	"It was nice . . . go out much."	*Ibid.*, p. 32.
19	"Made superior . . . the results."	*Ibid.*, p. 21.
19	"rather later . . . a child."	*Ibid.*, p. 23.

CHAPTER TWO

21   "The air is . . . I believe."   Anne Hoyt, pp. 44, 42.

22   "unbuttoned long . . . showed it to me."   (Y) Uncatalogued Wylie/Benét Collection. Undated interview with Miss Graeff.

22–23   "When I was seven . . . greater to the less. . . ."   Elinor Wylie, "Dedication," from *Trivial Breath* (New York: 1927), reprinted in *Collected Poems*, pp. 109–10.

23   Footnote   Henry Hoyt to Anne McMichael (n.d.) [June 20, 1881] (B).

24   "I realize . . . the school. . . ."   "In Memory of Florence Baldwin Nugent," pamphlet of Service (Nov. 7, 1926), p. [5]. All information about Miss Baldwin and her school was provided by Miss Sarah Morris.

24   "schools & colleges . . . sense."   Henry Hoyt to Anne McMichael Hoyt (May 9, 1910) (B).

24   "within three . . . station."   Miss Baldwin's School for Girls Prospectus, 1892–3, p. [3].

24   "A prominent place . . . English."   *Ibid.*

25   "I first read . . . understand those words."   Elinor Wylie, "Excess of Charity," *New York Herald Tribune, Books* (Feb. 27, 1927), p. 6. Later anthologized in *Collected Prose of Elinor Wylie* (New York: 1933), pp. 844–45. Review of the Julian Edition of Shelley.

25   "seven fits."   Elinor Wylie, "The Rainbow's Foot," *New York Evening Post, Literary Review* (Nov. 11, 1922), review of *Rainbow Gold* by Sara Teasdale.

25   "The sun had . . . upon a sail."   Written in the copy of *Incidental Numbers* (1912) that Elinor gave to Edmund Wilson, saying, "This is my first poem written at the age of eight." Copy sent to Nancy Hale from Edmund Wilson now at Smith College (Hale Papers).

25   "the woods . . . pine cones."   Anne Hoyt, p. 42.

26   "Nearly every . . . was added,"   *Ibid.*

26   "I was very carefully . . . connection with Elinor."   Interview with Mrs. Henry Goddard Leach, October 1974.

27–28   "Sleek-sides . . . myself in it."   Elinor Wylie, "A Narrow Escape" (1895), Unpublished (B).

28 "Great care . . . the building."   Miss Baldwin's School
Prospectus, p. 5.

28 "I planned to . . . sure.' "   Anne McMichael Hoyt,
Untitled, Unpublished memoir (B).

29 "I miss you . . . to next Fall?"   Elinor to Tirzah
Nichols (May 30, 1897), Hale Papers.

30 "I am coming . . . one of you."   Elinor to Tirzah
Nichols (Nov. 14, 1897), Hale Papers.

30 "had quite a . . . & pleasant."   Anne Hoyt, memoir
(B).

30 "This certainly can't . . . sentimentle [sic]."   Elinor to
Tirzah Nichols (Nov. 27, 1897), Hale Papers.

30 "a small . . . tutoring school"   Mrs. Mildred Brown to
author (April 30, 1975).

30 "When I heard . . . *very* much."   Elinor to Tirzah
Nichols (Dec. 27, 1897), Hale Papers.

30–31 "You are . . . water"   Dr. Nancy Potter, *Elinor Wylie:
A Biographical and Critical Study,* Ph.D. thesis, Boston
University, 1954, p. 7.

31 "Thanks to it . . . Donne."   Elinor Wylie, "The
Wickedness of Books," *Bookman* (February 1921), p.
512.

31 "It was September . . . between them."   Elinor Wylie,
"Excess of Charity," *Collected Prose,* p. 845. After
thirty years Elinor erred in her own favor. She claims
to have been eleven when this scene took place; the
youngest she could have been was twelve.

31 "she was . . . ever seen."   Horace Wylie, Untitled,
unpublished memoir (B).

32 "I am . . . Please do."   Elinor to Mama (Oct. 2, 1902)
(B).

33 "I have . . . of vipers!"   Family story.

34 "The girls . . . the production."   Papa to Mama (n.d.)
[?1902/3] (B).

34 "a cool, quiet . . . and debates."   "The Week", *The
Outlook* (Dec. 3, 1910), p. 759.

35–36 "Tonight we are . . . the other time."   Elinor to Mama
(n.d.) [July 18, 1903] (B).

36 "I hope I . . . expected welcome."   Joseph Hatton, *Sir
Henry Irving's Impressions of America* (London: 1884),
Vol. 1, p. 243.

36–37 "We went to . . . and well bred."   Elinor to Mama
(n.d.) [July 1903] (B).

37 "The only thing . . . since I landed."   Elinor to Mama
(June 2, 1903) (B).

37 "We really have . . . modernized lately."   Elinor to
Mama (n.d.) [?June 1903] (B).

39 "God knows the ... to climb ... "   Elinor Wylie,
"With a Bare Bodkin," Unpublished (n.d.) (Y).
39 " 'the brilliant ... the Administration,"   Edith
Wharton, *The Age of Innocence* (1920)
(Harmondsworth, England: Penguin Books, 1974), p.
180.
39 "delightful quietness"   Interview with Elinor Wylie,
Richmond *Times Dispatch* (April 4, 1926).
39 "the first dinner ... a success."   Nancy Hoyt, *Elinor
Wylie: The Portrait of an Unknown Lady* (Indianapolis:
1935), p. 22. Cited hereafter as Hoyt.
39 "all the young ... to know."   Interview with Mrs.
Henry Goddard Leach.
39 "I can remember ... radiant' "   Hoyt, p. 23.
40 "Yes, some blue ... hair."   Anne Hoyt, memoir (B).
40 "Before she came ... slightly austere. . . ."   Hoyt, p.
18.
41 "About this time ... year or more."   *Ibid.,* pp. 23–24.
41 *"Mrs Hichborn—ha!"*   Elinor to Mama (n.d.) [Dec. 13,
1906] (B).
42 "a Rudolph Valentino,"   Mama to Elinor (New Years
Day, 1924), (Y). Incorrectly dated by Mama; the year
is 1925.
42 "didn't they give ... —ha!"   Elinor to Mama (n.d.)
[Dec. 13, 1906], (B).
43 "a grand ... *perfect,"*   Elinor to Mama (n.d.) [Dec. 17,
1906], (B).
43 "Phil can ride ... I don't."   Elinor to Mama (n.d.)
[June 6, 1907], (B).
43 "very small ... outdoor amusements."   Hoyt, p. 24.
44 " 'I was so ... *them* again." ' "   Anne Hoyt, "The
Naked Truth," Undated, unpublished memoir (B).
44 "to be sure ... is crazy."   *Ibid.*
44 "My first news ... years old."   Henry Hoyt to WRB
(Sept. 24, 1907), Uncatalogued file (Y).
45 "Swear you won't ... [Phil] anyway."   Anne Hoyt,
"The Naked Truth" (B).
45 "Well as it ... as too good."   *Ibid.*
46 "Phil had a ... 'Philish.' "   Henry Hoyt to WRB
(n.d.) (Y).
46 "a life filled ... with supper."   Anne Hoyt, "The
Naked Truth" (B).
46 "with his own ... dementia-praecox."   *Ibid.*
46 "Phil has nervous ... Hell!"   Henry Hoyt to WRB
(n.d.) (Y).

46 "neglected her so . . . she hated." Horace Wylie,
    memoir (April 16, 1910) (B).
47 "I am really . . . good tempered." Henry Hoyt to
    WRB (n.d.) (Y).
47 "barely decent cheerfulness" Elinor to Mama
    (Thanksgiving) [?1911/12] (B).
47 "Reason is . . . emergencies." Elinor Wylie, *The
    Venetian Glass Nephew* (New York: 1925), p. 148.
48 "I thought at . . . followed her. . . . " Horace
    Wylie, Memoir (April 16, 1910) (B).
50 "Knew [Latin] . . . four hours." Horace Wylie,
    Autobiographical fragments (B).
50 "she had . . . Madonna," *Ibid.*
50–51 "Just to show . . . sorry for you." Horace Wylie,
    Memoir (April 16, 1910) (B).
51–52 "She was sitting . . . or well read?" *Ibid.*
52 "I kissed Elinor . . . Rock Creek Park." Horace
    Wylie, Autobiographical fragments (B).
52 "Song—For You" Elinor Wylie, "Song—For You,"
    Unpublished in this form (B).
53–54 "tried to hold . . . held on." Horace Wylie,
    Autobiographical fragments (Oct. 19, 1909) (B).
54 "To gradually . . . this winter." Horace Wylie,
    Autobiographical fragments [Oct. 20, 1909] (B).
54 "you don't . . . *that* way." Elinor to Horace (n.d.)
    [Oct. 18, 1909] (B).
54 "I am so . . . white . . . " Elinor to Horace (n.d.)
    [Oct. 20, 1909] (B).
54 "was cross . . . about it." Horace Wylie,
    Autobiographical fragments [Oct. 20, 1909] (B).
54 "Dear, I *am* . . . can live. . . ." Elinor to Horace
    (n.d.) [Oct. 22, 1909] (B).
54 "Saw her . . . through fortitude." Horace Wylie,
    Autobiographical fragments (B).
55 "please think . . . *your might.*" Elinor to Horace (n.d.)
    [Nov. 2, 1909] (B).
55 "she cried . . . was *perfect.*" Horace Wylie,
    Autobiographical fragments, "The Day of the Lunch"
    (Dec. 1, 1909) (B).
56 "I have been . . . to be home." Elinor to Horace
    (Dec. 8) [1909] (B).
56 "I am missing . . . fur coat." Elinor to Horace (n.d.)
    (B).
56 "We were sitting . . . going to die.' " Horace Wylie,
    Autobiographical fragments (Jan. 28, 1910) (B).
57 "I was sure . . . every second. . . ." Elinor to Horace
    (n.d.) [Feb. 25, 1910] "The Scolding Letter" (B).

57 "It was all love," Horace Wylie, Autobiographical fragments, "The Scolding Letter" (B).

58 "asked me for . . . You?' written." Horace Wylie, Autobiographical fragments (Feb. 14, 1910) (B).

58 "After sitting . . . *was sweet.*" Horace Wylie, Autobiographical fragments (April 9, 1910) (B).

59 "My love is . . . she is gone." Horace Wylie, Memoir (April 16, 1910) (B).

59 "I look to . . . me won't you?" Elinor to Horace (n.d.) [May 2, 1910] (B). From the four letters she sent to him after the Admiral's death.

60 "I am *so* . . . yes really. . . . " *Ibid.*

60 "If you don't . . . I love you?" *Ibid.*

61 "I am afraid . . . bless you." Elinor to Horace (June 6, 1910) (B).

62 "She disappointed . . . you terribly.' " Horace Wylie, Autobiographical fragments, "The Return from Abroad" (B).

62–63 "Listen my dear . . . wanted to see me." Elinor to Horace (n.d.) [Oct. 5, 1910], and Horace Wylie, Autobiographical fragments (same date) (B).

63 "O well . . . leave me!" Elinor to Horace (n.d.) [October 1910] (B).

65–66 "Please tear this . . . you so much." Elinor to Horace (n.d.) [Oct. 19, 1910] (B).

67 "dont worry . . . awfully lonely." Elinor to Horace (n.d.) [Nov. 18, 1910] (B).

67–68 "If we must . . . be unhappy." Elinor to Horace (n.d.) [Nov. 22, 1910] (B).

68 "Elinor described . . . blood pressure." Rebecca West to Dr. Nancy Potter (Nov. 2, 1953). Quoted in Dr. Potter's thesis, p. 17.

68 "The color of . . . of *yours.*" Elinor to Horace (n.d.) [December 1910] (B).

68–69 "There has been . . . I am winning." Philip Hichborn to Mama (Dec. 13, 1910) (B).

69–70 "O my dear . . . and save me." Elinor to Horace (n.d.) [December 1910] (B).

70 " 'don't let this . . . run away.' " Anne Hoyt, "The Naked Truth" (B).

71 "You must try . . . was silly . . . " Anne Hoyt to Katharine Wylie (Dec. 22 and Dec. 30, 1910), source anonymous.

71–72 "If I can . . . about the matter. . . . " President Taft to Mama (Dec. 26, 1910) (B).

73 "I am quite . . . deservedly exiled." Elinor to Mama
(May 10) [1912] (B).

73 "It is as . . . Hell outside." Elinor to Mama (May 28)
[1912] (B).

75 "But I shall . . . in His hands." Elinor Wylie, "From
Whom No Secrets Are Hid," *Incidental Numbers*
(London: 1912), p. 18.

76 "I can imagine . . . act of madness." Connie to Mama
(Jan. 4, 1911) (B).

76 "I don't ask . . . last June. . . ." Connie to Mama (Jan.
16, 1911) (B).

76 "Poor little Beeyup . . . he must feel." Connie to
Mama (Jan. 4, 1911) (B).

76 "Won't Phil . . . him go." Connie to Mama (Jan. 14,
1911) (B).

76 "No real or . . . you in Paris." Anne Hoyt, "The
Naked Truth" (B).

77 "The man an . . . to stand on." *Ibid.*

77 "one of the . . . often for months." Connie to Mama
(Jan. 14, 1911) (B).

78 "Would you and . . . me support you." Horace to
Katharine (n.d.), Source anonymous.

79 "I will not . . . do for you." Horace to Katharine
(n.d.) [March 20, 1911], Source anonymous.

79 "I will not . . . but desert her." Horace to Katharine
(n.d.) [March 25, 1911], Source anonymous.

79 "a reappearance . . . new, development" Anne Hoyt,
"The Naked Truth" (B).

80 "I drew it . . . cannot help it." Elinor to Horace (n.d.)
[April 14, 1911] (B).

80–81 "I have just heard . . . after all. . . . " Elinor to
Horace (n.d.) [April 24, 1911] (B).

81–82 "on the Cunarder . . . Henry White," Horace to
Katharine (n.d.) [April 1911], Source anonymous.

82 "I dare not . . . to give in. . . . " Elinor to Horace
(n.d.) [April 25, 1911] (B).

82 "Of course I . . . see you again." *Ibid.*

82–83 "Yesterday at 6 . . . (as usual)" Elinor to Horace
(n.d.) [April 28, 1911] (B).

83 "Aren't the papers . . . rather upset. . . ." *Ibid.*

83 "in which case . . . hope is small." *Ibid.*

84 "reproached himself . . . to return." Anne Hoyt, "The
Naked Truth" (B).

84 "Anything I can . . . her do so." Horace to Mama (May 23, 1911) (B).

85 "a couple of . . . the house." Elinor to Horace (May 24) [1911] (B).

85 "she might not . . . not desperate." Anne Hoyt, "The Naked Truth" (B).

85 "Listen my poor . . . do this thing." Elinor to Horace (May 24) [1911] (B).

85 "I'm perfectly well . . . my own darling." *Ibid.*

86 "—In the Wood" Elinor Wylie, "—In the Wood," Unpublished (B). Another version was published in *Incidental Numbers,* p. 25.

86 "quiet mountain . . . the rail-road," Anne Hoyt, "The Naked Truth" (B).

87 "if I were . . . madness or death" Horace to Katharine (n.d.) [Sept. 27, 1911], Source anonymous.

87 "The Last Word . . . flowers meant." *Ibid.*

87 "Every argument . . . was played out." Anne Hoyt, "The Naked Truth" (B).

88 "With your . . . for me." Katharine to Mama (n.d.) [September 1911] (B).

88 "stewardess's darling . . . adore him." Elinor to Mama (n.d.) [October 1911] (B).

88 "He is even . . . without end." Elinor to Mama (n.d.) [November 1911] (B).

88–89 "If it has been . . . to do it." Elinor to Mama (n.d.) [October 1911] (B).

89 "$4,000 a year . . . Graceless creatures." *Ibid.*

89 "a nuisance to me . . . a day, truly" Elinor to Mama (n.d.) [November 1911] (B).

90 "It is quite . . . explains itself." Elinor to Mama (Thanksgiving 1911) (B).

90 "Mrs H. Waring . . . of course," Elinor to Mama (Nov. 10, 1911) (B).

90 "You have got . . . it Waring!" Hoyt, *Elinor Wylie,* p. 31.

90–91 *"stuffed* with consumptives" Elinor to Mama (n.d.) [November 1911] (B).

91 "sort of wicked Baedeker" Elinor to Mama (n.d.) [?November 1911] (B).

91 "like a fever . . . at your *face!*" Elinor to Mama (Dec. 15) [1911] (B).

91 "I regret extremely . . . made her." Horace Wylie to Mama [November 1911] (n.d.) (B)

92 "threats of— . . . monster as I." Elinor to Mama (Nov. 23) [1911] (B).

92 "I would so . . . (my dear) Horace." Elinor to Mama (Thanksgiving 1911) (B).

93 "our steps to ... New Years presents." Elinor to Mama (Dec. 15) [1911] (B).

93 "unwell & ... one from which." Elinor to Mama (Dec. 29) [1911] (B).

93 "theatres & ... in the Sahara." Elinor to Mama (n.d.) [November 1911] (B).

93 "an extravagance ... the beginning." Elinor to Mama (Dec. 29) [1911] (B).

94 "From what I ... gentlemen's opinion." Baron Ferdinand von Stumm to Horace (October 1911) (B).

94–95 "I am hoping ... *one of them!*" Elinor to Mama (Jan. 19, 1912) (B).

95 "I am afraid ... it is disgusting." Elinor to Mama (n.d.) [Jan. 10, 1912] (B).

95 "with a full ... words can say." Elinor to Mama (n.d.) [Jan. 19, 1912] (B).

95 "I am glad ... please do." *Ibid.*

96 "It will be too ... would be enough." Elinor to Mama (n.d.) (B).

96 "Mrs. W. is ... long ago." Elinor to Mama (n.d.) (B).

96 "If only K. ... other children. . . ." *Ibid.*

97 "next to North ... in the world." Elinor to Mama (Dec. 29) [1911] (B).

97 "the most fairy-book ... in November" Elinor Wylie, "Shelley's Grandson and Some Others," *Bookman* (August 1923), p. 611.

97 "you could toss ... door" Elinor to Mama (Nov. 10) [1911] (B).

97 "& later with ... light as jade. . . ." Elinor to Mama (n.d.) [Jan. 10, 1912] (B).

98 "I think I keep ... tiger markings," Elinor to Mama (n.d.) (B).

98 "he comes right ... off the sill." Elinor to Mama (n.d.) (B).

98 "Dear Horace ... to me! ... " Elinor to Mama (n.d.) (B).

99 "we are simple ... can't be good." Elinor to Mama (n.d.) (B).

"the coldest weather ... of fires. . . ." Elinor to Mama (n.d.) (B).

99–100 "I often walk ... of a Horace." Elinor to Mama (March 7) [1912] (B).

100 "My headaches ... is Horace." Elinor to Mama (n.d.) (B).

100 "there were no ... & encouraged" Elinor to Mama (March 7) [1912] (B).

100–101 "If the Parkers ... up. Fools!" Elinor to Mama (March 18) [1912] (B).

101 "Of course you ... I now see."   *Ibid.*
101 "It will be ... it were *you.*"   Elinor to Mama (May 28) [1912] (B).
102 "I was awfully ... do *I* care?"   Elinor to Mama (July 12) [1912] (B).
102 "At present picking ... rather busy. ..."   *Ibid.*
103 "The rent,"   Source anonymous.
104 "I am not ... my mind. ..."   Washington *Evening Star* (March 28, 1912), p. 1.
105 "I knew this ... ever your Elinor?"   Elinor to Mama (n.d.) [April 1912] (B).
105 "It isn't fair ... than Martha's."   Elinor to Mama (April 4) [1912] (B).
105 "Of course ... to do it."   Carl Van Doren, *Three Worlds* (New York: 1936), p. 220.
105 "Naturally ... is worth anything."   Elinor to Mama (May 28) [1912] (B).
105–106 "dragged (that's) ... am with him."   Elinor to Mama (May 10) [1912] (B).
106 "I have lots ... & writing."   Elinor to Mama (n.d.) (B).
106 "I *will* write ... & so happy."   Elinor to Mama (n.d.) (B).
107 "Do you realize ... to what end?"   Elinor to Mama (n.d.) [May 1912] (B).
107 "We must go ... decision as final."   Elinor to Mama (July 31) [1912] (B).
107 "In September ... my birthday."   Elinor to Mama (Aug. 13) [1912] (B).
109 "thick brocaded ... what Holly needs."   Elinor to Mama (Dec. 27) [1912] (B).

CHAPTER FIVE

110 "People seem ... my time."   Elinor to Mama (Nov. 10, 1913) (B).
110 "This is one ... ever saw. ..."   Elinor to Mama (n.d.) [Jan. 6, 1913] (B).
110 "I am awfully ... tiring & dirty."   Elinor to Mama (Jan. 30) [1913] (B).
110 "It is so ... laugh at me."   *Ibid.*
110 *"And* it was ... which was worse,"   *Ibid.*
110–111 "came back ... Louis Fourteenth."   *Ibid.*
111 "not to get ... railway station?"   Elinor to Mama (Feb. 19) [1913] (B).

111–112 "I know all . . . *may they wave!*" Elinor to Mama (n.d.)
[June 1913] (B).

112 " . . . we would if . . . [Hichborn] again." Elinor
to Mama (March 11) [1913] (B).

112 "a flourishing . . . it dead. . . ." Elinor to Mama
[November 1911] (n.d.) (B)

112 "It is a . . . we haven't." Connie to Mama (March 3)
[1913] (B).

113 "a thick plaster . . . have ever seen. . . ." Hoyt, p. 39.

113 "I very nearly . . . young for that!" Elinor to Mama
(March 9) [1914] (B).

114 "I only have . . . make a burn." Elinor to Mama (Oct.
14) [1913] (B).

114 "Here I lead . . . little regretted." Elinor to Mama
(Oct. 21) [1913] (B).

114 "Horace is . . . a pest. . . ." Elinor to Mama (Nov. 4)
[1913] (B).

115 "I would so . . . in England." *Ibid.*

115–116 "for a few . . . heart & soul." Elinor to Mama (Nov.
10) [1913] (B).

116 "HOT WATER HEATING" Elinor to Mama (Dec. 1)
[1913] (B).

116 "have my leg . . . or 4 days." Elinor to Mama (Dec.
7) [1913] (B).

116 "under ether . . . like fire[?]" Elinor to Mama (Dec.
16) [1913] (B).

117 "We had to . . . plum pudding." Elinor to Mama
(Dec. 30) [1913] (B).

117–118 "She burned . . . no warmth," Interview with Mr.
Louis Untermeyer, January
1974.

119 "Elinor has had . . . surely arisen." Horace to Mama
(Jan. 27, 1914) (B).

121 "I got sweet . . . rather tired. . . ." Elinor to Mama
(Sept. 18) [1914] (B).

CHAPTER SIX

123 "I know . . . & frustration." Elinor to Eunice Tietjens
(April 16) [1923], The Newberry Library.

123 "It seems to . . . cruel mishaps. . . ." Elinor to Horace
(May 20, 1927) (B).

123–124 "Our house is . . . with fear." Elinor to Mama (n.d.)
[Fall 1914] (B).

125 "I do my hair . . . to *me.*" Elinor to Mama (Feb. 1)
[1915] (B).

125 "There is   . . .   could end!"   Elinor to Mama (March
22) [1915] (B).

125 "Summer at   . . .   into Fenway."   Horace Wylie,
Autobiographical fragments (B).

128 "Nobody knows   . . .   unrecognizable."   Elinor to Mama
(Nov. 4) [1915] (B).

128 "the other   . . .   the children."   *Ibid.*

129 "I am astounded   . . .   in the case."   Horace to Mama
(Jan. 13, 1916) (B).

129–130 "I do so   . . .   do you too."   Elinor to Mama (Feb. 8)
[1916] (B).

130 "The problem   . . .   had anywhere."   Elinor to Mama
(March 2) [1916] (B).

130 "we are   . . .   enjoying the change."   *Ibid.*

131 *"fine*   . . .   so   . . .   seems warm."   Elinor to Mama
(March 5) [1916] (B).

132 "took a bad   . . .   & dangerously."   Horace to Mama
(May 15, 1916) (B).

132 "How my heart   . . .   is all right."   Henry Hoyt to
Mama (May 16, 1916) (B).

132–133 "They occupied   . . .   perfectly good mother"
Transcript of Divorce Proceedings, Supreme Court of
the District of Columbia, July 1916.

134 "we couldn't very   . . .   own selves. . . ."   Elinor to
Mama (Dec. 22) [1916] (B).

134 "& if it   . . .   I'm dying to."   *Ibid.*

134 "has been *darling.*"   *Ibid.*

134–135 "would result in   . . .   house tomorrow."   Elinor to
Mama (Dec. 24) [1916] (B).

135 "I am heartbroken   . . .   about it."   Mama to Elinor
(Christmas Eve) [1916] (Y).

136 *"No one*   . . .   than he knows."   Elinor to Mama (Feb.
23) [1917] (B).

136 "I feel   . . .   began it all."   *Ibid.*

136 "trust to time   . . .   have children."   *Ibid.*

137 "If war breaks   . . .   than German."   Elinor to Mama
(March 1) [1917] (B).

138 "I intend to   . . .   provided thereby."   A copy of
Elinor's will, dated Nov. 15, 1916, was kept by
Horace and, in turn, placed among his papers at the
Berg Collection.

140 "we were swamped. . . . seriously affected."   Elinor to
Mama (Sept. 23) [1918] (B).

140 "tragedy, or   . . .   it failure?"   Elinor to Horace (May
20, 1927) (B).

140 "Horace will   . . .   them worse."   Elinor to Mama (Sept.
23) [1918] (B).

141 "The Room"   Elinor Wylie, "The Room," Unpublished
poem (B).
142 "Prayer"   Elinor Wylie, "Prayer," Unpublished poem (B).
143 "Somesville: no car."   Horace Wylie, Autobiographical
fragments (B).
143 "I am sure . . . never help."   Elinor to Mama (Dec. 3)
[1919] (B).
144 "I would for . . . my devotion."   Elinor Wylie, "The
Cloak," Unpublished poem (B).
144 "Our last . . . there [Somesville]."   Horace Wylie,
Autobiographical fragments (B).
145 "I was allowed . . . *very* good."   WRB to Stephen
Vincent Benét (Dec. 6, 1919) (Y).

BOOK THREE

CHAPTER SEVEN

147 "I think you . . . cowardly heart."   Elinor to WRB
(n.d.) [June 24, 1923] (Y).
147 "Went to a . . . was over."   R.S. Kennedy, *The Window
of Memory; The Literary Career of Thomas Wolfe* (Chapel
Hill, N.C.: 1962), p. 155. In *The Letters of Thomas
Wolfe,* ed. Elizabeth Nowell (New York: 1956), p.
121, the word "horrible" is deleted.
147 "I cannot . . . of life. . . ."   Elinor to Helen Young
(n.d.) [Nov. 5, 1927] (B).
"It was Horace . . . scholar of me."   Margaret
Widdemer, *Golden Friends I Had; unrevised Memoirs of
Margaret Widdemer* (New York: 1964), p. 268.
149 "I do not . . . never parted."   Elinor to Horace (May
20, 1927) (B). Printed in *Other People's Mail: Letters of
Men and Women of Letters,* ed. Lola L. Szladits (New
York: 1973), pp. 75–81. See Chapter six and Chapter
nine for the full text of this letter.
149–150 "noble ruin . . . New York."   Horace Wylie,
Autobiographical fragments (B).
150 "My mother . . . attractive sanctuary."   Hoyt, pp.
56–57.
150 "with some . . . interest accumulated?"   Horace Wylie,
Autobiographical fragments (B).
151 "a clerical . . . nominal salary."   Letter in Horace
Wylie, Autobiographical fragments (B).
151 "Elinor never . . . to cook,"   See Mrs. Eleanor Marsh
Wylie, *Memoir of Horace & Elinor,* Unpublished
typescript, p. 114 (B).

153 "was kind enough . . . few weeks." Elinor to Harriet
Monroe (Nov. 28) [1919] from U. of Chicago to
Newberry Library.

153 "I find . . . a group." Harriet Monroe to Elinor (Jan.
20, 1920) (Y).

153 "that it . . . *too* brilliant. . . ." Louis Untermeyer, *From
Another World* (New York: 1939),
p. 242.

153 "I also typed . . . as steel." WRB to Stephen Vincent
Benét (Feb. 15, 1920) (Y)

154 "Old Bill . . . -Hog Day." WRB included this couplet
in his entry for *Twentieth Century Authors*, eds. S.J.
Kunitz and H. Haycraft (New York: 1942).

154 "looks as . . . into place." See "The Literary Spotlight:
William Rose Benét," *Bookman* (October 1923), p.
138.

156 "to know . . . by heart." Leonard Bacon,
Semi-Centennial (New York: 1939), p. 163.

157 "Billy was . . . to vote." Kathleen Norris, *Family
Gathering* (London: 1959), p. 67.

157 "non-flying . . . non-combatant," Untermeyer, *From
Another World*, p. 240.

158 "From the . . . vividness pleased," William Rose
Benét, *The Dust Which Is God* (New York: 1941), p.
51.

158 "Yes, I . . . the underdog." "Henry," *Dry Points;
Studies in Black and White* by Henry Hoyt, preface by
William Rose Benét (New York: 1921), pp. 16,
9–10.

158–159 "Talk about . . . about it." Henry Hoyt to WRB
(n.d.) [February 1908?] (Y).

159 "Kindness was . . . aroused him." Untermeyer, *From
Another World*, pp. 236–37.

160 Footnote Norris, *Family Gathering*, p. 113.

161 "The petal . . . under glass." *Bookman* (October
1923), p. 136.

161 "At 1701 . . . other still." WRB to Frances Benét
(Oct. 30, 1919) (Y).

162 "immense charm" *Ibid.*

162 "I think . . . of richness." WRB to Frances Benét
(n.d.) [January or February 1920] (Y).

162 "quite a classical scholar." Benét, *The Dust* . . . , p.
226.

162 "suggested by . . . good title?" WRB to Stephen
Vincent Benét (Feb. 15, 1920) (Y).

163 "the bronze . . . china deer. . . ." Benét, *The Dust*
. . . , p. 237.

163	"the remote . . . of valour."	*Ibid.,* p. 319.
163	"You and . . . should be."	WRB to Elinor (May 15, 1920) (Y).
163	"This ms. . . . extra charge."	WRB to Elinor (Feb. 4, 1920) (Y).
164	"I am . . . ragged edges."	WRB to Elinor (n.d.) [Spring 1920] (Y).
164	"what I . . . your head,"	WRB to Elinor (May 15, 1920) (Y).
165	"You see . . . the end!"	WRB to Elinor (May 24) [1920] (Y).
165–166	"We are . . . Provincetown Players."	WRB to his parents (n.d.) [c. March 1920] (Y).
166	" 'Can't seem . . . my mind,' "	Benét, *The Dust* . . . , p. 225.
166	"I can't . . . that boy!"	WRB to Elinor (July 16, 1920) (Y).
167	"I'm tired . . . introduce myself!"	Interview with Mrs. Eugenia Bankhead, December 1974.
167	"the little . . . way through."	*Ibid.*
167	"one can't . . . rather loving"	Elinor to WRB (July 29) [1926] (Y).
167	"drive Buick . . . to Washington."	Horace Wylie, Autobiographical fragments, (B).
168	"Well, I'll . . . you—later."	Henry Hoyt, *Dry Points* . . . , p. 17.
168	"He could . . . that pain."	WRB to Stephen Vincent Benét (Aug. 30, 1920) (Y).
169	"(more or less) . . . of them"	Elinor to Martha Foote Crow (Nov. 27, 1920), Syracuse University.
169	"I lived . . . as yet"	Elinor to Harriet Monroe (January 1920) U. of Chicago.
170	"Rose is . . . beautifully fragile."	WRB to Elinor (Nov. 2) [1920] (Y).
171	"one of . . . the world."	Sinclair Lewis to Alfred Harcourt (Nov. 22, 1926). See Sinclair Lewis, *From Main Street to Stockholm: The Letters of Sinclair Lewis, 1919–1930,* ed. Harrison Smith (New York: 1952), p. 227.
171	"At that . . . popular reputation,"	Mrs. Eleanor Marsh Wylie (B).
171	"Isn't it . . . long time!"	Mark Schorer, *Sinclair Lewis: An American Life* (New York: 1961), p. 261.
172	"I admire . . . and character."	WRB to Mama (Oct. 13, 1920) (Y).
172	"My idea . . . do everything."	WRB to Elinor (Jan. 5, 1921) (Y).

172 "Well its . . . for something."   WRB to Elinor (n.d.) [?1921] (Y).

172 "I have . . . in Washington,"   Elinor to Martha Foote Crow (Jan. 3, 1921) and (Nov. 27, 1920), Syracuse University.

172–173 "You want . . . is nonsense,"   WRB to Elinor (n.d.) [?late December 1920] (Y).

173–174 "I shall . . . of them."   Elinor to Martha Foote Crow (Dec. 3, 1920), Syracuse University.

174 "You can . . . is true."   WRB to Elinor (n.d.) [January 1921] (Y).

174 "Come to . . . much twaddle."   WRB to Elinor (n.d.) [January 1921] (Y).

174 "She & . . . the trouble."   WRB to Elinor (n.d.) [late Autumn 1920] (Y).

175 " 'I can't . . . live/alone' "   Benét, *The Dust* . . . , pp. 260 and 262.

175 " 'the lesser . . . Troy (N.Y.)!!"   WRB to Elinor (Jan. 7, 1921) (Y).

175–176 "who made . . . her waist."   Hoyt, p. 63.

176 "I shall . . . so lovely."   Elinor to Martha Foote Crow (n.d.) [February 1921], Syracuse University.

176 "The ape . . . the period."   WRB to Elinor (n.d.) [c. March 17, 1921] (Y).

177 "Dmitri, the . . . great stuff."   WRB to Elinor (n.d.) [April 1921] (Y).

177 "Listen . . . I . . . or something."   WRB to Elinor (n.d.) [April 29, 1921] (Y).

177 "This novel . . . digging subways,"   WRB to Elinor (May 9, 1921) (Y).

177–178 "Be careful . . . simply existing"   WRB to Elinor (n.d.) [April 29, 1921] (Y).

179 "Lady Speyer? . . . parlor pagan."   WRB to Elinor (n.d.) [late December 1920] (Y.)

179 "Lady Speyer's . . . a blessing."   Elinor to Mama (May 30) [1921] (B).

179–180 "perfectly splendid . . . settles it."   *Ibid.*

180 "Alone"   Horace Wylie, Autobiographical fragments (B).

181 "It's new . . . been written."   Mahlon L. Fisher to Nancy Hale (May 17, 1937), Hale Papers. See also Elinor Wylie, *Last Poems of Elinor Wylie* (New York: 1943).

181 "I instantly . . . to her."   Ridgely Torrence to Nancy Hale (July 25, 1937), Hale Papers.

181 "I haven't . . . I've written."   Elinor to Mama (n.d.) [Aug. 30, 1921] (B).

182 "I certainly . . . to me."   *Ibid.*

182 "You better ... understand you." John Gordan, "A
Legend Revisited: Elinor Wylie," *The American
Scholar*, Vol. 38, No. 3, Summer 1969, p. 464.

182 "No, *don't* ... about time." WRB to Elinor (n.d.)
[October 1921] (Y).

CHAPTER EIGHT

184 "slightly like ... elementary geometry." Hoyt, p. 66.

184 "Amy the ... has brains." WRB to Elinor (n.d.) (Y).

185 "Not since ... of poems." Edna St. Vincent Millay to
Elinor (Nov. 27, 1921) (Y).

185 "The book ... cannot do." Edna St. Vincent Millay,
"Elinor Wylie's Poems," *New York Evening Post,
Literary Review* (Jan. 28, 1922).

186 "never falls ... and pure." Edmund Wilson, *Bookman*
(February 1922).

186 "My admiration ... very remarkable," Amy Lowell to
Elinor (Feb. 28, 1922) (Y). Amy Lowell's carbon
copies of her letters to Elinor are now at the
Houghton Library, Harvard, as are Elinor's letters to
her.

187 "I admire ... vary it." Quoted in Untermeyer, *From
Another World*, pp. 121–22.

188 "This character ... public actions." Carl Van Vechten,
Preface to *Jennifer Lorn*, in *Collected Prose of Elinor
Wylie* (New York: 1933), p. 8.

188 "although rather ... rather rare." Edmund Wilson,
The Twenties (New York: 1975), p. 78.

188–189 "My room ... likes it." Elinor to Mama (n.d.) [Nov.
2, 1922] (B).

189 "a mixture ... human being." Hoyt, pp. 69–70.

190 "almost skeletally thin" Wilson, *The Twenties*, p. 78.

191 "Here were ... and lively." Untermeyer, *From
Another World*, pp. 241–242.

191 "She gives ... is curled." Elinor Wylie, "Portrait,"
The New Yorker (March 19, 1927), p. 24, and again
(Dec. 29, 1928), p. 20. Also in *Collected Poems* under
the title "Portrait in Black Paint, With a Very Sparing
Use of Whitewash," pp. 276–79.

191 "You look ... other way?" Untermeyer, *From Another
World*, p. 230.

192 "a conglomeration ... swooning envoy." Louis
Untermeyer, *Bygones* (New York: 1965), p. 30.

193 "first got to know" Edmund Wilson to Nancy Hale (n.d.)
[July 25, 1937], Hale Papers.

193 "Bunny is funny ... ever thinking. ..."   Elinor to Mama (n.d.) [Nov. 3, 1922] (B).

194 "brilliant amateur"   Edmund Wilson, "In Memory of Elinor Wylie," *The New Republic* (Feb. 6, 1929), p. 316. Mary Colum's obituary of Elinor follows Wilson's in the same issue.

195 "they are ... any toothache."   WRB to Elinor (n.d.) [1922] (Y).

195 "no rudder ... she repented."   Interview with Laura Benét, October 1974.

195–196 "Mother had ... as 'bitch'. ..."   Stephen Vincent Benét to Rosemary Carr (n.d.) [1922] (Y).

196 Footnote   Rosemary Carr to WRB (n.d.) [c. Christmas 1922] (Y).

196 "Why get ... be *celibate!*"   Hoyt, pp. 73 and 75.

197 "I certainly ... to worry. ..."   Elinor to WRB (Sept. 14, 1928) (Y).

197 "If you ... enjoy life."   Mama to WRB (Aug. 23, 1922) (Y).

197 "supernumerary to that woman."   Interview with Laura Benét.

199 "The qualification ... can vouch."   John F. Porte, *Edward MacDowell: A Great American Tone Poet; His Life and Music* (London: 1922), p. 35.

199 "One may ... but excellent. ..."   Elinor to Horace (July 20) [1922] (B).

200 "she begged ... so little. ..."   Interview with Virginia Moore. I am indebted to Dr. Arnold Schwab for passing on this information to me.

200–201 "one walks ... one's eyelids. ..."   Elinor to Horace (July 20) [1922] (B).

201 "Full Moon"   Elinor Wylie, "Full Moon," *Black Armour* (New York: 1923), pp. 11–12. And *Collected Poems*, p. 47.

202 "Epitaph"   Elinor Wylie, "Epitaph," *Black Armour*, p. 16. And *Collected Poems*, p. 51.

203 "I have ... a history.'"   Horace to Elinor (n.d.) [July 23, 1922] (Y).

203 "When I ... costs $500. ..."   WRB to Elinor (n.d.) [July 1922] (Y).

204 "If this ... and stupidity."   Elinor to Burton Rascoe (Sept. 5, 1922), University of Pennsylvania Library.

204 "Elinor is ... in English."   Arthur Burton Rascoe, *A Bookman's Daybook* (New York: 1929), p. 36.

205 Footnote. "It is ... must part."   WRB to Elinor (n.d.) [Fall 1922] (Y).

205 "Listen— ... you think?"   Elinor to Eunice Tietjens (Halloween) [1922], The Newberry Library.

206 Footnote   Elinor Wylie, "Peregrine's Sunday Song," later "Peregrine," *Black Armour,* pp. 23–27. And *Collected Poems,* pp. 57–60.

206 "You are . . . not you."   Elinor to Horace (Halloween) [1922] (B).

206–207 "I have . . . and poetical."   Elinor to Mama (n.d.) [Nov. 3, 1922] (B).

207 "suddenly went . . . my forehead,"   Elinor to Mama (Nov. 21) [1922] (B).

207 "So no . . . and ribbon,"   Elinor to Mama (Dec. 28) [1922] (B).

207–208 "exactly how . . . soon, soon. . . ."   WRB to Elinor (Christmas Day) [1921] (Y).

208 "Crownie discovers . . . discover themselves."   Geoffrey T. Hellman, "Frank Crowninshield," *The Saturday Review Gallery* (New York: 1956), p. 226. First published April 10, 1954.

209 "at once . . . bent forward."   Wilson, *The Twenties,* p. 34.

209 "I am . . . I seem,"   Hellman, "Frank Crowninshield," p. 228.

209 "I have . . . like it."   Elinor to Horace (n.d.) [April 1923] (B).

209 "But I . . . days off"   *Ibid.*

210 "Star Among the Ash-Cans" and "Mr. Eliot's Slug-horn"   Typescripts (Y).

210–211 "I am . . . I haven't."   WRB to Elinor (Feb. 1, 1923) (Y).

211 "Bill is . . . petticoats [indec.]."   Elinor to Mama (Feb. 9) [1923] (B).

212 "I feel . . . feel most."   WRB to Elinor (n.d.) [Feb. 4, 1923] (Y).

212 "Have you . . . would despise."   WRB to Elinor (n.d.) [Feb. 5, 1923] (Y).

212–213 "And if you . . . a *home.*"   WRB to Elinor (n.d.) [February 1923] (Y).

213 "step all over Bunny."   Frank Crowninshield to Elinor (Nov. 4, 1923) (Y).

214 "Then the . . . her eyes."   Arthur Davison Ficke to Nancy Hale (June 23, 1937), Hale Papers.

214 "rather hard . . . quite instructive. . . ."   Elinor to Mama (Feb. 9?) [1923] (B).

214 "I don't . . . for good,"   Elinor to Eunice Tietjens (April 16) [1923] The Newberry Library.

214 "I'm glad . . . so desperately."   John Peale Bishop to Elinor (n.d.) [Spring 1923] (Y).

214–215 "I was . . . -rate poet.' "   Wilson, *The Twenties,* pp. 78–79.

215 "He killed . . . and Teresa."   Widdemer, *Golden Friends*, p. 261.

215 "I liked . . . bit astonished."   Hoyt, p. 76.

215 "snappy suit of clothes"   Elinor to Mama (n.d.) [June 1923] (B).

215 "Tears Eliot"   John Peale Bishop's name for T. S. Eliot.

216 "it is . . . written to-day."   Amy Lowell to Elinor (May 29, 1923) (Y), and Houghton Library, Harvard.

216 "Even when . . . literary dexterity."   Edmund Wilson, "The Magic Glass-Blower," *Vanity Fair* (July 1923), p. 19.

216 "there is . . . hard wit."   Mark Van Doren, review of *Black Armour* in *The Nation* (June 1923).

217 "contains not . . . profitable already."   Elinor to Eunice Tietjens (April 16) [1923], The Newberry Library.

217 "The book . . . E.W. & W.R.B."   Note by WRB (Y).

217 "most conspicuous . . . preparation."   Elizabeth Shepley Sargeant, *Fire Under the Andes* (New York: 1927), p. 114.

217 "I dread . . . at all."   Elinor to Horace (n.d.) [June 4, 1923] (B).

218 "a little . . . race-track."   Elinor to Mama (n.d.) [June 1923] (B).

219 "Publicity first . . . except passion."   Louis Untermeyer, "A Memoir," *The Complete Poetical Works of Amy Lowell* (Boston: 1955), p. xxviii.

219 "she always . . . intellectual conflict,"   William Rose Benét, "Amy Lowell," *Saturday Review Gallery*, p. 129. First published May 23, 1925.

219 "if you . . . me of!"   Amy Lowell to Elinor (June 23, 1923) (Y), and Houghton Library, Harvard.

220 "the poor . . . unbeautiful females,"   Elinor to WRB (n.d.) [June 25, 1923] (Y).

220 "remember that . . . more nourishing,"   Elinor to WRB (n.d.) [June 18, 1923] (Y).

220–221 "Funny . . . but . . . book-larning."   Elinor to WRB (n.d.) [June 13, 1923] (Y).

221 "The fact . . . own exuberance. . . ."   Elinor to Clifton Fadiman (April 14, 1928) (Y).

221 "Everyone—most . . . Persepolis,"   Elinor to WRB (n.d.) [June 24, 1923] (Y).

221 "if I . . . strange marriage. . . ."   Elinor to WRB (n.d.) [June 27, 1923] (Y).

221 "She always . . . count on,"   Dame Rebecca West to author (March 26, 1977).

222 "Your letter . . . between us."   Frances Benét to Elinor (March 4, 1923) (Y).

223 "I'm sorry . . . the dope." Elinor to WRB (n.d.) [June 15, 1923] (Y).

223 "That about . . . my darling." WRB to Elinor (n.d.) [June 18, 1923] (Y).

223 "I want . . . of October." Elinor to Mama (n.d.) [August 1923] (B).

224 "I had . . . breaking indeed." Elinor to Mama (n.d.) [Sept. 2?, 1923] (B).

224 "Ours will . . . of marriage . . . " Elinor to WRB (n.d.) [June 27, 1923] (Y).

225 "But if . . . be nobody." Horace Gregory, *Amy Lowell: Portrait of a Poet in Her Time* (Edinburgh: 1958), pp. 181–82. The comment was overheard by Amy Loveman.

225 "We hear . . . New Jersey." Elinor to Mama (Oct. 5) [1923] (B).

225 "walks in . . . lived here!" Elinor to Mama (Oct. 15) [1923] (B).

226 "were somehow . . . her Missy," Rosemary Benét Dawson to author (Feb. 21, 1975).

227 "Living with . . . flowery minefield." *Ibid.*

228 "I've been . . . our shadows?" Elinor to Mama (Oct. 28, 1928) (B).

229 "I feel . . . written myself." Max Beerbohm to Elinor (November 1923), Princeton University Library.

229 "In lieu . . . his unworthiness," Elinor to Horace (n.d.) [December 1923] (B).

229 "the whole . . . her life." Dr. Evelyn Helmick, *Elinor Wylie: The Woman in Her Work,* Ph.D. thesis, University of Miami, 1969, p. 82.

229 "If you . . . are diamonds." Elinor Wylie, "Symbols in Literature," *The English Review* (June 1928), p. 445. And *Collected Prose,* p. 879.

230 "The thinness . . . the interest," Potter, *Elinor Wylie: A Biographical and Critical Study,* p. 108.

230 "Of the character . . . of religion," Edmund Wilson, *The Shores of Light* (New York: 1952), p. 260.

230 "champion of . . . puzzling pride Potter, *Elinor Wylie,* p. 115.

230 "As a . . . to know." Elinor Wylie, *Jennifer Lorn* (New York: 1923), p. 235. And *Collected Prose,* p. 165.

231 "The only . . . and 'sophisticated.' . . . Sinclair Lewis to Elinor (Dec. 29, 1923) (Y).

231 "has that . . . *and Chloe.*" John Peale Bishop to Elinor (Dec. 23, 1923) (Y).

231 "credibility . . . enchanting tale." Carl Van Vechten, Preface to *Jennifer Lorn, Collected Prose,* p. 4.

232 "Carl Van ... young man."   Elinor Wylie, "Carl Van
        Vechten," *The Borzoi 1925: Being a Sort of Record of Ten*
        Years of Publishing (New York: 1925), pp. 232–33.

233 "I bless ... for *you.*"   Elinor to Carl Van Vechten
        (Nov. 28, 1923) (Y).

233 "in the opinion ... the book."   Elinor to Carl Van
        Vechten (Dec. 3) [1923] (Y).

233 "Jennifer Lorn ... & satire."   Carl Van Vechten to
        Hugh Walpole (Dec. 10) [1923] (B).

234 "But for ... been read."   Carl Van Vechten's copy of
        Jennifer Lorn (Y).

234 "My enthusiasm ... its own."   Van Vechten, Preface,
        Collected Prose, pp. 3–4.

234 "the fact ... four weeks."   Elinor to Carl Van Vechten
        (Jan. 13, 1924) (Y).

235 "Philip was ... good dancer."   Mama to Elinor (New
        Year's) [1924] (Y).

235 "I am ... MY turn."   Mama to Elinor (Dec. 26, 1924)
        (Y).

235 "that to ... Fordham Orphanage."   Kathleen Norris to
        Elinor (Nov. 27, 1923) (Y).

235–236 "The analysis ... Miss Fanny. ..."   Kathleen Norris
        to Elinor (January 1924) (Y).

236 "All the ... on him."   Mama to Elinor (Jan. 9, 1924)
        (Y).

236–237 "I dashed ... to me."   Elinor to WRB [April 3, 1924]
        (Y).

237 "shy questions ... electrified"   Emily Clark, *Innocence*
        Abroad (New York: 1931), p. 168.

237 "reformed and ... unanswerable surmise."   James
        Branch Cabell, *Some of Us: An Essay in Epitaphs* (New
        York: 1930), p. 16.

237 "Yes, I ... gunpowder magazine."   James Branch
        Cabell, *As I Remember It* (New York: 1955), p. 179.

238 "Dumbarton Grange ... of me."   Elinor to WRB
        (n.d.) [April 4, 1924] (Y).

239 "making it ... really touched."   Elinor to WRB (n.d.)
        [April 3, 1924] (Y).

239 "I used ... literary woman."   Clark, *Innocence Abroad*,
        p. 169.

239–240 "The poor ... well past."   WRB to Louis Untermeyer
        (June 5, 1924), University of Delaware.

241 "pure yet troubled genius"   Carl Van Doren, *Three*
        Worlds, p. 216. The passage on Elinor in Van Doren's
        autobiography appears in its third variation that year.
        "Elinor Wylie: A Portrait from Memory," appeared in
        the September 1936 issue of *Harper's Monthly*
        Magazine. And another essay on Elinor appeared as

the Preface to *The Venetian Glass Nephew* in *The Borzoi* *357*
Reader (New York: 1936).

Source
Notes

241 "By nature . . . its shadow." Van Doren, *Three Worlds,*
p. 97.
242 "an extremely competent editor" Rebecca West to author.
242–243 "I find . . . this letter." Elinor to Carl Van Doren
(Oct. 3, 1924), Princeton University. Appears in
Three Worlds, p. 223, and *The Borzoi Reader,* p. 122,
and in *Harper's,* p. 361. Van Doren occasionally
altered Elinor's letters in his regular use of them; the
originals have been used throughout this biography.
243 "She liked . . . the mail. . . . " Van Doren, *Three*
Worlds, p. 224.
243 "My book . . . want it." Elinor to James Branch Cabell
(Oct. 3, 1924), University of Virginia.

CHAPTER NINE

245 "Elinor Wylie . . . Bill Benét." Sara Teasdale,
Unpublished couplet, verified by Louis Untermeyer.
246 "There was . . . Rosalind Bailey." Thomas Wolfe, *The*
Web and the Rock (Harmondsworth, England: Penguin
Books, 1972), Chapter 30, pp. 540–42.
246–247 "They say . . . intense cold." Kathleen Coyle, *Immortal*
Ease (London: 1941), pp. 237 and 321.
247 "She wanted . . . of childlessness." Anne Parrish, *All*
Kneeling (New York: 1928), pp. 190 and 178.
247 "she couldn't . . . in consequences." Widdemer, *Golden*
Friends, p. 257.
247 "what really . . . suffering openly." Mary Colum, *Life*
and the Dream (New York: 1947), p. 339.
247 "half-woman . . . any way." Beatrice Kaufman to
Nancy Hale (July 8, 1937), Hale Papers.
248 "will leave . . . their hands," Elinor to Blanche Knopf
(Jan. 19) [1925], Humanities Research Center,
University of Texas.
249 "It seems . . . began talking." Blanche Knopf
Memorial Number *The Borzoi Quarterly,* Vol. 15, No.
3) (1966), pp. 14 and 10.
249 "Now that . . . Venetian glass." Elinor to Blanche
Knopf (Jan. 23) [1925], Texas.
249 "Nobody will . . . your time." Amy Lowell to Elinor
(March 23, 1925) (Y), and Houghton Library,
Harvard.
250 "Could I . . . the stage." WRB to Louis Untermeyer
(March 4, 1925), University of Delaware. And
Untermeyer, *From Another World,* p. 248.

251 "I do not . . . love and kisses."   Arthur Davison Ficke
to Nancy Hale (June 23, 1937), Hale Papers.

252 "better known . . . mirrored images."   Elinor Wylie,
The Venetian Glass Nephew (New York: 1925), pp. 68,
78–79, 146, and 182.

253 "For this . . . serious matters."   James Branch Cabell,
Some of Us, pp. 25–26.

253 "I must . . . allegorically, licentious."   Edmund Wilson,
Shores of Light, pp. 261–62.

254 "I wasted two weeks,"   Elinor to WRB (Aug. 4) [1925]
(Y).

254 "I was . . . my forehead."   Interview with Virginia
Moore.

254–255 "Posterity will . . . meant it."   Louis Untermeyer to
author.

255 "I'm sorry . . . from it."   Interview with Virginia
Moore.

255 "I cannot . . . this afternoon. . . ."   Elinor to WRB
(Aug. 4) [1925] (Y).

256 "I can't . . . of it."   Clark, *Innocence Abroad,* p. 173.

256 "I noticed . . . at nothing!"   Eunice Tietjens, *The World
at My Shoulder* (New York: 1938), p. 192.

257 "I find . . . to live. . . ."   Elinor to WRB (Aug. 4)
[1925] (Y).

257 "The joke . . . nice too."   Elinor to WRB (Aug. 6)
[1925] (Y).

258 "Elinor was . . . quite serious!"   Rebecca West to
author.

260 "I am . . . Jane Carlyle."   Elinor to Horace (June 12,
1927) (B).

261 "He looked . . . with silver."   Elinor Wylie, *The
Orphan Angel* (New York: 1926), p. 21.

261–262 "I am . . . & contented"   Elinor to Carl Van Doren
(August 12, 1925), Princeton University.

262 "the children . . . a way."   Elinor to Blanche Knopf
(Sept. 12) [1925], Texas.

262 "I know . . . to work."   Elinor to Blanche Knopf
(Sept. 14) [1925], Texas.

262–263 "greatest lyric . . . I am!"   Widdemer, *Golden Friends,*
p. 258. Grace Hazard Conkling's copy of "Wild
Peaches" is now at the University of Virginia
Library.

263 "Things are . . . out here,"   Elinor to Blanche Knopf
(Oct. 3) [1925], Texas.

263 "Things have . . . I suppose."   Elinor to Grace Hazard
Conkling (Oct. 8) [1925], University of Virginia
Library.

263 "the end ... of November." Elinor to Edmund
Wilson (Oct. 8, 1925). From Wilson's copy of
Elinor's letters for Nancy Hale, 1937, Hale Papers.

263 "Don't worry ... in England." WRB to Elinor (Oct.
12) [1925] (Y).

263 "So just ... possibly can." WRB to Elinor (Oct. 14)
[1925] (Y).

264 "Did we ... benign stupidity!" Elinor to Carl Van
Doren (Oct. 6) [1925], Princeton University.

264 "vitality ... was tired." Elinor to Carl Van Vechten
(Oct. 3) [1925] (Y).

264–265 "I very ... faulty, book." Elinor to Edmund Wilson
(Oct. 8, 1925), Hale Papers.

265 "I suppose ... sell matches?" Elinor to Carl Van
Doren [Oct. 5, 1925], Princeton University. Also in
Three Worlds, pp. 229–30.

265 "Come, let ... of malice!" Elinor Wylie, "Vale atque
Ave," New York *World,* May 21, 1926. Also
reprinted in *The Best in the World,* eds. John K.
Hutchens and George Oppenheimer (New York:
1973), p. 326.

266 "I send ... the extreme." Elinor to Blanche Knopf
(May 21, 1926), Texas.

266 Footnote Elinor to Blanche Knopf (March 5, 1926),
Texas.

266 "seen at ... country houses." Elinor to Mama (May
23, 1926) (B).

266 "I sent ... was sailing." Stephen Vincent Benét to
Rosemary Carr Benét [May 22, 1926] (Y).

266 "he won't ... other way." Elinor to Mama (May 23,
1926) (B).

267 "delicate artistry ... of character." *Times Literary
Supplement* (July 3, 1924), p. 418.

267 "It's an ... solid earth." *Times Literary Supplement*
(April 22, 1926), p. 300.

267 "your *Venetian* ... from home." Aldous Huxley,
Letters of Aldous Huxley, ed. Grover Smith (London:
1969), Letter no. 242, p. 265.

267 "English reviews ... been marvellous." Elinor to
Mama (May 23, 1926) (B).

268 "Curse their tea invitations—" Elinor to WRB (July 40)
[1926] (Y).

268 "Madame Hélène ... like that" Stephen Vincent
Benét to WRB (n.d.) (Y).

268 "metallic cuirass ... collar." Hoyt, p. 115.

268 Footnote Elinor Wylie, "My Silver Dress," *The New
Yorker* (May 8, 1926), p. 17.

269 "The upper ... green water."   Edith Olivier,
"Concerning Elinor Wylie," *Last Poems of Elinor Wylie*
(New York: 1943), p. ix.

269–270 "This is ... over-easefulness. ..."   Elinor to WRB
(July 18, 1926) (Y).

271 "I have ... White Aunts,"   Huxley, *Letters of Aldous
Huxley*, Letter No. 248, p. 270.

271–272 "the authoress ... her book."   Virginia Woolf, *A
Change of Perspective: The Letters of Virginia Woolf.
Volume III: 1923–1928.* (New York: 1977), pp.
279–80.

272 "If the ... opposite directions."   Elinor to Edward
Garnett (July 13, 1926), Humanities Research Center,
University of Texas.

272 Footnote   Elinor to WRB (Aug. 16, 1926) (Y).

272 "a bit scary ... it is."   Elinor to WRB (Aug. 8, 1926)
(Y).

273 "very pretty ... great bore."   Elinor to WRB (July
29) [1926] (Y).

273 "You've had ... three times.' "   Clark, *Innocence
Abroad*, p. 175.

273 "The only ... it so."   Elinor to WRB (July 29) [1926]
(Y).

273 "I have ... poor Nancy."   Elinor to Rosemary Benét
(Aug. 3) [1926] (Y).

274 "London at ... my nerves,"   Elinor to WRB (Aug. 8,
1926) (Y).

274 "I am here ... one of them."   Elinor to Rosemary
Benét (Aug. 17, 1926) (Y).

274 "Imagine being ... on earth—"   Elinor to Horace
(June 12, 1927) (B).

275 "By the way ... will you?"   Elinor to WRB (August
21, 1926) (Y).

275 " ... all Formosa's ... sweetly saltless."   Elinor
Wylie, "Love to Formosa," Unpublished poem (Y)
and (B).

275 "coming here ... & dryads."   Elinor to WRB (Aug.
21, 1926) (Y).

276 "& I ... you please."   *Ibid.*

276 "leads a life ... ghastly thought."   Nancy Hoyt to
Elinor (Jan. 4, 1926) (Y).

276 "the wonderful ... -Bronx splits."   Elinor Wylie,
"Sundae School," *The New Yorker* (Feb. 20, 1926), p.
29.

276 "I am ... out of date."   Kunitz and Haycraft, eds.,
Twentieth Century Writers, p. 1047.

277 "She looked ... be lionised."   Edith Olivier,
Unpublished diary (Saturday, Aug. 28, 1926).

278 "Miss W's . . . and herself."   Edith Olivier,
      Unpublished diary (Sunday, Aug. 29, 1926).
278 "moves serenely . . . perfect loveliness."   *Ibid.*
278 "I was . . . very bridal,"   Hoyt, p. 121.
280 "I suppose . . . the subject."   Elinor to Mama (Nov.
      22) [1926] (B).
281 "was entirely . . . little exaggerated."   Stephen Vincent
      Benét, Preface to *The Orphan Angel,* in *Collected Prose,*
      pp. 320 and 322.
281 "Elinor wrote . . . subtle spirit,"   Untermeyer, *From
      Another World,* p. 245.
281 "I declared . . . finest endeavors."   Cabell, *Some of Us,*
      pp. 17 and 19.
281 Footnote   James Branch Cabell, *Between Friends: The Letters
      of James Branch Cabell,* eds. Padraic Colum and
      Margaret Freeman Cabell (New York: 1962), p. 282.
282 "It has . . . angel live."   Huxley, *Letters of Aldous
      Huxley,* Letter No. 255, pp. 277–78.
282 "the oddest . . . interesting experiment."   *Times Literary
      Supplement* (Feb. 24, 1927), p. 124.
282 "But this . . . my dear."   Elinor Wylie, "A Red Carpet
      for Shelley," *The New Republic* (Jan. 12, 1927), p.
      218. Also *Trivial Breath* (New York: 1928), pp.
      68–71. And *Collected Poems,* pp. 156–59.
283 "The theory . . . her revenge."   Elinor Wylie, "Excess
      of Charity," *New York Herald Tribune, Books* (Feb. 27,
      1927). And *Collected Prose,* p. 843.
283 "I have . . . ridiculous mannerisms."   Elinor Wylie,
      "Mr. Shelley Speaking", *Bookman* (March 1927), pp.
      29–33. And *Collected Prose,* p. 847.
283 "When you've . . . blame you."   Wylie, "Mr. Shelley
      Speaking," *Collected Prose,* p. 853.
284 "She gives . . . sharp side."   Elinor Wylie, "Portrait,"
      The New Yorker (March 19, 1927), p. 24, and again
      (Dec. 29, 1928), p. 20. Also *Collected Poems,* pp.
      276–79.
284–285 "the piece . . . some quarters."   Elinor to Arthur
      Burton Rascoe (April 12, 1927), University of
      Pennsylvania.
285 "He told . . . was Elinor."   Hoyt, pp. 148–149.
285–286 "An awful . . . over it."   Mrs. Hoisington to Elinor
      (April 6, 1927) (Y).
286 "Please read . . . personal life."   Edna St. Vincent
      Millay to Elinor and League of American Pen Women
      (n.d.) [April 18, 1927]. See *Letters of Edna St. Vincent
      Millay,* ed. Allan Ross Macdougall (New York:
      1952), Letter No. 147, pp. 216–17. The original
      letter from Edna St. Vincent Millay to Elinor is at (Y).

287 "Oh, she ... be heralded." Edna St. Vincent Millay, "Sonnet in Answer to a Question," *Collected Poems* (New York: 1956), p. 371.

287 "She is ... Unflinchingly egoiste." Edith Olivier, Unpublished diary (July 28, 1927).

288 "I've been ... nine days." Elinor to WRB (May 2) [1927] (Y).

290 "How the ... goaded you." Horace to Elinor (March 1, 1927) (Y).

290–291 "Dearest Horace ... Answer it." Elinor to Horace (May 20, 1927) (B). Also Szladits, ed., *Other People's Mail.*

291 "I wish ... in love." Horace to Elinor (June 1, 1927) (Y).

291 "anti-Shelley ... every meeting." George Peregrine Young to Elinor (May 5) [?1927] (Y).

292 "Was it ... the world." Elinor to Horace (June 12, 1927) (B).

293 "great subject ... her gates." Edith Olivier, Unpublished diary (July 23, 1927).

293–294 "tried vainly ... cumulative effect." Edith Olivier, Unpublished diary (July 24 and 25, 1927).

294 "Talk with ... in her." Edith Olivier, Unpublished diary (July 25, 1927).

294 "Your cousin ... loveliest weekend." Elinor to Edith Olivier (n.d.) [July 27, 1927] (Y).

295 "How beastly ... one another." Helen Young to Elinor (July 28) [1927] (Y).

295 "I have ... trifling purposes." Metford Watkins to Elinor (March 17, 1928) (Y).

295–296 "I've the ... a parrot." The Hon. Sir Steven Runciman to author.

296 "No novel ... paper yet." Elinor to WRB (n.d.) [July 1927].

296 "The novel ... of Mr. Hodge." Elinor Wylie, "Advertisement," *Mr. Hodge and Mr. Hazard* (New York: 1928), p. vii. And *Collected Prose,* p. 647.

296–297 "You will ... and butter." Elinor to Helen Young (n.d.) [Nov. 5, 1927] (B).

297 "but you ... *point d'esprit.* ..." Ibid.

298 "Whatever might ... his armour." Wylie, *Mr. Hodge and Mr. Hazard,* p. 128.

298 "thin-skinned ... taste." *Ibid.,* p. 143.

298 "Mr. Hodge's ... opinions contemptible." *Ibid.,* pp. 188 and 190–91.

299 Presently he ... rusty needles." *Ibid.,* p. 36.

299 "the size . . . dog kennel."   Elinor to Rosemary Benét
                                        (Aug. 30) [1927].
299 "Is that . . . it is?"   Hoyt, p. 187.
299 "Anyone can . . . two tries,"   Horace Wylie,
                              Autobiographical fragments (B).
300 "As you . . . think of it?"   Elinor to Blanche Knopf
                                     (Oct. 20, 1927), Texas.
301 "After all . . . you are."   Mama to Elinor (New Year's)
                                            [1924] (Y).
302 "I will . . . enjoy there."   Mama to Elinor (Feb. 3,
                                               1928) (Y).
302 "The writer . . . comprehensive study."   Elinor Wylie,
        "Plans for Study," Proposal submitted to John Simon
        Guggenheim Memorial Foundation. Haverford
                                                College.
303 "It would . . . five years. . . ."   Elinor to Mr. Stimson
                           (at Knopf) (March 5, 1928), Texas.
303 "it has . . . moderate income."   Elinor to Rosemary
                                  Benét (April 28, 1928) (Y).
303-304 "I have . . . really rested."   Elinor to WRB (April 28,
                                               1928) (Y).
305 "I am . . . prefer girls."   Elinor to WRB (May 5,
                                               1928) (Y).
306 "of a . . . Poor Bill!"   Edith Olivier, Unpublished diary
                                           (May 8, 1928).
306-307 "Elinor is . . . hot whisky."   Edith Olivier,
                          Unpublished diary (May 9, 1928).
307 "I'm still . . . really dazzling."   Elinor to WRB (May
                                           16, 1928) (Y).
308 "I am too . . . enemy, Watson."   Metford Watkins to
                             Elinor (May 10) [1928] (Y).
308 "she replied . . . he was."   Robert Stopford to author.
309 "poor darling . . . Tamberlaine. . . ."   Elinor to WRB
                                      (May 29) [1928] (Y).
309 "the best . . . my life,"   Elinor to WRB (June 2)
                                            [1928] (Y).
309-310 "She suddenly . . . after all,"   Edith Olivier,
                 Unpublished diary (June 10 and 11, 1928).
310 "it seemed . . . pathetic relationship. . . ."   Mary
                     Colum, Life and the Dream, pp. 360-361.
310 "I . . . know . . . with her. . . ."   Henry deClifford
            Woodhouse to WRB (February 1929). Also Gordan,
                               "A Legend Revisited," p. 467.
311 "Elinor thinks . . . I feared."   Edith Olivier,
                  Unpublished diary (Sept. 12-14, 1928).
311 "got into . . . careful nursing."   Becky Woodhouse to
                             Elinor (Feb. 28, 1928) (Y).

312 "seven minutes ... best butter." Elinor to Horace
(Dec. 16, 1928) (B).
312 "Elinor ... alone ... reached home. ..." Hoyt,
p. 163.
312 "I had ... unadulterated hell. ..." Elinor to
Rosemary Benét (July 18, 1928).
313 "Mama has ... tout simple. ..." Ibid.
313 "The bad ... for it." Ibid.
314 "I hope ... was safe." WRB to Elinor (July 11,
1928) (Y).
314 "I can ... could do." Becky Woodhouse to Elinor
(n.d.) [?July 5, 1928] (Y).
314 "I would ... treacherous evil." Llewelyn Powys to
Elinor (n.d.) [July 1928] (Y).
314 "Isn't it ... praise me?" Elinor to Rosemary Benét
(July 18, 1928) (Y).
315 "We have ... an answer." Frances Benét to WRB
(Aug. 9) [1928] (Y).
315 "Lovers of ... and aberration." WRB to New York
Evening Post (Sept. 7, 1928).
315–316 "The wish ... mine is!" Elinor Wylie, "To the
Gentlemen of the Press," Unpublished poem
(Y).
316 "I have ... will approve." Elinor to Anna Hempstead
Branch (Aug. 28, 1928) (B).
317–318 "I do ... best friends." WRB to Elinor (Sept. 4,
1928) (Y).
318 "all went ... am childless." Elinor to WRB (Sept. 1,
1928) (Y).
319 "I am ... of accomplishment." Ibid.
319 "as if ... murder plans." Elinor to WRB (Sept. 10,
1928) (Y).
319–320 "—he is ... more exact." Elinor to Mama (n.d.)
[September 1928] (B).
320 "Of course ... a bit." Elinor to WRB (Sept. 14)
[1928] (Y).
321 "she lay ... a week?' " Rebecca West, "A
Commentary," Bookman (March 1929), p. 56. Later
included under the title "Manibus Dati Lilia Plenis"
in Ending in Earnest: A Literary Log (New York:
1931), pp. 16–22.
321 "This ... was ... grand holiday." Elinor to Mama
(n.d.) [September 1928] (B).
323 "The little ... my heart." Elinor Wylie, "Sonnet V,"
Angels and Earthly Creatures (New York: 1929), p. 7.
And Collected Poems, p. 176.
324 "I do ... (?)labour." Elinor to WRB (Sept. 10, 1928)
(Y).

324 "I really ... of Literature. ..." Elinor to Mama (n.d.) [Nov. 20, 1928] (B).

324 "had referred ... and ankles." Colum, *Life and the Dream*, p. 361.

325 "I want ... New York" Elinor to WRB (Oct. 26) [1928] (Y).

325 "When I ... of life?" Elinor to Harriet Monroe (Nov. 4, 1928), U. of Chicago.

325–326 "I stripped ... the city." Elinor to WRB (Oct. 31, 1928) (Y).

326 "Which comes ... any taste. ..." Elinor to Mama (n.d.) [Nov. 20, 1928] (B).

326 "and while ... Christmas plans." Elinor to WRB (n.d.) [November 1928] (Y).

327 "COULD YOU ... DONT WORRY" Elinor to WRB (Nov. 13, 1928) (Y).

327 "FRIGHTFULLY WORRIED ... POSSIBLY CAN" WRB to Elinor (Nov. 14, 1928) (Y).

327 "STOP CABLING ... ONLY DISCOMFORT" Elinor to WRB (Nov. 14, 1928) (Y).

327 "SORRY DARLING ... FINANCES" WRB to Elinor (Nov. 14, 1928) (Y).

327–328 "As you ... in England." WRB to Elinor (Nov. 14, 1928) (Y).

328 "and I ... you know." Elinor to WRB (n.d.) [?Nov. 8, 1928] (Y).

328 "I now ... Seidel Canby" Elinor to WRB (n.d.) [?Nov. 15, 1928] (Y).

328–329 "when Dr. ... is naturally." Elinor to Mama (n.d.) [?Nov. 20, 1928] (B).

329 "It is ... comfortable enough," WRB to Elinor (n.d.) [Nov. 14, 1928] (Y).

329 "So now ... the discomfort." Elinor to WRB (n.d.) [Nov. 23, 1928] (Y).

329 "Poor c. ... I like." Elinor to Mama (n.d.) [Nov. 20, 1928] (B).

331 "I am ... in dialect." Colum, *Life and the Dream*, p. 360.

331 "I was ... such luck." Elinor to Horace (Dec. 16) [1928] (B).

331 "Is that ... it is?" Hoyt, p. 187.

SELECT BIBLIOGRAPHY

Amory, Cleveland and Frederick Bradlee, eds.: *Vanity Fair, Selections from America's Most Memorable Magazine* (New York: 1960).

Bacon, Leonard: *Semi-Centennial* (New York: 1939).

Baltzell, E. D.: *Philadelphia Gentlemen; The Making of a National Upper Class* (Glencoe, Ill.: 1958).

Bankhead, Tallulah: *My Autobiography* (London: 1952).

Beaton, C. W. H.: *The Wandering Years; Diaries: 1922–1939* (London: 1961).

Benét, Laura: *When William Rose, Stephen Vincent and I Were Young* (New York: 1976).

Benét, Stephen Vincent: *Selected Letters of Stephen Vincent Benét*, C. B. Fenton, ed. (New Haven: 1960).

Benét, William Rose: *The Dust Which Is God* (New York: 1941).

——: *Fifty Poets* (New York: 1933).

——: *First Person Singular* (New York: 1922).

——: *Harlem* (New York: 1935).

——: *Merchants from Cathay* (New Haven: 1913).

——: *Perpetual Light* (New Haven: 1919).

——: *The Prose and Poetry of Elinor Wylie* (Norton, Mass.: 1934).

——: *Sagacity* (New York: 1929).

——: ed., with Henry Canby: *The Saturday Papers* (New York: 1921).

Bishop, John Peale: *Collected Essays* (New York: 1948).

Bogan, Louise: *Achievements in American Poetry, 1900–1950* (New York: 1951).

The Borzoi 1925; Being a Sort of Record of Ten Years of Publishing (New York: 1925).

Boyd, Ernest: *Literary Blasphemies* (New York: 1927).

——: *Portraits: Real and Imaginary* (New York: 1924).

Brenner, Rica: *Ten Modern Poets* (New York: 1928).

Cabell, James Branch: *As I Remember It* (New York: 1955).

——: *Some of Us: An Essay in Epitaphs* (New York: 1930).

——: *Between Friends: The Letters of James Branch Cabell*, Padraic Colum and Margaret Freeman Cabell, eds. (New York: 1962).

Canby, Henry S.: *American Memoir* (Boston: 1947).

Carpenter, Margaret: *Sara Teasdale* (New York: 1960).

Clark, Emily: *Innocence Abroad* (New York: 1931).

Colum, Mary: *Life and the Dream* (New York: 1966).

Coyle, Kathleen: *Immortal Ease* (New York: 1941).

Damon, S. Foster: *Amy Lowell* (Boston: 1935).

Deutsch, Babette: *Poetry in Our Time* (New York: 1956).

Farrar, John Chipman: *The Bookman Anthology of Essays* (New York: 1923).

Fenton, Charles B.: *Stephen Vincent Benét: The Life and Times of an American*

Man of Letters: 1895–1943 (New Haven: 1958).

Gordan, John: "A Legend Revisited: Elinor Wylie," *The American Scholar*, Vol. 38, No. 3, Summer 1969.

Gould, Jean: *Amy; The World of Amy Lowell and the Imagist Movement* (New York: 1975).

——: *The Poet and Her Book: A Biography of Edna St. Vincent Millay* (New York: 1969).

Grant, Jane: *Ross, The New Yorker and Me* (New York: 1968).

Gray, Thomas: *Elinor Wylie* (New York: 1969).

Gregory, Horace and M. Zaturenska: *A History of American Poetry* (New York: 1947).

——: *Amy Lowell; Portrait of a Poet in Her Time* (Edinburgh: 1958).

Hatton, J., ed.: *Henry Irving's Impressions of America* (2 vols., London: 1884).

Hoyt, D. W.: *A Genealogical History of the Hoyt, Haight, and Hight Families* (Providence, R.I.: 1871).

——: *The Hoyt Family* (Boston: 1857).

——: *Record of the Hoyt Family Meeting* (Boston: 1866).

Hoyt, Henry Martyn: *Dry Points; Studies in Black and White* (New York: 1921).

Hoyt, Nancy: *Bright Intervals* (New York: 1929).

——: *Elinor Wylie: The Portrait of an Unknown Lady* (Indianapolis: 1935).

Huxley, Aldous: *The Letters of Aldous Huxley*, Grover Smith, ed. (London: 1969).

Kellner, Bruce: *Carl Van Vechten and The Irreverent Decades* (Norman, Okla.: 1963).

Kennedy, R. S.: *The Window of Memory: The Literary Career of Thomas Wolfe* (Chapel Hill, N.C.: 1962).

Kenyon, B. L.: *Meridian* (New York: 1933).

Kunitz, Stanley J. and Howard Haycraft: *Twentieth Century Authors* (New York: 1942).

Lewis, G.: *With Love from Gracie* (New York: 1953).

Lewis, Sinclair: *From Main Street to Stockholm; The Letters of Sinclair Lewis, 1919–1930*, ed. Harrison Smith (New York: 1952).

Lowell, Amy: *The Complete Poetical Works of Amy Lowell* (Boston: 1955).

——: *Tendencies in Modern American Poetry* (Boston: 1921).

MacDowell, Marion: *Random Notes on Edwin MacDowell and His Music* (Boston: 1950).

Millay, Edna St. Vincent: *Collected Poems* (New York: 1956).

——: *The Letters of Edna St. Vincent Millay*, Allan Ross Macdougal, ed. (New York: 1952).

Monroe, Harriet: *A Poet's Life: Seventy Years in a Changing World* (New York: 1938).

——: *Poets and Their Work* (New York: 1926).

Morley, Christopher, ed.: *The Bowling Green* (New York: 1924).

Norris, Kathleen: *Family Gathering* (London: 1959).

Nowell, Elizabeth: *Thomas Wolfe* (New York: 1961).

Olivier, Edith: *As Far As Jane's Grandmother's* (London: 1928).

———: *The Love Child* (London: 1927).

———: *Without Knowing Mr. Walkley* (London: 1938).

Parrish, Anne: *All Kneeling* (New York: 1928).

Porte, John F.: *Edward MacDowell: A Great American Tone Poet; His Life and Music* (London: 1922).

Rascoe, Arthur Burton: *A Bookman's Daybook* (New York: 1929).

———: *Before I Forget* (New York: 1937).

———, editor: *Smart Set Anthology* (New York: 1934).

Rittenhouse, Jessie Belle: *My House of Life* (Boston: 1934).

The Saturday Review Gallery (New York: 1959).

Schorer, Mark: *Sinclair Lewis: An American Life* (New York: 1961).

Sergeant, Elizabeth Shepley: *Fire Under the Andes* (New York: 1927).

Speyer, Leonora: *American Poets* (New York: 1923).

Stoker, Bram: *The Jewel of the Seven Stars* (London: 1903).

Szladits, Lola L., ed.: *Other People's Mail: Letters of Men and Women of Letters* (New York: 1973).

Teasdale, Sara: *Collected Poems of Sara Teasdale* (New York: 1937).

Thurber, James: *The Years with Ross* (New York: 1959).

Tietjens, Eunice: *The World at My Shoulder* (New York: 1938).

Trelawny, Edward John: *Recollections of the Last Days of Shelley and Byron* (1858) (London: 1931).

Untermeyer, Jean Starr: *Private Collection* (New York: 1965).

Untermeyer, Louis: *American Poetry Since 1900* (New York: 1924).

———: *Bygones* (New York: 1965).

———: *From Another World* (New York: 1939).

———, ed.: *Modern American Poetry* (New York: 1964).

Upham, Charles: *Salem Witchcraft* (2 vols., Boston: 1867).

Van Doren, Carl Clinton, ed.: *The Borzoi Reader* (New York: 1936).

———: *Three Worlds* (New York: 1936).

Van Vechten, Carl: *Fragments from an Unwritten Autobiography* (2 vols., New Haven: 1955).

West, Rebecca: *Ending in Earnest: A Literary Log* (New York: 1931).

Wharton, Edith: *The Age of Innocence* (New York: 1920).

———: *The Custom of the Country* (New York: 1912).

Widdemer, Margaret: *Golden Friends I Had; Unrevised Memoirs of Margaret Widdemer* (New York: 1964).

Wilson, Edmund: *Letters on Literature and Politics, 1912–1972,* edited by Elena Wilson (London: 1977).

———: *The Shores of Light: A Literary Chronicle of the 1920's and 1930's* (New York: 1952).

———: *The Twenties* (New York: 1975).

Wolfe, Thomas: *The Web and the Rock* (New York: 1937).

———: *The Letters of Thomas Wolfe,* ed. Elizabeth Nowell (New York: 1956).

Woolf, Virginia: *A Change of Perspective; The Letters of Virginia Woolf 1923–1928,* Nigel Nicolson and Joanne Trautmann, eds. (New York: 1977).

Wylie, Elinor: *Angels and Earthly Creatures* (New York: 1929).

———: *Black Armour* (New York: 1923).

——: *Collected Poems of Elinor Wylie* (New York: 1932).
——: *Collected Prose of Elinor Wylie* (New York: 1933).
——: *Incidental Numbers* (London: 1912).
——: *Jennifer Lorn: A Sedate Extravaganza* (New York: 1923).
——: *Last Poems of Elinor Wylie*, Jane D. Wise, transcriber (New York: 1943).
——: *Mr. Hodge and Mr. Hazard* (New York: 1928).
——: *Nets to Catch the Wind* (New York: 1921).
——: *The Orphan Angel* (New York: 1926); published as *The Mortal Image* (London: 1926).
——: *Trivial Breath* (New York: 1928).
——: *The Venetian Glass Nephew* (New York: 1925).

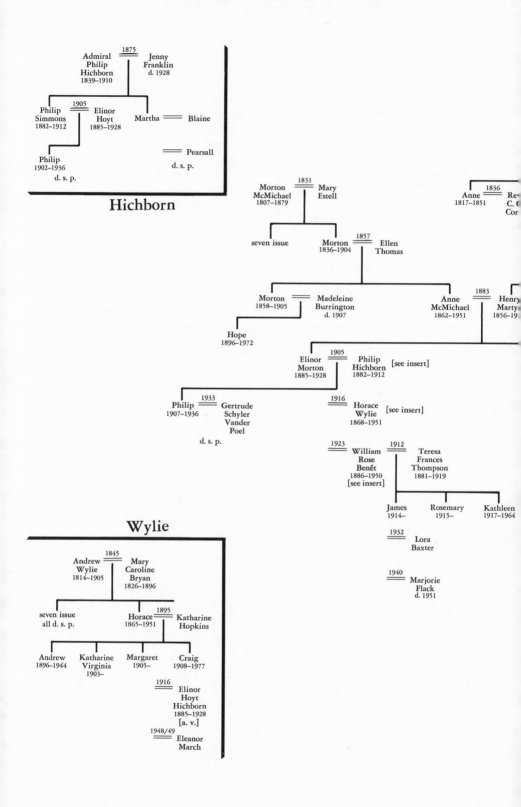

Hichborn

Admiral Philip Hichborn 1839–1910 — 1875 — Jenny Franklin d. 1928

Philip Simmons 1882–1912 — 1905 — Elinor Hoyt 1885–1928

Martha === Blaine

=== Pearsall d. s. p.

Philip 1902–1936 d. s. p.

Morton McMichael 1807–1879 — 1831 — Mary Estell

Anne 1817–1851 — 1836 — Re C. (Cor

seven issue

Morton 1836–1904 — 1857 — Ellen Thomas

Morton 1858–1905 === Madeleine Burrington d. 1907

Anne McMichael 1862–1951 — 1883 — Henry Marty 1856–19

Hope 1896–1972

Elinor Morton 1885–1928 — 1905 — Philip Hichborn 1882–1912 [see insert]

Philip 1907–1936 — 1933 — Gertrude Schyler Vander Poel

d. s. p.

1916 === Horace Wylie 1868–1951 [see insert]

1923 === William Rose Benét 1886–1950 [see insert] — 1912 — Teresa Frances Thompson 1881–1919

James 1914–   Rosemary 1915–   Kathleen 1917–1964

1932 === Lora Baxter

1940 === Marjorie Flack d. 1951

Wylie

Andrew Wylie 1814–1905 — 1845 — Mary Caroline Bryan 1826–1896

seven issue all d. s. p.

Horace 1865–1951 — 1895 — Katharine Hopkins

Andrew 1896–1944   Katharine Virginia 1903–   Margaret 1905–   Craig 1908–1977

1916 === Elinor Hoyt Hichborn 1885–1928 [a. v.]

1948/49 === Eleanor March

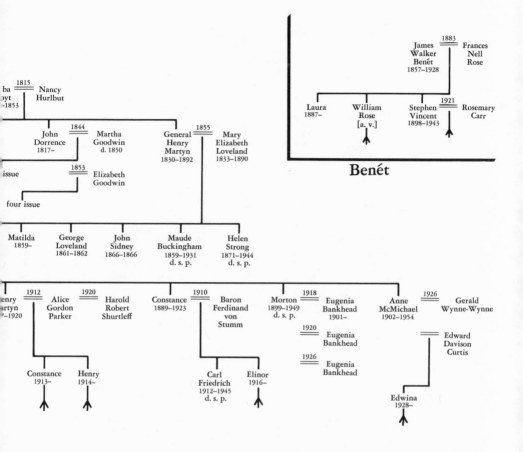

Benét

Elinor Wylie's Genealogy

INDEX

"Aaron Mordecai," 239
Accident, 312, 314–315
Adams, Franklin Pierce, 192, 225
Algonquin, 249
Aliens Restriction (Amendment) Order, 125, 127
Anderson, Tennessee, 257
Angels and Earthly Creatures, 316, 322, 331
Appearance, 31, 190–191
"Applewood Chair, The," 182, 255, 256
April, April, 282
Arms, Carolyn, 30–31, 33, 34
Arno, Peter, 285
Artistic ability, 19, 22
"As I Went Down by Havre de Grace . . .", 301, 303
"Atavism," 153
"August," 168
"Auspicious Monday," 165
Awards, 184, 325

Bacon, Leonard, 156
Baldry, Edith, 289, 320
Baldwin, Florence, 23–24
Bankhead, Eugenia, 166–167
Bankhead, Tallulah, 167, 273
Barcarole of James Smith and Other Poems (Herbert Gorman), 204
Beaton, Cecil, 270, 293
Beerbohm, Max, 229
Bell's Paralysis, 326
Benét family, 155–157, 195, 197, 222, 235
Benét, Stephen Vincent, 145, 157, 195–196, 244, 266, 281
Benét, William Rose, 40, 115, 144–145, 154–155, 157–166, 168–169, 172–178, 196–198, 205, 212–215, 221–229, 255, 323–331
Bennay Literary Agency, 163, 165, 176
Berners, Lord, 270
Birrell, Frankie, 293

"Birthday Cake for Lionel, A," 256, 283
Bishop, John Peale, 190, 214, 231
Bishop, Mrs. John Peale, 266
Black Armour, 168, 201, 206, 217
Blaine, James D., 64
Blake, William, 108, 186, 215
Blindness, 122–124
Blows, George, 321
Boissevain, Eugen, 251
Bookman, The, 178, 181, 186
Bowling Green: An Anthology of Verse (Christopher Morley), 164
Boyd, Madeleine, 289
Bradford, Irita, 242
Branch, Anna Hempstead, 316
Brenner, Rica, 186
"Bronze Trumpets and Sea Water," 186
Brook Corner, 119–120, 123–125
Brougham, Elinor, 270
Brown, Agnes, 26–27
Brown, Frank, 132
Brown, T. Whister, 26
Bryan, Mary Caroline, 49
Burglar of the Zodiac, The (William Rose Benét), 160
"Burtonage," 19

Cabell, James Branch, 229, 236, 237–238, 243, 253, 281–282
Caine, Christabel, 247
Canby, Henry Seidel, 163–164, 215, 242, 250, 287, 292
Carr, Rosemary, 195, 196
"Castilian," 155
"Casual Sonnet," 181
Cather, Willa, 265, 270
Century, The, 165
Character, 259–260, 284, 287
Childhood, 5–6, 13–38
Children, feelings about, 318; son, 44, 95–96, 105, 138, 235, 276, 332; W.R. Benét's, 226–229, 234–236, 243–244
Chilton, Eleanor, 320, 325, 330

372

Clark, Emily, 236, 237, 239, 258, 273, 301
"Coast Guard's Cottage, The," 301
Colefax, Sir Arthur and Lady, 270
Colum, Mary and Padraic, 200, 207, 245, 247, 250, 310, 324, 330–331
Conkling, Grace Hazard, 257, 262–263
Connelly, Mark, 266
Contemporary Verse, 153
Cowley, Malcolm, 216–217
Coyle, Kathleen, 246
Criticism of novels, 229–231, 233, 264–265, 267, 281, 282
Criticism of poetry, 185–187, 215–217
Crow, Martha Foote, 172, 173, 176
Crowninshield, Frank, 182, 208, 212

Damon, S. Foster, 250
de la Mare, Walter, 278
Deaths in the family, 67–68, 104, 122, 132, 168, 224, 259, 331
Dennis, William, 132–133
Dent, May, 268, 292, 299, 304, 325
Dial, The, 186, 233
Dickinson, Emily, 186, 187, 204
Divorces, 95, 103, 183, 203, 224, 254
Donne, 186, 215, 331
Doran, George, 215, 248, 267
Dos Passos, John, 207
Drinkwater, John, 268, 272
Dust Which Is God, The (William Rose Benét), 157

Easty, Issac, 9–10
Education, 19, 22–25, 30–34, 38, 40
Eliot, George, 162
Eliot, T.S., 153, 209
"Epitaph," 202
Evans, Charles, 272
"Excess of Charity," 283

Fadiman, Clifton, 221
"Fairy Goldsmith, The," 165
Falconer of God, The (William Rose Benét), 160
Fame, 245
Family, *see* Hoyt family
Farrar, John, 250
Ficke, Arthur and Gladys, 213, 251
"Fire and Sleet and Candlelight," 144, 153, 163

First Person Singular (William Rose Benét), 157
Fisher, Mahlon L., 181
Flack, Marjorie, 197
Frost, Robert, 250
"Full Moon," 201
Funeral, 331–332

Gardner, Mrs. Gibson, 170
Garnett, Edward, 272, 293
Gerald, 207, 221
Gilkyson, Bernice L.K., 180
Glasgow, Ellen, 238–239
Gorman, Herbert, 186, 220, 256
Graeff, Virginia, 22
Great White Wall, The (William Rose Benét), 160
"Green Hair," 170
Gregory, Alyse, 268
Grunberg, Louis, 201
Guion, Connie, 331

Harcourt, Alfred, 171, 184
Harper's Bazaar, 256
Health problems, 47, 89–90, 93, 99, 105, 111, 114, 116, 119, 122–124, 129, 132, 134, 136, 182, 200, 204, 207, 223, 243, 280, 300, 326, 331
Heggar, Grace, 162
Helen Haire Levinson Prize, 325
Helmick, Dr. Evelyn, 229
Hergesheimer, Joseph, 229, 236
"Heroics," 168
Heyward, DuBose, 220, 236
Hichborn family, 58, 59, 64
Hichborn, Philip, 41–48, 51, 84, 85, 95–96, 102–104, 108
Hichborn, Philip, III (Beeyup), 44, 95–96, 105, 138, 235, 276, 332
Hickey, William, 229
Hodgson, Ralph, 185
Holt, Roland, 176
Holton-Arms School, 33–34, 38
Hoofbeats (Philip Hichborn), 108
Hopkins, James, 133
Hopkins, Katherine, 50
"Hound, The," 207
Howard, Brian, 277–278, 293
Hoyt, (Anne) Nancy, 32, 108, 189–190, 196, 215, 278, 285, 313, 330
Hoyt family, 3–9, 12–20, 29, 32–35, 64, 67–68, 77, 96, 107, 135, 162, 167, 197, 313, 331–332
Hoyt, Henry, 13–14, 101–102,

112–113, 135, 158–159, 166, 168, 175
Huntsman, What Quarry (Edna St. Vincent Millay), 286
Huxley, Aldous, 267, 268, 271, 282

"In the Wood," 86
Incidental Numbers, 40, 52–53, 108, 153, 184
Ingpen, Roger, 278, 293
Innes, Hammond, 249
Irving, Sir Henry, 36

James, Henry, 162
Jennifer Lorn, 41, 217, 224, 229–231, 233, 236, 237, 253, 267, 300
Jungman sisters, 270, 293
"Juvenilia," 40

Kaufman, Beatrice, 247
Keats, J., 215
Kenyon, Bernice L., 179, 180–181
"King's Pity," 256
Knopf, Alfred and Blanche, 236, 262, 266, 300, 309, 329, 331
Kreymborg, Alfred, 186

Ladies' Home Companion, The, 182
Lady Stuffed with Pistachio Nuts, 221
"Lament," 220
Last Blackbird and Other Poems, 185
Last Poems, 164, 244
"Lauriers Sont Coupés, Les," 153
League of American Pen Women, 285
Lehmann, Rosamond, 270, 271
Lewis, Grace, 162
Lewis, Rosa, 326
Lewis, Sinclair, 157, 161–162, 170, 176, 215, 231, 281
Literary Guild, The, 283
"Lonesome Rose," 170, 309
"Love Song," 194, 206
"Love to Stephen," 244
Loveland, Mary E., 8
Loveman, Amy, 211, 315
Lowell, Amy, 186–187, 192, 215–216, 218–219, 225, 248, 249–250
Lynd, Robert and Sylvia, 267, 293

MacDowell Colony, 198–199, 200, 218, 220, 254, 256, 262
MacDowell, Edward, 197
MacLeish, Archibald, 216

McDonald, Mary Ann, 17–18, 22, 228
McKinley, President, 29, 34
McMichael family, 3–6, 9–13
"Madman's Song," 165, 185
Main Street, 170
Mann, Thomas, 249
Marinoff, Fania, 233
Markham, Mrs. Edwin, 176
Marriages, 42–48, 133, 224
Marsh, Eleanor Taylor, 51, 202
Mary Tamberlaine, 309
Mary's Husband; A Farce Tragedy, 218
Melcher, Helen de Selding, 134, 139
Merchants from Cathay (William Rose Benét), 160
Millay, Edna St. Vincent, 169, 184–186, 197, 213, 215, 251, 262–263, 285, 286–288, 303, 319–320, 332
"Miranda's Supper," 239, 301
Miscarriages, 142, 239
Monroe, Harriet, 153, 169, 186, 325
Moons of Grandeur (William. Rose Benét), 160–161
Moore, Douglas, 219–220
Moore, Virginia, 199–200, 254
Morley, Christopher, 154, 183, 204
Mr. Hodge and Mr. Hazard, 295, 296–299, 307, 309, 325
Mr. Shelley Speaking, 283
Mumford, Claire, 225
"My Silver Dress," 268

"Nadir," 181
"Nancy," 165
"Narrow Escape, A," 27
Nathan, Robert, 229, 311
Nation, The, 178
Nets to Catch the Wind, 176, 184, 185, 186, 189, 216
"Never Ask the End," 220
Nevin, Arthur, 201
New Republic, The, 168, 178, 181, 201, 202, 229, 264, 282, 283, 330
New York Herald Tribune, 282
New Yorker, 265, 268, 276, 284, 285
Nichols, Tirzah, 29–30
Nicolson, Harold, 292
"Ninety-nine Cream Bottles," 256
Norris, Kathleen, 157, 164, 235

Odell, Mrs. George, 170–171
Olivier, Edith, 196, 269, 276–278, 293, 304, 306, 309, 311, 325, 329
Olivier, Lord, 293–294
"One Person," 301, 322, 330
Orphan Angel, The, 260–261, 265, 272, 280, 281–282, 293
Osler, Sir William, 89, 93

Parker, Alice, 100–101, 102
Parker, Dorothy, 165, 251, 280
Parrish, Anne, 247
Paterson, Isabel, 298
Pearsall, Martha, 104
Penguin Club, 171
"Peregrine's Sunday Song," 206
"Peter and John," 301
Playboy, 207
Poetry magazine, 152, 169, 205, 325
Poetry readings, 250
Poetry Society, 173, 175, 176, 178, 184
"Poet's Club, The," 248
Poiret, Paul, 268
Porter, John Addison, 28–29
"Portrait," 284, 285, 289
Potter, Nancy, 230
Pound, Ezra, 153
Powys, Llewelyn, 272, 293, 301, 314
Poynyard, Gerald, 199
"Prayer," 142
Pregnancies, 43–44, 119–122, 131–132, 141–142, 239
"Proud Lady, A," 186

Ramsey, Janet, 257
Rascoe, Arthur B., 203–204, 284, 285
"Red Carpet for Shelley, A," 281, 282
Regina Watson Studio, 220, 256
Reviewer, The, 236
Reviewing books, 209, 282–283
Robeson, Paul, 321
Robinson, E.A., 154, 200, 254
Rockylane, 311, 314
"Room, The," 141
Roosevelt, President Theodore, 34, 39
Root, Esther, 225
Rose, Frances Neill, 156–157
Rothenstein, John, 267, 268
Rotherfield Greys, 305, 311, 317, 324

Runciman, Steven, 270, 293, 296, 308, 311, 325
Russell, Mrs. Charles Edward, 170

Sackville-West, Anne and Vita, 292
Sanctuary in Porcelain (James Branch Cabell), 237
Sargeant, Elizabeth Shepley, 217
Scandal, 71–72, 83–84, 88, 96, 103, 127, 139
"Sea Lullaby," 144, 153
Shakespeare, William, 162
Shay, Frank, 179
Shelley, fascination with, 257–261, 280, 281, 282–284, 295, 300, 332
"Silver Filigree," 153
Sitwell, Edith, 268
Sitwell, Sacheverell and Georgia, 270, 272, 293
Smart Set, The, 181
Smith, Logan Pearsall, 255
Social Register, removing name from, 103
"Song," 52–53
Sonnet, The, 181
"Sonnet in Answer to a Question" (Edna St. Vincent Millay), 287
Sonnets, 321–323, 329, 330
"South of the Potomac," 164
"Spell, The" (Henry Hoyt), 168
Speyer, Edgar and Leonora, 178–179, 224
Squire, J.C., 273
Stagg, Hunter, 236
"Star Among the Ash-Cans," 209
Starr, Jean, 192
Stein, Gertrude, 162, 232
"Still Colors," 153
Stillborn child, 122
Stoker, Bram, 36, 37
Stopford, Robert, 308
Stowers, Deborah, 7
"Strange Song, A," 301
Stroke, 331
Suicides in family, 104–105, 168, 224, 259, 313–314
"Sundae School," 276
Symbols in Literature, 229, 253

Taft, President, 71–72
Teasdale, Sara, 204, 245
Tennant, Stephen, 270, 271, 287, 293, 320
Thompson, Teresa, 159–160
Three Worlds (Carl Van Doren), 241

Tietjens, Eunice, 205, 214, 217, 256
Times Literary Supplement, 267
"To Elinor Wylie" (Edna St. Vincent Millay), 287
"To the Gentlemen of the Press," 315–316
Torrence, Ridgley, 181, 330
Towne, Mary, 9
Trivial Breath, 300, 303

Untermeyer, Louis, 118, 154, 159, 170, 184, 186, 187, 190, 191–193, 215, 217, 219, 229, 239, 254, 281
"Unwilling Admission," 229
"Useful Gift—Why Not, The," 265

Van Doren, Carl, 105, 108, 204, 241, 247, 254, 257, 262, 264, 266, 280–281, 310, 311
Van Doren, Mark, 216
Van Vechten, Carl, 188, 204, 229, 231, 232–234, 236, 245, 248, 264
Vanity, 191, 204, 245
Vanity Fair, 194, 206, 208, 209, 218
"Velvet Shoes," 144, 153
Venetian Glass Nephew, The, 199, 202, 242, 243, 248, 249, 251–253, 264–265, 267, 277
Vogue, 182
von Stumm, Carl H.F., 77, 94
von Stumm, Constance, 75–76, 77, 79, 121–122, 135, 206, 224

Wainwright, Dr., 326, 327
Walpole, Hugh, 233, 236, 292
War, 120, 121–122, 124, 125, 136–137
Waring, Mrs. H., 90, 115

Waste Land, The (T.S. Eliot), 209–210
Waterman, Savrina, 98
Watkins, Metford, 294–295, 307–308
Wayfarer's Bookshop, 170–171
Wells, H.G., 188, 268
Wells, Winifred, 180–181, 188
West, Rebecca, 68, 221–222, 242, 248, 258, 268, 274, 321
Wharton, Edith, 104
Whistler, Rex, 270, 293
Wickedness of Books, The, 178
Widdemer, Margaret, 199, 215, 247
"Wild Peaches," 263
Wilder, Thornton, 197
Wilson, Edmund, 186, 188, 190, 193, 208, 213, 214–215, 216, 245, 248, 253, 264, 266, 284
Wilson, President, 137
"Winter," 144
"With a Bare Bodkin," 168
Wolfe, Thomas, 147, 233, 246, 264
Woman's Home Companion, 255, 256
Woodhouse, Becky, 305–306, 310, 311, 312, 314, 316, 318, 328, 329
Woodhouse, "Cliff," 306, 309, 310–311, 316, 317, 323, 324, 325, 329, 330
Woolf, Leonard and Virginia, 271–272
Wylie family, 49, 58, 162
Wylie, Horace, 48–145, 202, 289–291, 316
Wylie, Katherine, 48, 58, 63, 71, 75, 76, 80, 87, 91, 96, 103, 128, 132
Wynne-Wynne, Gerald, 278

Young, George, 274, 291, 294, 325
Young, Helen, 274, 295, 296, 304, 325